Gordon Weaver, born 1939, left school when aged 15 years. Served as a RAF national serviceman in Malaya 1959-62 and afterwards became a salesman. Read for a degree as a mature student graduating in political science. Later studied law (CPE) and successfully completed the Law Society's Diploma in Legal Practice. Worked as a university researcher and lecturer in colleges of further education, teaching sociology, politics, history and law.

He now provides legal advice (part-time) for refugees. This is his first book but he has produced a research paper on Birmingham minority group politics; an article on religion and the law; and two book reviews on sociology and politics. He has two children and three grandchildren.

CONAN DOYLE AND THE PARSON'S SON

THE GEORGE EDALJI CASE

Gordon Weaver

Conan Doyle And The Parson's Son

The George Edalji Case

Vanguard Press

A CIP catalogue record for this title is
available from the British Library

ISBN 1 84386 241 7

Vanguard Press is an imprint of
Pegasus Elliot MacKenzie Publishers Ltd.
www.pegasuspublishers.com

First Published in 2006

Vanguard Press
Sheraton House Castle Park
Cambridge England

Printed & Bound in Great Britain

DEDICATION

This book is dedicated to victims of injustice and intolerance everywhere.

CONTENTS

PREFACE

In 1980 while researching for a paper 'The Police, Political Groups and Young Blacks in Handsworth' in the Birmingham Reference Library, I came across a collection of newspaper cuttings that included a reference to a solicitor from South Staffordshire sentenced to seven years penal servitude for maiming a horse in 1903. What caught my eye was the ethnic origin of the convicted man – his father was an Indian and his mother English. Not a particularly unusual combination for a person's ethnic origins in late-twentieth century Britain but in South Staffordshire in the first decade of the twentieth century it was something of a novelty. A reference to Sir Arthur Conan Doyle's involvement increased my interest. In an autobiography, 'Memories and Adventures', Conan Doyle wrote of a serious miscarriage of justice and of his own contribution in securing a pardon for George Edalji, the convicted solicitor. A small book reproducing several articles written by Conan Doyle for the Daily Telegraph in 1907, providing details of this miscarriage of justice, was also at hand.

I thought little of this case for close on twenty years until it suddenly came to mind when I was researching another topic in the same library. Curious as to what happened to this young solicitor, I began to enquire into the case. After reading copies of Birmingham newspapers published at the time covering the trial and related issues, I visited a number of libraries in South Staffordshire collecting information on the case and used the considerable quantity of records kept at the Public Record Office at Kew – correspondence from Conan Doyle; from the chief constable of Staffordshire; and comments by officials and advisers at the Home Office; as well as many other documents. What became apparent was that the arrest, trial and imprisonment of George Edalji was the culmination of a series of problems faced by the Edalji family over many years in the Great Wyrley area of South Staffordshire. From the late 1870s, considerable conflict existed in the parish between Reverend Edalji and several prominent persons and interest groups that brought with it a campaign of harassment and intimidation directed against the Vicar and his family, which continued on and off for close on twenty years.

Surprisingly, given the significance of the case, which drew notable lawyers, writers and scholars into the fray at the time, very little has been written on the case itself. Apart from references made to the case in numerous biographies of Sir Arthur Conan Doyle, which offer little to the complexity of the case, there have only been the most limited attempts at dealing with the Edalji case. In the later stages of the twentieth century, apart from a few short articles produced in magazines, all that is available is an introduction to Conan Doyle's newspaper articles on the case; a chapter in a book on Doyle; and a paper presented to a police conference. These rather short inadequate contributions and the paucity of information contained within them, in effect apologias to the Staffordshire police, have been addressed in the final chapter of my book where the reader can judge for himself/herself the merit of their contributions in relation to the reality faced by the Edaljis.

I would like to thank the staff at the Birmingham Reference Library, Birmingham Hall Green Library, Walsall Library, Wolverhampton Library, Cannock Library, Great Wyrley Library, Wm Salt Library at Stafford, Colindale Newspaper Library, the British Library and the Public Record Offices at Stafford and Kew. They probably would not remember me as I pottered away collecting information but I have not forgotten their politeness and consideration.

Gordon Weaver - 24 October 2004

Abbreviations

ACD	Sir Arthur Conan Doyle
AL	Anonymous Letter
BME	Birmingham Midland Express
BSE	Birmingham Sunday Echo
BWM	Birmingham Weekly Mail
BWP	Birmingham Weekly Post
CA	Cannock Advertiser
CCC	Cannock Chase Courier
DC	Daily Chronicle, London
DE	Daily Express, London
Despatch	Evening Despatch, Birmingham
DM (Lon)	Daily Mail, London
DN	Daily News, London
DPP	Director of Public Prosecutions
DT	Daily Telegraph, London
E & S	Express & Star, Wolverhampton
EN	Evening News, London
ES	Evening Standard, London
Gazette	Birmingham Gazette
HO	Home Office
Law Jnl	Law Journal, London
LCJ	Lord Chief Justice
LM	Lichfield Mercury
Mail	Birmingham Daily Mail
MG	Manchester Guardian
Mercury	Birmingham Sunday Mercury
MM	Martin Molton
PMG	Pall Mall Gazette, London
Post	Birmingham Post
PP	Parliamentary Papers
PRO	Public Record Office
PW	Pearson's Weekly, London
RN	Reynold's News, London
SA	Staffordshire Advertiser, Stafford
SCICG	Southern Cross or Indian Church Gazette
SDA	Slater's Detective Agency, London
SS	Staffordshire Sentinel, Stoke
UDSB	United District School Board
WO	Walsall Observer

Introduction

Great Wyrley, in South Staffordshire, was principally an agricultural and mining parish and, like other agricultural areas, suffered from outbreaks of cattle maiming as a form of social protest, which usually represented expressions of group disputes or individual grievances. This particular parish was unlike others insofar as it had a Parsee-convert to Christianity as its Anglican minister – an appointment, in the post mid-Victorian era, not likely to be greeted with universal approval by the parishioners at a time when a more strident racism began to develop in Britain.[1] The ethnic origins of the vicar, Shapurji Edalji, were undoubtedly a contributory factor in the conflict that raged in the parish over the three decades after the outspoken reverend took up the living at St Mark's Parish Church in 1876. The tribulations suffered by, and causing so much anxiety to Reverend Edalji and his family during this time, were eventually overshadowed by the consequences of a cattle-maiming scourge inflicted on the parish in 1903 that catapulted the Edalji family into national prominence in which even the reigning monarch, King Edward VII, had a part to play. Between the 1st February 1903, when a horse belonging to Mr Holmes was maimed, and the 29th June 1903, when two horses owned by Mr Blewitt were similarly mutilated, a string of atrocities was committed against a total of eight animals: five horses, one sheep and two cows belonging to local tradesmen, farmers and colliery owners. These mutilated animals were found either dead or dying of wounds inflicted to their abdomen, practically disembowelling them, committed by someone skilled in wielding a large curved-blade weapon.

When the first maiming took place it raised little public interest since it was attributed to someone holding a grudge against the owner. However, when five animals had been butchered, the police took the offences seriously enough to draft twenty special police officers into the neighbourhood[2] and in collaboration with a few civilians began patrolling the locality during the night. Catching the maimer became the main priority for the police and was the principal issue of concern for the villagers, yet by the time Blewitt's horses were killed on the 29th June, the extensive surveillance exercised by the police and the greater vigilance shown by the local populace had failed to stem the atrocities.

---

[1] *Lorimer, Doug A, [1978] Colour, Class & the Victorians, Univ of Leicester, p208.*

[2] Post, 23 Oct 1903

Nor had a single clue turned up to identify the architect of the maimings or give a hint as to the motive behind the attacks.[3] The failure of the police to detect the maimer caused widespread alarm amongst the residents, an environment described by one reporter as akin to a 'reign of terror' with villagers perceiving the maimer to be a lunatic with a mania for shedding blood and in possession of supernatural powers that enabled him not only to accomplish the mutilations on widely dispersed farms but also to avoid detection. This image of the maimer was responsible for triggering off additional fears amongst villagers of the attacker extending his list of victims to include women and young children in order to satisfy his lust for blood.[4]

During this period of bloodletting, the police, whose competence came under fire from locals for not running the culprit to earth, ran the rule over a number of suspects, mostly boisterous young men, but made no arrests. However, within a day of the Blewitt incident, the police focused their attention on the vicarage at Great Wyrley, where a highly improbable suspect, a young solicitor, George Edalji, lived with his father, mother and younger sister. Apparently, George Edalji's name had been mentioned to the police as a possible suspect by a local Justice of the Peace - more than likely to be Mr J T Hatton, a local landowner and director of a colliery, who was no fan of Reverend Edalji's, having crossed swords with him in the past, and who was the only JP living in the immediate area. On the same day, 'coincidentally', an anonymous letter went to Sergeant Rowley at Hednesford police station pointing the finger at a passenger on the evening train from Walsall, a train used by George Edalji, and rumours began to circulate around the district about the vicar's son being under arrest. When these rumours reached the ears of George Edalji, on the advice of associates, he placed advertisements in the local newspapers offering a reward for information leading to the discovery of the person spreading the rumours.[5]

Over the next five weeks, several anonymous letters and postcards were sent to the police; to George Edalji; and to a Hednesford schoolboy named Wilfred Greatorex. The author(s) claimed that George Edalji, Wilfred Greatorex and several other local inhabitants were involved in the outrages and in one of the letters a threat was made to kill Police Sergeant Robinson, stationed at Cannock, a parish adjacent to Great Wyrley. Several of the people named in the letters received visits from the police; George Edalji was visited three times, but

---

[3] Mail, 2 July 1903

[4] Mail, 2 July 1903; Post, 19 Aug 1903

[5] Despatch, 3 Sep 1903

nothing of substance came from these inquiries. The final anonymous missives were sent out on the 4th August; one received by George Edalji accused him of sexual immorality with the daughter of the vicar of Hednesford parish and another sent to the police gave 'information' on the departure of 'PB' from the area as nothing more could be done, i.e. no further maimings would be carried out while the police were patrolling the area.[6] Despite notifying this cessation of activity, two weeks later the maimer struck yet again.

On the morning of the 18th August, a horse belonging to the Great Wyrley Colliery Company was discovered disembowelled in a field. As soon as the news reached the police, Inspector Campbell, the senior police officer in the district, embarked on three courses of action. Firstly, he immediately despatched a constable to Great Wyrley railway station to intercept George Edalji *en route* to his office in Birmingham. However, George Edalji declined the police invitation to delay his journey and proceeded on his way to work. Secondly, the inspector sent another police constable to inspect the field where the maiming was carried out. Thirdly, following a fleeting visit to the scene of the crime, Inspector Campbell went straight to the vicarage to gather evidence against George Edalji and, after being informed of the police constable's abortive trip to detain George Edalji at the railway station, the inspector lost no time in going to Edalji's office in Birmingham where he took him into custody.

George Edalji was arraigned before the Cannock magistrates the next day and remanded in custody for an offence under the Malicious Damages Act 1861 relating to the maiming of the Great Wyrley Colliery horse. Several days later, an additional charge of threatening to kill a police officer under the Offences Against the Persons Act 1861 was preferred against him – a charge having the primary purpose of implicating him in writing the anonymous letters.

Edalji was tried at Stafford Quarter Sessions in October 1903, found guilty of maliciously causing injury to the colliery horse and sentenced to seven years penal servitude. During the trial, which attracted the attention of the national press, a barrister, who read the daily reports of the proceedings, suspected that Edalji was the victim of a serious miscarriage of justice and, after contacting Reverend Edalji, took up George Edalji's case. As there was no criminal court of appeal at the time, representations for a review of the case had to be made to the Home Office, which for a variety of reasons associated with the bureaucratic ethos of 'closing ranks,' rejected several of George

---

[6] Despatch, 22 Oct 1903

Edalji's petitions for a free pardon. However, after three years and some misgivings by the Home Secretary over the severity of the sentence, Edalji was released under license. Edalji's release inspired the existing national campaign seeking redress for him and, significantly, added the name of Sir Arthur Conan Doyle to the list of many prominent people already involved in the campaign. Eventually, a reluctant and grudgingly qualified pardon was granted to Edalji but without any compensation for his three years imprisonment and loss of reputation and earnings.

How did so unlikely a candidate as George Edalji become a scapegoat for both the Staffordshire Ripper and the malicious scribe(s) who successfully railroaded him into one of His Majesty's prisons for the maimings and anonymous letter writing? To understand the social forces acting to the detriment of not only George Edalji but also the Edalji family as a whole requires more than an examination of the events of 1903, it is necessary to turn the clock back 27 years to the time when George Edalji's father, Shapurji Edalji, became vicar of St Mark's Church in the parish of Great Wyrley.

Chapter I

Sowing the Wind

(i)   Arrival in the Home of the Raj

Reverend Shapurji Edalji, born a Parsee in 1843, travelled a long and circuitous route from his birthplace in India to the straggling mining and farming district of Great Wyrley, South Staffordshire, where he became the parish vicar at St Mark's Church in December 1875. In India, Shapurji was a scholar attending the Bombay Free Kirk College and, in his youth, converted to Christianity. Shapurji's dedication to Christianity went beyond mere membership of a congregation, to him his conversion was a calling and he set his sights on bringing the word of God to his fellow countrymen in the Indian sub-continent. On the recommendations of his tutors, Shapurji became a beneficiary of a scheme for accomplished 'Hindoos, Mahomedans or Parsees' to undergo a three years training course for the Ministry in the United Kingdom as preparation for missionary work in India.[7] Shapurji financed his passage from India to attend a course of religious instruction at St Augustine's College, Canterbury, through the sale of a Dictionary of 'Guzerate and English' compiled by the budding theologian.[8] Upon his ordination in the Anglican Church, his anticipated return to India as a messenger of the Christian gospel did not come to pass. The prospective proselytiser fell foul of a system that based its legitimacy on the alleged racial superiority of Europeans and its disdain for Indian civilisations.[9] This was a system fostered by Governor Arthur Wellesley when establishing Imperial rule throughout India, which was reinforced and strengthened following the Indian uprising of 1857. Legitimised by imperialist ideology, the policies of the Christian Missionary Society and the Society for the Propagation of the Gospel played their part in supporting the system by insisting on European missionaries bringing Christianity to the 'heathen masses' of India –

---

[7] Mrs C Edalji to HO, 8 Jan 1904, HO No 48, file 984; The Hon I J Gibb, SCICG, 5 Jan 1867; Mrs C Edalji to J B Stone and others, 26 & 27 Jan 1904, J B Stone Collection, p 164 in Birmingham Library Archives;

[8] Mrs C Edalji to J B Stone and others, 26 & 27 Jan 1904, J B Stone Collection, p 164 in Birmingham Library Archives; C Edalji to HO, 8 Jan 1904, HO No 48 File 984

[9] Edwardes M, Red Year, [1975] Sphere Books, London, p 17

21

save their souls for God but contain their social aspirations for equality of treatment. These restrictions, thwarting the original aspirations of the prospective missionary, propelled Shapurji in the direction of saving the souls of the 'quasi-heathen masses' of England.

Shapurji Edalji accepted temporary posts in a number of parishes in England,[10] and during a second spell in Liverpool became acquainted with Charlotte Stoneham, the younger of two unmarried daughters of Reverend Thompson Stoneham, vicar of Ketley parish in Shropshire. The route from Bombay to the twenty-nine years old Charlotte was paved to some extent by an old friend of the Stonehams, the vicar of St Clement's in Toxteth, Liverpool, Reverend G A Sandberg, for whom Shapurji acted as curate. Soon after a visit made by the Stoneham family to Toxteth in 1872, and a return visit to Ketley by Shapurji making a 'guest appearance' as preacher, Charlotte and Shapurji were engaged. Two years later, receiving the blessings of both Charlotte's parents and the good wishes of their friends, the couple were married in what was described in the local Shrewsbury Chronicle as "one of the (parish's) most notable weddings."[11] The ceremony was performed by the bride's uncle, Reverend E B Compson, Vicar of Hillesley, Gloucestershire, whilst another of Charlotte's clerical uncles, Reverend J Compson, vicar of St Mark's Church, Great Wyrley, putting into practice a characteristic of Victorian society as common then as it is today - nepotism, arranged with the patron of the living at St Mark's for his ministry to pass to Shapurji, as a wedding gift to the couple, when he vacated the post. A happy and useful life full of good works, in line with the protestant ethic, was forecast for the couple, as informed opinion, at least in Ketley, Shropshire, thought "Parsees were a cultivated race with many good qualities."[12] The feelings of the people of Ketley, if indeed they were so fair-minded, were not in conformity with the attitudes of the rest of the country at that time.

British society was not partial to English women marrying Indian men. Imperialist ideology viewed 'inter-racial' sexual relations and marriage as violating the English woman's whole nature as a woman and, ironically and ambiguously since both Shapurji and Charlotte were devout Christians, as threatening the whole integrity of the Christian nature. This code of belief, hatched in India during the Wellesley

[10] At Burford, Oxford, Farnworth, Liverpool, St Levan and Bromley St Leonard.

[11] Shrewsbury Chronicle, 26 June 1874

[12] M S Stoneham to J B Stone, 27 Jan 1904, J B Stone Collection, p 165, in Birmingham Library Archives.

regime, permeated down from the upper layers of British society to the 'masses', receiving a further boost in 1883 following the Hume case when the wife of an English administrator in India was caught by her husband *in flagrante delicto* with an Indian servant and was forced to perjure herself by claiming to have been raped.[13] Historians researching into the influence of the attitudes of ex-patriots on British society, found that even the "more insular Englishmen absorbed the racial attitudes of their countrymen overseas" through reading the observations of colonial and overseas adventurers recorded in numerous articles and press reports.[14] t

The Edaljis arrived in Great Wyrley for Shapurji to take up the living in December 1875 – Reverend Compson was about to resign on grounds of ill-health and he died shortly afterwards. Charlotte was in the final stages of her first pregnancy with the future George Edalji and a few days before George saw the light of day through the windows of the vicarage on the 22 January 1876, Reverend Edalji was initiated into the Ministry by Bishop Hobhouse of the Lichfield diocese. What the Vestry Committee or the parishioners really thought of the appointment of an Asian to the post of vicar is difficult to determine at first hand but it could hardly have been an inviting one. Given the prevailing attitudes of the time, Reverend Compson's wedding present to the happy couple was undoubtedly a contributory factor in generating a discordant attitude amongst the parishioners, especially as the more influential of them might have their own favoured nominee marked down as a replacement for the previous ailing incumbent. Shapurji had 'inherited' the less than enviable position of an Indian Christian-convert preaching to a Midland farming and mining community less than twenty years after the Indian uprising of 1857 and the ideological consequences of that rising on British citizens both in the Raj and in the mother country.

Sir Arthur Conan Doyle, as well as other prominent figures, writing in the early 1900s, cited racism as responsible for the perennial problems faced by the Edalji family after the reverend's arrival in Great Wyrley and he believed that placing an Asian clergyman married to an English woman with children of that union, "in a rude, unrefined parish

[13] The Hume case, Times 30 Jan 1883; see Victorian Uncovered, Channel 4, 3 April 2001 for an interesting account of the case.

[14] Deighton, H S, [1959] 'History and the Study of Race Relations', Race I, pp15-25

was bound to cause some regrettable situation."[15] The future Lord Birkenhead, F E Smith, who eventually became Lord Chancellor, thought Shapurji's appointment unlikely to be popular with a provincial community.[16] Two relatively recent contributors[17] to the Edalji case have challenged the view that racism was the root cause of the Edalji's difficulties but both of these latter day critics with their impressionistic contributions have ignored the prevailing ideology of the time – the jingoistic, imperialistic bigotry and self-interest that passed itself off as the 'civilising mission.'

For Charlotte, not a complete stranger to the parish having visited it as a child,[18] Great Wyrley, though not far distant in miles from Ketley, was a different world compared to the tranquil England of the Shropshire countryside. This parish, unlike the 'leafy' parish of mid-Shropshire, must have been seen by this middle Englander as a stepping stone to a more suitable setting expected for a clergyman with published religious texts already to his credit. However, Great Wyrley with its trials and tribulations originating from a host of less than Christian-spirited opponents became the final destination of Sharpurji's journey from Bombay as he was to remain there until his death in 1918, never to return, or even to visit, his homeland.

(ii)   Congregating Enemies

(a) Burghers, Bureaucrats and Aristocrats

The two clerics, Edalji and Compson, far distant in their respective birthplaces, were also far distant in their dispositions. Reverend Compson, the incumbent since the sanctification of the Church in 1845, appeared to be less concerned with the activities of the larger ratepayers, churchwardens and poor law guardians on the Vestry Committee than would be the new reverend, an entirely different kind of 'shepherd of his flock' compared to his predecessor. By the time Reverend Edalji took up his post, the Vestry Committee dominated by the interests of the Great Wyrley Colliery, represented by J T Hatton and D M Munro, had a free hand in conducting its affairs with the

---

[15] Doyle described it, not particularly eloquently, "as a coloured clergyman with a half-caste son". Doyle, AC, Memoirs and Adventures,[1924]Hodder & Stoughton, London p216

[16] F E Smith, Hansard, 18 July 1907, v 178, c 1007

[17] Dr P Lester and M Harley, see Appendix II

[18] Mrs C Edalji to Home Office, 8 Jan 1904, HO No 48, File 984

compliance of Reverend Compson, a situation the committee would undoubtedly wish to maintain with any successor. When Reverend Edalji began to demonstrate a more single-minded, interventionist approach in pursuit of what he interpreted as right and became an outspoken critic of the dominant members on the Vestry Committee who ran Great Wyrley, these members lamented the passing of the previous incumbent's more acquiescent approach by criticising the new vicar for ruining the way parish matters had been handled over the previous thirty years under Reverend Compson.[19] Over the next two decades, Reverend Edalji's more vigorous approach caused him to fall foul of a variety of interests – local burghers and small businessmen on the Vestry Committee; officials both in the Staffordshire County Education Authority and the National Education Department; Lord Hatherton, doyen of Staffordshire society and political life, the largest land owner in the area, proprietor of many industrial ventures,[20] and whose son was to play a part in the George Edalji prosecution over 20 years later; members of non-conformist religions; local representatives of the Miners' Federation; and a few members of the working classes.[21]

Reverend Compson's acquiescent approach to secular parish affairs was illustrated by an issue coming before the Vestry Committee in 1872. A trustee of the estate of the late Joseph Brown, holder of the rights to the coal, ironstone, other minerals and mines lying under the land at Cheslyn Hay and owner of the surface land for agricultural use, was a small time trader and insurance agent, Mr Thomas Cash Barton, who claimed the rights over those assets. Whatever entitlements Barton thought he had were successfully challenged by the Vestry Committee

---

[19] Vestry Minutes (originals) 4 Mar 1880, Stafford PRO

[20] Lord Hatherton held interests in railways, canals, coal, brickworks, stone quarries, gravel and sand pits, ironstone, waterworks and water mains, and tithes from tenant farmers and other occupiers of property throughout South Staffordshire.

[21] Conflicts over apparently non-racist issues often obscure the racist dimension underpinning those conflicts. In these situations, even though the principal objective behind the harassment may be one other than racism, e.g. an economic one, racism is used as a means of achieving the principal objective. This is made possible by the racist's knowledge that the ethnic minority victim is unlikely to secure support from members of the dominant group either because of the racist feelings of the individuals in that group and/or in not wanting to be seen assisting a minority member at the expense of a member of the dominant group. This is not an uncommon occurrence and has been addressed in a number of articles on race relations in recent times.

and it took possession of the rights to the minerals and surface land on behalf of the ratepayers of Great Wyrley. The Committee then sold the assets, although their sale appeared to be for reasons other than the general well-being of all the parishioners, and, in February 1874, invested the proceeds in securities with the nett returns going towards liquidating the parish poor rates – dual benefits accruing to Vestry Committee members and the limited franchise they represented. Some Committee members obtained direct benefits by acquiring mineral rights and land; to others went the benefits of a reduction in the poor rates; and for Reverend Compson, not overlooked by the Committee, a £20 annuity for life. The driving force behind the Committee's pursuit of Joseph Brown's land was J T Hatton and D M Munro. The former was to become both a substantial landowner and a leading shareholder in the Great Wyrley Colliery Company after agreeing to lease the mineral rights to the colliery. The latter held the post of general manager of that colliery.[22]

Reverend Edalji's attempt to exercise control over those things rendered unto him – church matters, ruffled the feathers of Messrs Hatton and Munro, who must have viewed the reverend's approach as threatening the free hand they had exercised with the previous incumbent to pursue their own pecuniary interests. The reverend embarked on a course of action unlikely to endear him to the parties involved when he attacked Hatton and Munro from the pulpit for failing to seek his approval when arranging a money collection in the church for a former churchwarden.[23] At a later date, the churchwardens were reluctant to carry out their parish duties because of what they described as the "unpleasantness and increasing troubles surrounding the office", and the loss of honour and dignity associated with the posts, putting the blame on the vicar for being remiss in his duties. However, this loss of dignity did not prevent Messrs Hatton and Munro, whilst occupying those 'undignified' roles, from unequivocally pursuing the interests of the Great Wyrley Colliery Company by pressing for the sale of mining rights still held by the parish, despite opposition from the Cannock Board of Guardians, who blocked the sale. A deputation to the board led by Munro and lobbying by Hatton managed to overturn the decision. On another occasion, the reverend, concerned with the lack of

---

[22] Vestry Minutes (originals): 15 Jul 1873; 1 Aug 1873; 27 Nov 1873; 27 Feb 1874. Of the 283 shares in the new company, 96 were held by Vestry Committee members, of which J T Hatton held 60 and B Gilpin 30 - see File BT 31/30869/9669 at the PRO

[23] J E, Calf Heath and Reverend Edalji, Gazette 21 and 26 Feb 1907

control exercised over the Vestry's bank funds, refused to nominate one of the churchwardens, required as signatories for operating the bank account, but was out manoeuvred and both Hatton and Munro were appointed.[24]

Isolating himself from the dominant interests in the parish, Reverend Edalji was soon to extend that isolation when he wanted to reopen the Church School at Great Wyrley. The Vestry Committee inevitably lined up against him in opposing the proposal on financial criteria and the non-conformists on the chapel committee did likewise by opposing the Church of England's monopoly over religious education in the school.

Another similar dispute that became a long running saga over the next thirty years, involved a number of parties and interests centring on the newly created United District School Board (UDSB).[25] A pecuniary dispute arose between the ratepayers of Cheslyn Hay and Great Wyrley over the relative contribution to be paid by the two districts to provide education under the UDSB. Great Wyrley's representatives opposed the scheme because of the higher proportion of funding they would have to pay compared to their less affluent neighbours. However, once the UDSB was operating, the Board wanted control of the Cheslyn Hay National School but as the school was under the trusteeship of the vicar, curate and churchwardens it could not be taken over without the permission of the reverend, who wanted to retain control of religious education.[26] The reverend's almost demagogic desire to maintain an Anglican influence over educational provision and his insistence, contrary to statutory requirements, in wanting to employ only teachers of the Anglican faith again brought him into conflict with the non-conformists.

The issue went up to the officials at the National Education Department, who tried a legal manoeuvre to prise the school away from

---

[24] Vestry meetings in CA 27 July 1878; 14 and Dec 28 1878; 24 April 1879; 4 Mar 1880

[25] Parishes were entrusted with the provision of education and religious instruction for children and adults of the 'labouring, manufacturing and other poorer classes' overseen by a directly elected United District School Board (UDSB).

[26] The Reverend Edalji followed a line carved out by another clergyman, Dr Whiston, some years before, who had 'the audacity' to tell the members of the Rochester Chapter they were breaking their own laws as the dean and canons, by taking a disproportionate share of cathedral revenues for themselves, were depriving their scholars of funds. Arnold, RMC, [1961] The Whiston Matter, Camelot Press, London, p47

the reverend's grasp. However, this impractical man, a term coined to describe the reverend by an Education Department official, had done his homework and reminded the authorities he was prohibited under statute from relinquishing control of the church school.[27]

The UDSB changed tack and directed its attention with a show of considerable enthusiasm to purchasing or leasing a particular site on which to build a new school with a government loan. As this represented a charge to ratepayers, support for this scheme from the habitually mercenary ratepayers of Great Wyrley suggested some other motive might be behind their decision to secure this site. Despite the National Educational Board initially vetoing the plan due to the land to be purchased being excessively overvalued, after further representations, permission was granted in the face of strong objections from the reverend.

Unable to outwit the UDSB, the reverend decided to join them and in September 1886 was elected to the Board - an election overshadowed by accusations against Cheslyn Hay candidates of gerrymandering to ensure all its candidates were elected.[28] Playing a cat and mouse game, the reverend changed direction on the church school by proposing that the land revert to Lord Hatherton and the proceeds from the sale of the school buildings be used to benefit the parishioners. However, Lord Hatherton, who had originally donated the land with a reversion clause,

---

[27] UDSB minutes 21 Dec 1880; Correspondence between the Reverend, the School Board and the National Education Board, 18 Feb 1880, 4 Jan 1881, 29 Mar 1881, 4 April 1881, 9 April 1881, 19 May 1881, 31 May 1881. In ED/397, 9268 PRO; Wildman Burnett, Great Wyrley to National Education Dept, 12 Jan 1880; National Education Dept Minutes, 12 and 17 Jan 1880; Yarde (HMI) to National Education Dept, 3 Feb 1880; National Education Dept note, 24 Feb 1880; Reverend Edalji and Secretary, National Education Dept, 18 Feb 1880 and 3 May 1880; Shorthand notes in Attorney-General v Rev Edalji, 4 Jul 1907; J Hale, Cheslyn Hay, to Education Dept, 10 Oct 1879; Yarde, HMI to National Education Dept, 13 Oct 1879. All in document ED/397, File 9268, PRO; Walter B Yarde to National Education Dept, 12 Mar 1881; National Education Dept to Rev Edalji, 18 Mar 1881, in ED/397, 9267 in PRO; T R Dolby (UDSB) to National Education Dept, 31 May 1881, 9 Jul 1881, 20 Jul 1881; Public Works Loan Board to National Education Dept, 15 Sep 1882 - All in ED/397, 9268. CA reports on UDSB meetings 12 Feb 1881, 31 May 1881, 13 Aug 1881, 20 Aug 1881, 29 Oct 1881; UDSB minutes 21 Dec 1880; Report of Public Inquiry, 16 Nov 1906, pp 13/14/15/17/20/21 in File TS 18/251, PRO;
[28] CA 18 and 25 Sep 1886, and 2 Oct 1886

wanted both the land and the buildings to be returned to him and was prepared to resort to law to get them, so the reverend dropped the idea, thereby, preventing the site from reverting to Lord Hatherton.[29] Over a number of years, Reverend Edalji's actions stored up considerable resentment among a number of influential people.

Overall, this was an extremely stressful period for the reverend, resulting in attacks of lumbago, bouts of insomnia, and eventually a stroke. His daughter, Maud, also suffered serious illness during this period, resulting in Mrs Edalji moving in to the children's bedroom. As a consequence, George Edalji, then nine years old, went to sleep in the same room as his father, a room immediately adjoining the room now occupied by the mother. This family matter came back to haunt the Edaljis almost twenty years later when these sleeping arrangements, which continued until 1903, prompted tasteless slurs against Reverend Edalji.[30] In the meantime, however, more than slurs invaded the Edalji household. A new group of enemies and a precedent for the future entered the scene.

(b)   Working Girl Threatens Revenge: the Foster Affair[31]

The education issue temporarily subsided and the Edalji's were brought face to face with a new and different problem beginning in August 1888. Over the next twenty years, anonymous letters were to descend on the Edaljis and, to a lesser extent, on other inhabitants of Great Wyrley and the surrounding areas. The letters of 1888/9, subsequently referred to by Sir Arthur Conan Doyle as the first series to distinguish them from the letters of 1892-5, 1903 and 1907, began in a fairly innocuous way but eventually developed into threats on Reverend

---

[29] Correspondence between Rev Edalji and Charity Commissioners, 8 Dec 1886, 7, 11 and 22 Jan 1887 in ED 397/9238

[30] See Chapter 13 section (iv)

[31] CA 12 & 19 Jan 1889; LM 18 Jan 1889; Gazette 1 & 21 Feb 1907; C Edalji, Truth, 23 Mar 1905; Rev Edalji to Upton, 15 Jan 1889; Supt Barrett's report, 9 Dec 1892, in Capt Anson to HO, May 1905, HO No 124, File 985

Edalji's life.[32]

The early letters in the first series began with requests for the reverend to order a Wolverhampton newspaper, the Express & Star, and although they also contained a threat to smash the vicarage windows if he failed to comply, Reverend Edalji dismissed the letters as foolish. The situation reached a more critical level in December when threats were made to shoot the reverend if he refused to order the newspaper and when the windows at the vicarage were actually broken in line with the previous threat, Reverend Edalji became reluctant to carry out his parish visits for fear of being shot. Graffiti, denouncing the Edalji's as "wicked," was scribbled on the outside and inside walls of the vicarage suggesting the culprit had access to the vicarage. The Edaljis' maidservant, 17 years old Elizabeth Foster, in the Edaljis' employ for a few months, received letters written under the pseudonym 'Thomas Hitchins'. Hitchins, claiming to be the author of the letters sent to her 'Black master', accused her of writing on the walls and he threatened to shoot her when her 'Black man' was out. When learning of these threats, Mrs Edalji showed consideration and compassion by allowing Elizabeth Foster to sleep in the same room as herself and her daughter, Maud. The threats of violence prompted the reverend to call in the police and Sergeant Upton, who was to figure significantly in the 1892 – 5 events, went with Police Constable Daley to the vicarage to question the occupants. The police then set a watch on the vicarage but no new letters arrived. However, when the surveillance was abandoned, anonymous letters began to turn up in the yard, outbuildings and inside the vicarage, increasing suspicions of it being an inside job. On New Year's Day, 1889, a letter to Elizabeth Foster was found in the hall of the vicarage with the gum on the envelope flap still wet. The following day, a letter addressed to the reverend, written on a fly leaf from one of the children's school exercise books, was found on the doorstep after George Edalji, almost thirteen years old, claimed to have seen what looked like a man's shadow through the glass door leading on to the hall. Almost immediately, Mrs Edalji came across Elizabeth Foster

---

[32] The second series, between 1892 and 1895, included crude, pornographic and blasphemous letters, undoubtedly written by more than one scribe. The third series in 1903 dealt principally with cattle maimings and to a lesser extent contained crude accusations of sexual impropriety as well as criticising a number of local people. The fourth series in 1907 appeared to have been written to hamper the campaign to get a free pardon and compensation for Edalji for the miscarriage of justice inflicted upon him.

coming from that direction. The same morning, George found another letter written on a leaf torn from an exercise book kept in the vicarage and on the 3rd January, a letter addressed to Reverend Edalji was found by George and Elizabeth, who were together at the time. The common denominators were Elizabeth Foster and George Edalji. Both were in the vicarage on all three occasions and both had access to the nursery and to the study where the exercise books were kept. It looked like either Elizabeth Foster was responsible or George Edalji was the culprit and doing his best to fit her up.

The police were again called in and a specimen of Elizabeth Foster's handwriting was taken, which the constable thought showed a similarity to the writing in the anonymous letters. The following day, Police Sergeant Upton visited the vicarage and took samples of handwriting from all the people residing there. He, too, found Foster's writing to be similar to that in the letters. After consulting the reverend, who concurred with Sergeant Upton's assessment, Foster was charged with sending threatening letters. Reverend Edalji offered to drop the charge against her if she confessed. However, protesting her innocence and in a panic for being either found out or unfairly charged, she ran to the safety of her aunt's house near to the vicarage.

Pleading not guilty when she came up before the magistrates at Cannock Police Court on the 14th January 1889, Foster was faced by five prosecution witnesses: Reverend Edalji, Mrs Edalji, George Edalji, Sergeant Upton and Police Constable Daley. None of these witnesses could claim any expertise in handwriting, offering merely lay opinions – a feature to be associated with the anonymous letters throughout the whole period when many people from a wide range of occupations professed views on the authorship of the numerous letters that were to flood the area. The defence argued that it was not possible to convict a person merely by comparing handwriting and if the case was sent to the Assizes it would mean ruin for the girl's parents. The reverend agreed to the prosecution's suggestion to reduce the charge to one of using threats and Foster, pleading guilty to the lesser charge on the advice of her solicitor, was bound over to keep the peace. Showing no sign of contrition, perhaps there was no reason to do so, Foster threatened to have her revenge on the Edaljis some day. Reverend Edalji believed that Elizabeth Foster sent letters to herself in the name of Thomas Hitchins in order to deceive him – a conclusion that came home to roost when the police, using a similar lay person's knowledge of handwriting, reached similar conclusions about George Edalji's alleged responsibility for writing the 1903 series of anonymous letters. After Foster's conviction, the reverend congratulated Sergeant Upton for tracing the letters to their author – an indication that the reverend had confidence in the police and that the police in South Staffordshire had no particular axe to grind against the clergyman and his family prior to Captain Anson, the newly appointed Chief Constable of Staffordshire, taking a particular interest in the Edalji family.

(c) Miners and Mining Employers

Reverend Edalji not only fell foul of working people but also came into conflict with the leaders of organised labour. His temperament and tendency to vacillate brought him into a dispute with the leadership of the local Miner's Federation after chairing a meeting of the Federation held in the Great Wyrley National School on the 7th November 1889. During that meeting the miners' representatives called for the eight hour day and a withdrawal of labour "until concessions (are) made." Following the meeting, the reverend tried to distance himself from the use of strike action as a weapon in industrial conflict by claiming to be ignorant of that proposal prior to Albert Stanley, a miners' representative, making the appeal from the platform. In a rejoinder, Stanley drew attention to the posters put out before the meeting, which the reverend must have seen, and he also made the point that no one would assume Reverend Edalji was complicit in the miners' strike proposal merely by occupying the Chair. The reverend responded by accusing Stanley and Rogers, another miners' representative, of misleading him into believing the aim of the meeting was to raise money for the relatives of miners recently killed at the Longton mines in Staffordshire and he excused his own failure to make a protest against the proposal for a strike at the meeting on the grounds of not wishing to mar the harmony of the meeting. The last word on the issue went to another contributor, John Piggott, who revealed that Reverend Edalji, prior to the meeting, had enquired as to the objects of the meeting and was told what they were, consequently, stripping the reverend of his plea of ignorance. Piggott also made the allegation that "Reverend Edalji belongs to a class whose opinion is ever wavering and who side with one party and apologise to the other for doing so."[33]

The reverend also clashed with the management of one of the collieries. A few weeks before the Miners' Federation meeting, at the inaugural meeting of the UDSB, Reverend Edalji, wanting the Board to have a fresh start, opposed the nomination of Mr C Browell, General Manager of the Great Wyrley Colliery Company, as chair of the

---

[33] CA 16 and 23 Nov 1889; 7 and 14 Dec 1889

USDSB because of his authoritarian manner towards staff under the Board's jurisdiction and he also opposed the nominee for vice chair for being of the same class as Browell. Instead, the reverend's support went to Mr Rogers of the Miners' Federation. The reverend and Rogers found themselves on the same side again some time after the Miners' Federation meeting when both severely criticised Browell for acting illegally in removing one of the board's teachers and, following their protests, Browell resigned, adding yet another discordant voice to the reverend's collection.[34] But by far the greatest opponent of the Edalji's held 'court' in Stafford in the 'palace' at police headquarters.

(d) The Aristocratic Policeman

The second son of the Earl of Lichfield, Captain Anson, was commissioned as a lieutenant in the army on the 14th August 1876, eventually making it to captain. His service, apart from a brief spell in Egypt in 1884, was confined to UK military establishments at Aldershot, Woolwich, Bristol and Stafford. He left the army in 1888 securing the post of chief constable for Staffordshire by 'beating' sixty-seven other applicants to the post, although his competitive prowess over the other candidates may have something to do with the fact that his father wielded considerable influence in the shire.

The captain introduced the Staffordshire constabulary to military style discipline, apparently receiving in return respect and loyalty from his men. He was to show skills more inclined towards administration - a bureaucrat, rather than an ability to display initiative and originality, distrusting those with deductive powers, such as detectives, which resulted in him blocking the formation of a CID in Staffordshire. He also allowed his image of what he thought physically attractive to influence his professional activities, not considering anyone suitable as a police officer if he had "deformities of the face or who are from any cause unsightly, and men who stammer,"[35] which undoubtedly influenced his attitude to those with similar characteristics who came under suspicion in Staffordshire – possibly deriving from Lombroso (1836-1909) the Italian criminologist, who claimed criminal types could be determined by physical characteristics. The chief constable's views were not untypical of the attitudes of late-nineteenth and early-twentieth century Britain popularised in literature where villains were caricatured

[34] CA 5 Oct 1889; 19 and 26 July 1890; 9, 16 and 23 Aug 1890; 6 Sep 1890; 11 Oct 1890

[35] M Harley, An Infamous Anson, Staffs History, Spring 1985, p37

as foreign and/or physically disabled or repellent. It was little wonder that George Edalji attracted suspicion and dislike from this 'font of wisdom' for his perceived less than attractive physical appearance linked, through populist mythology, to his 'racial' origins.

Captain Anson, when hearing of Reverend Edalji's ethnic origins in the wake of the Foster case, betrayed his own ethnocentric attitude towards the cleric by asking, "how this 'Hindoo', who could only talk with a foreign accent, came to be a clergyman of the Church of England and in charge of an important working class parish."[36] The captain's attitude locked into those perceptions of the period by which "gentlemen by disposition were white and that a black or brown skin, irrespective of an individual's wealth, learning or manner, marked that individual as a member of an inferior order."[37]

Captain Anson's viewpoint, contaminated as it was by that late-Victorian malady associated with imperial jingoism, found its way down through the bureaucratic structure to interact with similar attitudes embraced by the lower ranks of the Staffordshire police force, not unusual since their attitudes would be consistent with those displayed in other sectors of British social life. Following the Foster conviction, the captain expressed regret that one of his officers, Sergeant Upton, took part in getting her convicted. A curious remark considering the captain acknowledged Sergeant Upton was 'doing his duty', and it could only have signified that his regret had more to do with his attitude to the Edaljis than concern for Elizabeth Foster. The captain's criticism of Sergeant Upton found its way to the sergeant and may account for the open antagonism displayed towards the Edaljis by the local police from then on because prior to Captain Anson's appointment as chief constable there was no evidence of any conflict between the Edaljis and the police.

At a later date, Captain Anson disingenuously claimed not to have been aware of the Foster affair when it happened, yet at an even later date when put under considerable pressure in the wake of the Edalji conviction, he asserted Foster's innocence and believed the whole Edalji family were equally aware of her innocence. Captain Anson's speculative judgements based on his feelings hardly fell into the definition of police work and his belief that the reverend, an Anglican minister, and Mrs Edalji, a respectable daughter of a country vicar, would be prepared to accuse Foster when believing her to be innocent

[36] Capt Anson to HO, 30/ 31 Dec 1906, HO File 989, Part 2
[37] Lorimer, Doug A, [1978] Colour, Class & the Victorians, Univ of Leicester, p15

fitted in with his own malevolent and derisory attitude towards a 'Hindoo' clergyman and a woman, who married a 'Hindoo'. His attitude towards the Edaljis had been nurtured in the fertile grounds available in Victorian Britain enabling racism to flourish and was an undoubted contribution towards the difficulties faced by the reverend and his family.

Destined to hold an obsessive antipathy to the Edaljis, the chief constable entered the Great Wyrley scene and lined up against the Reverend and George Edalji - a powerful adversary and one who would use that power to try to rid the area of the Edaljis. Captain Anson was destined to become the most significant opponent of George Edalji, stretching from 1889 until as late as 1935, representing over half a lifetime of contempt and malice towards the Edaljis.[38]

The reverend's original sin arousing such animosity in Captain Anson was for being none other than a 'Hindoo clergyman' speaking the English language with a foreign accent. Nor was he a punkawallah or dhobiwallah showing due deference or subservience to the folk of South Staffordshire as might be demanded of an Indian colonial subject. Within this conflict-ridden environment laced with Victorian jingoism, the fusion of economic interests and ideology put the Edaljis on the rack and it was open season on them with the police turning a blind eye to their difficulties. South Staffordshire, like the rest of late Victorian England, was fertile ground for the imperialistic, jingoistic, racist ideology seeping into a growing literate population feeding off 'Penny Dreadfuls'.[39]

During these early years, the reverend appeared to invite conflict, perhaps in line with his calling not to shrink from perceived and real injustices or it may have been a result of a pedantic, dogmatic individualism with a tendency to inconsistent behaviour towards those with whom he came into contact. However, whatever qualities Reverend Edalji displayed to adversaries, the issue overlaying all others related to his ethnic origins and the racist milieu prevalent at the time. The antagonistic fruits growing out of the seeds planted during this and earlier periods were to burst forth onto the scene with a vengeance within the next two years.

---

[38] Anson lived to be 91 years of age, dying in 1947, having survived an air raid in 1941 in London in which his wife and daughter were killed

[39] E J Hobsbawm argued that the spread of compulsory state education was a potent force for creating national loyalty and all that goes with it in transmitting dominant ideas. Hobsbawm, E, The Age of Capital [1975] Weidenfeld & Nicholson, London, pp94-7

Chapter II

The Whirlwind Cometh: The Harassment of the Edaljis

(i)   The Eye of the Storm Hovers Over Walsall Grammar School

Three relatively uneventful years followed on from the 'Foster affair' until Reverend Edalji, still displaying a single mindedness and pedantic attitude, resurrected the educational issue in early 1892. The reverend received permission from the Home Secretary and the Charity Commissioners to sell Cheslyn Hay National School providing no objections were raised by local people or from the representatives of the new Lord Hatherton. The reverend, cavalier in his attitude to previous events and misreading the situation yet again or perhaps he thought his proposal might bear fruit as *a fait accompli*, chose not to discuss the proposal with Lord Hatherton's representatives. He later claimed, rather naively or misleadingly, that he thought it unlikely for any opposition to arise to his proposal. Consequently, in April 1892, he published a notice of intent to sell the property.[40] Various objections to the reverend's proposals were received, including one from E A Foden, the agent of Lord Hatherton, who had no intention of forgoing his rights of reversion to the property; another came from the Bishop of Lichfield; and several others from Great Wyrley parishioners, who thought the school should be preserved for Church purposes. As a consequence the Charity Commissioners withdrew their support and the scheme was abandoned.[41]

One parishioner emerging from the shadows, a member of the Vestry Committee, was Mr W H Brookes, a local grocer, who on several occasions in the future was to show an incredible animosity towards Reverend Edalji and George Edalji. Brookes, with two other parishioners, unimpressed by the performance of the vicar and the two churchwardens, accused all three of neglecting church work. Brookes, objecting in the name of the 'Anglican Holy Alliance' of religion and property, thought it a sin to sell schools established to carry out the church's divine mission of uplifting the morality and spirituality of the

---

[40] Reverend Edalji to the Charity Commissioners, 14 Jan 1892, in File TS 18/251 PRO
[41] Public Inquiry 16 Nov 1906, p28, in File TS 18/251 PRO

parish, which, he claimed, had been successfully carried out under the previous ministry. Criticising Reverend Edalji directly for making no serious effort to carry on Reverend Compson's work, Brookes, as did Hatton and Munro a dozen years before, harkened back to some 'golden age' before Reverend Edalji came to St Mark's Church – the time when the previous incumbent made no attempt to question the pursuit of vested interests on the Vestry Committee. Expressing, perhaps, a latent wish on Brookes' own part to see the back of the reverend, he considered that any replacement acting "as an energetic clergyman", another side swipe at the reverend, would need the school to look after the moral and spiritual welfare of his flock.[42]

In the midst of the disagreements involving the reverend, the managing authorities and various interests associated with the national school and disenchanted parishioners; the parish of Great Wyrley and surrounding areas were hit by a wave of anonymous letters descending predominantly on the Edalji family and occasionally on to other people. In the three and a half years from the first anonymous letter in July 1892 to the last one in December 1895, the Edaljis reaped a bigoted whirlwind from a number of authors writing in a variety of handwriting styles and under a number of pseudonyms, sometimes invoking the Almighty, the Prince of Darkness and God-Satan.

What prompted the reign of paper terror in this South Staffordshire parish that had seen more than its fair share of conflict between the man of cloth in the vicarage and a variety of interests embracing the aristocracy, large and small businessmen, working people and their representatives, religious conformists and non-conformists, cannot be specifically determined. The reverend had shown himself to be an uncompromising and pedantic opponent of vested interests and his predisposition towards single-mindedness may have fuelled the 'paper bombardment'. However, this in no way detracted from the racism underpinning the antagonism fostered by the chief constable, who was instrumental in setting the guidelines for police action or, more accurately, inaction and the accompanying distress heaped upon the Edaljis.

Sir Arthur Conan Doyle, writing over twenty years later, searching for a motive for the salvo of paper raining down on the heads of the Edaljis in the 1890s, alighted on the differing party political affiliations shown during the general election campaign of July 1892 – an election

---

[42] Correspondence with the Charity Commissioners, 28 July1891; 23 Nov 1891; 20 and 21 April 1892; 21 Sep 1892; 26 Nov 1892 and Public Inquiry 16 Nov 1906, p27, in File TS 18/251 PRO; CA 14 and 21 April 1892

campaign that fostered considerable hostility between the contending parties.[43] Doyle concluded that party politics was the motive behind the anonymous letters because the first letter arrived two days after Reverend Edalji, a sometime champion of the labouring classes, had presided over a Liberal Party political meeting in his schoolroom. Party affiliations may have played some part in the antagonism shown towards the Edaljis, especially as Reverend Edalji had shown himself to be a veritable 'thorn in the side' of the local burghers, principally Unionists, who wanted him out of the parish altogether, but not all his adversaries were Unionists. The anonymous letters and the 'dirty tricks' campaign played on the Edalji family may well have originated amongst a kaleidoscope of particularised interests, Unionist, Liberal or non-party, accumulated by Reverend Edalji over the years each with his or her own reason for harming the Edaljis. Perhaps, some opponents turned a blind eye to those whom they suspected of the harassing the Edaljis, or took advantage of the harassment by furtively encouraging other malcontents or mercenaries to extend and intensify the campaign. Or they used their influence to dissuade the local police from either taking the issue seriously or taking any action against the real perpetrators.

At the outset of the campaign, the letters gave no indication of having any political motives. In fact, when the first letters burst on to the scene they were fairly mundane and juvenile with the bile directed at Fred Brookes, son of W H Brookes and a pupil at Walsall Grammar School. When another schoolboy from the same school, Fred Wynne, also received a couple of letters and the contents of the letters referred to the firing of Hatton's rick and damage to railway compartments, the letters appeared to be linked to a schoolboy dispute involving these two boys and another named Royden Sharp, who was later to be removed from that school for swearing, lying, cheating, falsifying marks and forging letters.[44] Prior to the advent of these letters, Sharp had reported Brookes and Wynne to a railway guard for breaking a window of a carriage when all three were travelling in the same compartment. However, Sharp was found to be the culprit and had to pay restitution to the railway company as he was forced to do on another occasion after cutting the window straps in another carriage. The twelve year old Sharp had a propensity for falling foul of the law having previously been bound over for twelve months for firing a rick belonging to J T Hatton in early 1892, which, in another anonymous letter, was blamed

[43] DT 11 Jan 1907; CA 2, 9, 30 July 1892 and 6 Aug 1892
[44] ACD to HO, Case Against Royden Sharp, undated 1907, HO File 988

on Fred Brookes.[45] In the wake of that court case, Sharp, touting a newspaper report of the incident around the school for master and pupils to see, gave the impression of being proud of his notoriety.[46] The scribe also claimed that he and his mates damaged three compartments in the presence of George Edalji, who had stared at him but failed to recognise him,[47] which was more than possible because George Edalji was extremely short-sighted and, if the story was true, might not have seen, let alone recognise, the vandals. But would Sharp make it so clear that he was one of the authors unless seeking the very notoriety as was alleged after the rick firing incident.

The principal targets in the early letters appeared to be the Brookes with Lucy Brookes, previously brought before the UDSB for mistreating children in the local school,[48] placed first in the catalogue for abuse, followed by Mrs Brookes, Bloody (Mr) Brookes, and only at the end came the Edaljis.[49] George Edalji was named on the writer's assumption of a friendship existing between Fred Brookes and George Edalji since a death threat made against the latter was only to be carried out if he continued to speak to 'the grocer's kid'.[50] In fact as late as the 16th November 1892, Edalji's place within the letters seemed to be determined by this assumed friendship. Reverend Edalji also figured in the letters on a similar ground, accused of being unchristian for letting his "bloody blasted dam bloody currst buger bleeding blasting kid talk to the grocer's kid."[51]

George Edalji then began to occupy a more prominent place alongside Fred Brookes. When Fred Brookes was accused of the authorship of the 'Foster' letters, George Edalji was named as the party posting them[52] and rumours were circulated around the area about George Edalji and Fred Brookes being responsible for all the letters.[53] The letters continued to contain juvenile threats to pull the legs off a railway employee if he did not leave money at Wyrley station, and adolescent sexual fantasies were introduced involving George Edalji

---

[45] CA 7 May 1892; ALs Oct to Dec 1892, in HO File 990

[46] Fred Wynne to ACD, 2 Feb 1907 in ACD to HO, 17 Nov 1907, HO No 300, File 987

[47] ALs Oct to Dec 1892, in HO File 990

[48] CA 15 Mar 1890

[49] AL 29 Sep 1892 in HO File 990

[50] W H Brookes was a local grocer

[51] ALs in HO File 989 Pt 2 and HO File 990

[52] AL 29 Oct 1892 in HO File 990

[53] CA 14 Jan 1893; Report of Sergeant Upton, 8 Dec 1892 in Captain Anson to HO, May 1905, HO No 124, File 985

and Fred Brookes having sexual relations with each others' sisters, one of whom, Maud Edalji, was only 10 years old at the time.[54] The author raised the stakes by revealing an intention to wreak vengeance on the two boys for some injury caused by Mr Brookes and Reverend Edalji to a relation of the author's some twenty years earlier and for some more recent harm done to the author. The letters were often written in two distinct types of handwriting, one writer demonstrating a low level of education and the other from the pen of a more educated person suggesting at least two people were involved, a young person and an adult.

With the anonymous letters increasing in number and tone, Reverend Edalji brought in the local police. Sergeant Upton, of 'Foster' fame, questioned George Edalji and Fred Brookes and examined samples of their handwriting as he did with the handwriting of all the members of the Edalji family, none of which was similar to the writing in the anonymous letters.[55] In an attempt to track down the culprit, subsequent police enquiries having failed to discover any real clues as to the writer's identity, the police sought the help of the post office authorities to trace the author(s). However, no clues came from this co-operative venture because the letters temporarily ceased when the post office became involved. If any connection existed between the intervention of the post office and the cessation of letters despatched by post, then the author(s) must have known of the post office's intentions. However, this did not narrow the field of suspects since, given the police's lack of discretion, the news of this new approach to the problem could easily have found its way into the ears of a number of people in the area and village gossip being what it was the post office's proposed course of action would soon become common knowledge. The last posted letter had gone out on the 19th October 1892 and until Christmas envelopes and letters were deposited by hand in the vicarage drive and on the premises.[56]

The scribe(s) worked overtime during the dark and fog-ridden nights of November and December[57] - an aid to the deliverer(s) in

[54] ALs 8, 11 and 16 Nov1892 in HO File 990; CA 16 May 1893

[55] Report of Sergeant Upton, 8 Dec 1892, in Captain Anson to HO, May 1905, HO No 124, File 985

[56] Captain Anson to HO, 2 May 1905, in Observation on articles in Truth, produced by Bettany of the HO, 9 May 1905, Blackwell Papers, Appendix VII, England: HO Case of George Edalji – memos and papers, Bp 2/4 (19) p 52

[57] Rev Edalji to Capt Anson, 22 Dec 1892, HO File 990

avoiding detection as he, she or they deposited seventy-four small envelopes replete with abusive and foul comments scribbled on them. A regular huckster's shop of items also found their way around the environs of the vicarage, including pieces of coal, a pocket knife, blue crayon, a bundle of leather bootlaces, a leather purse, an empty phial, spoons, collar studs, a small thermometer. The huckster even went to the trouble of putting excreta in brown paper and leaving it on the vicarage doorstep. Apparently a fan of one of the Edaljis' ex-servants, this new 'postboy' attached a note to the kitchen door with the message "God Bless Lizzie Foster." The writer(s) had an obsession with sexual activity, especially adulterous sex and sex outside of marriage, displaying an adolescent sexual interest in Fred Brookes, Maud Edalji, George Edalji and Lucy Brookes and expressing a particular fascination about people urinating, going beyond the written word to include drawings of Fred Brookes and George Edalji, with a blacked-in face, carrying out this bodily function. Apart from this example of George Edalji with his face blackened, only a couple of other references were made to race, a drawing of "The Black Man", Reverend Edalji, and a threat to Mrs Edalji that, "Unless you run away from the Black I'll murder you and Mrs Brookes." Both Mrs Edalji and Mrs Brookes were damned for giving birth to their children outside of marriage with Mrs Edalji receiving an additional scathing as the reverend's mischief-making wife, who should be sent away, otherwise she would be shot as "She is a cant (cunt), liar, divil (devil), confounded hypocrite, silly blasted bloody fool" - a letter written by someone apparently unable to spell 'cunt' or 'devil' but able to spell 'confounded hypocrite.' The reverend was also advised to send away those old splitters (informers) Fred Brookes and George Edalji, another possible connection with Sharp or Foster.[58]

In the midst of these nocturnal deliveries, a breakthrough appeared to have arrived with the resurrection of the Walsall Grammar School connection.[59] An anonymous letter went to the headmaster, Mr Aldis, threatening to kill him and to set fire to the school – another link to Royden Sharp, who, however, was now a boarder at a school in Lincolnshire. The letter was shown to the Cannock police, who also received a 'tip off' that Wynne was a collaborator in writing the

[58] ALs, mostly undated in HO File 990, originals sent by Captain Anson to Blackwell at HO, 3 Dec 1907

[59] Mr Aldis to Captain Anson, 1 Jan 1893 in Captain Anson to Blackwell, 19 Nov 1903, HO File 989 Pt 1; Fred Wynne to ACD, 2 Feb 1907 in HO File 989 Pt 1

anonymous letters. This 'tip off' came from an eye witness, a clerk named Tandy working at Walsall Post Office, who identified Wynne as the boy asking for a letter at the post office connected with the anonymous letter writing. This 'tip' sparked off a trip to the school by Sergeant Upton on the 10th November 1892 to confront Wynne with Tandy. After providing Sergeant Upton with a sample of his handwriting, Wynne was suspended from school but, after further enquiries, he returned to school and no more was heard of it. Fred Wynne might well have been a participant as he knew of Sharp's misdemeanours, as did many others of course, and it was Wynne, antagonistic to Sharp over the railway carriage incident, who claimed Sharp paraded himself around the school basking in the 'glory' of firing Hatton's rick. The early letters sent to the Brookes' and Edaljis' could have been written by Wynne with a couple to himself to give the impression Sharp was the culprit.

The headmaster was convinced but had no proof, a salient feature infecting everyone throughout this long drawn out saga, that Wynne was an accomplice of the author as were both Fred Brookes and George Edalji, but an accomplice of whom? Royden Sharp, whose previous history of misdeeds at Walsall Grammar School included writing anonymous letters, was now ensconced in a boarding school at Wisbech, Lincolnshire. Could the headmaster have meant one of Sharp's brothers, Walter, who had also attended the school, and was known in the past to jump to the defence of his younger brother? But this made no sense whether or not Walter was the scribe since why would Wynne, Brookes or Edalji assist the anonymous letter writer to make such claims against themselves and/or their families. It is also difficult to understand why the headmaster included George Edalji. Edalji was not a pupil at the school and had never attended there, so the headmaster could know little about him, especially as Edalji had no close friend or companion at the school. If Edalji was an accomplice what function did he perform? Posting the letters? To do this, the myopic Edalji would have to travel considerable distances away from the Great Wyrley to Walsall to Birmingham railway route as many of the pre-hand delivered missives, which had only just ceased, were posted in diverse places across the West Midlands. Nor could he have been an accomplice in writing the letters because his handwriting did not match that of the scribe, although that was yet another lay assessment.

To all intents and purposes, George Edalji was outside the frame and the central actors in the anonymous letters saga were connected with the grammar school in Walsall, which events in December 1892 seemed to confirm. However, George Edalji was to be catapulted into centre stage in the most unconvincing way through the local gossip channels.

(ii) The Rumour Machine

The failure to link pupils at Walsall Grammar School to the anonymous letters may have resulted from a lack of desire on the part of the local police to have anything distract attention from a more vulnerable target and one to satisfy Captain Anson's prejudices concerning the 'Hindoo' clergyman. Sergeant Upton may have wanted to match up to Captain Anson's expectations of an Edalji being responsible for the letters and to redress his 'error' in the eyes of the chief constable for assisting the 'Hindoo vicar' in the conviction of Elizabeth Foster – little point in attracting the chief constable's displeasure yet again. Sergeant Upton may also be seeking to curry favour with local people by making amends for the role he played in the conviction of 'one of their own', Elizabeth Foster. Whatever motivated the sergeant to focus solely on George Edalji, he became a potent force in spreading rumours around the area about the vicar's son being the scribe despite knowing that George Edalji's handwriting did not fit the bill and the letters were connected with Walsall Grammar School.

Sergeant Upton spun a tale to Mr W H Brookes about seeing George Edalji posting a letter in the pillar-box near Great Wyrley station. The sergeant, apparently unseen by George Edalji, a not too difficult task to achieve considering Edalji's extreme short-sightedness, was himself so sharp-sighted as to be able to distinguish the type and colour of the envelope 'posted' by George, which Mr Brookes confirmed matched the envelope recently sent to him with an anonymous letter inside.[60] This particular piece of detective work on Sergeant Upton's part was told to Mr Brookes in 1892 although it did not come to light until November 1903 when Mr Brookes tried to get the story published in the Birmingham Daily Mail shortly after the campaign to get George Edalji released from prison had begun.[61] If Sergeant Upton had discovered the culprit's identity it was truly an incredible piece of detective work outstripping anything previously

---

[60] W H Brookes to Mail 23 Nov 1903, HO File 989 Pt 2

[61] The Birmingham Daily Mail refused to publish the letter because of the possibility of a libel suit being brought against the paper on behalf of George Edalji. BDM to WH Brookes, 25 Nov 1903, HO File 989 Pt 2

done by the police up to that point, or for that matter thereafter.[62] Furthermore as the letter must have been posted prior to the 16th October, after which posted letters temporarily ceased, then there was no possible reason for the police to accept the post office's offer to track down the culprit(s). Sergeant Upton certainly looked to be massaging public opinion against George Edalji because he failed to mention his findings to his superior officers at the time nor did he mention it in either of his two written reports submitted to Superintendent Barrett in December 1892. Nor was Mr Brookes likely to be the sole beneficiary of Sergeant Upton's revelations as rumours of George Edalji's guilt soon began to circulate around the parish. Brookes should have exercised more caution in accepting this 'tit-bit' of information because from previous experience he knew that Sergeant Upton was prone to stretching the truth when seeking an arrest. Brookes had witnessed several people being charged by the sergeant for allegedly gambling on licensed premises and in court had disputed Sergeant Upton's version of the facts, which resulted in all the alleged gamblers being discharged.[63] Nonetheless, Sergeant Upton's 'disclosure' convinced Mr Brookes, who wanted to see the back of Reverend Edalji, that George Edalji was the author of the anonymous letters. Brookes mustered his own 'proof' of George Edalji's guilt - a reference to Brookes' 'sour look' in one of the letters, which Brookes attributed to an incident involving himself and George Edalji after travelling in the same train from Walsall to Great Wyrley. After getting off the train, George Edalji smiled across at Brookes who, according to Brookes' own description, returned George Edalji's gesture with a 'sour look'. A more unpleasant incident occurred shortly afterwards. While sitting in a railway carriage, Brookes saw George Edalji walking up and down the platform "prying into every carriage… with that cunning look for which he was so noted." Brookes, whose "feelings and passions got the better of him, alighted from the train and rushed at George Edalji." With the schoolboy responding with a bow and a smile, Brookes attacked him with fists flailing. Edalji successfully avoided the blows and the now exhausted Brookes, dropped his arms, ceased his threats and Edalji "sneaked off into the

---

[62] The explanation for Sergeant Upton's astuteness might reside in the possibility that the sergeant or a collaborator was responsible for the letter sent to W H Brookes, which would account for the clear description of the envelope. This tactic of sending out 'anonymous' letters was not unknown to the Staffordshire police force as events in 1903 would amply demonstrate.

[63] CA 27 Nov 1886

railway carriage." The incident, according to Brookes' account, was a watershed as he claimed the anonymous letters and other forgeries ceased forthwith,[64] a claim far from the truth because the letters continued for years afterwards and Brookes was again referred to as 'sour face' in letters in 1894 and 1895.

Mr Brookes ignored the possibility of his 'sour look' being the face he showed to others, including a pair named Holmes and Mears, whom Brookes accused of stealing from his shop. More significantly, Mr Brookes' actions and his terminology tell more about Brookes than it does about George Edalji. What kind of man would scowl for no apparent reason at a smiling youth, the son of the local vicar and a neighbour, and physically attack an inoffensive youth who politely bowed and smiled at him. Perhaps Mr Brookes was impelled into this belligerent and unreasonable behaviour by Sergeant Upton's remarks to him, yet even this explanation seems unlikely to be the sole reason for Brookes' violent behaviour. More than likely, Brookes, too, was infected with a less than tolerant attitude towards his Asian and Euro-Asian neighbours as expressed in his less than favourable comments towards Reverend Edalji over the Cheslyn Hay school issue. Referring to George Edalji "prying into every carriage" and the "cunning look for which he was noted", when the lad, well known locally as extremely short-sighted, was more than likely looking for a seat on the train, could be explained as part of Brookes' stereotypal image of the devious 'Oriental'.

A case was being manufactured against George Edalji and not even Sergeant Upton's visit to Walsall Grammar School a couple of weeks later and the identification of one of its pupils in an incident involving anonymous letters made the slightest difference. The sergeant had begun to backtrack on his own contribution in securing the conviction of Elizabeth Foster in 1889 by suggesting that if she was not guilty of sending those threatening letters, they must have originated from within the Edalji family.[65] This was a surprising evolution in the field of detection when more likely suspects for the recent spate of letters were available at Walsall Grammar School.

(ii) A Key, some Excreta and a Leaflet

---

[64] W H Brookes to Mail, 23 Nov 1903, HO File 989 Pt 2

[65] Report of Sergeant Upton, 8 Dec 1892, in Captain Anson to HO, May 1905, HO No 124, File 985; Reverend Edalji to Captain Anson, 22 December 1892, HO File 990

George Edalji and Fred Brookes remained the anonymous letter writers' favourite targets and the scribes widened the circulation of disdain for the two boys. Writing under the names of Fred Brookes and George Edalji, the scribes contacted the Daily Argus admitting authorship of the recent anonymous letters and the Foster letters of 1888/9, which the Argus found space to publish. Both parents commenced legal proceedings against the paper for damages for libel but this action appeared to have been abandoned after the Daily Argus offered a reward for the identity of the person sending in the forged confession.[66]

In a manner similar to the police when they directed sole attention to George Edalji because of the previous anonymous letter scandal at the vicarage, Reverend Edalji, also without any evidence, fixed his attention on the person convicted of sending those 1888/9 letters, Elizabeth Foster. The reverend wanted Elizabeth Foster arrested but the police only offered to issue a warrant for a prosecution by Reverend Edalji, who must have thought better of it, since, like police suspicions about George Edalji's alleged guilt, there was no evidence. However, Superintendent Barrett agreed to maintain the police watch on the vicarage in the evenings, which was to produce some bizarre incidents.[67]

In the seven days from the 11th to the 18th December 1892, the various 'droppings' continued to fall in and around the vicarage. In addition to the usual scribbled paper and coins, a key was found on the doorstep, excreta daubed on the outside of the windows and a leaflet placed in the vicarage hall. The three incidents, taking place in quick succession, conveniently arrived on the scene at a time when the police were at their wits end and being ridiculed for their incompetence throughout the district. Sergeant Upton, needing an arrest, put the blame on someone inside the vicarage – when at a loss choose the easy and popular route, find a scapegoat, so the sergeant settled on George Edalji as the culprit. From then on the die was cast, sealing George Edalji's fate, as nothing would persuade the police to consider alternatives.

The three-strike saga began after Police Constable Poole, on watch at the vicarage, claimed to have found a key on the back doorstep on the 12th December and no one had been seen to pass in or out of the house between the time George Edalji went in and when the key was found.

---

[66] DA 30 Nov and 7 Dec 1892 in Report of Sergeant Upton, 8 Dec 1892, in Captain Anson to HO, May 1905, HO No 124, File 984;

[67] Superintendent Barrett's report, 9 Dec 1892 in Captain Anson to HO, May 1905, HO No 124, File 985

PC Poole handed the key to the reverend, who in turn passed it on to Sergeant Upton, who boasted he would "soon find out where it came from." A week later, still not having discovered the ownership of the key, Sergeant Upton predicted that George Edalji not only wrote the anonymous letters but also the owner of the stolen key would be found at Mason College, where George Edalji studied – another ingenious piece of deduction linking it to an educational establishment but unfortunately for the sergeant it came from a different scholarly institution. [68]

By the 19th December, this 'forecast' and sweeping conclusion was proven to be in error and Sergeant Upton was completely on the wrong track. From information coming through the police 'grapevine' the key was eventually traced to none other than Walsall Grammar School, a long way away from Mason College. Yet how did the police 'informant' come by this information? The most reasonable explanation for someone knowing of the key's origins was that either the informant took the key or knew who did – scholars or previous scholars at the school, which disqualified George Edalji.

Two days after the 'key incident', 'the excreta incident' occurred, yet again investigated by Sergeant Upton but not until the 17th December between 8 pm and 10 pm, corresponding to the time the initial incident occurred three days before. The sergeant thought it impossible for anyone to throw excreta on to the upstairs window from outside the vicarage as the window was partly covered by a yew tree. When Reverend Edalji suggested that the perpetrator might have climbed the tree before flinging the excreta, Sergeant Upton later claimed to have examined the tree, finding no evidence of such an attempt. Doubts can be entertained over the sergeant's findings since the examination of the tree took place three days after the event and at night. Sergeant Upton then interviewed George Edalji and, determined to pin both offences on him, told Reverend Edalji within earshot of his son, who was in bed, of the police's intention to watch the vicarage in the mornings but not in the evenings – an oral snare having the purpose of seeking to trap the youthful George.[69]

The following evening, Sergeant Upton and PC Jackson arrived at the vicarage at 8.25 pm and, according to the sergeant, thoroughly

[68] Report of Sergeant Upton, 19 Dec 1892 in Captain Anson to HO, May 1905, HO No 124, File 985; C Edalji to HO, 30 Nov 1903, HO No 17, file 985

[69] Report of Sergeant Upton, 19 Dec 1892 in Captain Anson to HO, May 1905, HO No 124, File 985;

examined all the vicarage doors finding nothing there. There was a half-inch space between the front door and the doorstep, which enabled the two officers when lying down to peer through the gap to see some distance into the hall. At 9 pm, someone went upstairs in slippers as if going to bed. Shortly afterwards, the police still peering under the door saw Reverend Edalji go into the backyard with the servant girl presumably to lock up. On his return, the reverend went into the dining room and shut the door. The police then heard someone come down the stairs in stockinged feet and heard that person breathing. They waited until the person left the hall and then Sergeant Upton, using his lamp, looked under the door and saw something resembling a letter. Instead of banging on the front door, both police officers rushed immediately to the side door of the vicarage and knocked it, explaining to the vicar, who was having supper with Mrs Edalji, what they had heard. This came as a surprise to the Edaljis since, according to them and contrary to the police's story, they were sitting in the dining room with the door open – a precaution taken to reassure the servant, working in the adjoining kitchen, who was extremely nervous due to recent events. This concern for the servant was consistent with the reverend earlier going outside in the dark with her to lock up and with the protective approach previously taken on behalf of Elizabeth Foster in 1888/9 by Mrs Edalji. Neither of the Edaljis saw nor heard anyone in the hall and from where the Edaljis were sitting it was impossible for any of the children to come down without being seen, especially if the child had allegedly made enough noise for the policemen waiting outside the front door to hear it.

Sergeant Upton asked the reverend to see if anything was in the hall and, 'voila', an envelope with a leaflet and some faeces inside was found close to the front door. The sergeant more than implied that one of the Edalji children was responsible and, accompanied by Reverend Edalji, went upstairs to speak to them. George Edalji, lying in bed, denied going downstairs or putting down any paper in the hall. Sergeant Upton went to examine the water closet and saw that the contents of the toilet pan had been covered with brown paper to conceal the fact that it had been disturbed. This presumption, which the police failed to examine at close hand, in no way established that the excreta came from the Edalji toilet. If the faeces in the envelope had their origins in the Edaljis' water closet, as was later implied, they would more than likely be damp and attract comment but nothing was said by either of the police officers at the time.

Sergeant Upton tried to convince Reverend Edalji that his son had put the leaflet in the hall and he wanted to search the vicarage for other leaflets. However, the reverend refused to accommodate him as the police had questioned George Edalji on two previous occasions without producing anything concrete and an unusually angry Mrs Edalji spoke of the impossibility of anyone coming down the stairs without either Reverend Edalji or herself seeing them. The reverend, doubting the veracity of the police officer's story, thought it physically impossible for anyone to "hear stockinged-feet and breathing" through a thick outer door a dozen feet from the bottom of the stairs shielded behind another closed inner door, which also made it impossible for the police to see if the dining room door was closed. The closed intermediary door in the hall would also make it difficult for either of the two police officers to see Reverend Edalji go outside with the servant, suggesting that when they did go outside the officers were watching from around the back of the vicarage.

The reverend thought it questionable for the police to go around to the side door when they could have raised the alarm at the front door where they were positioned. Not mincing his words, Reverend Edalji put it to Sergeant Upton that he was trying to frame his son by pushing the leaflet himself under the door from the outside. Sergeant Upton defended himself by arguing there was insufficient space under the door to slide a leaflet through, whereupon, Shapurji went outside and pushed the leaflet under the door to show how it could be accomplished. Interestingly, the police officers claimed to have laid down to look through the gap under the door, so it seemed as if they were grasping at straws by claiming it was not possible to push an envelope under the door and if they heard stockinged-feet and breathing why did they not, as the reverend asked, alert those inside by banging on the door or shouting. [70]

Mrs Edalji, in keeping with a certain quality in her character not to think the worst of people, which she held firmly to until Captain Anson's cavalier disregard for her and her family completely exorcised it, offered a novel account of the leaflet incident. Mrs Edalji suggested that as George slept in a room over the hall and tended to walk, or more specifically thump in his stockings to the window to blow out the candle, that might be the sound the police heard. [71]

Notwithstanding the suspect nature of the police version of these three incidents, George Edalji's fate was well and truly sealed.

Captain Anson's contribution to these events displayed not only his ignorance and lack of interest in establishing the facts but also his lack of impartiality as he accused George Edalji of taking the key from the school, described by Captain Anson in a letter to Reverend Edalji, as "the school George Edalji attended, Walsall Grammar School." In what appeared to be an attempt to silence or to intimidate the reverend, the captain raised the possibility of taking out a summons against George Edalji over the theft of the key, a non-starter showing the captain to be unaware that George Edalji had never set foot on the premises nor had any real friends who could have given him the key. When it became known to Captain Anson that George Edalji was a student at Mason College Birmingham, he refused to accept that he could possibly be wrong and used a sleight of hand or mind in an attempt to rescue his completely unviable conclusions. Sidetracking the

---

[70] In 1907, a pseudonymous letter writer, Martin Molton, claimed that Sergeant Upton left his post at the front door leaving PC Preston on guard. During his absence the leaflet was put on the doorstep. After criticism from the sergeant for failing to detect the culprit, PC Preston pushed the envelope under the door. If this had any truth, either the depositor stayed to watch the police from somewhere outside the vicarage, or someone in the vicarage pushed the leaflet under the door to the outside and would know the police pushed it back inside. If the sergeant's story was a fabrication, he was trying to set up George Edalji by bringing the leaflet with him to push under the door. The writer also claimed the letter in the hall was in the same handwriting as previous anonymous letters, which was off the mark since the pamphlet was merely a printed document with no handwriting on it and it was PC Jackson on watch with Sergeant Upton not PC Preston. Report of Sergeant Upton, 19 Dec 1892 in Captain Anson to HO, May 1905, HO No 124, File 985; Martin Molton Letters, Blackwell Papers, England: HO Case of George Edalji – memos and papers, Bp 2/4 (19) p 57

[71] Reverend Edalji to Captain Anson, 22 December 1892, HO File 990

glaring deficiencies in his position, he claimed that George Edalji knew how the key turned up on the vicarage doorstep and he conjured up a new conclusion of at least two people being involved, a conclusion he was forced into since he was adamant one the culprits was George Edalji. But who were the others – Fred Brookes or Fred Wynne or Royden Sharp, all pupils at the school and all suspected by the police as well as the school headmaster of involvement in the anonymous letters, none of whom would have any difficulty in taking the key off the board where it was kept. Royden Sharp, could still be considered as a suspect for the theft of the key since the teachers at the school were unsure how long the key had been missing and he might have taken it prior to his enforced withdrawal from the school before passing it on to his brother, Walter. Fishing for information, a sign that Captain Anson had nothing substantive, he asked George Edalji how he got hold of the key and promised that if the incident had been merely a practical joke no further action would ensue. However, if George Edalji failed to admit to his part in the deception, those involved would be regarded as thieves and proceedings taken against them.

Ultimately forced into acknowledging that someone other than George Edalji had taken the key, actually saying it was "tolerably clear" the key was taken by a boy at Walsall Grammar School, Captain Anson showed a considerable reluctance to admit that others might be involved in the other incidents and in the anonymous letter writing. Unable to surmount his less than adequate and prejudicial assessment of the situation, the captain arrived at the conclusion that there was no connection between the "key matter and other annoyances to which you (the Edaljis) had been subject." To say the least, this was a remarkable and anomalous admission because Captain Anson was saying that if George Edalji was in some way involved in the 'key' incident, as he believed him to be, then by the captain's own 'logic', Edalji was unconnected to the leaflet incident or any of the anonymous letters flooding the area. Behind this misguided 'logic' was the inference that the police knew who was really involved in the 'key' incident and it was not George Edalji but the police were not going to admit that. Even though Captain Anson believed George Edalji to be nothing more than a bit player in the 'key' incident, he was unrelenting in his persecution of this boy for this crime and appeared not to be interested in anyone else including the one who must have taken the key from the school. Consequently, the police dropped the 'key' issue unconcerned that the harassment of the Edaljis was continuing in full flow.[72]

Captain Anson also refused to accept the dissimilarity between George Edalji's handwriting and the writing in the anonymous letters, describing the sample of handwriting provided by the sixteen years old George Edalji as resembling 'a round hand' of a boy of aged eleven or twelve years implying that George Edalji had disguised his handwriting to deflect suspicion from himself.[73] Not a particularly convincing argument as it ignored George Edalji's acute myopia and astigmatism, a possible reason for his writing to have taken on this particular 'rounded form.'

The way others more likely to have committed the crimes were overlooked, as during the animal maimings of 1903, put into context the way the Staffordshire constabulary from Captain Anson downwards behaved towards George Edalji. He was always the object to be spoken of with no mention of how he felt about the continuous unsubstantiated allegations, threats and attempted assaults – a studious young man of sixteen years caught up in events not of his making but of course he was an outcaste to the 'real' people. In fact, as a result of police accusations, George Edalji became increasingly apprehensive of what the police might do and say about him – almost resignation, which might explain his apparent detachment when arrested, tried and convicted in 1903.[74]

(v) The Reverend Casts his Stone

The reverend had been doing his own scratching around, casting his net wide to gather up suspects, identifying Holmes and Mears, whom Mr Brookes had previously accused of theft from his shop, and George Greensill, attributed with writing the newspaper confession, as co-conspirators. Elizabeth Foster was also accused of conspiring with her brothers, relations and friends as potential scribes seeking revenge for the perceived injustice meted out to her. The reverend's lantern also fell on Daniel Cotton, one time church organist at St Mark's, who left eighteen months before when the reverend refused to exclude Fred

---

[72] Captain Anson to Reverend Edalji, 20 Dec 1892 and 24 & 26 Jan 1893, HO File 990; Report of Sergeant Upton, 8 Dec 1892 in Captain Anson to HO, May 1905, HO No 124, File 985; Truth, 9 Feb 1905; Gazette 1 Feb 1907; Aldis to Captain Anson, 1 Jan 1893 in Captain Anson to Blackwell, 19 Nov 1903, HO File 989 Pt 1; Yelverton, in BME 28 Nov 1903

[73] Ward, Dr J, The Story of George Edalji, Paper to the Police History Society [1993] p2 at Wm Salt Library, Stafford

[74] M Edalji to the Home Secretary, 8 Feb 1956, HO File 45/24635

Brookes from the church choir.[75] The reverend passed on the names of his suspects to Sergeant Upton but the police had made up their minds on who to blame for the anonymous letters and other incidents. One group escaping the reverend's attention was the Sharps of Hednesford, who did not enter the equation, at least outside of police circles, until fifteen years later when Sir Arthur Conan Doyle unconvincingly offered up the Sharp brothers as authors of the anonymous letters.[76]

When rumours claiming that "The police caught George Edalji with a letter in the house" reached the reverend's ears, he had no doubts about Sergeant Upton's role in originating these rumours and he asked the sergeant to distance himself from the rumours if he was not responsible[77] – a request left unsatisfied, which confirmed to the reverend that Sergeant Upton was culpable. Nor should any doubts be entertained as to Sergeant Upton's role in the rumours given his comments to Mr Brookes about George Edalji. The reverend followed up by asking the chief constable to produce the evidence on which he came to suspect his son and he also reported his suspicions of a frame up carried out by Sergeant Upton.[78] An invitation was also extended to Captain Anson to visit the vicarage to see for himself the physical impossibility of Sergeant Upton's claims but the captain was not about to take up any offer from the 'Hindoo parson'. Taking a leaf out of the anonymous scribe's book, Reverend Edalji wrote to the local press publicly denouncing the rumours as a mistake or something worse on the part of the police. As the reverend put it, "The wish was father to the thought."[79] Not to be outdone by the police's cavalier attitude, Reverend Edalji went a step further by threatening to inform Lord Hatherton of the incapability of the chief constable and the local police in detecting the real culprit, which found its way to Captain Anson exacerbating even further the flawed relationship between the captain and Reverend Edalji.[80]

---

75 Reverend Edalji to Captain Anson, 22 December 1892, HO File 990
76 ACD to HO, 7 Feb 1907, HO File 989 Pt 1
77 Reverend Edalji to Captain Anson, 22 December 1892, HO File 990
78 Ibid; Despatch 31 Jan 1907
79 CA 28 December 1892
80 Report of Sergeant Upton, 19 Dec 1892 in Captain Anson to HO, May 1905, HO No 124, file 985; the reverend wrote to Lord Hatherton at a time when he was threatening his Lordship's reversion rights to the church school property. Correspondence with the Charity Commissioners, July1891 to 26 Nov 1892 and Public Inquiry 16 Nov 1906, p27, in File TS 18/251 PRO

The reverend, yet again, had tweaked the moustache and punctured the ego of a leading member of the Staffordshire aristocracy, reinforcing Captain Anson's less than favourable state of mind towards this Asian upstart, who was audacious enough to launch an attack on Captain Anson and his faithful retainers in his Staffordshire Constabulary fiefdom. This petit-bourgeoise 'Hindoo' Christian, by questioning the integrity of Staffordshire police officers, displayed an 'uppityness' far in excess of his 'station in life' – a quality unlikely to endear him to this second son of a peer of the realm.

Sergeant Upton, later to be eulogised in several of the subsequent anonymous letters – almost a reward it seemed for allegedly 'catching' George Edalji, had already beaten the reverend to the punch by sending a report of the 'triple events' to Superintendent Barrett but omitting any reference to his alleged sighting of George Edalji posting an anonymous letter to Mr Brookes from the station pillar box. The superintendent, in turn, despite the absence of firm evidence to connect George Edalji with the anonymous letters, praised his sergeant for discovering the real offender and took it upon himself to declare the case closed as "no outsider could possibly do such things." In spite of more suitable candidates being available for that dishonour, Superintendent Barrett, offering himself up as a 'lay expert', one of a whole range of such experts to surface over the next fifteen years, informed Captain Anson that the contents of the anonymous letters pointed to someone with knowledge of almost everything taking place in the vicarage on a daily basis and the author's objective was attributed to causing annoyance rather than harm.[81] The Superintendent had overlooked the fact that the information contained in the anonymous letters would be known to many people living in the vicinity of the vicarage and/or attending St Mark's Church. He was obviously not familiar with scandal-mongers, of which Sergeant Upton appeared to be a prime example, who kept their ears metaphorically stuck to the letter boxes and took great delight in broadcasting local gossip to all and sundry. Sergeant Upton's report was passed on to Captain Anson without any of the details being subjected to critical examination but it was enough to convince the chief constable, who needed little to persuade him of George Edalji's authorship not only of the anonymous letters but also for everything else happening in the area. Instead of inquiring into the reverend's allegation against Sergeant Upton, Captain Anson decided it did not warrant serious consideration. The sergeant had at least achieved a

---

[81] Superintendent Barrett's Report, 9 Dec 1892 in Captain Anson to HO, May 1905, HO No 124, File 985

measure of personal success by removing some of the displeasure Captain Anson felt for his part in the Foster affair.

By the end of 1892, when a new scribe entered the arena, the framework for inflicting harm on the Edaljis was now firmly established and the police contemptuously and maliciously threw the Edalji family to the wolves or, in this case, to the Staffordshire bull terriers.

Chapter III

The Whirlwind Arriveth: The Isolation of the Edaljis

(i)   The Paroxysm of the Scribe

The aggressive posture displayed by the police towards the Edalji family, orchestrated by the chief constable, broadcast to all and sundry that it was open season on the 'Hindoo' family. A spate of anonymous letters, around a dozen, descended on the vicarage between the 20th December 1892 and the 2nd January 1893. The last one offered a temporary respite to the family by promising a cessation in the harassment for a few months, while the author took temporary leave of the area – an indication of an individual or members of a group, perhaps a family, constantly on the move in search of employment or a boy returning to boarding school. As the promised respite by the author(s) did not materialise, was it merely another hoax to give the Edaljis a false sense of security in believing their ordeal was over? Or was it an indication that the author(s) were handing over to another scribe because the letters arriving between the end of December 1892 and the end of March 1893, while retaining links with the earlier ones, introduced an entirely different dimension. The threats to George Edalji and Fred Brookes; protestations over the alleged victimisation of Elizabeth Foster; and the sexual crudity remained but new features surfaced from the dark interior of the author's psyche - religious ranting, self-persecution and grotesque violence.[82] The religious contributions entered the letters shortly before the end of the year when the author wrote of God and Christ (28 December), and continued with 'Christ' (13 January), Pharisees and hypocrites (17 January), 'God allelulah' (sic) Christ (25 January), Christ (14 February) and God Almighty (undated but before March 1893) accompanied often by the expression "ha ha ha". The new scribe appeared intoxicated with religion and exhibited a paroxysm associated with early Methodism and

---

[82] ALs 22 Jan, 5 Feb, 17 and 29 Mar 1893, undated ALs and numerous others in HO File 990; CA 7, 14, 21 Jan, 25 Mar and 8 April 1893; F E Smith, Hansard, 18 Jul 1907, v 178 c 1007; Capt Anson to HO, May 1905, HO No 124, File 984; Carr, J D [1949] The Life of Sir Arthur Conan Doyle, John Murray, London, p220

Methodist revivalism noted for emotional violence, vivid descriptions of sudden death and catastrophe, and the rhetoric of the enormity of sin with the dramatic offer of redemption.[83]

George Edalji and Fred Brookes continued to be the prime targets for the new scriptwriter but the stakes were raised against them with promises of an unpleasant end either in death or disgrace. The dislike of the two boys appeared to have its origins in the past actions of their parents as mentioned once in a previous letter. Mr Brookes, for his behaviour on New Years' day in 1873, and similar behaviour by Reverend Edalji in 1876, which the author claimed had damaged his brother's name and prevented him from becoming a gentleman.[84] Not without a certain self-indulgence, the new scribe, using a religious turn of phrase, wrote of Reverend Edalji as a "hypocrite and liar, how can you preach as you do? I was hungry and you fed me not, naked and you clothed me not, in prison and you visited me not…God help all the poor souls whom you have accused." His rantings continued with "I do not think hell is such a bad place after all and I long, yes I long, to be there rolling in the flames of Hell fire that shall never be quenched…never, never, never, I know that I am lost, oh, oh, oh, Christ, Christ, Christ help me! Oh I am lost, God have mercy, Christ help, every day, every hour, my hatred is growing against George Edalji and Fred Brookes. If I could get into an empty railway compartment with them I would do for them both" and then to die on the scaffold accompanied by the exultant shouts of the Reverend and Mrs Edalji and many others. Hostility was directed at Mrs Edalji, whom the author threatened to make it so hot for her that she would flee the place and he cautioned her not to let "the Black person read this (letter)" otherwise "your kid will be before the magistrates." The scribe also wanted Reverend Edalji to follow in the footsteps of other male parishioners and have sexual relations with Lucy Brookes. The bitterness and hatred mingled with promises of violence erupting from the wrath of God embraced many people in the parish, whose excommunication the writer sought. These included George Edalji, Maud Edalji, Fred Brookes, Mr and Mrs Brookes, Messrs Hatton, Bowen, Sambrook and many others.

---

[83] Southey R [1889] Life of Wesley and the Rise of Progressive Methodism, Cavendish, London, p382ft

[84] Thomas Cash Burton fell foul of the Vestry Committee, of which Mr Brookes was a member, in 1873 but that was before Reverend Edalji became parish Minister. If the claim was genuine both Mr Brookes and the Reverend would know who it was unless the slight was so insignificant, other than to the scribe, that it went unnoticed

Boasting of the ability to imitate the Reverend and George Edalji's handwriting, the writer displayed another side to his or her character – hatred was not the only theme in these letters. Sergeant Upton was eulogised and attracted the affectionate comment of "I love Upton better than life itself for his kindness that night because for my sake he lost promotion." The three police officers – Upton, Jackson and Preston, who were on watch at the vicarage when the key and leaflet were found, were awarded the honour of the 'Noble Trinity' with Upton as God.

The Upton-Foster theme was pursued in the Lichfield Mercury, which, in a repeat performance of the 'conning' of the Daily Argus, published an apology in the names of George Edalji and Fred Brookes for writing all the anonymous letters. The 'repentant' boys requested that all charges against Sergeant Upton and Elizabeth Foster be dropped. This 'apology' was exposed as a fraud in the next edition of the paper following a complaint from Reverend Edalji.[85] A curious mix up had arisen following the initial publication of the boy's 'apology'. Reverend Edalji handed a telegram into the post office addressed to the Lichfield Mercury requesting the retraction of the forged confession. At the same time, another telegram was handed in addressed to a gentleman at the Lichfield Brewery. The reverend's telegram was sent to the brewery and on the following day he received a letter from a solicitor demanding substantial damages for libel and threatening Reverend Edalji with the 'Queen's greeting in default.' It took some time for the other party to accept the reverend was not at fault.[86] Reverend Edalji was certainly at the tail end of a terrible spate of ill fortune.

Towards the end of March, either a substitute writer took over or the scribe, who had brandished the pen since Christmas, began to suffer more extreme delusions as the letters took on an increasingly rabid form. This was the start of the pseudonymous letters signed 'God-Satan', which arrived at the vicarage on and after the 29 March 1893. God-Satan, who also used the term 'ha ha ha', claimed to have arrived in the district barely seven and a half months before, in mid-August 1892 and was handed the task of writing the letters from now on because of his ability to put what the original scribe dictated to him into 'proper' English. His 'employer' held a deep-seated hatred for Mr Brookes and also for Reverend Edalji, referred to as a "Parsee, Pharisee or whatever you are." The new transcriber, a self-confessed rake, thief,

---

[85] LM 3 & 10 March 1893

[86] Despatch, 31 January 1907

liar and jailbird, wrote of descending into hell in a golden chariot to watch thousands of creatures being tortured, who, as Christ had reputedly explained to him, were mainly grocer's kids and "common printers who print what they should not," introducing a new adversary, Withington, proprietor of the Cannock Advertiser, described as a "grasping money making vulgar printer...biggest liar and cheat in Cannock." He then listed twenty-six people, in addition to Satan and all his angels, in the circle of hatred, which must have been the enemies of the person for whom he had assumed the role of amanuensis, or his own enemies if he was in fact the same post-Christmas scribe now suffering from an intensifying psychiatric disorder. Those incurring the wrath of God-Satan included Reverend Edalji, Charlotte Edalji, George Edalji, Maud Edalji (horrid little girl) Lucy Brookes, Fred Brookes (grocer's kid), W H Brookes, Mr Hatton (fool of a farmer), Mrs Hatton (lady), Mr Wynne and railway employees, postmen, gravediggers and washerwomen. Mrs Edalji fared badly being referred to as "your damned wife" and described as a "Vile, ill tempered, mischief making wife spreading heinous charges against the police." God-Satan was not averse to demonstrating his interest in explicit sexual practices expressed in an extremely crude manner focussing attention on Lucy Brookes, who was again the practitioner as well as the recipient of future sexual favours. One noticeable absentee in this array of people against whom the writer(s) held grudges, as was the case in all the previous and subsequent anonymous letters, was the name of Horace Edalji, the second son of the Reverend and Mrs Edalji. Conversely, the writer expressed love for: Sergeant Upton, 'Lizzie' Foster, the Cannock police, friends, a brother in the church, the memory of dead kinsman, four railwaymen, some post office employees, thus showing that his, her or their writings were not all ill tidings and signals of despair.

The God-Satan letters contained Latin and French, absent in previous missives, indicating that these latest letters were written by a person of some education, thought to be either a clergyman or a lawyer or other man of learning. The careful omission of punctuation coupled with accurate spelling and sound grammatical construction were the signs of an educated and practical writer, who, if the handwriting was disguised, showed someone skilled in disguising his handwriting carefully.[87] One such person fitted that description – James Morgan, aged 50, an educated man, accustomed to writing with accuracy and elegance, possessing the ability to write in various handwriting styles, previously in a good position but now of reduced circumstances

---

[87] Truth 16 February 1905

working as an insurance agent but having connections with the local press as a newspaper reporter.

(ii) The 'Convert Crusader' and The 'Infidel'.

Reverend Edalji, in his constant search for the author, had heard the name of James Morgan, who kept a journal containing a variety of his handwriting styles, being bandied about as the unknown missive writer. The reverend invited Morgan to the vicarage, an invitation described by Morgan as a commandment from "His Holiness the Pope of Great Wyrley to attend his chateau".[88] The visit led to a discourse between the reverend and Morgan in the columns of the Cannock Advertiser from the end of April until the beginning of June 1893, coinciding with the use of God-Satan in the anonymous letters.

The clergyman suspected Morgan on both spiritual and earthly grounds. He believed Morgan to be an infidel, capable of making the blasphemous comments in the letters, and Morgan wrote in a similar hand to the writing in the anonymous letters. Morgan did not hide his dislike of the reverend and his family, or for that matter the congregation at St Mark's Church but did deny responsibility for the letters[89] and whilst declaring his opposition to practices associated with the Anglicans and Methodists, saw no justification for being cast as an infidel. Morgan thought the scribe knew what was going on in the church unlike himself who was not a churchgoer. Nor did he have a brother as did the scribe appear to have. Morgan also believed the issue of handwriting was a matter for experts and, to rub salt into the wounds, displayed his dexterity by writing his rejoinder in one of his numerous styles of handwriting with a sprinkling of Latin and French. The use of Latin and French to embellish the contents of Morgan's letter was pointed out by the reverend as a feature of the anonymous letters, which prompted Morgan, no doubt mocking the reverend, to reel off a whole paragraph in Latin in a follow up letter.

Morgan had flights of fantasy concocting stories shown to be no more than figments of his imagination. He wrote of a visit from Reverend Edalji, George Edalji, Mr Brookes and Fred Brookes, who went to accuse him of writing letters after observing him returning from Walsall where the letters were posted. This account was a complete fabrication publicly refuted by both Mr Brookes and the reverend as

---

[88] CA 29 Apr 1893
[89] Rev Edalji to Capt Anson, 22 Apr 1893, HO File 990

never having taken place.[90] Morgan's response to the rebuttal was to disavow writing the 'accusative' letter, a denial he was later to retract, and, in his defence, admitted being "a bit mixed up when he wrote it" – a similar admission of confusion was to be made by the author of the 1903 anonymous letters. Morgan, appearing not to be completely labouring under any confusion, took a swipe at the reverend and Mr Brookes, referring to them as "a real live vicar and his jackal", who wanted to injure him in "the eyes of these vile, lazy, pettifogging, ignorant collier folk of which there are a sight too many in Wyrley Bonk for my liking...(where) Even the dirty, defiled, unwanted children of these vulgar, ignorant fools, the miners, make fun of me." Morgan, later, also denied writing these derogatory attacks on the working class of Great Wyrley.[91]

The Elizabeth Foster issue entered into the correspondence on two occasions. The anonymous scribe wrote to Reverend Edalji on the 23rd May in support of the ex-servant. The reverend saw to it that the letter was published in the Cannock Advertiser on the 27th May. In the same edition of that paper, which meant Morgan could not have read the anonymous letter in the paper prior to sending in his letter, Morgan also dug up the Foster affair, claiming to have discovered the truth about the Foster letters in February 1892, but without disclosing the source of this new-found 'truth'. His story was that while sharing a railway compartment with George Edalji and Fred Brookes, Morgan ordered them to write out a confession but he never produced the confession and it was obviously another Morgan fabrication. Morgan also adopted a pro-Sergeant Upton line, alleging that the sergeant was reluctant to arrest Elizabeth Foster but the reverend, "his spouse and cubs" gave evidence despite the absence of any proof. Morgan's claim of cautioning the two boys was also made in an anonymous letter in the pre-November 1892 period and it drew Mrs Edalji into the debate when she, too, wrote to the Cannock Advertiser denouncing the alleged confession as part of the fraud being perpetrated against the two boys.[92] Harsh words indeed from the genteel Shropshire lady, an indication of the stress the family was put under while the police continued to turn a blind eye to their difficulties.

Towards the end of this exchange, Morgan launched a bitter attack on Reverend Edalji in a letter strewn with religious and philosophical

---

[90] CA 29 Apr, 6 & 13 May 1893

[91] CA 13 May &10 Jun 1893

[92] CA 27 May & 3 June 1893

rantings.[93] This brought the Morgan-Edalji literary confrontation to an end. A mixed up individual with strong views on religion, dexterous in his handwriting, knowledgeable in French and Latin, Morgan was never quite sure what he had or had not written or whom he had visited or who had visited him or whom he had or had not denounced. He was undoubtedly a bitter man, a *déclassé* fallen scholar, at odds with the world and almost everybody in it. He may have written some of the anonymous letters or been an *agent provocateur*, a fellow traveller jumping on the anti-Edalji bandwagon, or part of some conspiracy against the Edaljis, whose dislike of the world and those in it found its outlet on a vulnerable target.

During this interchange of correspondence, the reverend contacted Captain Anson, speculating that this newly discovered suspect was writing anonymous letters for someone else and he asked the police to make enquiries although he doubted that the police would act. Not unexpectedly, the chief constable rejected any possibility of Morgan being the author of the anonymous letters but accepted that the letters from Morgan in the Morgan-Edalji correspondence published in the Cannock Advertiser were written by Morgan although Morgan himself was not sure whether or not he was the author.[94] Captain Anson was as dismissive of Morgan's guilt, despite Morgan's self-acknowledged prowess in handwriting styles, as he was convinced of George Edalji's guilt, despite there being no resemblance between George Edalji's handwriting and the writing in the anonymous letters.

(iii) The Harassment takes on a New Phase

The ending of the *contretemps* between Morgan and Reverend Edalji brought no respite for the Edaljis as it was succeeded by a new source of discomfort for them – a number of crude letters and a procession of hoaxes in which the hoaxer exhibited a considerable depth of imagination with letters purported to have been written by the Edaljis. These letters went to clergymen; solicitors; newspapers – inserting birth, marriage or death notices or matrimonial proposals; to tradesmen – ordering wines, spirits, medicines, books, furniture, clothes, musical instruments; and to an undertaker to collect a body of a family member – the addresses of these trades people no doubt gleaned

---

[93] CA 3 June 1893

[94] Rev Edalji to Capt Anson, 22 Apr 1893, HO File 990; Capt Anson to Rev Ed, 5 Sep 1893, HO No 124, File 985

from trade directories.[95] The crude letters were divided into two groups: letters including both the Edaljis and Brookes; and others concerning solely the Edaljis.

A few examples of the letters, allegedly 'signed' by the reverend and entirely different in content and style from the rambling ranting letters of God-Satan, give an idea of the nuisance caused to the Edaljis and to others. One gentleman arrived in great haste at the vicarage from Lincolnshire after receiving a letter informing him that a woman refusing to identify herself by name was found dying in the vicarage garden and had asked for the Lincolnshire gentleman by name. A clergyman in Essex was asked to apologise immediately by telegram for making hints in his sermons about the reverend's chastity, otherwise, face exposure for his own adultery and rape. Another clergyman from the North of England, a recent visitor to St Mark's Church, received a letter calling him a damned thief for stealing a prayer book from the church.[96]

One ingenious hoax brought a female detective to the vicarage summoned so she thought to assist Mrs Edalji in gathering proof of her husband's infidelity. Mrs Edalji's first realisation of something amiss came when she received an unusual letter from this detective, Elizabeth Baker,[97] confirming an appointment to meet her. Apparently, a letter claiming to be from Mrs Edalji, of the 5th June 1893, was sent to Slater's Detective Agency in London about matrimonial difficulties allegedly faced by Mrs Edalji. The writer, writing in a fluid, clear, not particularly flowery style but written by a person with some education, disclosed that for the last eleven months[98] her husband had treated her coldly and had rebuffed her when she asked about a lady with whom he was sitting on the couch holding hands. Disgraceful letters written by this unknown woman to her husband were later found by 'Mrs Edalji'.

When Miss Baker explained the reasons for her visit, the reverend told her of the hoaxes played on them and about the forged letters sent out in their names. Subsequently, the agency compared the handwriting on the letter ostensibly sent by Mrs Edalji with a specimen of a genuine letter received by Reverend Edalji and found them to be identical. No record exists as to whose handwriting the reverend provided to the agency but given that at the time Reverend Edalji suspected Morgan, it

---

[95] Rev Edalji, Times 16 Aug 1895;

[96] Despatch 31 January 1907; Mercury 31 Oct 1903; Carr, J D [1949] The Life of Sir Arthur Conan Doyle, p220

[97] Baker to Mrs C Edalji, 14 June 1893, in HO File 990

[98] Since July 1892 when the first anonymous letters began to arrive

was highly probable the specimen was one of Morgan's multi-style examples, although Rogers, a local councillor and official in the Miners Federation, was mentioned in the letter from Slater's. The Agency asked for Rogers' address and the names and addresses of others whom the reverend suspected and it would test their handwriting.[99] The hoaxes played on the Edaljis were part of a nation-wide campaign of harassment against the Edaljis but excluding the Brookes family as the main target, which suggested that other participants than the original letter writers became involved in the harassment.

The Brookes family were not completely overlooked. Some hostility was directed towards Mr Brookes, described as the 'sour faced scoundrel', coming months after Brookes was supposed to have put an end to 'George Edalji's' writings. Particularly offensive letters went out under the names of Shapurji Edalji, W H Brookes, Fred Brookes and George Edalji, posted at Dudley, to a number of parsons, Members of Parliament, solicitors, station masters and Justices of the Peace, accusing the recipients of adultery with their servants and drinking their wives' urine. Several dates, 12th December 1892 (key incident), 20th August 1892 and 12th June 1893 were recalled as days of "merry things", which appeared to have some significance to the actual writer. The Edaljis' servants were also targets with threats of vengeance to be delivered upon them,[100] offering up the possibility of Elizabeth Foster or one of her supporters being involved.

For another two years, the harassment conducted through the medium of hoaxes and anonymous letters plagued the Edaljis without any attempt made by the police to relieve their situation. In 1895, Mrs Edalji continued to be targeted with severe punishment destined as her lot – a form of punishment predicted to hit 'the Black' even harder.

Both Brookes and Reverend Edalji were reminded of incidents they allegedly figured in twenty and twenty-two years before, and Brookes yet again was described as the 'sour faced' grocer in a letter from God-Satan.[101]

Trying to stall the harassment and inconvenience and to warn traders to be cautious over any letter received in his name, Reverend Edalji rather belatedly wrote to a number of provincial and national newspapers, which published his letter under the headings of

---

[99] Pseudonymous letter signed Mrs C Edalji to SDA, 5 Jun 1893; and correspondence between SDA and Rev Edalji, 14, 15 and 30 June, 5 and 10 July 1893 in HO File 990

[100] 26 July 1893, in Yelverton to HO, 5 Mar 1904, HO No 81 File 985

[101] 7 Jun 1893, 12 April & 11 May 1895

'Persecuting the Reverend Edalji' or 'A Strange Hoax', listing the hoaxes played on the family and those in which his name was used to commit hoaxes on others.[102] The vicar's excursion into the national press did not bring any abatement in the supply of anonymous letters, which continued to delve into the depths of human depravity. A direct response to the reverend's letters to the press brought to the Edalji's servant, Nora, one of the most crudest letters of the whole series from someone claiming to be a Thomas Hitchings, chief constable of West Bromwich, specially commissioned by the Home Secretary to prevent any more young girls from being enticed into hell.[103] Reverend Edalji, referred to as the 'infernal blackman', was described as the most immoral man in creation responsible for starving, beating and torturing every girl employed at the vicarage and soon to be arrested for "vile... gross immorality with persons using vaseline in the same way as did Oscar Wilde and Taylor."

The writer invited Nora to put the bits of paper enclosed in the letter under the carpets, throw the cat down one of the WC's in her master's yard, for which she would be rewarded with £50. Also suggested was for Nora to report finding Mr Brookes sleeping with Mrs Edalji under Nora's bed at the vicarage and that they held Nora down and outraged her before she managed to escape through the bedroom window where she met George Edalji, Fred and Edgar Brookes, who wanted to take Nora upstairs and similarly ravage her and drink her urine. Nora, eulogised as "You most lovely, most sweet...creature whom I loved directly I saw you," was told she owed a "Duty to yourself. God our crucified saviour, (to) stop the vile career of the blackguard and murderer, this pharisee." The letter ended with a culinary instruction to "Put shit with anything you may cook for the family and save all your piss and put it to boil potatoes."

The reverend was also accused, by a pseudonymous G Robinson, of committing criminal acts of the type that ruined Oscar Wilde with a youth H E in a house in Beaumont St, Liverpool, where Reverend Edalji had lodged whilst curate as St Clements Church.[104] The spurious accusation of sodomy levelled against the reverend was to emerge from

---

102 Rev Edalji in The Standard, 25 July 1895; CA 3 Aug 1895; Sunderland Echo and Times 16 Aug 1895; Mercury 31 Oct 1903

103 17 Aug 1895, HO No 127, File 985 – Thomas Hitchins was a name used in the 1888/9 series

104 26 Sep 1895, original kept by Staffs police, in Ward, Dr J, [1993] The Story of George Edalji, Paper to the Police History Society p 10 at Wm Salt Library, Stafford

the shadows less than a decade later from an entirely different quarter.

The offensive invective raged on, "Revenge on you hellish bastard you seem to think I have forgotten your loathsome carcase still defiles the soil…In order to dispel any misgivings…I am taking steps to warm your temper again…." The author linked a paragraph in the Birmingham Daily Mail of the 21st September 1895, which referred to an unnamed gentleman in South Staffordshire, undoubtedly Reverend Edalji, who was the subject of hoaxes until it was discovered the perpetrator was his own son. The article also referred to the gentleman opposing the activities of the school board,[105] which at the time of the letter was again engaged in serious internal conflict over the burden imposed on the Great Wyrley ratepayers.[106] Interestingly, the reference to Reverend's Edalji's troubles and the identification of the culprit as his son was accepted without question by the author of the article in the newspaper – another recipient apparently eager to accept the police's unsubstantiated allegations against the reverend's son.[107]

The resurrection of the type of letters sent out in the 1892/3 period slamming the Brookes and the Edaljis, accompanied the return of Royden Sharp to the Great Wyrley area from Wisbech. Sharp became an apprentice to a butcher called Mellor, who later made some interesting observations about Sharp's behaviour whilst in his employ, and such was Sharp's general anti-social behaviour that his father's trustee, a relative, Mr Greatorex, and Sharp's elder brother, Frank, decided to resolve the problems by sending him to sea.

(iii) Captain Anson's Kangaroo 'Court-Martial'

Towards the end of series two, correspondence between the Edaljis and Captain Anson resumed but it merely confirmed the contemptuous disregard the chief constable felt for the 'Hindoo' vicar and his family. In response to the reverend's further requests for assistance, Captain Anson dispatched the deputy chief constable in April 1895 to tell the reverend that the culprit was either the reverend himself or his son George.[108] This dismissive response, as ever lacking any substantive evidence, did not deter the reverend or Mrs Edalji. In July 1895, Reverend Edalji locked horns with Captain Anson yet again.

---

[105] AL, in Statutory Declaration, 2 Jan 1904, HO No 45, File 984

[106] Correspondence between Great Wyrley Parish Council, UDSB and Education Dept, 5, 22 & 27 Jul 1895, and 23 Aug 1895, ED/397, 9268

[107] 'Table Talk', in Mail 21 Sep 1895

[108] Capt Anson to HO, May 1905, HO No 124, File 984

Mr Perry, who knew the chief constable, broke the news to the reverend that Captain Anson was claiming to know the offender's name, prompting the reverend to write immediately to the captain. Captain Anson denied telling Mr Perry anything other than his suspicions but would say no more to the reverend until he (Anson) was able to prove those suspicions and he promised a dose of penal servitude for the offender. Two and a half years after deciding George Edalji was the culprit, Captain Anson now admitted he had no proof against him. However, the captain did say more and in a rather surprising and contradictory statement, which made no sense at all, he claimed that the anonymous letter writer had avoided committing any offence in law but had made himself liable to the most serious punishment. In later correspondence, in 1903, Captain Anson made it clear to a barrister supporter of George Edalji, an ex-chief justice of the Bahamas, the 'dose of penal servitude' was meant for George Edalji. Therein lay the key to the captain's determination to get Edalji convicted for cattle maiming in 1903 and his subsequent behaviour towards Edalji and Edalji's supporters.

Captain Anson went as far as to blame the reverend and Mrs Edalji for the crude letter sent to the Edalji's servant. The captain's accusation was based on what he saw as the refusal of both parents to accept that the letter was written with the connivance of someone intimately acquainted with the Edalji household. If nothing else Captain Anson's ineptness was consistent, dogmatically clinging to the thesis that George Edalji was responsible without any supportive evidence as the captain himself had admitted. In a reply to Mrs Edalji, who had written to say it was "cruel on your (Anson's) part to do nothing" and politely adding that "your conduct and that of the police has been most trying throughout," Captain Anson informed her of his intention to disregard any further letters from her unless she gave an assurance to the police that she and the reverend were doing their best to help. However, he made it clear that he would "use any means possible to prevent annoyance to outsiders who are in no way connected with your family." The captain's policing methods were naught but a variation of a 'means test' – prove beyond doubt that you deserve police assistance and it might be given.

Captain Anson's letter to Mrs Edalji was a brash and arrogant way of dealing with the years of harassment inflicted on the Edaljis and it betrayed the captain's own views on people like the Edaljis. Captain Anson had based his whole approach to the anonymous letters on the strength of one report from a police officer, Sergeant Upton, with an axe to grind and a predisposition to overlook more likely candidates.

However, it was unlikely that the captain really placed much reliance on Sergeant Upton's report as such and his ready acceptance of it can be traced to his own jaundiced worldview.

When tackled by Reverend Edalji for his curt and dismissive response to Mrs Edalji, Captain Anson refused to enter into any discussions. However, after making his suspicions about George Edalji clear to the reverend, the captain could not resist adding insult to the reverend's injuries, by referring to the author of the anonymous letters as a "crazy, half-witted lunatic" fit only for an asylum.

Captain Anson offered the reverend the opportunity of disclosing the identity of any person he suspected of being the letter writer and it would be investigated but this was so much 'chaff to the wind' since when the reverend offered possibilities of how the envelopes with the reverend's address on them could have been appropriated and used by the scribe, the captain rejected them out of hand as of no consequence. This was not surprising since the police had previously failed to act on the reverend's list of suspects given to Sergeant Upton or on the reverend's suspicions about James Morgan. To the chief constable, the culprit was someone with access to the reverend's immediate surroundings but excluded all who did not have the name 'Edalji' or, more specifically, George Edalji.[109]

In this exchange of letters, Captain Anson retained his arrogant and pompous attitude and there was no sign of the gallantry that one would expect to be shown by the second son of an aristocrat to a woman from 'middle England', the wife of a Church of England clergyman. But of course Mrs Edalji had, no doubt in Captain Anson's eyes, surrendered any right to that kind of respect by violating the English woman's whole nature as a woman in marrying a 'Hindoo parson' whose presence in Great Wyrley was a source of mystery, and distaste, to the noble chief constable. Aware of the antagonism amongst local burghers towards the reverend over the 'Education' issue and of the reverend's inability to mobilise any support in his favour, Captain Anson, using his position to block any action to ease the Edaljis' problems, demonstrated that he was less of a gentleman and more of a bully.

Interestingly, the Edaljis, despite differences in the ethnic origins of four members of the family when compared to the local population, appeared more in tune with the acceptable image of being 'English'

---

[109] Correspondence between Capt Anson and the Rev & Mrs C Edalji, 25 July and 3, 4, 5, 9 & 19 Sep 1895 in Capt Anson to HO, May 1905, HO No 124, File 985

than the majority of the population in South Staffordshire, adopting a life-style associated with middle England, the England of the shires, the England of 19th century literature, thoroughly loyal to King, country and the church – the middle England patriots. It was almost with a tinge of regret that Mrs Edalji disclosed the family's inability to enter 'society' because of the reverend's inadequate financial resources and this genteel lady, no stranger to the racism so evident in her life, said many years later that prejudice was the motive against George Edalji and expressed shock and grief that English people could be prejudiced against someone merely because they were not English.[110]

If Captain Anson had given the issue serious and unprejudiced thought he would have realised that the religious content in the letters, a form of Methodist revivalism was not within the framework of the Edaljis' Anglican beliefs. Instead, the captain made up his mind as to the culprit's identity on inadequate information, reneging on detective work – an anathema to the captain anyway,[111] and had placed the onus on the victims to unquestionably prove their innocence rather than the police proving the family were guilty. At a much later date, the captain claimed that George Edalji's mania for writing anonymous letters was common knowledge to those in the area. If this was the case, surely the police would have caught him during the three and a half years when anonymous letters were flooding the area but nobody did and, if he was the guilty party, it was a remarkable achievement for the youthful and myopic George Edalji during the years of the 'paper assault' to avoid being caught. A more accurate assessment was that local people thought George Edalji had a mania for writing anonymous letters but this was a pattern of thinking nurtured by the police on uninformed speculation and hearsay – *Ansonspeak* for police work.

The reverend may have played a part in fostering negative attitudes against himself and his family during his tenure at the vicarage. His somewhat erratic way of doing things, his insularity in dealing with people with whom he entered into commitments or had a commitment to serve, attracted a lot of enemies. A certain pedantism, a 'stickler for the rules', a brusque, sometimes insensitive approach evident in the reverend's make-up, were no doubt reinforced by the inherent prejudicial attitudes shown towards him. His relations with the School Board, the Board of Education, Lord Hatherton over the CHNS,

---

110 Mrs C Edalji to HO, 8 Jan 1904, HO No 48, File 984; Mrs C Edalji to J B Stone and others, 26 Jan 1905, J B Stone Collection, p 166,

111 Harley, M [1985] An Infamous Anson, Staffordshire History, Spring, p39

Munro and Hatton over church collections, Browell on the UDSB, Stanley and Rogers of the Miner's Federation, Elizabeth Foster and James Morgan demonstrated this but it was observable in other areas over which he had more control. The termination of a lease for the Great Wyrley National School house made between the reverend and Mr and Mrs Harvey within ten days of signing the agreement because he had suddenly decided to use the house for a Sunday school showed that his single-mindedness sometimes overrode consideration for others. This decision aroused the anonymous scribe to encourage Mrs Harvey to commit acts of vandalism on the property similar to acts committed in 1888/9 and 1892.[112] Nor had the more recent bout of sparring with Captain Anson mellowed Reverend Edalji or shaved off the outer casing of his dogmatism that stifled what should have been a charitable approach by the reverend when applying the law governing church burials. Under the Burial Laws Amendment Act 1880, nonconformists were allowed to use Anglican burial grounds but the reverend's refusal to allow a non-sectarian hymn to be sung at the funeral of a Methodist child soured relations between him and Methodist churchgoers.[113]

Shortly after this latest display of dogmatism the anonymous letters were to come to an end.

(iv) The Scribe gets Writer's Cramp:

The final two anonymous communications came within five days of each other and followed on from an anonymous letter resurrecting the tirade of hatred towards Brookes on the 14th December 1895. The penultimate letter, posted on the 19th December 1895 at Stafford Station on the rail route to Liverpool, revealed links with the 1892 letters by referring to 'certain little accidents' which the reverend and Brookes were allegedly involved in twenty and twenty two years before respectively, although this information could have been culled from copies of the letters published in the Cannock Advertiser. Writing as God-Satan, his thoughts dwelt on revenge against Edalji, Brookes and Browell, threatening them with fire and brimstone and, less metaphorically, proposing to send out an increasing number of letters and postcards to facilitate the ultimate arrest of Reverend Edalji or his

---

[112] Rev Ed to Mr Harvey, 11 Oct 1894; AL to Mrs Harvey, approx Oct 1894, Capt Anson to HO, May 1905, HO No 124 File 985
[113] J Whitehouse, Mr W Morgan and Mr Williams, Methodists, CA 2 Nov 1895; CA 16 Nov 1895; Rev Ed, CA 9 Nov 1895

possible committal to a lunatic asylum.[114] Five days later, 24th December 1895, a bogus advert, offering up an Irish orphan girl aged seven years for adoption, was submitted to the 'Blackpool Times' in the reverend's name. These last two letters came at a time when Royden Sharp went to Liverpool to board the 'General Roberts' as an apprentice ship hand, which set sail on the 30th December 1895. Around the same time, Sergeant Upton left the district for a new post, a promotion, not too far away in West Bromwich.[115] After this – silence for several years until June 1903, shortly after Royden Sharp returned to the area and Sergeant Upton had left the police force on grounds of ill health after being charged with drunkenness in charge of a horse and cart.[116]

After three and a half years the police were no nearer to catching the perpetrator than they were in 1892, undoubtedly hampered by Captain Anson's concentration on George Edalji, which was fuelled by prejudice and unsubstantiated suspicions. Captain Anson had received additional specimens of George Edalji's handwriting in 1894 and claimed to be even more convinced of his guilt – a surprising admission since the samples were notes taken from George Edalji's law exercise books and the writing in those books bore no resemblance to anything in the anonymous letters. No doubt the captain would argue that George Edalji had disguised his writing in the anonymous letters but if that was the case Captain Anson needed to provide some similarities between the law notes and the anonymous letters to support his claims – something he singularly failed to do.[117]

One thing the police never stopped to consider was how George Edalji would be able to spend time and money to write and post so many anonymous letters when he had been studying for his matriculation between January 1892 and Midsummer 1893 and for part of his law qualifications as an articled clerk between October 1893 and the end of 1895, time consuming and exacting activities. Another point overlooked by the police was that the cost of postage and adverts must have been considerable, well beyond George Edalji's means since the

---

114 J B Stone collection, p 168; The author may have spent time in an asylum as had Foster's aunt.

115 W Greatorex to ACD, 3 Apr 1907 in ACD to HO, 17 Nov 1907, HO No 300, File 987

116 Mrs C Edalji to HO, 30 Nov 1903, HO No 17, File 984

117 Capt Anson to HO, 2 May 1905, Observations on 'Truth', England: HO Case of George Edalji – memos and papers, Bp 2/4 (19) p 52; Capt Anson to Blackwell, 25 Mar 1907, HO File 989 Pt 2

Edalji children did not receive pocket money to spend.[118] George Edalji undoubtedly fitted into the category of financially dependent on his father while at college and undergoing training for his articles. Not only that, how did this studious student and industrious articled clerk find the time to make the necessary journeys all over the West Midlands where the anonymous letters were posted. Moreover, why would George Edalji express such hatred towards his family and accuse his father of homosexual practices. Perhaps, if he was subjected to some form of sexual abuse himself, as was suggested by a police officer several years later, it might be considered as a plea for help but, if so, why write of it only at the very end of this series of anonymous letters. Captain Anson, like others in the case, delved into psychological explanations in an ill-informed manner believing that George Edalji "was possessed with a blind fury against his father for being his father and being black. He had no friends, and associates, and no doubt would suffer chaff at school for being a semi-oriental and I imagine could not forgive his father." Captain Anson, no more adept in the field of psychological analysis than in detective work, in expressing this pseudo-psychological viewpoint failed to explain the author's deep-seated hatred of Mrs Edalji unless the captain believed George Edalji hated her as well for marrying an 'Oriental'. Furthermore, how would the equally intense dislike of Maud Edalji and the hatred shown to the Brookes, amongst others, be interpreted by the Anson school of psychology. At a later date in 1903, this so-called 'father-hating, friendless and isolated' George Edalji was alleged to be a member of a gang of local 'roughs' scouring the countryside at night maiming animals. Not a particularly illuminating analysis and saying more about the workings of Captain Anson's own mind than of George Edalji's.

---

[118] M Edalji to Home Secretary, 8 Feb 1956, HO File 45/24635, 227924/18

Chapter IV

The Lull

The intervening years between the cessation of the crude campaign of harassment against the Edaljis and the commencement of a new campaign against George Edalji in 1903, witnessed a significant degree of success for the vicar's son. He was an excellent student, winner of the Birmingham Law Society's first prize in three successive years, 1896,1897,1898; completed his articles; set up in a law practice in Birmingham in 1898 by his father; and in December 1900 published a handbook on railway law for passengers. The handbook, 'Man in the Train', was described by the Cannock Advertiser as interesting and useful, and reported it as "somewhat gratifying to the public of this district that 'one of us' has been the author"[119] – at least someone locally identified George Edalji with the local community, not a widely held viewpoint in the district towards members of ethnic minorities.

Over the years, the few ethnic minority members living or passing through the district, predominantly Jewish people appeared as particular targets for local hostility. This showed not only their personal vulnerability in the area but also confirmed their situation in South Staffordshire to be consistent with the prevailing attitude at the national level, which by the end of the 19th century was showing an increase in racial phobia – a bigoted reaction to Jewish immigration.[120] The robbing of Lazarus Pappe, a travelling jeweller, of £5 in a public house was referred to in the local press as "The Jew and his £5 note" and "The true type of a Jew's love of money." After describing the scenario where the jeweller tried to sell a watch in a public house, an offer declined by the clientele, the paper asked "Did he leave?" answering it thus: "But no, he was a Jew, and having seen the money, he must have it, so he re-entered the public house and said 'Vell, I vill let you have de watch for de 10 shillings" after which he was robbed. "But Jews will be Jews" was the parting shot from the news reporter. At a later date, a Jewish hawker, S Goldstein, was assaulted and robbed by a soldier, who described it as "having a bit of fun," and for this 'congenial' mugging the soldier received merely a minimal fine. When Ralph Gordon, an itinerant, was

---

[119] CCC 26 Jan 1901
[120] Ganier, B [1972] The Alien Invasion: The Origins of the Aliens Act of 1905, London; Goddard J [1971] The English and Immigration 1880-1910, London

abused in the street by some local lads, the police sergeant, referring in court to the condition of the victim, described it as "The Jew was bleeding at the nose."[121]

Sandwiched between these two last incidents, in December 1900, some local men assaulted George Edalji, threatening him with further violence when Edalji naively asked for their names. The offence took place at Snareshill, about three miles from the village, while George Edalji was on one of his 'walks', which Captain Anson sought to make great play of several years later. The magistrates, although describing the assault as a serious offence deserving prison, were content merely to fine the assailants.[122] Although a majority of police cases centred on the drunk and disorderly, the assault on George Edalji differed from the usual drunken fracas occurring between young men coming to blows after arguments in local public houses. The following year, George Edalji was again singled out, this time by a fellow solicitor and clerk to the Walsall justices, C A Loxton, a confidante of Captain Anson's, who accused Edalji of daubing 'immoral and offensive' graffiti about Loxton and his bride-to-be on the walls in the locality.[123] This accusation was either an outgrowth of existing ill-feeling between the two or was the initial spark of an antagonism having significant negative consequences for George Edalji at the height of the cattle maiming and anonymous letter affairs in July 1903 and, possibly, in 1907 when anonymous letters began to turn up during the campaign to secure a free pardon for Edalji. In 1903, Loxton, in collaboration with Captain Anson, was to act against George Edalji in a manner that would have caused considerable concern at the Incorporated Law Society for a breach of professional ethics on Loxton's part. Another would-be enemy of George Edalji surfaced in 1902. In the course of his business George Edalji corresponded with John England Hart, a local butcher, regarding a libel case taken against Hart. This civil suit provoked considerable animosity on Hart's part towards Edalji, as Hart later admitted, and Edalji's letter to Hart provided him and his friends with a sample of Edalji's handwriting, which may have had some bearing on the events of 1903.[124] Around the time of the libel case a friend of Hart, Royden Sharp, of railway 'vandalism' fame, returned to the South Staffordshire area after spending some time on a cattle ship travelling between Liverpool and the USA.

---

[121] CA 7 and 14 Sep 1889, 10 Mar 1900, 2 Aug 1902; CCC 15 Mar 1902;
[122] CA 8 Dec 1900
[123] Captain Anson to Blackwell, 15 Mar 1907, File 989 Pt 1
[124] ACD to HO, 2 Aug 1907, HO No 271, File 986

George Edalji managed to get himself into another predicament at the end of that year, which Captain Anson made use of at a later date in an attempt to discredit him in the eyes of officialdom during the campaign for his release from prison. A solicitor colleague of Edalji's, John William Phillips, misappropriated funds to the value of over £900 entrusted to him by three clients. Following an order in Chancery to repay the money in August 1900, Phillips absconded leaving George Edalji in a perilous position. Showing himself to be a trusting and generous person, albeit a naïve and foolish one, Edalji had agreed to stand surety for Phillips and in order to honour the bond, Edalji borrowed from moneylenders at exorbitant interest rates. In January 1902, Phillips was eventually located, arrested and was on the receiving end of twelve months hard labour. Phillips was treated leniently[125] because of ill health, which had left him with one good eye, one sound ear and one lung whereas George Edalji was left with one large debt. In an attempt to cover the repayments on the loan George Edalji speculated on the stock market and by the end of 1902, a firm of London stockbrokers filed a judgment summons against him for £350. In January 1903, his creditors filed a bankruptcy petition but were prepared to withdraw it if Edalji could raise £105 quickly.[126] Obviously desperate, as bankruptcy would bring an end to his career in law, Edalji took a course of action that he, himself, thought distasteful but justified it to himself on the grounds that his debts were not his fault. As a last resort, since he claimed to have no one else to approach, he canvassed notable people for donations, referring to them as subscriptions.[127] These appeals can only be described as 'begging letters' and, to one contributor who came to his aid, it presented a picture of George Edalji holding a child-like faith in the generosity of people and a certain naiveté in expecting to raise £105, the sum required, by 5/- donations – a not unreasonable assessment of George Edalji bearing in mind he was conned into this debt by putting his faith in a colleague.[128]

Why George Edalji resorted to this undignified method of seeking relief from his debts when his mother had some private means, albeit limited, as did his aunt, both of whom eventually funded his defence in 1903, is not known. Could it be that a strict patriarch in the form of

---

[125] Arthur S Francis received five years penal servitude for a similar offence in Mar 1902, Post 15 Mar 1902

[126] Capt Anson to Lord Desart, DPP, 6 Feb 1905, HO No 118, File 985

[127] G Edalji to J B Stone, MP, 29 Dec 1902 in JB Stone Collection, p163

[128] W G Devon Astle, solicitor, 7 and 9 Jan 1903 in Dawson to Gladstone, 12 Feb 1907, File 989 Pt 1

Reverend Edalji propelled George Edalji into this course of action to recoup his losses because he was reluctant to let his family know of his generous but foolish act? The admonitions of family members for his ill-judged generosity would surely be less than the ignominy of humbling himself to strangers.

Several years later, a rather bizarre allegation was made of George Edalji trying to resolve these financial difficulties by wagering fifty guineas with three bookmakers at Christmas 1902 to maim six horses, six cows and six sheep in the Great Wyrley parish before the end of 1903.[129] However, this allegation needs to be taken with caution, if not dismissed altogether, since the accuser waited well over four years before bringing it to the attention of the police in an anonymous letter and the claim had a somewhat ridiculous ring to it, since it could be anything up to twelve months before George Edalji collected his winnings, assuming he was able to win the bet, when his need for money was immediate. In 1908, a resident of Great Wyrley told George Edalji of a similar wager made in December 1902 between three local men to maim animals but this revelation also needs to be taken cautiously.

---

[129] AL signed Martin Molton to Capt Anson, received 7 Jan 1907, MM Letters, England: HO Case of George Edalji – memos and papers, Bp 2/4 (19) pp57/8

Chapter V

The Breezy Trail to the Vicarage

When the first animal, a horse belonging to Joseph Holmes, a local shopkeeper, was disembowelled on the 1st February, it raised little interest amongst the local populace. Not surprising, really, since premeditated animal mutilation was no stranger to agricultural societies. It served as a form of class-consciousness "motivated, like arson, by social protest or simple revenge (in that) killing the animal is the symbolic murder of the owner."[130] By the end of the 19th century the transformation of the United Kingdom into an industrial society made it a less common feature of social discontent and to some extent, as a remnant of that tradition of protest, owed its continued existence to individual vendettas amongst rural folk or those with close attachments to the rustic scene. The maiming of animals was also an expression of the harsh reality of working class alienation and, as such, cruelty to horses was not unknown amongst local miners. Cannock magistrates, including J Williamson and J T Hatton, later to sit on the Bench at George Edalji's arraignment, recognised its prevalence when referring to the "great deal of cruelty to animals in the pits of which very little was known outside."[131] The local newspaper, the Cannock Advertiser, often reported convictions for cruelty to horses carried out by members of the working classes.

The mood of the locals in South Staffordshire changed after a succession of animals met similar fates, most of them attacked within a half-mile radius of St Mark's Vicarage at Great Wyrley. By the 6th June, three horses, three cows and a sheep had met premature and gory ends,[132] the news of each new maiming spreading through the area like wild fire; a topic of conversation re-ignited amongst local residents after each new incident. In order to explain the maimer's success, the locals

---

130 Archer J [1985] "A fiendish outrage? A story of animal maiming in East Anglia 1830 – 1870", Agricultural History Review, pp 147 – 157

131 F D Bumstead, JP, CA 20 July1901

132 a horse belonging to E Thomas, the Landywood baker and parish councillor on Easter Saturday, 10 April; a cow owned Mrs E Bungay on 2 May; a horse owned by Henry Badger, a Great Wyrley publican, and a sheep belonging to T J Green, a farmer on the 14 May; two cows, the property of Captain Harrison of Brownhills Colliery, on the 6 June. Mail, 2 July 1903

conjured up the image of a lunatic with a mania for shedding blood and endowed with almost supernatural powers to enable him to avoid detection. The demon-like qualities attributed to the maimer stoked-up widespread alarm in the locality creating an atmosphere not unlike a reign of terror and provoking fears of the perpetrator turning his attention to women and children. The only clue uncovered by the local police was the sighting of a ne'er-do-well miner, Farrington, seen in the vicinity and close to the time of the first two maimings by the horses' owners. The police appeared not to follow up this potentially fruitful avenue or at least did not give serious attention to it.[133]

On the 8th June, two days after the latest maimings, a team of specialist officers from the Staffordshire Constabulary were drafted into the neighbourhood and a feeling of security embraced the locals, who thought that even if the police failed to catch those responsible at least it might deter further crimes. Despite the extra police vigilance, within three weeks this confidence was shattered, replaced yet again by a feeling of alarm, when two horses belonging to Mr Blewitt were found disembowelled, on the 29th June, in a manner resembling the previous maimings.

A number of men working the night shift at the colliery were within thirty yards of the maimings and police patrols were operating in the area until daybreak but no suspicious characters were seen during the night. As with all previous maimings no evidence of any kind was uncovered at the crime scene, although any evidence of the slaughterer's presence in the field was quickly contaminated by the large numbers of people flocking to the crime scene as soon as news of the maiming began to circulate. The only piece of concrete evidence the police had to rely on was that all five horses, three cows and one sheep were killed by a large sharp edged knife with a scimitar-like blade, most likely wielded by a powerful man.

Unable to marshal any evidence, the police could well have posed a number of questions about the perpetrator. How did the maimer manage to conceal the blood on his clothes? Did he live alone or were others protecting him? The maimer must also have been familiar with the routes taken, able to find the way in pitch darkness along narrow winding lanes, over fields, paths, stiles and gates, through gaps and hedges and across rough and broken ground, where police officers were patrolling or keeping watch. When reaching the fields, the maimer(s) had to approach the animal in a manner not likely to cause alarm,

---

[133] Farrington was convicted in April 1904 of killing two sheep - see Chapter XI

indicating some familiarity with animals, especially horses, and to have access to a scimitar-like weapon and the ability to use it, perhaps a member of the sabre-wielding local yeomanry or a butcher or slaughterman. If a gang was responsible did it contain members with these differing skills as local farmers thought at least two people would be required to carry out the maimings, one to hold the animal and put it at ease while the other did the deed?[134]

Two local men did spring to the minds of the local constabulary, Royden Sharp, one-time apprentice butcher and mate on a cattle ship recently returned to the area, and a friend of his, John England Hart, a butcher from nearby Cheslyn Hay, who, possessing skills in dealing with horses, provided a service to local gentlemen by breaking in their steeds. Captain Anson was of the opinion that both these men were involved in some way in the maimings.[135] Another possible suspect, as later events would amply demonstrate, was Harry Green, whose father, T J Green, lost a sheep to the maimer. Young Green was a member of the Staffordshire Yeomanry, a cavalry regiment, whose members were adept in the use of the sabre, the type of weapon capable of causing the wounds. A further suspect was Farrington seen in the vicinity of the first two maimings.[136] The police thought the motive might be a grudge against the owners but the failure to find any such link let these suspects off the hook.

With these more likely candidates in the frame and gangs of 'exuberant' young men at large in the district,[137] it was to George Edalji whom the police honed in on. George was a timid person, lacking physical courage,[138] a man who never had anything to do with horses, alive or dead, nor proficient in sword wielding skills. Nor was he able to roam about the countryside during the night looking for animals to maim because of acute myopia and astigmatism. He was a middle class professional operating within an urban environment and unconnected with either agriculture and rural protest or mining and working class alienation. So why did the police focus attention on this meek, mild mannered, myopic solicitor, selecting him as the prime candidate for the crime of animal maiming? Had the police found George Edalji holding a grudge against the owners – a disparate group, thereby, connecting

134 DT 22 Jan 1907
135 Capt Anson to Blackwell, 26 Aug 1907, HO File 989 Pt 1; Capt Anson, notes on ACD letters, undated, HO File 989 Pt 2
136 DM (Lon) 29 Aug 1907; Tribune 31 Aug 1907
137 J E Wilkes, AMICE, SS 16 Jan 1907
138 M Edalji, Statutory Declaration, 2 Jan 1904, HO No 45 File 984

him to the maimings? No such evidence was ever presented for what was later described as a motiveless series of crimes.

The police had turned in the direction of the young solicitor, propelled by three interconnected factors that shunted him firmly into the frame. A Justice of the Peace in the reverend's parish, almost certainly J T Hatton, who had crossed swords with Reverend Edalji many times in the past, informed the police of his suspicions about George Edalji. The content of this information was never made public but later disclosures suggest he accused Edalji of 'being seen' in the district late at night. The intervention of the Justice of the Peace sparked off a spate of rumours about the arrest of George Edalji as the Great Wyrley maimer and the author of a series of anonymous letters, which began to descend on various people in the area.[139]

Having become the butt of public indignation due to their failure to catch the perpetrator[140] and without any clues to identify the maimer, the police turned towards George Edalji, the easiest of scapegoats and a member of an unpopular family. This animosity towards the family was nurtured over the years by Captain Anson, whose dislike of the Edalji family and George Edalji in particular was well known to the local police and local inhabitants. Captain Anson later wrote of his surprise upon hearing that George Edalji was a suspect and thought it improbable for such a serious offence being committed by Edalji because he had a fairly good position as a solicitor. However, the newly promoted Inspector Campbell, in charge of the investigation locally, held none of these alleged reservations and quickly accepted there might be some substance in the reports of George Edalji's suspicious habit of late night 'prowling', a highly subjective, value-laden and criminalising term – fixing the date of these suspicions at mid-June 1903.[141]

Several years later, Captain Anson, in a confidential statement to the Home Office, which naturally prevented any challenge to its veracity, embellished the allegations of George Edalji 'prowling about'. Edalji was apparently seen very late at night on the 29th June in the field where Blewitt's animals were killed and footprints were allegedly traced from the site of the Blewitt maiming, across the field up to the

---

[139] All the Anonymous Letters are in HO No 30 File 984; and in HO File 990

[140] Mail 2 July 1903

[141] Capt Anson to HO, 20 Mar 1907, HO No 192, File 986

vicarage garden,[142] but this revelation came at a time when the captain's reputation was on the line and he seemed prepared to conjure up anything in defending himself against accusations of the police railroading George Edalji.[143] Other people were alleged to have come forward claiming to have spotted Edalji 'prowling' around the locality at night. However, these claims were highly suspect since they flew in the face of earlier police statements that no one was observed in suspicious circumstances, conveniently ignoring the sightings of Farrington. Nor were these claims produced prior to, or during, Edalji's trial.[144]

These 'sightings' were only written down in 1907 by people, some of whom were not favourably disposed towards Edalji, and were only offered up by the chief constable in his correspondence with the Home Office in highly dubious circumstances. They came in the wake of the public disclosure in the Daily Telegraph of the acute myopia and astigmatism afflicting George Edalji's eyesight that made it impossible for him to undertake the journeys necessary to commit the maimings. One statement came from a suspect, Jack Hart, who held a grudge against Edalji, and another contribution came from a prosecution witness, Thacker, whose evidence against George Edalji at the trial was contradicted by other witnesses. From the contents of the statements, Edalji's movements were hardly descriptive of the movements of a maimer since they consisted of sightings of Edalji in 1902 and 1903 walking on main roads several miles distant from his home and far from the scene of any maiming, without Edalji trying to conceal himself and on one occasion was walking with a book under his arm.[145] If Edalji had been prowling the district searching for animals, surely he would have acted more surreptitiously than was apparent from the ease with which he was allegedly seen. Nonetheless, as a result of 'breakthrough

---

[142] Mail 2 July 1903; CA 4 Jul 1903; Capt Anson to HO, 20 Mar 1907, HO No 192, File 986

[143] Captain Anson claimed a similar tracking exercise had been undertaken from the scene of a previous maiming, without disclosing which one, also leading to the vicarage – the same caveat about the captain's motive must also apply to this.

[144] Mail 2 July 1903; CA 4 Jul 1903; Capt Anson to HO, 20 Mar 1907, HO No 192, File 986. It could be argued that they were not introduced because of their inadmissibility as Edalji was charged only with the August maiming. However, such a claim could not be sustained since every animal maimed was mentioned at Edalji's trial even though it was inadmissible evidence. See Chapter IX

[145] See Chapter XIII

evidence' from a Justice of the Peace informant, the police discounted all other possibilities and Captain Anson consented to a surveillance of George Edalji's movements and for a very close police watch to be placed on the vicarage from the 29th June 1903.[146] Some disparity existed in police accounts covering the period of police surveillance since another claim placed the duration of the surveillance as two to three weeks from the Blewitt maiming and another claim fixed the surveillance as two to three weeks preceding and including the 18th August. Another version from Captain Anson fixed the length of the observation on the vicarage as lasting from the 6th August, the day when the police intended to arrest Royden Sharp on suspicion of sending out a batch of anonymous postcards, until the 18th August.[147] This disparity surfaced from the contradictory evidence supplied by the police at Edalji's arraignment and trial and should be assessed in the context of the police manipulating evidence for its own purposes.[148] It seems likely that the vicarage was watched shortly after the 29th June when Edalji's name was 'dropped' to the police as the maimer until 5 am on the 18th August. Despite conducting a nightly surveillance duty between 10 pm and 5 am at the vicarage, the police never saw George Edalji either coming out of or going into the vicarage during the night, not even when he was allegedly 'prowling' the district late at night.

At other times, the police went from house to house raking up any gossip against the Edaljis. Innocuous bits of information about George Edalji's so-called interest in the maimings were gathered up by the police and amplified at Edalji's trial as confirmation of his involvement in those maimings. Apparently, in a conversation with a general dealer from Bridgtown, David Hobson, one of Edalji's clients, Edalji mentioned the maimings three days before the attack on Blewitt's horses, and on the day after the attack when travelling in a train passing the spot where the outrages occurred, Edalji remarked to his fellow passengers that the horses belonged to Blewitt, having heard the news of the maimings while waiting at the station. Considering that the maimings were the main talking point in the district for most inhabitants, if the criterion for guilt was in taking an interest in the

---

[146] Evidence at Cannock police court in Capt Anson to HO, 20 Mar 1907, HO No 192, File 986

[147] Brief for the Prosecution, Capt Anson to HO, 30 Mar 1907, HO No 195, File 986

[148] The four different versions gave the commencing date of the police watch on the vicarage as (i) 29 June, (ii) sometime between the 13 and 20 July, (iii) sometime between the 28 July and 4 August, and (iv) 6 August

maimings then virtually the whole population of the district would have ended up in Stafford gaol. The police, in an unfair and disingenuous manner, blew Edalji's 'interest' in the maimings out of all proportions, unlike the Lord Chancellor, who, in a report to the Director of Public Prosecutions in 1904 thought Edalji's remarks to be perfectly natural comments for any local person to make about the maimings.[149]

When rumours of George Edalji's arrest for cattle maiming began circulating in the district,[150] George placed little significance on them, believing them to be the work of the cattle maimers, but he was urged to offer a £25 reward for information on the identity of the rumourmonger. The monetary inducement advertised in local newspapers brought no reward either for George Edalji or for a potential informant as no response was forthcoming.[151] This particular episode was hardly novel since rumours about the Edaljis and their affairs seemed part and parcel of the local sport as all manner of accusations were levelled against them over the years, not only amongst locals but also at the highest levels of the Staffordshire administration and judiciary.[152] No doubt Captain Anson was a willing contributor at this end of the social scale as were the two Lord Hatherton's, father and son, whom Reverend Edalji in the 1880s and 1890s had rubbed up the wrong way on more than one occasion.

The initiator of the rumour may have been the person supplying 'information' to the police or someone who had noticed police surveillance on the vicarage on his own nocturnal wanderings, or who was privy to police suspicions through connections with the police, or who was merely reproducing local gossip emanating from any of those sources. In other words, it could be anyone with some kind of grudge or 'hang up' concerning the Edalji family or George Edalji in particular and there seemed to be an abundance of people qualifying under those headings.

Accompanying the rumours of George Edalji's arrest, a steady flow of anonymous letters were sent out over the next five weeks, ceasing a couple of weeks before the 17/18th August maiming. Those seeking to direct attention to George Edalji must have known the police suspected he was the author of anonymous letters circulating the area in 1892 and this new series was a master stroke in ensuring he would be

---

[149]Lord Chancellor, 30 Jan 1904, HO No 63, File 985

[150] Mail 21 Oct 1903

[151] Post 19 Aug 1903

[152] Sir Reg Hardy to Under Secretary of State, 18 Dec 1903, England, HO Case of George Edalji – memos and papers, Bp 2/4 (19) p3

pursued to the limit. For George Edalji, knowing the police would see him as the prime suspect for any anonymous letters, to deliberately send letters around the area accusing himself of the maimings was rather akin to putting his head into a noose and was not the likeliest of actions for the solicitor to undertake. One thing was certain, whoever penned the anonymous letters and whatever the motive inducing their appearance, the letters nailed down the coffin lid on Edalji's freedom since, as far as the police were concerned, the missives fed the deep-rooted belief in Edalji's culpability for the previous letters and by the strangest of police logic to his responsibility for the maimings.

As for the letters, the first three had nothing in common and were undoubtedly written by three different people. The first to hit the area went to Sergeant Rowley at Hednesford police station, the day after the Blewitt maiming, in printed capitals, tipping off the police to an alleged suspect with "eagle eyes and ears as sharp as a razor and fleet of foot as a fox," travelling on the evening train. The scribe taunted the police by claiming they would never 'gess' the identity of the writer – a spelling of 'guess' used in the 1890s anonymous letters. A different style and carrying an entirely different message came on an anonymous postcard to Blewitt and Co on the 4th July, signed John L Sullivan, linking the maimings, the Jack the Ripper crimes and the Phoenix Park murders to the 'Irish Fenions'.[153] Neither of these letters was attributed to George Edalji by the handwriting expert, Gurrin, when he was called to give evidence at Edalji's trial.

The increased notoriety attaching to the district provided a particular aid to any anonymous letter writer. An article in the Birmingham Daily Mail on the 2nd July ensured that details of the maimings, if not already known, became widely available and provided a resource base for anyone who chose to write anonymous letters. None of the letters that were subsequently to find their way to the police; to a schoolboy named Wilfred Greatorex – a relation of Royden Sharp; and to George Edalji; under the pseudonyms of Wilfred Greatorex, 'Lover of Justice' or just left unsigned, provided any inside knowledge of the maimings, offering only information known to the majority of the inhabitants of the area and presented in a 'Boy's Own' magazine fantasy style that saturated the letters.

Sergeant Robinson, mistakenly referred to as an inspector, at Hednesford police station was the beneficiary, three days later, 7th July, of the first 'Wilfred Greatorex-signed' letter and the hotch-potch of information contained within it. Describing himself as having a

153 Post 4 Sep 1903

"daredevil face," he name-dropped several local people as gang members - Browell, General Manager of Great Wyrley Colliery Co; Edgar, a porter at Wyrley station; Edalji, the lawyer; Fred Wootton from Cheslyn Hay post office and the Captain, who had carried out the maimings at full moon to give the impression of having been done by a 'looney.'' He offered to provide additional information if the police visited him on Thursday or Friday after he had spoken to his 'strict and nasty' father, which was the type of behaviour Greatorex senior was alleged to have shown towards Royden Sharp, his nephew, in the 1890s, resulting in bitter antipathy between the two.[154] The author went out of his or her way to defend the honour of the Hattons by exonerating them from any involvement in "killing the cows".

This letter was in four pieces placed inside an envelope imprinted with the name EC Osborne and Son, a supplier of stationery in Birmingham. One piece bore the words "Your affectionate friend Fred Wootton"; a postscript was written on another EC Osborne and Son envelope as part of the message. Edalji's office address was written on it in pencil but with blotches of ink partly covering Edalji's name and address giving the impression of an unsuccessful attempt to block out these words – a ploy used in 1895 to incriminate the Edaljis. Several young people were mentioned including Westwood Stanley, son of Albert Stanley the miner's agent and a local councillor, and Quibell, son of the vicar of Hednesford, all of whom travelled each day on the morning train bound for Walsall, as did George Edalji, but as they were considerably younger than Edalji it was unlikely for Edalji to have formed any kind of social bond with them.[155]

The style of this letter was grammatically different from the previous two and had all the hallmarks of being written by someone used to reading boy's adventure stories about gangs, secret oaths, maimings and intrigue – a youth, perhaps. This was the first of the letters that Gurrin, the handwriting expert, attributed to George Edalji's penmanship acting in collaboration with a co-author.

This letter provided the police with the opportunity to call on George Edalji on the 8th July when, according to one account, his home was under surveillance. Inspector Campbell, accompanied by PC Cooper, impressed on Edalji the police's determination to find the person responsible for spreading the rumours about Edalji but this sympathetic approach failed to convince Edalji that it was anything more than mere pretence on the inspector's part. Showing Edalji only

---

154 Capt Anson to ACD, 14 Jan 1911, HO No 315 File 987
155 Wilkes, AMICE, SS 16 Jan 1907

the Osborne and Son envelope with the postscript on it, the inspector asked if he could throw any light on the letter. Unable to do so, Edalji asked to see the rest of the letter, which contained Edalji's name amongst others as a co-participant in the maimings. Inspector Campbell, not wishing to disclose the contents, put him off by telling him the rest of the letter, like the postscript, was nonsense. The inspector also speculated on Edalji being a future recipient and in the event of him receiving any anonymous letters to let the police know but not to tell anyone about the 'Greatorex' letter. Apparently the inspector noticed that every time he spoke a smile surfaced on Edalji's lips, interpreted by Inspector Campbell as a sign of guilt!

Everyone in the district was talking about the mutilations, therefore, Edalji, sharing the same interest, asked the police a number of questions about the progress of the case – were they still watching the area; if it was risky work; if a knife or other weapon had been found; if the maimings were linked to the phases of the moon; and he offered up the suggestion of using bloodhounds as his contribution to catching the maimer. The lunar motive was mentioned in the undisclosed contents of the 'Greatorex' letter but this did not necessarily link Edalji to the letter because the 'moon link' was a view prevalent in the district and was mentioned in the Birmingham Daily Mail article even though no such connection with the phases of the moon existed.[156] The police also paid visits to the other people mentioned in the letter.

An unsigned letter went to the Police Sergeant at Hednesford on the 10th July. This letter, referring to the proposed visit on Thursday or Friday and his own daredevil face,[157] showed the author to be familiar with the contents of the previous 'Greatorex' letter. He was also aware of the police visits to Edalji, Wootton, Fereday, Stanley and Quibell and that the writing on the envelopes had been shown to them. A special mention was made to a proposed trip by George Edalji "to Brum on Sunday night to see the Captain near Northfield" to find out how to continue the maimings with so many detectives about. A seemingly more terrifying threat concerned the gang's intention to "do twenty wenches like the horses before next March." However, the fear of this possibility had already been aired by locals and reported in the Birmingham Daily Mail on the 2nd July, and may well have its origins in either source. He claimed to know and to have visited all the 'toffs' in the locality: Squire Hatton's, the Great Wyrley vicarage, Quibell's

[156] Dates of new moons, 28 Jan; 29 Mar; 27 Apr; 26 May in Blackwell to Capt Anson, 23 Nov 1907, HO No 300 File 987
[157] CA 5 Sep 1903

vicarage and the headmaster of Rugeley Grammar School, George Edalji's old school. The sons of Mr Stanley and Reverend Quibell were given a special mention and a clean bill of health for not knowing anything.

Sergeant Robinson came in for a considerable amount of abuse, interspersed with foul language, followed by a threat to murder him, even "if I get a thick bit of rope around my neck for it. But I think they wouldn't hang me but send me to sea."[158] The writer appeared unsure of things, changing his mind by denying that he had killed Blewitt's horse himself and forgetting that Robinson was only "a common sergeant and not an inspector." Both comments connected this letter with the 7th July letter or with someone who had seen the letter. His memory was also suspect as he claimed not to remember writing that letter but thought he might have done. Temporary amnesia was a feature of the letters written to the Cannock Advertiser in 1893 by James Morgan, whom Reverend Edalji suspected of writing some of the anonymous letters during the 1890s.

The scribe tweaked the whiskers of the uniformed police and the plainclothes detectives patrolling the area by boasting of the gang's ability to avoid them and he criticised the police for assuming that the gang "aren't as sharp and a damn sight sharper than all the detectives." For the second time, the author referred to being 'sharp', which several years later was suggested as a surreptitious attempt to point the finger at Royden Sharp or even of Sharp having fun with the police by naming himself. The term 'sharp' was a link with the first anonymous letter of 30th June, therefore, whoever wrote this letter knew of the first one – a letter that Gurrin, the expert, testified was not the work of George Edalji. However, this most recent unsigned letter was identified by Gurrin as being another of George Edalji's letters – an ambiguous analysis on his part to say the least.

As these two letters were thought to be written by different people, the person writing the later letter must be someone either in league with the author of the earlier letter or in collaboration with a police officer because the police had the collection of anonymous letters in its possession. The second option excluded George Edalji and as for the first option, only if this 'loner', Edalji, was collaborating with someone could responsibility for the letters be laid at the vicarage door. Edalji had no close friends other than his sister, Maud, but if she was the collaborator it meant there were two aberrant adult children of the

---

[158] In 1895 Royden Sharp was sent to sea by Greatorex because of anti-social behaviour.

parish vicar and no one at the time was inclined to make this suggestion. Interestingly, four years later after George's release from prison and during his campaign for a pardon, Captain Anson, in what appeared to be an act of desperation, accused Maud, in a letter to the Home Office, of writing the anonymous letters for George Edalji to post.

The inspector was the next recipient of a 'Greatorex' letter posted on the 15th July. Apparently written in the same handwriting as the previous two, the writer expressed his willingness to reveal the 'Captain of the Gang's' name for a monetary consideration. It resembled the style of some of the 1893 letters – the self-destructive comment of throwing himself under a train at Hednesford station, having his brains blown out by the captain for refusing to carry on with the maimings, self-delusions and claimed amnesia but without the religious mania. The letter exhibited a 'Boy's Own' melodrama referring to the gang, the glory and the excitement of this 'splendid sport.' He apologised for threatening to murder the sergeant; and the sons of Stanley and Quibell were again exonerated from any culpability for the maimings.

This letter contained four pieces of paper, including a stamped envelope sent to Greatorex at the GPO in Walsall with a crude attempt to blot out Greatorex's name. For Edalji to have pulled off this stunt, he would have to address the envelope to the GPO in Walsall and collect it himself.[159] If Edalji had collected mail addressed to Greatorex surely, given the publicity surrounding the anonymous letters and Edalji's 'Eastern' appearance, the clerk at the GPO would surely have remembered, as happened in 1892 when Fred Wynne was identified by a GPO clerk for collecting a letter linked to the anonymous letter writer. This letter, too, was attributed by Gurrin to George Edalji's penmanship.

A different kind of letter, signed by 'Lover of Justice' posted at Rugeley, Staffordshire, on the 23rd July, went through the postal system *en route* to George Edalji, as Inspector Campbell had predicted a couple of weeks before. The writer, claiming not to know Edalji, admitted to not liking natives such as Edalji but believed everyone deserved fair treatment, especially as he thought Edalji had nothing to do with the crimes in spite of others being convinced of his guilt – an undoubted allusion to Inspector Campbell as later events revealed. He disclosed that the police were now watching another suspect as the police surveillance on Edalji had come up with nothing against him. Obviously

---

[159] Points under Consider by Attorney-General, England, HO Case of George Edalji – memos and papers, Bp 2/4 (19) App V, p 43;

trying to impress Edalji, he mentioned the additional pieces of paper bearing Edalji's name and address in one of the anonymous letters and of receiving this information from a policeman. In conclusion, he advised Edalji to take a holiday and by being out of the way would be beyond suspicion when the next maiming occurred, which was expected by the police to take place at the end of the month.

After turning it over in his mind and deliberating on what was erupting around him - the rumours and now the 'Lover of Justice' letter, Edalji speculated, that C A Loxton, a solicitor, with whom he had a personal dispute a couple of years before,[160] was collaborating with some other person – a police officer, in order to get him convicted or to cause him some other serious harm.[161] Edalji had seen Loxton's handwriting on business correspondence and knew Loxton had samples of his (Edalji's) handwriting. An eminent KC, Sir George Lewis, entering the arena four months later, also suspected this letter originated from 'someone in the know', who, apprehensive of Edalji leaving the district before another outrage was committed and knowing something of Edalji's character, probably thought that if Edalji was told to go away he would remain.[162] Edalji and Sir George were right on track as Captain Anson was the author of this letter with Loxton as the scribe.

Captain Anson, not believing George Edalji to be the maimer, was driven by his longstanding antagonism towards the Edaljis to try to trick George Edalji into giving himself away as the anonymous scribe.[163] He suspected Edalji of taking advantage of the situation to resume his 'old habit' of writing anonymous letters and that Edalji had written the self-incriminating letters in order to deflect attention from himself. Captain Anson's motive behind the 'Lover of Justice' letter was to "puzzle Edalji into taking some step to assist the police in clearing up some doubtful points" but failed to say what points were doubtful, not a particularly surprising omission since the police had only rumour and dubious speculation, and the Captain's bigotry, to go on. To carry out his scheme, Captain Anson enlisted the assistance of Loxton to whom he dictated the fake 'Lover of Justice' letter, by which name it came to be known. Nor could Captain Anson resist the temptation, even in a

[160] See G Edalji's comment on Loxton, 18 Aug 1903, Depositions, 3/4 Sep 1903; and Sir R Hardy's notes on the trial, both in HO File 990; G Edalji to HO, 13 Jun 1907, HO No 249 File 986

[161] Despatch 14 Feb, 2 May and 18 May 1907

[162] Despatch 14 Feb 1907

[163] Ward, Dr J, The Story of George Edalji, Paper to the Police History Society [1993] p 3 at Wm Salt Library, Stafford

letter feigning support for Edalji, of making a disparaging reference to 'Natives', a completely irrelevant remark for the purpose of the letter and perceived by the ex-Chief Justice of Bahamas, without knowing the origin of this letter, as betraying the author's racist disposition towards George Edalji.[164]

With no proof whatsoever of Edalji committing the maimings or writing the anonymous letters, Captain Anson allowed his own prejudices to propel him on a course of harassment and attempted entrapment. This seemed par for the course in Edwardian England because one leading magistrate, Sir Albert Rutzen, a relative of Captain Anson and later to figure in the Edalji case, when trying a case involving a Scotland Yard detective-sergeant who sent a forged telegram to a suspect to effect an arrest, decided that police forgery was an acceptable practice and not in any way prejudicial to the suspect.[165]

At George Edalji's request, Inspector Campbell and PC Cooper made a second visit to the vicarage on the 27th July. He showed the 'Lover of Justice' letter and asked them to trace the author. Edalji made a few off the cuff enquiries about the maimer, asking if the inspector thought more than one person was involved and if they were still looking for the maimer now that he appeared to have moved from killing cattle to writing anonymous letters. The inspector confirmed that the police believed more than one person was responsible but the district was not now under surveillance as the anonymous letter writer had named Hednesford and Littleworth as new target areas. Inspector Campbell was feeding Edalji a line because the police were watching the fields in Great Wyrley and, possibly, the vicarage by then, if the second statement on police surveillance was accurate.

Sandwiched between the 'Lover of Justice' letter and the police visit to the vicarage, two missives were posted on the 25th July, a postcard informing the inspector at Cannock that the maimings were moving from Great Wyrley to Littleworth, and a letter to Wilfred Greatorex warning him of warrants issued for his arrest together with

---

[164] Capt Anson to HO, 2 May 1905, File 988; admitting authorship; Yelverton in Petition to HO, Nov 1903, HO No 17 File 984.

[165] De Rutzen had to determine whether the "making of writing to the prejudice of another man's right", under 47 & 48 Vict Chap 76 s 11, applied when Detective-Sergeant Ward sent a forged telegram to someone he suspected of a crime to effect an arrest. De Rutzen considered the forgery to be so trivial to the victim's rights that he dismissed the charge against Ward! BME 18 Aug 1903; Times 19/20 Aug 1903

George Edalji and Fred Wootton, and that everything necessary to save themselves had been disclosed to Edalji, whom Greatorex was advised to contact on the 5.55 pm train from Walsall. The author accused Greatorex of involvement in the maimings basing his accusation on the visit a sergeant and a detective had made to Greatorex's house.[166] This was another letter written by someone with knowledge of the police visits to the Greatorex abode. The scribe was also aware of the advice given to George Edalji in the 'Lover of Justice' letter – advice with which only George Edalji, his family, Captain Anson, Loxton and local police officers would be acquainted.

It was now George Edalji's turn to receive a letter bearing the postmark 29th July and signed Wilfred Greatorex, written on a book wrapper addressed to Greatorex and written in a similar vein to the one sent to Greatorex four days before. This letter, attributed to Edalji by Gurrin, made use of the words 'sharp' and 'aren't as sharp', linking the author to the 10th July letter or more likely copied from those letters for effect. However, the letter exhibited a clear *volte face* on the standing of Stanley and Quibell in the author's eyes. The 'new' writer displayed an extreme anti-socialist bias 'identifying' the maimers as the sons "of that socialist scheming miner's agent (Stanley) who is always making strife, a dirty fucking swine, as bad as Frank Smith, another durned socialist," and Quibell, "the ranting parson" (vicar of Hednesford), also a socialist. Young Arthur Quibell was accused of starting the rumour against George Edalji in retaliation for an alleged offensive remark made by Edalji about Frank Smith and Arthur Quibell's sister. More filthy abuse was directed at the two parents and it was anticipated that their sons would finish up on a training ship. This denunciation of the sons of socialists was in sharp contrast to the defence of these boys in the letter of the 15th July. Could it be that someone other than the author of the previous pre-'Lover of Justice' 'Greatorex' letters was the penman of this latest letter. If Edalji wrote it, he would have to post it in Birmingham to himself, cut off the address after receiving it, then write Greatorex's name and address on another part, which even the Attorney-General, at a later date, thought not likely.[167] Greatorex later denied receiving a book through the post so knew nothing of the wrapper on which the letter was written.[168] George Edalji wrote immediately to Greatorex discounting any possibility of boys being

[166] CA 5 Sep 1903
[167] Points under Consider by Attorney-General, England, HO Case of George Edalji – memos and papers, Bp 2/4 (19) App V, p 44
[168] Mail 4 Sep 1903

involved in the anonymous letters as he was convinced that it was "someone in a very different position", a hint of Edalji's suspicion of police and/or Loxton involvement. Edalji invited Greatorex to call at his home but by that time Greatorex was on his way to the Isle of Man. Edalji also dropped a note to Inspector Campbell.[169]

The contents of the two letters show significant similarities:

The Lover of Justice letter	The Greatorex letter
(Anson/Loxton)	(unknown)
(i) Horrid crimes that everyone talks about	horrid crimes everyone is shocked at
(ii) The people… do not think you are the right sort	none of the people think you are right sort
(iii) I think you still did it	think you did it
(iv) Horse is murdered	murdering the horses

Captain Anson seized on these similarities to lay the blame for the anonymous letters firmly on Edalji's shoulders. The commonalities in the two letters did indicate that they were written by and/or for the same person or by someone having seen the 'Lover of Justice' letter. Captain Anson and Loxton were in the frame under the first option. George Edalji, possibly members of the Edalji family, and police officers, as the letter was taken to Cannock police station, came into consideration for the second option. But why would Edalji send out a letter with contents similar to the 'Lover of Justice' letter – a letter Edalji knew he had not written. If he was responsible for the other anonymous letters why provide this kind of evidence to assist the police in catching him, especially as he suspected the origin of the 'Lover of Justice' letter lay with Loxton in collaboration with the police. Captain Anson had sent the 'Lover of Justice' letter "to puzzle" Edalji but a more likely explanation was that both letters were sent by Loxton to George Edalji

---

[169] Gaz 23 Oct 1903; Post 21 Oct 1903; Mail 4 Sep and 21 Oct 1903

with similar information in them in order to claim that Edalji was the only person who could be responsible for the second letter – a set up.

The 'Lover of Justice' letter was never presented for 'expert' examination and no comparison was ever made with any of the other letters, so it is not possible to either link it with, or dissociate it from the later anonymous letters but the likelihood of the Greatorex letter of the 29th July being another Anson-inspired, Loxton-scribed fabrication drawing on the contents of previous letters should not be ruled out. The condemnation of Stanley and Quibell as socialists may be a reflection of Captain Anson's dislike of this brand of radicalism, an admission the Captain made at a later date.[170] As in his reference to 'Natives' in the 'Lover of Justice' letter, this letter provided him with an opportunity to display his prejudices and/or more practically to isolate Quibell, a man with a social conscience, from the Edalji camp and to feed old antagonisms, such as the Reverend Edalji v Stanley dispute of the 1890s.[171] Perhaps, in a more sinister vein, the 'Lover of Justice' letter was one of several letters initiated by Captain Anson and written by Loxton to get Edalji that "dose of penal servitude" the captain had laboured after for such a long time. If these letters were constructed by Captain Anson and Loxton to fabricate a case against Edalji, they could not have hit on a scheme more suitable for the purpose of railroading him.

A few days passed before a postcard carrying a Wolverhampton postmark, signed by Wilfred Greatorex went to George Edalji's office in Birmingham, and another postmarked Walsall went to Inspector Campbell from someone claiming to be a schoolboy. The one to Edalji contained crude sexual innuendoes about Edalji's alleged nightly

---

[170] Capt Anson to Blackwell, 26 Aug 1907, HO File 987

[171] In fact, Albert Stanley was a virulent opponent of socialism and the Independent Labour Party of which Quibell was a member. This linking together of two spokespersons of differing working class based ideologies was obviously done by someone with an obsessive anti-socialism, who did not know the finer points of working class politics. Gregory, R [1968] The Miners and British Politics 1906 - 14, OUP, London, p169.

A 14 weeks discourse between Frank Smith, of the Independent Labour Party, and a writer using the pen-name, 'Trade Unionist", was carried on in the pages of the Cannock Advertiser. The Trade Unionist was very articulate and informed, knowledgeable about union and religious matters, as well as strongly opposed to the ILP, a curriculum vitae remarkably similar to Albert Stanley's. CA beginning in November 1901; Gregory R, ibid

conduct with Quibell's sister, said soon to be marrying Frank Smith, the socialist. Edalji was also accused of reverting to his old game of writing anonymous letters, scribbling on walls and killing cows. In Inspector Campbell's postcard, a reference was made to 'PB' having moved away as there was nothing to be done at Littleworth while the police were about, showing a link with the 25th July postcard. The capital letters 'PB', easier to copy, appeared to ape Edalji's writing to fix the authorship on him. Both postcards were again put down to Edalji by Gurrin.

The police claimed, a point taken up later by the prosecution at Edalji's trial, that Edalji had sent the obscene postcard to divert suspicion away from himself. However, while self-incrimination may be a ploy to feign innocence, it made no sense for a young solicitor to accuse himself of immorality on open postcards to be seen, no doubt to his acute embarrassment, by the postman and the caretaker at his Birmingham office. Convinced that Edalji was the author, police officers thought the 'scribbling on walls' referred to the events involving Elizabeth Foster and the Edalji's in 1888. However, scribbling of graffiti on walls was also an unsubstantiated accusation made against Edalji by Loxton in 1901. Not disclosed at the time nor ever made public, was that these postcards were two of several similar postcards sent out on the same day to a number of local people, including a banker. These postcards were date-marked 9.30 am on the 4th August, when George Edalji and his sister, Maud, were on their way to Aberystwyth having left home just before 5 am returning around 12 midnight. A seemingly perfect alibi for Edalji matching the alibi of Greatorex holidaying in the Isle of Man since the 31st July and not due to return to the district until the 18th August.[172]

Was it possible for Edalji to have posted the postcards on the 4th August in the Walsall and Wolverhampton postal areas whilst *en route* to Aberystwyth? Captain Anson thought it was and he tried to explain away the anomaly, not at the time but after Edalji's imprisonment, by disclosing that letters posted in various villages, 2½ to 3 miles from Great Wyrley bore a Wolverhampton postmark while those within that radius were postmarked Walsall. The captain claimed that all postboxes were cleared before 12 noon on the 3rd August, consequently, letters posted after that time would not reach either the Walsall or

---

[172] Gazette 23 Oct 1903; Despatch 3 Sep and 21 Oct 1903; E and S 3 Sep 1903; Mail 4 Sep, 21 and 22 Oct 1903; CA 5 Sep 1903; Capt Anson to HO, 9 Jan 1908, HO File 989 Pt 1; Observations of 'Truth', in England, HO Case of George Edalji – memos and papers, Bp 2/4 (19) App VII, p51

Wolverhampton post offices until the following morning of the 4th August. According to Captain Anson's hypothesis, George Edalji would have seventeen hours, between midday on the 3rd August and 5 am on the 4th August, when he left for his day trip, to post the letters. Taking into account that George Edalji was under police surveillance, rumours were circulating in the area about him and people were apparently reporting sightings of him miles away from the vicarage, not one person saw him 'prowling' around the area up to three miles away from the vicarage to post these postcards. After all, George Edalji was quite a distinctive person to go unnoticed. It was more likely that the person who posted the letters lived close to the border between the two postal districts.

George Edalji again invited the police to call on him, which the unaccompanied PC Cooper did on the 6th August, a sign perhaps that police interest was waning or they had another suspect in mind. In fact, on that same day, Inspector Campbell interviewed Mr Greatorex, a bank manager and unrelated to Wilfred Greatorex, about a postcard he had also received bearing a 4th August postmark. Mr Greatorex was informed that the police had evidence of Royden Sharp being the author and he was to be arrested that evening.[173] For some undisclosed reason, after Sharp was questioned by Inspector Campbell, nothing further was done and the focus returned to George Edalji who became Inspector Campbell's only suspect. Interestingly, after the questioning of Sharp, the anonymous letters and postcards ceased until after the arrest of George Edalji. George's temporary absence from the area when these postcards were posted; the suspicion attaching to Royden Sharp; and the scribe knowing where the police were watching and how to avoid them; which Edalji, as the police admitted, was completely unaware of, did not deter Captain Anson from accusing Edalji of responsibility for the letters.

The anonymous letters must have been written by at least four people. The first sent to Sergeant Rowley pointed the police in the direction of a passenger on the Walsall train, a letter that preceded by a couple of days the rumour of Edalji allegedly being arrested. The second to Blewitt merely raved on about Jack the Ripper and the Phoenix Park murders. Distinctly different were the next three providing information on the gang and other information written in the mould of a 'Penny Dreadful'. Following the 'Lover of Justice' letter compiled and written by Captain Anson and Loxton, the letters and postcards took on a different form, doing an about face on Stanley and

173 Capt Anson notes on ACD letters (undated) HO File 989 Pt 2

Quibell, attacking socialists and including references to the letters sent out prior to the 'Lover of Justice'. These later letters had the appearance of being the work of someone who had seen the previous letters and were written to make it look as if all the letters came from the same source with the objective of establishing a connection between all the letters in order to pin them on to George Edalji. While not discounting Edalji as a possible scribe, it was just as likely, or more than likely in view of the origins of the 'Lover of Justice' letter, that Loxton or some other accomplice of Captain Anson wrote them. The last postcards, which the police thought were written by Royden Sharp, introduced a new dimension of crude sexual references and recalled previous letters sent to the Edalji family between 1892 and 1895.

In spite of George Edalji being under the spotlight, the police did not have a unified front about matters in Great Wyrley. A difference of opinion existed between Captain Anson, who did not believe Edalji to be the maimer but only the scribe, and Inspector Campbell, who was sure Edalji was both the maimer and scribe – an opinion probably in tune with the prejudices of local police officers and some of the burghers. The police, not highly thought of in the district due to their continued failings, realised they were the ones in the firing line. Naturally anxious to divert public attention away from the abject failings of the Staffordshire police's detection techniques later described by one observer as "like watching an elephant imitating a tiger in the tracking of a deer,"[174] Inspector Campbell needed to make an arrest. His chance came on the morning of the 18th August when another disembowelled horse was found and he lighted on the easiest of prey, a scapegoat, one whom the local police knew would be a favourable candidate for Captain Anson given his known dislike of the Edalji family and of George Edalji in particular. While Captain Anson, on holiday in Scotland from the 11th August, was shooting grouse, his men in South Staffordshire were shooting fish, or one particular fish, in a barrel in Great Wyrley.

---

[174] DTel 17 Jan 1907

Chapter VI

The Storm: The Arrest of George Edalji

The evening prior to the maiming, the last evening of freedom for George Edalji for the next three years, began with his arrival home just after 6 pm, followed by his usual practice of putting on an old coat - the one examined by the police on the following day and taken away as part of the 'evidence' of Edalji's guilt for the maiming. Between 7 pm and 8 pm each evening, Edalji saw clients at the vicarage, on this occasion the client was David Hobson, a general dealer from nearby Bridgtown, who arrived at 7.15 pm and left at 7.55 pm.

After donning a blue serge jacket and a pair of boots, George Edalji left the vicarage to walk to a shoemaker's shop in Bridgtown owned by Mr Hands. The evening was fine but, as it had been raining during the day, puddles were strewn along the route. Edalji arrived at the shop about 8.30 pm leaving shortly afterwards to return home, seeing and being seen by a number of people on the return journey. As he was early for supper, he decided to walk past the vicarage and stroll to the entrance of Green's farm, a short distance away, before turning back towards the vicarage reaching there at 9.30 pm. When the Edaljis' servant, Dora Earp, returned to the vicarage around 9.50 pm, she served supper to the family and afterwards George chatted to Maud before retiring at 10.45 pm to one of two small beds in a bedroom shared with his father, which had been the usual arrangement since 1885. Reverend Edalji went to bed at 11 pm and, as usual, locked the door leaving the key inside the lock. The reverend, apparently a light sleeper due to regular attacks of lumbago, woke up at 4 am and remained awake until it was time to get up.

When the Edaljis were settling down to their usual evening routine, supper at 10 pm, the police began the nightly surveillance of the vicarage – a ritual often proving itself unrewarding as not once during their vigil had George Edalji been seen to leave the vicarage. On a very dark and stormy night, Inspector Campbell, Sergeant Robinson and Police Constable Cooper were in the churchyard sharing a view of the front and side doors of the vicarage. Three additional officers, located on the other side of the house, made up the usual complement of officers on duty at the vicarage. With this level of surveillance, the police considered it not possible for anyone to leave the vicarage without being seen.[175] Another fourteen men were on duty in other parts of the district, including Sergeant Parsons, Police Constables Weaver and Bradley on watch from around 10.15 pm to 5 am at the field where a horse, soon to become the maimer's next victim, was stabled. Sergeant Parsons saw the horse uninjured at 11 pm and when the officers went off duty at 5 am the horse was said to be fine. Captain Anson claimed at a later date that earlier in the month he had visited the police's observation positions and withdrew the men from the vicarage, setting them to watch a number of fields where the animals were kept out at night. However, even if he did give this order, being in Scotland at the time, Captain Anson would not know if Inspector Campbell reinstated the watch on the vicarage, and the evidence provided by police officers in their depositions to the court and in the brief for the prosecutor, confirmed that the vicarage was under surveillance on the night of the 17/18th August.[176]

After the police officers left their guard duty, Henry Garnett, a youth on his way to work at 5.40 am, crossed the field near the colliery and found the horse slashed across the stomach with a lump of fat hanging out of the cut. On hearing of the crime, Inspector Campbell despatched Police Constable Cooper to the scene and, despite having no evidence to connect George Edalji or anyone else for that matter to the crime, he sent Police Constable Marklow to the railway station to delay George Edalji's departure for Birmingham. When Constable Cooper arrived at the scene at 6.20 am, he discovered blood smeared on the grass where the perpetrator's hands, apparently covered in blood, were wiped. By the time Inspector Campbell, together with Sergeant Parsons turned up at the field at 7 am, the constable had discovered several different types of footprints in and around the shed where the horse was kept, suggesting that either more than one person was involved in the crime or curious workers, about fifty in all, as they walked along the paths on their way to work, had already contaminated the scene. The senior officers were shown a considerable quantity of blood on the ground where the horse had been standing when it was attacked as well as two particular sets of footprints from amongst the many sets that were said to be present in the shed. A similar set of footprints to those found in the shed were also spotted in the slate coloured mud in the

---

[175] Capt Anson to HO, 30 Mar 1907, HO No 195, File 986; Sgt Robinson, Depositions of Committal Proceedings App I: England, HO Case of George Edalji – memos and papers, Bp 2/4 (19) p.12; Sgt Robinson, Despatch 3 Sep 1903, and CA 5 Sep 1903
[176] Capt Anson to HO, 20 & 30 Mar 1907, HO No 192 & 195, File 986;

corner of the field. [177]

In the meantime, George Edalji, wearing the same old jacket worn when he saw David Hobson the previous evening, ate breakfast at 7.10 am served by Dora Earp, who later recollected that the jacket did not appear to be damp nor had any hairs on it. Conforming to his usual practice, Edalji dressed into his business clothes and left for the railway station at the usual time of 7.39 am – George Edalji was undoubtedly a creature of habit. At the station, *en route* to his office in Birmingham, Edalji was approached by Constable Marklow, waiting at the station for well over an hour, and asked to delay his journey as Inspector Campbell wished to speak to him. Edalji, believing it had something to do with the anonymous letters and not the maiming, which he had just heard about from other passengers, declined the request because of the amount of work awaiting him at his office. [178] If Edalji was guilty of the maiming, he might be expected to return home to dispose of any incriminating evidence[179] unless, if he was the scribe, he went to his office in Birmingham to remove any evidence that might link him to the anonymous letters, which was unlikely given that Edalji believed the police were collaborating with Loxton to set him up and he was hardly likely to leave incriminating evidence around the office.

Back in the field where the maiming took place; after viewing the scene for around twenty minutes, which yielded several footprints and a considerable amount of blood but absolutely nothing else, Inspector Campbell, taking Sergeant Parsons and Constable Cooper with him, went to the vicarage arriving at around 8 am, demonstrating very clearly that he had decided in the event of any future maiming George Edalji would top the list of suspects. From then on, the inspector set about 'proving' Edalji's guilt in whatever way could be contrived and irrespective of the scarcity of corroborating evidence. Inspector Campbell informed Mrs Edalji of another animal maiming and asked if anyone had claimed the reward offered by George Edalji for

<hr>

177 PC Cooper and Insp Campbell, Depositions of Committal Proceedings App I: England, HO Case of George Edalji – memos and papers, Bp 2/4 (19) p.12-18, and HO File 990; Edalji, Rev S [1905] Miscarriage of Justice: The Case of George Edalji, United Press Association, London, pp24/5; Statutory Declarations to HO, 2 & 7 Jan 1904, HO No 45/6, File 984; Edalji Petition, 27 Feb 1904, England, HO Case of George Edalji – memos and papers, Bp 2/4 (19) p45; Post, 5 Sep & 23 Oct 1903; DT 12 Jan 1907
178 Mrs C Edalji, Dora Earp and others, Statutory Declarations, 2 & 7 Jan 1904, HO No 45/6, File 984
179 Edalji Petition, 27 Feb 1904, England, HO Case of George Edalji – memos and papers, Bp 2/4 (19) p46

information on the rumour-monger eliciting a negative reply from her.[180]

The next item on Inspector Campbell's agenda was to look at George Edalji's clothes; consequently, Mrs Edalji gave him four suits, a pair of trousers and the old jacket, which she gave to the police with an openness entirely inconsistent with the duplicity the police later attached to the family's actions. The old jacket worn by George Edalji around the vicarage and adjoining gardens, which he wore the previous evening when seeing Mr Hobson, attracted the inspector's attention. According to the inspector, he found a dark reddish stain having the appearance of partly dried blood 4" long and a ½" wide on the right cuff; a similar stain but not so big on the left cuff; a handkerchief in the pocket with a similar brownish coloured stain; whitish coloured stains on both jacket sleeves; a white mark about 1½" in diameter on the vest (waistcoat) believed to be horse's saliva; and a horse hair just below the left shoulder. [181]

The reverend disputed that the reddish stains were blood; Mrs Edalji thought the white stains probably came from some sort of milk-based food and the 'hair' on the jacket looked more like a thread; and Maud Edalji believed the 'hair' to be a roving. Inspector Campbell insisted it was a 'hair' but the reverend took the jacket and vest to the window for a closer inspection and claimed to see no hair at all. With a dispute over the existence of a 'hair', instead of sealing the 'hair' in a packet as should have been done with this type of forensic evidence, the inspector instructed Constable Cooper merely to wrap the jacket and the vest in the brown paper supplied by Mrs Edalji,[182] and by the time the jacket reached Dr Butter, the police analyst, there were twenty-nine hairs on the jacket as well as four on the vest!

All the previous maimings suggested a long curved knife with a strong handgrip was used, yet the police threw scientific evidence aside believing Edalji had committed the outrage with a dagger, picking up on local rumours of the Edaljis carrying around such a weapon, fitting into prevalent folklore of Asians always carrying knives about their

---

[180] PC Cooper and Insp Campbell, Depositions of Committal Proceedings App I: England, HO Case of George Edalji – memos and papers, Bp 2/4 (19) p.12-18, and HO File 990; Statutory Declarations to HO, 2 & 7 Jan 1904, HO No 45/6, File 984;

[181] Statutory Declarations, 2 & 7 Jan 1904, HO No 45/6, File 984; Truth 12 Jan 1905; Gazette 23 Oct 1903; CA 22 Aug 1903

[182] Statutory Declarations, 2 & 7 Jan 1904, HO No 45/6, File 984; Capt Anson to HO, 20 Mar 1907, HO No 192 File 986

persons. Inspector Campbell wanted to see George's dagger but all that could be mustered was a small blunt botany trowel belonging to Maud Edalji, a keen botanist well known in the district for wandering around the countryside collecting specimens, or perhaps she, too, was in the habit of prowling![183] None of the officers mentioned that any item of clothing - the jacket, vest or trousers, was damp but an old pair of boots with some mud on the lower part of one of them temporarily attracted Constable Cooper's attention before he lost interest and discarded them. As the police left, the constable took the jacket and vest with him but not the trousers, suggesting they were not of sufficient importance to their enquiries and signifying they were neither wet nor had mud on them. Five minutes after the police left Constable Cooper returned to take the boot with a worn down heel, although at the time a boot with a worn down heel held little significance for the police. If the police had noticed footmarks of any particular significance in the field and the boot had as much mud on them as was later claimed, why did they not hone in on it immediately rather than leaving it to an afterthought before taking it away. Edalji's boots were in no way unique, a ready-made pair from a store in Walsall, merely one of scores of the same size and pattern in general use.[184]

Constable Cooper, having placed the jacket, vest and boot on a cart, returned to the field at 9.30 am to find people still walking along the footpath towards the colliery. He spent the time between 9.30 am and 11 am looking for footprints and made comparisons by pressing the heel of Edalji's boot into the ground.[185] Using this method inevitably caused the boot to become muddier maybe reaching right up to the top of the boot as was its state when it was introduced as an exhibit at the trial.

Also in attendance at the field was the veterinary surgeon, Robert M Lewis of Cannock, who, on examining the horse at 8.30 am, found a wound similar to those on all the previous maimings, that is, a wound inflicted by a curved weapon with concave sides attached to a handle to

---

[183] BWM, 23 Mar 1907; Edalji, Rev S [1905] Miscarriage of Justice: The Case of George Edalji, United Press Association, London, p35; Despatch 14 Feb 1907; Statutory Declarations, 2 & 7 Jan 1904, HO 45/6 File 984

[184] Statutory Declarations, 2 & 7 Jan 1904, HO No 45/6, File 984; Truth, 12 Jan 1905

[185] Depositions of Committal Proceedings App I: England, HO Case of George Edalji – memos and papers, Bp 2/4 (19) p18; and HO File 990; Capt Anson to HO, 20 Mar 1907, HO No 192 File 986

give the user a good grip.[186] When the veterinary surgeon had completed his examination, William Cooper, the horse slaughterer, removed the carcase to his slaughterhouse, where an employee, William Bruton, cut off a piece of the horse's hide for the police to use as a specimen for analysis. At 11 am, Constable Cooper left the field to call at the slaughterhouse to collect the piece of hide before taking the clothes and the hide to the Cannock police station around 11.30 am.[187] Carrying the hide and the clothes together was sufficient to introduce the possibility of cross contamination and should have rendered the forensic evidence associated with the coat inadmissible.

While Constable Cooper had been eagerly trying to match the boot to a footprint, Inspector Campbell and Sergeant Parsons, keen to speak to Edalji, sped off to Birmingham arriving at Edalji's office in Newhall Street at 10.30 am. The Inspector divulged the reason for their visit and revealed the 'results' of their inspection of Edalji's old jacket. Edalji thought the stains on his clothes were possibly grease, milk or oatmeal and any hairs on the jacket must have rubbed on to his clothes while he was leaning on gates and fence rails near the vicarage. Edalji informed them that the only time he went out on the previous night was on his trip to and from Bridgtown and he had not worn that jacket on the trip.[188]

When Inspector Campbell accused Edalji of writing the anonymous letters, Edalji made a very perceptive observation. He referred to letters received from Loxton in a professional capacity showing similar handwriting to the 'Lover of Justice' letter and speculated on Loxton having some connection with the anonymous letters, adding that Loxton would be made to "sit up" before he had done with him.[189] These two statements were to be given an entirely different interpretation by the police at a later date. Not satisfied with Edalji's explanation, the inspector arrested him for the maiming without cautioning him and when Edalji asked if this was the only charge to be brought against him, the inspector refused to discuss the matter as Edalji was now in custody. Edalji was relieved of the keys to his office;

186 Post 23 Oct 1903

187 Capt Anson to HO, 20 Mar 1907, HO No 192 File 986

188 Depositions of Committal Proceedings App I: England, HO Case of George Edalji – memos and papers, Bp 2/4 (19) p14; Despatch, 3 Sep 1903; BME 20 Aug 1903; CA 22 Aug 1903

189 Hardy's notes of Trial, HO File 990; Gazette 23 Oct 1903; Depositions of Committal Proceedings App I: England, HO Case of George Edalji – memos and papers, Bp 2/4 (19) p14; and HO File 990

also taken was a piece of paper with the numbers of banknotes to the value of £220, which Edalji held on behalf of a client, kept in a cash box in one of his desk's drawers. The police, so intent on charging Edalji hence their speedy visit to his home and office, had conducted the whole of this interview without taking any notes, relying solely on their memories to recall the contents of this crucial meeting when Edalji came to trial. Edalji was then escorted to the police station in Birmingham where he spent 1½ hours in a cell. While cooling his heels, Edalji, in protesting his innocence to one of the officers, mentioned not being surprised at the turn of events because of the earlier rumours circulated about his alleged arrest.[190] The trio left Birmingham on the 12.40 pm train arriving at Cannock police station around 1.30 pm where Edalji was eventually cautioned and formally charged with maiming a horse sometime during the previous night. Later in the day, Edalji was given access to a legal representative, Litchfield Meek, a local solicitor.[191] When the news of George's arrest reached the Edaljis, Mrs Edalji, no stranger to the racism so evident in her life, attributed the arrest to the prejudice directed at her son over the years.[192]

With Edalji locked up, Inspector Campbell, probably realising that minimal stains and 'a hair' was somewhat thin evidence upon which to prosecute a case against Edalji, led a team of a dozen officers back to the vicarage to search for a weapon used in the maiming. Between 2.30 pm and 5 pm they went like a fine toothcomb through the whole premises – vicarage, schoolroom, churchyard, pond and pig sties. Unaware of the veterinary surgeon's findings, the inspector's interest, giving up on the idea of a dagger, settled on four old razors, all more or less stained. As with the hair on the jacket, the inspector was to claim later that a dispute arose between himself and Reverend Edalji as to the state of the razors. The inspector's version was that the razors were wet

---

[190] CA 22 August 1903; Depositions of Committal Proceedings App I: England, HO Case of George Edalji – memos and papers, Bp 2/4 (19) p14; and HO File 990; Rev Edalji to HO, 12 Dec 1903, HO No 28, File 984; Gazette, 23 Oct 1903; LM 11 Sep 1903

[191] Umpire 18 Nov 1906; CA 22 August 1903; Despatch 14 Feb 1907; Edalji Petition, 27 Feb 1904, and Depositions of Committal Proceedings App I both in England, HO Case of George Edalji – memos and papers, Bp 2/4 (19) p14 & 45; and HO File 990;

[192] Mrs Edalji to HO, 8 Jan 1904, HO No 48, File 984; Mrs Edalji to J B Stone, 26 Jan 1904, J B Stone Collection p 164; Depositions of Committal Proceedings App I: England, HO Case of George Edalji – memos and papers, Bp 2/4 (19) p14; Statutory Declarations, 2 & 7 Jan 1904, HO No 45/6, File 984

and had hair on them, not a particularly unusual condition for shaving equipment; the reverend claimed the razors were dry not having been in use for years. While this dispute was in progress, Reverend Edalji was alleged to have taken the razor into his hands and proceeded to rub off the stains with his thumb, a claim later denied by the reverend gentleman.[193] This dispute was in fact irrelevant because the type of weapon capable of causing the wound was something other than a blunt old razor. The police eventually abandoned the search having found nothing more than four old razors. They took the other boot and the pair of trousers with them when they left. The police later claimed the trousers had been cleaned but if one of the Edaljis did take the trouble to clean them why did the police not comment on it at the time and, if the Edaljis had cleaned the trousers, why did they not take the trouble to clean the other boot if it was as muddy as the police later claimed it to be?[194]

It had been a busy day for Inspector Campbell and Sergeant Parsons, both of whom left the vicarage before the search was completed to return to the field. Sergeant Parsons arrived at 4 pm and accompanied by Constable Cooper went along the route allegedly taken by the maimer making impressions in the soil with both boots as they went along. When Inspector Campbell reached the field some time later, he and Sergeant Parsons retraced the footprints from the site of the horse's mutilation. The 'discoveries' allegedly made by the police officers during their trek over the grasslands of Great Wyrley were no mean achievements. Their feat was accomplished by tracking the footprints across one field of grass, over a stile to a footpath, into another field, out of that field through a gap into a cornfield, which was partly cut, halfway up the cornfield where the tracks disappeared. They picked up the track again on the other side of the field, went up the hedge side, through another gap into a clover field, along the hedge to a gate at the top of the field, over the gate into a field adjoining the

---

[193] Statutory Declarations, 2 & 7 Jan 1904, HO No 45/6, File 984; Edalji, Rev S [1905] Miscarriage of Justice: The Case of George Edalji, United Press Association, London, p33; Depositions of Committal Proceedings App I: England, HO Case of George Edalji – memos and papers, Bp 2/4 (19) p14

[194] Committee of Inquiry into the case of G E T Edalji, (Wilson Committee) Home Office, May 1907, London; Depositions of Committal Proceedings App I: England, HO Case of George Edalji – memos and papers, Bp 2/4 (19) p14; Statutory Declarations, 2 & 7 Jan 1904, HO No 45/6, File 984

vicarage and then on to a public footpath where the tracks were lost. The footprints were then rediscovered leading in the direction of Green's farm down the lane not far from the vicarage.[195] All this was achieved over fields where only two or three days before grass had been cut and reapers had been trampling.[196] Curiously, when these officers followed the footprints, they were under the impression that Edalji had killed the horse on his way back from Bridgtown but they made no effort to trace the footprints backwards from the scene of the crime to the place near Benton's Farm where Edalji allegedly left the route on his return journey to the vicarage. The method used by these two officers to compare the footprints in the earth with Edalji's boot was to press Edalji's boot with a heavy hand into the soft reddish, sandy soil alongside the original print. Assuming they actually carried out a comparison, the footprint used for comparison may well have been a print of Edalji's actual boot made by Constable Cooper in the morning or by Sergeant Parsons a half-hour or so before when carrying out similar comparisons. According to Inspector Campbell, in spite of the heavy rain falling during the night, the track was apparently so hard that to provide a cast of the footprint by cutting out a portion of the path with a footprint on it would have required a pickaxe, contradicting his other claim that the ground was so wet it was impossible to take a sod, and another police claim of making the comparisons by pressing the boot into the <u>soft</u> earth (My emphasis). The police were unable to decide what the state of the ground was like. Furthermore, the fields were described as sandy rather than clay, yet Edalji's boots, according to another police witness, had clay on them. The pinnacle of the police's skill in collecting evidence was shown by the way they established the dimensions of the footprints, which were apparently carried out by using "bits of stick and straw" as a measure.[197]

With the police 'work' at the crime scene completed, the officers returned to the police station and at 6 pm Constable Cooper handed over the jacket, vest, trousers, razor and a piece of the horse's hide to Inspector Campbell, who according to his deposition, passed them over to Dr Butter, the police analyst, on the 21st August for examination. Yet, Dr Butter claimed to have examined all the items on the evening of

---

[195] Depositions of Committal Proceedings App I: England, HO Case of George Edalji – memos and papers, Bp 2/4 (19) p14

[196] Mail 22 Oct 1903

[197] Mail 21/22 Oct 1903; Insp Campbell, Depositions of Committal Proceedings App I: England, HO Case of George Edalji – memos and papers, Bp 2/4 (19) pp15/18/21; and HO File 990

the 18th August, finding two spots of mammalian blood on the jacket about the size of an old silver threepenny bit (1cm) of indeterminate age, which may have been the result of Edalji having a nose bleed. The spots were much smaller than the police claimed and were hardly consistent with the butchering of animals over many months. Dr Butter also found grey stains on the vest, twenty-nine reddish coloured hairs about a half-inch long on the jacket and four on the vest matching the hair on the sample of the dead horse's hide. Apparently, Dr Butter wanted the coat to be examined independently, so the police took the jacket to Birmingham on the 22nd August. However, their search for an independent forensic expert was as equally fruitless as their other efforts in the case, and the items were returned to Dr Butter for analysis, a surprising decision because Dr Butter had already carried this out, whether on the 18th or 21st August. Particularly surprising was the failure to get some other specialist to examine this evidence because in cases requiring forensic examination on behalf of the Staffordshire police, the County Analyst for Warwickshire was called in. The failure on this occasion to 'locate' an independent analyst looked too much like the police wanting to keep this part of the evidence in their own hands, even refusing George Edalji's quadruple requests to have his own analyst attend the examination.[198]

Why did the police, if the usual procedure was for this kind of evidence to be sent to Birmingham for analysis, give the jacket to Dr Butter to examine on the evening of the 18th August prior to sending it to Birmingham? How could such a large number of hairs be found on the coat when only a few hours before there was a disagreement over whether or not a single hair was actually on the coat? If so many hairs had been on the coat when Inspector Campbell examined it at the vicarage, then no dispute between him and the Edaljis could possible have arisen because not even close and partisan relatives would be able to deny and dismiss the existence of such a substantial quantity of hairs.

According to Captain Anson, whose source of information must have been Inspector Campbell, the dispute over the hairs could be explained away on the grounds that it was easy for the Edaljis not to see them as the hairs were very short and "were not readily seen without a close inspection," overlooking that Reverend, Mrs and Maud Edalji all made a careful examination of the jacket and that Dr Butter found twenty-nine hairs on the jacket and four on the vest later in the day,

[198] Gazette 21/22 Oct 1903; BME 22 Oct 1903; Depositions of Committal Proceedings, HO File 990; Post, 5 Sep 1903; Capt Anson to HO, 20 Mar 1907, HO No 192, File 986; Harley, CA 4 Nov 1983; Despatch, 14 Mar 1907

hardly not noticeable! If so many hairs had been on the jacket it would be impossible not to see them and all the inspector would have had to do was to bring in an independent witness; Dora Earp, the Edalji's servant, was available to verify his 'find' but he did not trouble to avail himself of this opportunity.[199]

In the light of strong denials by the Edaljis and the failure of the police to bring in an independent witness to arbitrate on the dispute, serious doubts can be entertained as to the existence of any hairs on the coat when the police examined it at the vicarage. If this was the case, the only ways in which the hairs could later get on the coat was either by (a) being rubbed off in transit when the hide and Edalji's clothes were taken in the same package to the analyst – cross contamination, which was thought to be a scientifically unlikely prospect by a police-employed veterinary surgeon, who reckoned it would take forty-eight hours for hide from a dead horse rubbing against cloth to come off, or (b) being inadvertently transferred from the uniforms of those police officers who examined the slaughtered horse and also handled the clothes, which can be discounted because the police denied going near the animal, or (c) the hairs were deliberately placed on the coat by the police and they required a credible witness, Dr Butter, to state that numerous hairs were on the jacket at a time not too distant from when the Edaljis examined the coat – a line of thought that leads on to the probability that the hairs and the jacket first came into contact with each other after the police collected the sample of horse hide from the slaughterers. Moreover, given that the police based their case on an evening maiming during Edalji's return trip from Bridgtown when he was wearing the blue serge coat, how did so many of the dead horse's hairs get on a jacket that Edalji could not possible have worn to do the maiming? In 1907, Sir Arthur Conan Doyle thought the hairs 'found' on the jacket were unrepresentative of the variety of hairs the maimer would get on his clothes and too closely resembled the hairs cut from the carcase of the horse as they were all similar in colour, length and structure. Doyle also made the point that even the most skilful operator would not be able to rip up a horse with a razor on a dark night and have only two spots of blood, the size of a three-penny bit, to show for it. A reasonable expectation of such a maiming, according to a leading veterinary surgeon, would be for the jacket and the trousers to have

---

[199] Capt Anson to HO, 20 Mar 1907, HO No 192, File 986; Capt Anson to Simpson, 12 Mar 1907, File 989 Pt 2; Sgt Parsons, Mail 21 Oct 1903; Dr Butters, Gazette 5 Sep 1903

considerable bloodstains on them.[200] The forensic evidence accumulated by the police was far from satisfactory and posed serious questions about malpractice.

Another task facing the police was to place Edalji at the scene of the crime when the maiming was committed. The veterinary surgeon's report placed the time of the maiming at within six hours of his examination made at 8.30 am, therefore, the offence was committed between 2.30 am and 5.40 am when the horse was found. This put the police in a quandary because, according to Sergeant Parsons, the horse was still alive at 5 am and police surveillance on the vicarage until 5 am made it extremely unlikely, if not impossible, for Edalji to be responsible. He would only have a time frame of 5 am to 5.40 am to carry out the deed over a route that the myopic Edalji would have found virtually impossible to traverse in the time available and at a time when local workers were making their way to work. It would also be extremely risky for Edalji because he would not to be able to see sufficiently far in order to avoid people or to know whether or not he had been seen during his rapidly executed journey. If police officers made an error at 5 am in saying the horse was still alive then the time of the maiming could be put at between about 2.30 am and 5 am. If the horse was killed between these times, the noise made by the horse while being disembowelled might be shielded by the heavy storm raging that night from 11.40 pm until after the police ceased watching at 5 am.[201] But could George Edalji have committed the crime between 2.30 am and 5 am?

For George to reach the field and commit the crime, he would have to avoid the police watch on the vicarage; find his way along a colliery tramway littered with obstacles at every step; cross the main line of the London and North West Railway with its signal wires and fences; negotiate rows of metal sidings, points and sleepers; descend a flight of steps under an archway; elude the police patrols around the field; make his way into the field, grope about until he found the horse and maimed it; then avoid the police patrols yet again and return by another and equally difficult route over open country where there were no paths of any description, having to cross three or four ditches and find his way through several gaps in the hedges; steal past the police watch on the vicarage for the second time and sneak into the reverend's

---

[200] Capt Anson to Simpson, 12 Sep 1907, File 989 Pt 2; Mail, 21 Oct 1903; Yelverton to HO, 9 Jan 1904, HO No 49, File 984; ACD, DT 11/12 Jan 1907; Edward Sewell, MRCVS, sworn declaration, Despatch 14 Mar 1907
[201] Despatch 25 Apr 1907

room before 4 am when the reverend was awakened by a lumbago attack.[202]

The difficulties facing anyone trying to negotiate these hazards were magnified in the case of George Edalji because of his acute astigmatism and myopia, a permanent structural eye condition, which prevented him from seeing objects clearly unless only a few feet away and in the absence of light, such as in the dusk or at night, it was practically impossible for him to find his way about any place with which he was not perfectly familiar. To negotiate this route with so many obstructions required a special kind of athletic performance and would have been quite an achievement for the astigmatic and myopic solicitor known to be no athlete.[203] Even if Edalji had been able to overcome his medical condition, after such an expedition his clothes would surely be drenched and covered in mud laced with grass, corn and clover from the fields, a quite different condition from their state when examined by the police around 8 am the following morning. Not only that, would not the incessant rain have washed away any evidence of footprints?

Detractors have disputed the level of difficulty faced by Edalji in pursuing a venture of this kind. Captain Anson, apparently, found 'it a curiously easy walk and especially to anyone who knows the ground',[204] although it is not known if the chief constable actually did the 'walk' or carried it out by proxy since both Sergeant Parsons and Constable Cooper did make the journey on the 27th August and could have described it to the captain. However, the police officers followed the route from Benton's Farm to the field – a route that had nothing to do with the maiming. If Captain Anson actually walked the route himself, it would have been along the wrong route in the daytime and he was free from astigmatism and myopia, except that type of myopia associated with narrow-mindedness, partiality and bigotry.

To lay the crime at Edalji's door, the police, even more disreputably, decided to create an alternative time sequence by fixing the time of the offence at between 9 pm and 9.40 pm when Edalji was travelling from Bridgtown to the vicarage. Disreputable because police

---

202 Statutory Declarations, 2 & 7 Jan 1904, HO No 46, File 984; Churton Collins, Gazette, 6 Feb 1907

203 Kenneth Scott, opthalmic expert, DT 21 Jan 1907; ACD, DT 11 Jan 1907; G Edalji, DT 15 Jan 1907

204 Capt Anson to HO, 22 Dec 1903 and 4 Jan 1904; Capt Anson to Blackwell, 9 Aug 1907, HO File 989 Pt 1; Depositions of Committal Proceedings App I: England, HO Case of George Edalji – memos and papers, Bp 2/4 (19) pp17 & 22; and HO File 990

officers knew the animal was said to be fine at 11 pm and 5 am and they were also familiar with the veterinary surgeon's report. However, it was on this premise that the police case was constructed using the evidence of those people seeing Edalji at different places along the route from Bridgtown to the vicarage.

George Edalji was observed between 8.50 pm and 9 pm by five people at different stages on his return journey going towards Great Wyrley. No one else saw Edalji on his travels after that until two local men spotted him near the vicarage. William Thacker claimed to having seen Edalji near the Great Wyrley churchyard going in the direction of the vicarage around 9.40 pm. However, Walter Whitehouse said that he saw Thacker near the vicarage at 9.25 pm and five minutes later, at 9.30 pm, saw Edalji walking at a leisurely pace coming from a direction other than the one where the horse was maimed and he watched him go through the vicarage gate. If Whitehouse was correct, Thacker must have seen Edalji earlier than he stated, at approximately 9.20 pm.[205]

The amount of free time available to Edalji between 9 pm and when seen going into the vicarage offered up two alternatives. The greatest time that Edalji was walking unseen would be between 9 pm in Station St and 9.40 pm at the churchyard, giving a maximum of 40 minutes unseen. The least time on his own would be about 20 minutes if he was actually seen by Thacker around 9.20 pm *en route* to the vicarage. However, this nit-picking exercise to dissect the walk in order to show whether or not Edalji had the time to commit the crime was irrelevant and the police knew that it was.

There was no possibility of the police constructing a case against Edalji on the basis of his committing the offence between 9 pm and 9.40 pm on the 17th August, yet it was on this ground that the police pursued him. The police's insistence on this time-frame can only be understood in terms of the police's absolute certainty that Edalji did not nor could not have left the vicarage during the night of the 17/18th August because of the police surveillance at the vicarage.[206] George Edalji was in the 'fortunate' position of having several police officers able to provide him with an alibi for his whereabouts during the early hours of the 18th August even if a question mark hung over the

[205] Post 5 Sep and 23 Oct 1903; E & S 23 Oct 1903

[206] A later claim by the police that no officers watched the vicarage on the night of 17/18 August flew in the face of police depositions prior to Edalji's committal and trial, and police evidence given on oath at the committal proceedings. Sgt Robinson's evidence, Depositions of Committal Proceedings, HO File 990

reliability of the alibi given by his father, who may have been dissembling over the lumbago attack to bolster his son's defence. Despite the police knowing the time constraints for committing the offence and the type of weapon likely to have caused the injuries, they persisted in the claim that the maiming occurred on the evening of the 17th August with the use of a razor. This they did despite the police doubting that a razor could have been used to commit the offence because on the 19th August they went to Edalji's office in Birmingham in search of a weapon capable of disembowelling a horse.[207]

Searching Edalji's office proved just as fruitless as their other attempts at finding evidence to incriminate him but they took the opportunity to pick up samples of Edalji's handwriting and some of his papers, which became exhibits at the trial. The police had now searched the vicarage and Edalji's office but not a scrap of paper was found connecting him with the anonymous letters nor any real evidence to connect him with the maimings.

The police case against Edalji was extremely weak and in order to 'get at him' they used a highly dubious avenue of linking him to the maiming through the services provided by the writer of the anonymous letters, who had put the blame for the maimings on Edalji acting in collusion with a few other named individuals, whom the police left virtually alone. The police arrived at the conclusion, or so they said, that Edalji wrote the letters to throw them off his scent since it was thought Edalji would hardly be likely to deliberately incriminate himself for the maimings, but by naming himself in the letters it would encourage the police to visit him so that he could find out how much the police actually knew. This was one avenue the police had no difficulty in travelling along pushed by Captain Anson with his obsessive belief that Edalji wrote the 1892 to 1895 anonymous letters and his antagonistic attitude to the 'Hindoo' parson and his English wife.

The police investigation following the 18th August maiming was not carried out for the purpose of finding the guilty party but to find evidence against George Edalji, so found a Home Office Committee of Inquiry in 1907,[208] and the police investigation provided little chance for George Edalji to be treated impartially, so thought Sir Arthur Conan Doyle also in 1907.

---

[207] Edalji, Rev S [1905] Miscarriage of Justice: The Case of George Edalji, United Press Association, London, p36; Rev Edalji to HO, 12 Dec 1903, HO No 28 File 984

[208] Committee of Inquiry into the case of G E T Edalji, (Wilson Committee) Home Office, May 1907, London.

Chapter VII

Stacking the Deck: Arraignment, Committal and Pre-Trial

When news of George Edalji's arrest began to spread through the district, it caused something of a sensation because, despite the rumours circulating in the area in early July, few people gave any credence to the possibility that he had anything to do with the maimings. The arrest also created a stir in local legal circles where he was well known and respected, although one particular solicitor would not be at all surprised by the news since he was a willing aide in the attempt to entrap a fellow member of the Incorporated Law Society. Captain Anson, too, albeit disingenuously, expressed an element of surprise because he claimed to have held the opinion that unless Edalji was caught red-handed he was too sharp to expose himself to any possibility of arrest when, in fact, he had actually thought Edalji had no involvement in the maimings.[209]

The arrest generated considerable interest and the following day large crowds of onlookers gathered on the roads leading to the vicarage to catch a glimpse of the Edaljis on the way to the police court for George's arraignment. Another crowd waited outside Cannock police station for a chance to see George Edalji *en route* to the police court.[210] As George Edalji threaded his way through the sightseers to reach the court about fifty yards from the police station only one old woman shouted abuse at him but the police quickly stepped in to silence her. On reaching the court, George managed to have a brief word with his parents before settling down in front of the magistrates comprising J T Hatton, the most likely candidate as the initial informant against Edalji; Mr J Williamson; and Colonel R S Williamson, politically all Unionists. Mr Burke appeared for the prosecution with Litchfield Meek, of Birmingham and Norton Canes, appearing for the defence.[211]

Inspector Campbell presented the forensic evidence, which consisted of one of the four razors, the jacket with miniscule stains on it, the boots with mud on them but nothing was mentioned about footprints or hairs on the coat – a surprising omission in the light of the

---

[209] Gazette 20 Aug 1903; Mail 19 Aug 1903; Capt Anson to HO, 20 Mar 1907, HO No 192, File 986

[210] Gazette 20 Aug 1903

[211] Ibid; Post 4 Sep 1903; Umpire 31 Oct 1906

quantity of hairs allegedly found by the police analyst on the jacket during his examination the previous night, nor did the police release any information concerning the time of the maiming. The inspector later excused himself for omitting the footprint evidence on the grounds that it was still "fresh in his mind," a rather strange remark to make because it takes no great leap of the intellect to conclude that if it was 'fresh in his mind' it would be more likely for him to mention it – one of many strange claims to emerge from police evidence before the legal case was over.[212] The failure to introduce any evidence of hairs on the jacket may be due to the clothes not really being seen by Dr Butters until the 21st August, although the police's later contradictory statements merely confuse the issue as to whether or not the analyst saw the forensic evidence before the arraignment. A more likely reason for these pieces of 'evidence' not finding their way into the proceedings could be put down to the fact that only later did the police realise the evidence so far collected was extremely weak and suddenly these 'key' elements were 'detected' or, more likely, 'fabricated.'

The defence thought there was no case for Edalji to answer because an alibi was available for the hours between 9.30 pm and 6.30 am, a time span during which Edalji's legal representative thought it reasonable to assume the offence was committed, and he asked for the charges to be dismissed. However, the magistrates, two of whom, J Williamson and Hatton, were clearly aware of the cruelty that miners inflicted on their horses "of which very little was heard outside"[213] and this was a colliery-owned pony, ordered the court to reconvene the following week to hear evidence and, at the chief constable's request, refused the defendant bail. George Edalji, after shaking hands with his father and kissing his mother, was taken to Hednesford railway station *en route* to Stafford gaol.[214]

On the following Monday, Cannock, whose predominantly mining population was in the throes of the summertime slack period, hosted a local flower show and, as a result, people flocked through the town giving it the appearance of a general holiday. Not even the rain was sufficient to dampen the interest of the many men, casting aside their mining clothes to become holidaymakers, or the spirits of their wives

---

[212] Gazette 20 Aug 1903; Insp Campbell, Depositions of Committal Proceedings App I: England, HO Case of George Edalji – memos and papers, Bp 2/4 (19) p16

[213] FD Bumstead, sitting with Williamson and Hatton, at Cannock Police Court in a horse cruelty case in 1901. CA 20 July 1901

[214] Gazette 20 Aug 1903; CA 22 Aug 1903

and children who accompanied them. The huge crowd lining the streets greeted George Edalji as he was taken in a four-wheeled cab from which a clutch of small boys clung to the back as it hastened from Cannock railway station to the courthouse.[215] When Edalji and his police minders reached the court, the crowd in its eagerness to get a glimpse of Edalji pressed forward so forcefully that the cab door broke from its hinges but, according to the majority of press reports, this was no demonstration of hostile feeling, simply one of curiosity.[216]

Among those in court were the other four members of the Edalji family, including the almost imperceptible Horace making a temporary entrance on to the scene. Also in attendance were Captain Anson, Mr Longden (deputy chief constable) and Superintendent Barrett[217] – an unusually large presence of senior police officers – a reflection, perhaps, of their desire to bask in the glow of 'success' following the cloud of derision that hovered above them during their previous failings.

The magistrates again included J Williamson and Colonel Williamson but J T Hatton was replaced by Mr E A Foden, another Unionist and the agent for Lord Hatherton – an adversary of Reverend Edalji. The legal representatives remained the same. The hearing was brief dealing mainly with the application for bail. The usual legal games were played with the police keen to have Edalji remanded and the defence asking for bail as a further remand would have a ruinous effect on Edalji's law practice. Bail was fixed at £200 to be paid by George Edalji with three other sureties of £100, one of whom must come from outside the Edalji family. After representations from the defence, the bench agreed to allow the whole amount to be paid by the Edaljis but the omniscient chief constable made known his opposition to the granting of bail so George Edalji was remanded to Stafford gaol until the next hearing. Frustrated by the chief constable's intransigence,

---

[215] Despatch 24 Aug 1903; Post 25 Aug 1903

[216] CA 29 Aug 1903; Some later commentators have claimed the door of the police cab was torn from its hinges in an expression of popular fury directed against this young Black man in danger of being lynched. However, this erroneous description of events, likening it to a lynch mob scene in the Deep South of the USA, was taken from a solitary sensationalist account published in the Wolverhampton Express & Star newspaper. E & S 24 Aug 1903; See Mackenzie, Compton [1962] On Moral Courage, Collins, London, p 171; Carr, J D [1949] The Life of Sir Arthur Conan Doyle, John Murray, London, p 224

[217] Gazette 25 Aug 1903

Reverend Edalji took a side swipe by remarking to reporters that "You might as well live in Turkey,"[218] which at the turn of the century was noted for its despotism.

A similar ritual was performed the following Monday, 31st August, when George Edalji, retaining the same self-possessed demeanour despite looking a trifle worn, was driven from the railway station in a cab to be greeted by a large crowd outside the court. The Edaljis, minus Maud, were in attendance as was Captain Anson.[219]

The number of magistrates had grown, now consisting of the ever-present J Williamson and Col Williamson and three newcomers, Mr A Lane; with the Honourable E C R Littleton and Lieutenant Littleton, sons of Lord Hatherton, managing to squeeze their way on to the Bench.[220] Another short hearing followed with the new prosecuting counsel, Mr Barnes instructed by the chief constable, seeking another remand in order to lay a charge of 'threatening to murder Sergeant Robinson' against George Edalji,[221] almost certainly pushed by Captain Anson to connect the maimings with the author of the anonymous letters to satisfy the captain's obsessive determination to see George Edalji taste his "dose of penal servitude" promised to him several years before.[222] The link being forged between the two crimes, given the paucity of direct evidence against Edalji for the maiming, was a means to get at him by the backdoor.

Bail was fixed on the same terms but George Edalji surprised the court by refusing bail even though surety was available from relatives and well-wishers. Expecting the worse if he was out on bail, Edalji had decided it would be an advantage to be in gaol in the event of a fresh outrage.[223]

For the third trip to court on the 3rd September,[224] George Edalji

---

[218] CA 29 Aug 1903; Gazette 25 Aug 1903; Post 25 Aug 1903

[219] Mail 31 Aug 1903; Despatch 31 Aug 1903; Gazette 1 Sep 1903

[220] CA 5 Sep 1903

[221] Post 1 Sep 1903

[222] That Captain Anson held obsessive grudges against any one who crossed him or even disagreed with him became patently evident in the years following the George Edalji trial

[223] Gazette 1 Sep 1903; PC Meredith, Gazette 22 Oct 1903

[224] Details of the committal from: CA 5 Sep 1903 and 21 Feb 1907; Despatch 3 Sep 1903; Gazette 4/5 Sep 1903; E & S 3 Sep 1903; DM (Lon) 4 Sep 1903; Mail 3 Sep 1903; Post 4/5 Sep 1903; BME 5 Sep 1903; LM 11 Sep 1903; Times 5 Sep 1903; Depositions of Committal Proceedings App I: England, HO Case of George Edalji – memos and papers, Bp 2/4 (19) and HO File 990

travelled by rail from Stafford to Cannock and on to the courthouse in a closed cab. As on previous occasions, and for the two days of the hearing, a large crowd besieged the courthouse but there was no demonstration as Edalji passed into the building. Horace Edalji, an early arrival, took his seat at the rear of the crowded court, whose numbers were swelled by the presence of many women with their long Edwardian dresses not so much walking but giving the impression of floating through the crowds into the court. Elizabeth Foster, a face from the past seeking what she thought was her pound of flesh with the same determination as shown by Captain Anson, was seated among the witnesses for the prosecution. As to be expected, the Reverend and Mrs Edalji were among the spectators as were the chief and deputy-chief constables. George Edalji, looking younger than his 28 years, minus the beard sprouting around his face since his arrest, dressed in a black and white check suit much too short at the wrist and ankles, appeared to be as unconcerned with the situation as on previous occasions.

The magisterial merry-go-round continued its rotation with two different members on the bench, Messrs M Wolverson and T Evans, sitting with the ever-present J Williamson. Mr Barnes of Lichfield prosecuted the case, while Mr W J Gandy, instructed by Litchfield Meek, appeared for the defence.

Although George Edalji was charged with only one maiming, the prosecutor, Mr Barnes, when opening the case, inappropriately referred to the charge against Edalji as not an isolated offence but the eighth in a series of maimings over a period of six months in Great Wyrley and he went on to give details of all the previous maimings. The next act of dishonesty came when the prosecutor, who may not himself have been aware of the deception, placed the time of the outrage at sometime between 9 pm and 9.30 pm on the 17th August, informing the Bench that Edalji had admitted to being out and about at that time and witnesses would be called to testify to the time and place of Edalji's movements on that evening. Other witnesses were to be called to give evidence about the surveillance placed on the vicarage; the footprints, the stains and the hairs on Edalji's clothing and razor; the muddy boots; and on other matters. Noticeably, between the arraignment on the 19th August and the committal hearing on the 3rd September 'evidence' concerning the footprints and the horse's hairs had entered into the proceedings – careful detection or out-and-out fabrication? Barnes also had an expert witness on hand to show George Edalji was the person responsible for the anonymous letters and he listed the letters and postcards to be brought home to Edalji's penmanship.

Police witnesses consisted of Sergeants Rowley, Parsons and

Robinson, Inspector Campbell and Constable Cooper – two noticeable absentees were Constables Weaver and Bradley, who had been on guard duty at the field during the night of the maiming. Police evidence covered the visits to see George Edalji at the vicarage; to the scene of the maiming; to the vicarage in search of evidence; to Edalji's office; as well as comments on the footprints and the condition of the jacket, vest, trousers and boots. The police officers certainly did not get their act together because while they tried their level best to corroborate each other's stories, contradictions appeared between the evidence in the depositions and the evidence given in court on what they claimed to have heard, seen or discovered.

Although not challenging, as inadmissible, the references made by the prosecutor to all the maimings and the anonymous letters, defence counsel did object to the evidence of the police officers' conversations with George Edalji up until the time he was charged and cautioned at Cannock police station on the grounds of inadmissibility but was overruled by the bench – a foretaste of the way the 'judiciary' appeared to openly welcome any inadmissible, or other dubious, evidence worming its way into the proceedings right up until Edalji was convicted seven weeks later.

Sergeant Robinson confirmed that the vicarage was under observation for the whole night on the 17/18th August and, although unsure of the number of men actually observing the vicarage, he was certain no one could have left the house from the side he was watching without being seen. His evidence confirmed the sheer impossibility of George Edalji carrying out the offence at the time it was actually committed and it threw light on why it was crucial for the police to tie George Edalji to a crime committed between 9 pm and 9.30 pm on his way back from Bridgtown. Inspector Campbell also confirmed the police surveillance on the vicarage albeit reducing it to one man to whom he gave specific instructions to carry out this duty. He made this claim even though he was one of three men watching the vicarage according to Sergeant Robinson's evidence. Sergeant Parsons then contradicted both his fellow officers by reducing the number even further by claiming no watch was placed on the vicarage on the 17th August – an interesting conflict of evidence since Sergeant Robinson and Inspector Campbell were part of the surveillance team that night whereas Sergeant Parsons, by his own admission, was in charge of the men patrolling in another area and had kept no records of police duties. As someone in charge of the officers on watch, Sergeant Parsons did not seem to know much about what went on. Police officers were also at odds with each other over the duration of the watch on the vicarage.

Inspector Campbell put the time scale at about 2 or 3 weeks prior to the 18th August, that is, from about the 28th July or 4th August, whereas Sergeant Parson's said the watch was carried out for two or three weeks from the 29th June. Did no one keep any records?

When it came to the actual time of the offence, Inspector Campbell was less than honest in claiming that the maiming occurred between 9 pm and 10 pm. Aware that Constables Weaver and Bradley reported seeing the horse alive at 11 pm, and knowing the horse could not have been maimed until after 2.30 am, Inspector Campbell misled the court by suggesting the horse was already injured when seen by the two police officers – a claim not earning much credit for the inspector and having all the hallmarks of a conspiracy to suppress the facts. The presence and acquiescence of the chief and deputy chief constables, who were also aware of the time of the maiming, during Inspector Campbell's performance did not bring much credit to them either.

As several police officers were undoubtedly colluding to present a false picture of events, the reasonable person might also suspect these same officers of being quite capable of fabricating the forensic evidence regarding the hairs on the coat, the footprints and the mud on the boots. When the prosecution turned towards this evidence, Inspector Campbell claimed the jacket was damp, hairs were on the jacket and vest, the trousers were muddy and damp around the bottom edges, and mud covered the boots right to the top, whereas Sergeant Parsons admitted that the police paid little attention to the trousers on their first visit to the vicarage and did not bother to take the trousers with them, a rather surprising admission if the trousers had been so wet and muddy. Sergeant Parsons tried to explain away this inconsistency by claiming that the absence of mud on the trousers was due to them being cleaned between the first and second police visit, which did not explain why the police failed to take them on their first visit in the morning if they were so muddy, nor why this 'cleaning' was not pointed out to the Edaljis on the police's second visit. Furthermore, if George Edalji had scrambled through field and hedgerows getting his boots in such a muddy state surely his jacket and trousers would be equally muddy yet no mud was on the jacket and obviously none on the trousers. As for the boots, the police would have been expected to comment on their alleged 'muddy' state when Constable Cooper examined them at the vicarage and not leave it to an afterthought to come back and take only one of them.

Constable Cooper dealt with the search for footprints, the methods used for comparing the prints with the boots and the tracking of the footprints between the field and the vicarage. He admitted that between the discovery of the maiming and his comparison of the footprints, a number of people had passed over the spot on their way to work, which would certainly have contaminated the crime scene, but he denied that any other footprints were near the impressions he made. Sergeant Parsons referred to two sets of footprints at the shed, one with the imprint of a light boot without nails, the other with the heels worn down and he saw similar footprints in the corner of the field. He also said that Edalji's boots had clay on them and had only one heel worn down when he saw them at the vicarage although the fields were described as sandy rather than clay and the footprints he 'found' in the field had both heels worn down. The officers also contradicted each other when defending themselves for not providing a sample of the footprint. The track was described as extremely hard, on the one hand, and as very wet, on the other, making it impossible in both circumstances to obtain a sample. Contradictions also arose when dealing with the razors: Sergeant Parsons referred to one or two hairs on one of the razors, which the reverend had tried to wipe off, whereas Inspector Campbell never mentioned any hairs, speaking only of the razors being stained and wet with the appearance of having recently been washed.

Both Constable Cooper and Sergeant Parsons claimed to have walked from Benton's Farm to the scene of the crime and then on to the vicarage, the route George Edalji was alleged to have taken, in 21 and 21½ minutes, without either officer mentioning the time of the day or the weather conditions prevailing when they made this trek. Nor did they disclose whether or not they simulated a person with acute myopia and astigmatism. Irrespective of these caveats undermining their veracity, this was yet another irrelevant piece of information as their walks were from Benton's Farm where George Edalji was alleged to have been around 9 pm before cutting off to go to the field to kill the pony. If George Edalji was responsible his route to and from the scene would be entirely different, starting out from the vicarage during the night.

The examination of the forensic evidence also brought contradictions but this time between Inspector Campbell and the police analyst, Dr J K Butter of Cannock. The inspector claimed to have handed the forensic evidence to Dr Butter, for analysis on the 21st August but this did not tally with the doctor's own disclosure of having examined the articles on the 18th August. Dr Butter had found: (i) bloodstains much smaller than claimed by the police, approximately a half inch in diameter; (ii) grey coloured stains on Edalji's vest not being horse's saliva but starch; and (iii) twenty-nine reddish coloured, uniformly half inch long hairs on the jacket matching the hairs on the dead horse's hide.

The selection of the witnesses called in to testify seeing George Edalji on his journey back from Bridgtown on the 17th August – William Banbury, Frederick Bruton, Miss Biddle and William Thacker, gave evidence to bolster the deception over the time of the maiming, whereas other witnesses, Harry Loach, Fred Cope, Walter Whitehouse and John Hands, whose evidence cast serious doubts on the police theory were not called.

The most significant absentee from the prosecution's witnesses was the veterinary surgeon. Instead of calling him, the prosecution relied on William Cooper, the horse slaughterer, to testify to the horse being maimed by a sharp knife. The replacement of the professional expert by the slaughterman was further confirmation of a 'fit-up' under way since the police obviously did not want the time of the incident nor the type of weapon used to be brought to the attention of the court. Although the veterinary surgeon's evidence was not presented, his findings were known to the magistrates,[225] as shown by the annotation in the depositions noting Lewis's evidence, which really should have raised serious doubts in their minds as to the plausibility of the prosecution's case when deciding on whether or not to commit Edalji for trial.[226]

The anonymous letters attracted a great deal of attention and their introduction, inadmissible as they were since they had nothing to do with the maiming for which George Edalji was charged – the maiming of the 17/18th August, was an attempt to place in the minds of the magistrates a strong suspicion that the author of the letters was involved in the maimings and that George Edalji was responsible for those letters despite no connection being established between the maimer and the author as one and the same person. Sergeant Rowley; Joseph Southam, employed at Blewitt's colliery; and Sergeant Robinson gave evidence on the letters they received, despite these letters not being attributed to Edalji by the handwriting expert. Wilfred Greatorex junior, was also called and he denied writing the letters bearing his name; was in the Isle of Man when the 4th August postcard was posted; and had no knowledge of the letter in which a wrapper addressed to him formed the last page. He did travel in the same train with the boys named in the letters and had heard Edalji's comment as they passed the place where

---

[225] In fact, one magistrate had not fully read the depositions because he asked why the veterinary surgeon was not called in to examine the horse, only to be put right by the other.

[226] Magistrates written comments on the Depositions of Committal Proceedings, HO File 990 alongside PC Cooper's statement

Blewitt's horses were maimed but other than that could throw no light on the letters. Inspector Campbell described the police's visit to the vicarage, accusing Edalji of wanting to know more about the letters than a person would normally be inclined to ask. But this was grasping at straws as many people in the locality were curious about the maiming and the anonymous letters so why should George Edalji be an exception, especially as he was named in the letters and had been a recipient?

The prosecution brought in a Treasury handwriting expert with nineteen years' experience, Mr Gurrin, renown for his evidence in several prominent cases: *Moat Farm; Fazet v Dougal; and Adolf Beck*,[227] to testify that the handwriting, although disguised, exhibited a number of peculiarities that could be matched to Edalji's writing. Gurrin concluded that with the exceptions of an envelope in the Osborne and Son letter; the 3rd July postcard (Southam's); and a letter dated 30th June (Rowley's); all the other correspondence was in Edalji's handwriting. This differed from the prosecution's opening address when he claimed that all the anonymous letters were written by Edalji and had called two witnesses, Sergeant Rowley and Southam, to give evidence on these unattributed letters. The missives attributed to George Edalji were the letters of the 7th, 10th, 15th, 25th and 30th July; and the two postcards of the 4th August for which the police two days afterwards had intended to charge Royden Sharp as being the author.

No mention was made, naturally, of whether or not Captain Anson had passed on to Gurrin his own suspicions about the authorship of the 1892 – 5 anonymous letters but, given the captain's way of operating and with his malevolent streak, it would be most unlikely for the chief constable to pass up the chance of familiarising Gurrin with his own pet, jaundiced hypotheses, as he did to everyone else involved in the case.[228] Whether such information would have influenced Gurrin's professional approach to his subject cannot be conclusively determined but later events would show Gurrin was significantly influenced by

---

[227] He was also an adviser to the Home Office, Scotland Yard, the Post Office, Bankers' Association, Admiralty, War Office, Bank of England – a considerable amount of accreditations but in the not too distant future this 'Hall of Fame' was not to count for much as far as Adolph Beck was concerned, see Chapter XI

[228] In 1907, Captain Anson, pursuing the identity of a fanatical religious scribe writing from California on the Edalji maimings, thought to be one of the Sharp brothers, disclosed the alleged past history of George Edalji and anonymous letter writing to the Marshall of Long Beach, California

prior assumptions about the people whose handwriting he was examining.

The second charge of threatening to murder Sergeant Robinson was heard by the same magistrates – an action later criticised by legal experts on the grounds that the two charges should have been dealt with by separate sessions. Sergeant Robinson reported the alarm he felt after receiving the letter; Greatorex junior denied writing it; and Gurrin's unsurprising contribution was to say it was in George Edalji's handwriting. Inspector Campbell, having seen Edalji's writing, also claimed this letter to be in Edalji's handwriting. Interestingly, the inspector had previously accepted that the handwriting in both the 'Lover of Justice' letter written by Loxton and the 15th July letter 'signed' by Greatorex, which Gurrin attributed to George Edalji, were written by the same person – although merely a lay opinion it was still allowed to carry some weight when it concerned George Edalji.

Upon the conclusion of the prosecution's case, defence counsel, Mr Gandy, asked for both charges to be dismissed as the evidence was insufficient for any jury to convict Edalji; the bench gave his application for a dismissal short shrift and accepted a *prima facie* case had been made. Edalji, committed for trial at the Stafford Quarter Sessions, proclaimed his innocence and reserved his defence. Bail was set at the same terms but Edalji once again declined bail.

The venue chosen by the magistrates was unusual because crimes of this seriousness, cattle maiming and threatening to murder a police officer, were heard before a judge at the Assizes. According to authoritative legal sources: 'Russell on Crime', the leading legal text of its day; the Lord Chief Justice's opinion given six weeks after the trial; Sir George Lewis, a leading criminal lawyer at the time, involved in the Sir Charles Dilke and Mrs Crawford cases; and advice given to Herbert Gladstone, when assuming the post of Home Secretary in 1906; important cases such as Edalji's should have been tried at the Assizes.[229] The question searching for an answer is why did the magistrates commit the case to a lower level tier in the judicial hierarchy and who was the influential voice behind their decision?

A case heard by a judge at the Assizes would not have served the interests of the chief constable, who had waited ten years to settle an old score irrespective of whether Edalji was guilty or not. Any judge worth

---

[229] Yelverton, DT 14 Jan 1907; LCJ to HO, 11 Dec 1903, HO No 26a, File 984; CA 27 Aug 1904; Sir G Lewis to Yelverton, 17 Jan 1904, HO File 984; Sir G Lewis, DT 27 Aug 1904; Mallett, Sir Chas [1932] Herbert Gladstone, a memoir, Hutchinson, London, pp215/6

his salt would have required a more substantive level of evidence to be entered into the court than was available to the prosecution before asking Edalji's defence to address the charges or allowing a jury to deliberate upon it.

With the evidence against George Edalji predominantly circumstantial, lacking corroboration except from other police officers, who often contradicted each other, and the rest of the evidence mostly inadmissible, for the prosecution to stand any chance of securing a conviction a hearing chaired by someone lacking the necessary skills to identify and exclude inadmissible evidence and without the experience to instruct the jury correctly would be a considerable asset.

To secure the chief constable's ends, the case had to be committed to the Quarter Sessions, whose chair, Lord Hatherton, was no fan of the Edaljis – his predecessor's and his own more recent dealings with Reverend Edalji over the land reversion issue was a testament to that. In what seemed a noble gesture by the nobleman, Lord Hatherton excused himself from the proceedings. He was later to claim that he chose not to hear the case personally because: (i) he was resident in the immediate neighbourhood of the maimings, and "he always made it a rule not to try cases from that particular neighbourhood," (ii) the committal was made in the petty sessional court of which he was the chairman, although he had taken no part in the deliberations, and (iii) he had knowledge of the Edalji family having heard much local talk about them over the years.[230] Lord Hatherton's reasons for distancing himself from the Edalji case did not square with his later involvement in two other cattle maiming cases involving local men from the same area – Farrington in 1904 and Morgan in 1907. Nor did it explain why Lord Hatherton as Chair of the petty sessional court did not advise the magistrates to refer the case to the Assizes. More significantly, His Lordship's withdrawal provided the opportunity to hand responsibility over to Sir Reginald Hardy, vice chair of the Quarter Sessions, deputy lieutenant of Staffordshire and vice chair of the Staffordshire County Council, to hear the case even further down the judicial chain in the Second Court of the Quarter Sessions. Sir Reginald was also a lieutenant-colonel and commanding officer of the Staffordshire Imperial Yeomanry and yeoman had been suspected of being involved in the maimings.

The prime mover for having the case heard at the Quarter Sessions was the chief constable, who several months later boasted to Home

---

[230] Horton, asst magistrates clerk, Gazette 21 Jan 1907; Sir Reg Hardy to HO, 18 Dec 1903, England: HO Case of George Edalji – memos and papers, Bp 2/4 (19) p3

Office officials about the influence he could wield in determining the venue for crimes such as these, [231] aided and abetted by Lord Hatherton, who ensured the Edalji case went to the Second Court of the Quarter Sessions. Not even the reservations held by the counsel for the prosecution, Mr Disturnal, who at a pre-trial conference with the chief constable proposed having the case heard at the Assizes, made any impression. Captain Anson, assuming the mantle of spokesperson for the defence as well as the prosecution, advised him that George Edalji wanted to be tried at the Quarter Sessions as the Assizes were not due to be held for another two months.[232]

The cavalier disregard shown towards using appropriate procedures and the choice of Sir Reginald Hardy to hear the case confirmed that some aristocratic lobbying had taken place between the 19th August and the 3rd September to seal George Edalji's fate. In the light of Captain Anson's influence and his later track record, little doubt can be entertained that in any meetings with the justices in Staffordshire, Captain Anson, whose family held considerable sway in the county, would not let the opportunity slip by to discuss the maimings and to exert influence on anyone involved in the proceedings.

As senior members of the legal profession later acknowledged, a vice chairman of Quarter Sessions without any real legal experience should not have been given jurisdiction in such a grave case and, given the strong local feeling, the trial should have been transferred to a jurisdiction where less excitement and prejudice prevailed.[233] The Anson-Hatherton-Hardy axis put George Edalji into the hands of a person ill equipped and without the required level of legal expertise to deal with this type of case.

Sir Reginald Hardy's inadequacy was undoubtedly recognised since it led to Mr Blakiston, the clerk of the peace at the Staffordshire Quarter Sessions, who had accompanied the chief constable of the prosecuting authority to the pre-trial meeting with the prosecuting counsel, to absent himself from the trial. Instead, Mr Bertram Brough, a junior member of the Bar, by special arrangement was appointed to sit as legal adviser to Sir Reginald Hardy, advising him on points of law

---

[231] Correspondence between Capt Anson and Simpson (HO) 25, 29, 30 & 31 Mar 1904, HO No 87 File 985

[232] Disturnal to Chambers, HO, 19 Mar 1907, File 989 Pt 1

[233] Sir G Lewis, CA 27 Aug 1904; Law Jnl, Vol 42 No 2410, 19 Jan 1907 p29 and No 2144, 16 Feb 1907 p 103

and evidence arising in the court during the Edalji trial[234] – an arrangement later claimed to have been made before it was decided for Sir Reginald to hear the case.[235] This claim was just not true since Sir Reginald Hardy, admitting to his lack of competence and experience in trying a case of such seriousness, agreed to take the case only if Mr Bertram Brough assisted him. This arrangement had no legal precedence because the court duties of a clerk were administrative not judicial – keeping the records of the court, calling the jury into the box, arraigning the prisoner, taking the plea, announcing bills returned by the Grand Jury, taking the verdict and recording the sentence,[236] but it did confirm Sir Reginald Hardy's lack of competence. Sir Reginald's 'suitability' was placed into its true perspective by one ex-colonial chief justice who commented that "a gentleman who declares his incompetence by asking a practicing barrister…to advise on points arising in a case is hardly the person whose opinion would (be) receive(d) with confidence in a case of so serious a felony."[237]

The attempted entrapment of George Edalji through the 'Lover of Justice' letter was also a talking point at the pre-trial conference. Mr Disturnal wanted Captain Anson to serve notice on the defence for the letter to be produced at the trial; otherwise, it might be suspected that the prosecution did not want the letter produced in court. Of course, Captain Anson wanted the letter to stay where it was and for his part in the whole sleazy affair not to enter the public domain, although making it seem that his only concern was for Loxton, who was anxious to keep his identity secret and not to be seen as being involved in the police pursuit of Edalji. The captain's view prevailed.[238] Loxton was undoubtedly reluctant to have his role in this affair exposed as the Incorporated Law Society would obviously have something to say about his unprofessional conduct in colluding with the police in a highly dubious venture to entrap a professional colleague by using a forged letter "to the prejudice of another man's right."[239] This arrangement for hiding Loxton's involvement was conducted in the presence of the clerk

---

[234] Unnamed members of the Staffordshire Quarter Sessions to Yelverton, and B Brough to Yelverton, in Yelverton to HO, 5 & 7 Dec 1903, HO No 20 & 23, File 984; C Brough to Yelverton, Dec 1903, HO No 23 File 984

[235] Capt Anson to HO, 20 Mar 1907, HO No 192, File 986

[236] Justice's Clerks' Act 1877, ss40 and 41 Victoria, Chapter 43

[237] Yelverton to HO, 7 Dec 1903, HO No 23, File 984

[238] Captain Anson to Blackwell, 21and 23 Apr 1907, File 989 Pt 1

[239] Definition of forgery under 47 & 48 Victoria, Chapter 76 section 11. See Rutzen in the case of Det-Sgt Ward, Times 19/20 Aug 1903

of the peace. Since Captain Anson was not ill-disposed to letting the clerk know the origin of the 'Lover of Justice' letter, it would be reasonable to assume that the captain's attempted entrapment would not be kept from those higher up in the Quarter Sessions chain of command, that is, Lord Hatherton and Sir Reginald Hardy, in the run up to the trial. It could also reasonably be expected for the chief constable to exert as much influence as possible on anyone involved in the proceedings or likely to give specialist evidence at the trial, for example, the handwriting expert, by providing them with his version of events. As the aftermath of George Edalji's conviction would show, Captain Anson was not averse to 'massaging' or even 'fabricating' facts to present Edalji in the worst possible light and it should not stretch the imagination too much to believe Captain Anson was capable of doing the same before the trial in contact meetings with members of the judiciary in whatever capacity they met, professional or social. The likelihood of this prospect was only too evident in the contents of the brief produced for the prosecutor; the hand guiding the penholder who wrote out that brief can be seen to be none other than Captain Anson's.

The 'case' history in the brief irrelevantly retreated into the 1890s with accusations against George Edalji of writing anonymous letters and playing practical jokes, which was erroneously claimed to have ceased in 1892 when the police caught him placing leaflets under the door of the vicarage, yet another misrepresentation since Edalji was never connected in any meaningful way to the anonymous letters.[240] Loxton's unsubstantiated allegations against Edalji in 1901 of writing libellous statements on the walls and gateposts around Great Wyrley also found their way into the brief. A rather inane inclusion was the description of George Edalji "carrying in his face manifest traces of his Eastern parentage – a swarthiness of complexion, very noticeable thick protruding lips and a peculiar panther like walk."[241] This overly subjective, prejudicial view firmly located Edalji in the mould of a Captain Anson 'Lombroso' creation. This contribution from the captain, grossly irrelevant to the charge, except perhaps for the stealth like qualities attributed to Edalji, which at a 'pinch' in the *Ansonian* scheme of things, might be considered a skill suitable for 'prowling' the countryside looking for prey. Can there be any doubt that Captain Anson was the inspiration behind the brief? The compiler of this

---

[240] This was the second claim of someone allegedly thwarting George Edalji in 1892, W H Brookes was also to make this claim.

[241] Captain Anson to HO, sending the Brief, 30 Mar 1907, HO No 195, File 986

scenario fantasia was determined to provide the prosecution with an extremely jaundiced picture of George Edalji to be matched only by the prosecution's equally devious performance at the forthcoming trial.

As part of the prosecution's attempt to fix the time of the maiming at between 9 pm and 9.30 pm on the 17th August, it was confirmed in the brief that the vicarage was under a nightly surveillance between the 6th and 18th August, which included the night of the maiming, and a watch was also maintained on the fields.[242] No mention was made of any conversations taking place between the police and the Edaljis during the police's two visits to the vicarage on the 18th August, suggesting nothing of significance passed between the parties during these visits. Perhaps, Captain Anson was leaving his options open to allow for unconfirmed comments to be included in the court hearing without being tied down by statements in the brief. Four years later, Captain Anson threw up the excuse for the omission from the depositions of the conversations between Inspector Campbell and the Edaljis at the vicarage as due to the conversations not being evidence, a rather bizarre claim considering the conversations, albeit unwritten down police versions, were given considerable prominence at the trial.

George Edalji's defence team were provided with a number of Aunt Sally's to knock down but seemed reluctant to take the steps necessary to line up the targets. Apparently, the defence team was so confident of Edalji having no case to answer and the charges against him would be dismissed that he was advised not to call any witnesses.[243] However, Edalji insisted on calling witnesses capable of dismantling the police theory on the time of the maiming but he complied with counsel's advice not to call expert witnesses for the handwriting or for his eye condition, even though the plea of defective eyesight was entered on Edalji's brief by his solicitor. Vachell decided not to use Edalji's myopia believing that rebuttal evidence might be presented by people claiming to have seen George Edalji walking about in the dark.[244] An interesting forecast because Captain Anson made such a claim four years later, which did not really amount to much but it does suggest that Vachell, prior to the trial, had been told of these alleged sightings and allowed his defence of Edalji to be influenced by these claims. Notwithstanding this, any attempt by the prosecuting counsel at rebuttal could easily have been demolished by evidence from

[242] Ibid

[243] CA 15 Dec 1907; DT 15 Jan 1907

[244] Letter from someone with knowledge of the Defence, probably Hazel, the MP for West Bromwich, Gazette 21 Jan 1907

any one of a number of specialist oculists, and surely the defence knew the difference between strolling leisurely down main roads and making the hazardous trek on a dark, stormy night to carry out the maiming, especially by a man whom they described in the brief as no athlete and very short-sighted. Edalj's counsel also failed to obtain access to the anonymous letters in spite of promising the Edaljis he would do so.[245] Nor did he follow up his request to see the letters made at the committal proceedings. The defence did eventually and unsuccessfully point out to the court that the letters were inadmissible as far as the mutilation charge was concerned since the maiming was never mentioned in those letters[246] but failed to make any provision for a handwriting expert should the letters be admitted into evidence, offering up the excuse of the high cost for such a service.[247] The defence made no representations for the case to be heard at the Assizes, overlooking the possibility of the case coming before the less than competent vice chair of the Quarter Sessions. The impression emerging was of a set of defence lawyers giving less than their best to a fellow lawyer and appearing to take into account too much of the information flowing from the prosecution to the defence's ears concerning Edalji's 'eyesight' and the 'anonymous letters' as will be illustrated later.

---

[245] Rev and Mrs Ed, in HO Memo for consideration of Home Sec, undated, HO No 127, File 985; DT 15 Jan 1907
[246] CA 15 Dec 1907
[247] Despatch 30 May 1907

Chapter VIII

Injustice is a Darker Shade of Green

The chief constable may have occupied the dominant position in believing that the law, however misapplied, was on his side but Reverend Edalji had the pulpit and believed God to be on his. The Man of God made full use of his calling to the packed congregations now turning up at St Mark's Church by constantly invoking his son's case and offering prayers for the deliverance of the innocent. His prayers seemed to be answered with an incident that cast long shadows over Captain Anson's desire to remove George Edalji from South Staffordshire. During the night of the 21st September, in spite of the continued presence of policemen patrolling the area, a horse belonging to the Green family paddocked in Benton's field, the alleged starting point for George Edalji's maiming excursion, was killed within a half mile of the previous maiming. According to the veterinary surgeon, this maiming took place around midnight although a night watchman at Gilpins, a factory close to the field, heard a squeal around 1.30 am.[248]

News of the killing quickly spread throughout the district bringing out a large number of spectators − well dressed ladies, cyclists of both sexes, people in traps, cabs, wagonettes, brakes and charabancs. Civilian spectators were not the only ones to show a presence, the police came out in considerable strength, dozens of officers scouring the district and, as with previous maimings, not a single piece of evidence was discovered at the scene of the crime. Leading lights in the Crown's case against Edalji − Mr A W Barnes − the solicitor, Captains Anson and Longden, visited the scene, although Captain Anson did not stay long in the area and returned to his Staffordshire headquarters the following day leaving the latest enigma to occupy the time of the Deputy Chief Constable Longden but, before departing, the captain offered a £50 reward for information leading to a conviction.[249]

The police, as ever, found itself in a quandary as the latest maiming served to undermine the prosecution's case against Edalji. Edalji was in Stafford Gaol and not even Captain Anson could argue that he managed to evade his guardians on this occasion. Responsibility for the crime pointed in the direction of someone familiar with handling

---

[248] BME 24, 28 & 30 Sep 1903; BWM 26 Sep 1903
[249] BME 23 & 24 Sep 1903; BWP 26 Sep & 3 Oct 1903

horses as the latest equine victim was reputed to be extremely spirited because only a few days prior to the maiming, four people had tried to catch it without success. One previous owner of the horse suggested that such a spirited horse would require more than one person to be involved in its slaughter – an informed view of the horse's temperament raising the possibility of a gang being involved, including someone with considerable knowledge of dealing with horses.[250]

A large number of police officers remained in the area to guard against further maimings – a rather pious hope since the maimer appeared to be able to breach police lines at will to commit these outrages. The local population, lacking confidence in the police's ability to solve a mystery terrorising the whole district, was hardly impressed by this show of force. Women and young girls were reluctant to venture out after dark and any local incident was interpreted within the context of the communal paranoia. When a local child walking with her mother, Mrs Handley, the wife of a local miner, was jostled by three men, it was reported as an attempt to strangle the child. With no evidence of marks on her throat, Inspector Campbell and Captain Longden put the incident down to a bout of drunken behaviour by the men involved.[251]

Constantly slated for lacking any systematic approach for tracking down the offender, the police brought in a number of suspects for questioning. A man named Darby, a name to be used as a pseudonym for a large number of letters soon to flood the area, after hinting to his co-drinkers in a public house that he was the leader of the gang, was questioned by the police. Darby's excursion into animal maiming was found to be nothing more than the usual *braggadocio* 'tavern-talk'. An unnamed member of the local yeomanry had his sword examined but it was found to be too blunt to slice open an animal as well as being free from any traces of blood. With the police suspecting that the maimer used a curved sword, it brought members of the yeomanry, known to be a boisterous group of young men, into the frame. Police officers began to accept the possibility of a gang carrying out the maimings and, with an element of desperation, meted out to suspects hauled into the police station the kind of treatment that led to a wave of indignation against the police. Joseph Greenall, captain of the local cricket team, sought legal advice after being taken to Cannock police station by Captain Longden where, he claimed, he was bullied for one and a half hours to

[250] BWP 26 Sep 1903

[251] ACD attributed this attack to R Sharp and J Hart, although the basis of the claim lay in the realm of detective fiction. BME 23, 24 and 26 Sep 1903; BWM 22 Aug 1903; Case Against Sharp by ACD, HO File 988

make statements about the maimings, of which he was completely ignorant, before being released.[252] Another suspect, Harry Green, of the local yeomanry was not to be so fortunate.

When news of the maiming reached the ears of the Edalji family their spirits were lifted. Mrs Edalji, hoping that the suspicion directed at her son would now be removed, sent a telegram to him with the news. Reverend Edalji, caught by surprise since he believed a conspiracy was operating against his son and, adopting a rather naïve stance considering what the Edalji family had experienced over the previous twenty years, trusted in justice eventually being done, or, perhaps, this was hope born of sheer despair. Not so optimistic as his parents, George Edalji's hopes were not raised by this latest bloodshed and he thought it unlikely for the police to drop the charge after rigging the evidence against him. He was open minded, or naïve enough, to believe that the Green maiming was evidence of the perpetrator having no personal spite against him, otherwise, he thought, another animal would not have been killed so soon after his arrest and while he was still in jail.[253]

The maimings triggered off a new wave of anonymous letters. Harry Green received an offer from a writer in Brierley Hill prepared to betray the leader of the gang for £20, while his father, T J Green, was sent a letter of an entirely different order threatening to maim his other ten horses. Harry Green was to receive five letters within the next three days, which he took on a daily basis to Inspector Campbell at Cannock police station. On seeing the first letter, Inspector Campbell thought the writing looked nothing like George Edalji's, which considering Edalji was in gaol hardly constituted a distinctive piece of detective work. After seeing the fifth letter, the inspector told Green to "Let the letters stop," suggesting that he believed Green to be involved in some way. Green denied all knowledge of the letters but his constant visits to the police station gave the impression of wanting to be near to the police to find out what they knew – the very thing George Edalji was accused of doing with regard to the other maimings.[254]

A breakthrough arrived when a witness, Mr Copestake, claimed to have seen Harry Green, whom the police had high up on its list of suspects, near the field where the maiming took place. There seemed to be little mileage in this sighting because Green said he stopped to look

[252] BME, 1 Oct 1903; 3 Oct 1903; Despatch 2 Oct 1903

[253] BME, 23 Sep 1903; E & S 23 Sep 1903; BWM, 26 Sep 1903; G Edalji to Mrs C Edalji, 22 Sep 1903, HO No 57, File 985

[254] Yelverton to HO, 4 Dec 1903, HO No 29, File 984; BWM 25 & 26 Sep 1903

at his horse about 10.20 pm on his way home[255] but over the next few weeks, Harry Green was placed firmly in the frame for this latest outrage. The story about to unfold consists of an unusual set of disclosures and admissions, packaged in alternative versions from the Green family, the police and a friend of Harry Green named Arrowsmith.[256]

Arrowsmith's version began at noon on the day Green's horse was found. Harry Green arrived at the shop managed by Arrowsmith and owned up to killing his own horse. Green implicated several well-known local men who had apparently drawn straws to decide who would carry out the killing. Afraid the police might blame him and one of his associates, possibly Jack Hart, Green revealed that in the event of the police charging him with the maiming one of his pals would get him out of it by maiming another horse to clear him.[257] Green showed Arrowsmith a letter he intended to send out containing the message, "If you want the bloody horse killer it is the bloody old man at the vicarage," but changed his mind when the 'public-spirited' Arrowsmith threatened to denounce him as the maimer if Green refused to send out an alternative letter exonerating George Edalji. A worried Harry Green contacted an unknown person about Arrowsmith's threat and a letter written on a telegram form posted in London was despatched to Green pointing out that the police had made a mistake in arresting Edalji. The writer also included a threat to slaughter women and children in the middle of October.

During the following week, Green and Arrowsmith met several times to discuss the maimings and other related issues. When Green informed his family of Arrowsmith's interest and of their conversations being recorded by a third party, whose identity was not disclosed,

---

[255] PC Meredith, Yelverton to HO, 4 Dec 1903, HO No 29 File 984

[256] Yelverton to HO, 4, 16 & 17 Dec 1903, HO No 29, 31 & 33, File 984; Affidavits, TJ Green, S E Green, C M Green, 15 Dec 1903, and H Green to PC Meredith, 22 Sep 1903, HO No 31 File 984; Despatch 8 May 1907; CA 14 & 28 Nov 1903; BME 9 Nov 1903; Fred W Peake, Green's brother-in-law, CA 21 Nov 1903; Capt Anson to HO, 22 Dec 1903, HO No 39, File 984; BWP 24 Oct & 7 Nov 1903; Rept of Chief Constable, 22 Dec 1903, England: HO Case of George Edalji – memos and papers, Bp 2/4 (19) App II, pp36/7; Arrowsmith to ACD, 3 Mar 1907, File 989 Pt 1; Arrowsmith to Anson, 19 Sep 1907, File 989 Pt 2;

[257] Interestingly, the prosecution used this idea in the trial against George Edalji to suggest that the Green maiming was carried out by gang members to help George Edalji – maybe it was from the reports made to the police by Arrowsmith that this prosecution hypothesis originated.

Green's family suspected a trap was being laid for him. Arrowsmith then began corresponding with Harry by letter, a novelty in their friendship, and the Green family advised Harry to make notes of any future conversations with the shop manager. The family were right to be suspicious because Arrowsmith, inspired by the £50 reward offered by Captain Anson for information, was reporting these conversations to Inspector Campbell and Superintendent Bishop. On hearing of Arrowsmith's disclosures, Captain Anson was full of praise for this 'highly respectable man', as Arrowsmith was described by the captain at the time, only for the captain to change his opinion at a later date when Arrowsmith began to aid the George Edalji campaign in 1907. Captain Anson responded by arranging for Green to be invited to the police station on the 29th September. Under the pretext of asking if he had received any more anonymous letters, the police wanted to check out Arrowsmith's revelations, or perhaps some other shady purpose was on the cards since the contents of the Green-Arrowsmith conversations put a sabre right through the case Captain Anson was fleshing out against George Edalji.

According to Green, this pretext was quickly dropped and he was interrogated in a locked room by three senior officers, Superintendent Bishop, Inspector Campbell and Captain Longden. He was offered £50 to admit to committing the maiming otherwise he would face ten years penal servitude. Superintendent Bishop, leading the interrogation, threatened to confront him with several members of the yeomanry, who had all claimed to have seen Green killing his own horse. He then took Green into another room and applying a softer, kindlier manner, a tactic obviously not unknown in those days, made it clear to Green that he would be in Stafford gaol on a serious charge if he (Bishop) had not intervened. The 'sympathetic' Bishop tried to coax Green into making a confession, promising him in return that no prosecution would ensue. The alternative to this offer was to charge Green whether guilty or not. After this 'side' interview, lasting about thirty minutes, back they went to join Captain Longden and Inspector Campbell. The 'softly softly' approach was replaced with a more severe interrogation but Green continued to maintain his innocence. The soft approach was resumed by Superintendent Bishop followed by another bout of the Campbell-Longden bullying technique.

Around 7 pm, after three hours of continuous questioning, the police assured Green that killing this horse was no offence – an issue for the Society for the Prevention of Cruelty to Animals to decide whether or not to prosecute, and he would be free from a Society prosecution if he could prove the horse was his own property. The police chose to ignore the fact that the owner of the horse was not Harry Green but his father, therefore, this defence was inappropriate. Nor could owners claim exemption from prosecution for cruelty to their own animals as attested to by the many cases brought before the Cannock courts at the time.

After offering Green this deal, Inspector Campbell started to write out a confession for Green to sign. Green, obviously not putting too much reliance on police promises or perhaps not personally guilty of the actual maiming, refused to sign the confession. He denied discussing the maimings with Arrowsmith except the point about drawing straws – a most significant admission because this 'lottery' was to decide who would kill Green's horse and it confirmed the existence of a group of men or 'gang' prepared to kill animals. According to the police, when Green declined to sign the confession, Arrowsmith was brought in to confront him. In the presence of the three senior police officers, Arrowsmith read out the notes of his conversations with Green, who quickly admitted everything. Having played his lucrative part in denouncing Green, Arrowsmith left the police station and Green put his signature to the confession in front of the three officers, who then took it along to Captain Anson waiting in an adjoining room. The confession read: "I, the undersigned, am in no way connected with the person or persons connected with maiming of cattle in Great Wyrley, except the last one, which was my property. I make this admission on the thorough understanding that no prosecution shall follow." A sparse confession giving no details of the maiming, nor information on the weapon used, nor any motive for the killing of his father's horse.

This was a curious state of affairs because these senior police officers were offering Green immunity from prosecution if he admitted killing the horse and denied killing any other without the police showing any interest in investigating whether or not the latest killing was part of the whole series of animal maimings in the locality. Captain Anson later claimed, albeit mistakenly because he went on to retract it, that Green killed his own horse as he was afraid of being found out for making a fraudulent claim for compensation from the government for alleging that his horse had sustained injuries during Yeomanry training, surely an indictable offence for fraud if it had been true.

The determination shown by this high powered team of interrogators to obtain this confession and then to sweep the affair under the carpet clearly demonstrated the importance the Staffordshire police, especially Captain Anson, attached to a confession classifying the Green maiming as a separate and distinct aberration to be isolated from the 18th August maiming and all the other maimings. This subterfuge served its purpose and left the police free to continue the prosecution or, more aptly, persecution of George Edalji. This was no error of judgement on the part of the police but a deliberate conspiracy to get Edalji that 'dose of penal servitude' with the confession acting as a weapon held over Green's head to keep him in check.

Harry Green returned from the police station in an agitated state, showing signs of weeping, and complaining of the way the police treated him. According to Captain Anson, Green went off to see Arrowsmith to tell him he (Green) was getting off lightly having signed a confession and making no mention of the police coercing him into making the confession. Green disclosed his intention "to take off as soon as possible" giving South Africa as his destination and that when he drew his first month's salary in South Africa he intended sending Superintendent Bishop £5 because of the courteousness shown to him. This was a highly unlikely story bearing in mind Arrowsmith had 'sneaked' on him and it placed a question mark not so much against Arrowsmith's contribution but against what Captain Anson claimed Arrowsmith had reported. Captain Anson had this tendency to quote third party information without the third party knowing of it or being able to comment on its veracity.

Whatever method used by the police to prise a confession out of Green, the confession itself was inadequate. Not completely satisfied that Green had disclosed everything he knew or had done, the police visited Green's home on several occasions seeking an additional statement until Harry Green's father called in a solicitor to put a stop to it. To get around this, Superintendent Bishop waylaid Green in Cannock and 'invited' him to the police station under the pretext of the chief constable wanting a sample of his handwriting to compare with the anonymous letters, a ruse to get Green to make a second confession in his own handwriting. The police later claimed to have no reason for questioning the accuracy of the first confession, yet they duped Harry Green into signing another one, by explaining the need for a new confession on the ambiguity in the wording of the first.

Superintendent Bishop dictated a statement, in reality a confession, and Green, whom the police had 'over a barrel' because of the first confession, wrote it out and signed it. The confession read: "I H Green of High House Farm Great Wyrley had a horse turned out in my father's field, which had been injured in the Yeomanry training. Thinking it would never recover I killed it. I do not require any compensation from the local funds or from the military authorities. I passed Copestake when I was leaving the field, sorry for what I done and I have been to Mr Benton and told him. The horse was killed to keep the game rolling". Green's signature was then added to the confession. Despite having a second bite of the cherry, the second confession still contained serious flaws. Superintendent Bishop noticed the absence of any reference to a weapon and he asked Green what weapon had he used to kill the horse. Green, waking up to the reality behind the 'test' of his handwriting, denied killing the horse. Inspector Campbell, thinking the omission unimportant, suggested it be left out and it was. Mr Benton would also have something to say about his name being included.

From then on, the police stuck to Green like glue. Superintendent Bishop accompanied Green to the shipping agents in Walsall to find out Green's plans for his trip to South Africa and on the 7th October helped him to transfer his ticket to another ship. Just as Green was about to set sail for South Africa, Captain Longden contacted him to say he could not leave as he was an important witness in the Edalji trial. According to Captain Anson, Green was anxious to get away from the area and the police had great difficulty in preventing him from sailing before the trial. However, it was more likely that having realised the possibility of Edalji's defence team issuing a subpoena for Green to appear as a witness, the police decided to detain him in case his absence led to insinuations against the police for letting him leave the jurisdiction. Captain Anson also claimed it was essential for Green to be on hand in case the defence wanted to call him as a witness – an extremely noble gesture on the captain's part and completely out of character. Green, disturbed at what he thought was in store for him, went to see Meek and Walker, Edalji's solicitors, who passed him on to a Birmingham solicitor, Hallam. Hallam wrote to Superintendent Bishop, on the 18th October 1903, accusing the police of extorting a confession from Green and advising the Superintendent of Green's intention to take steps to retrieve his ticket, which had been impounded by the police.

Curious about what Edalji's defence team might throw at them following the retraction of Green's confession; about Green's sudden attachment to the Edalji camp; and about Green's threats against the police; the police arranged for its informant, Arrowsmith, to invite Green to call on him two days before the Edalji trial began with Inspector Campbell hiding in a cupboard listening to the conversation. Green was alleged to have spoken of his trip to the solicitor in Birmingham and of Vachell's intention to take up his case against the police for forcing the confession out of him. Surprisingly, Green was supposed to have disclosed to this police informant his intention to take up writing anonymous letters again but asked Arrowsmith to keep quiet about it and when Arrowsmith made the accusation that Royden Sharp was captain of the gang, Green, quite uncharacteristically, turned on him fiercely and they almost came to blows.

These latter disclosures in the Green-Arrowsmith conversations were, to say the least, questionable. Could any reasonable person believe that Green, after his recent dealings with the police and knowing of Arrowsmith's role in reporting their earlier conversations, would admit to being the anonymous letter writer? If the disclosures were true, Captain Anson's failure to pin the authorship on Green confirmed that his leniency towards Green was to ensure nothing would be allowed to disturb the case against Edalji. If Green's confession was irregularly obtained and untrue, little reliance could be placed on the evidence collected against George Edalji by the very same officers. If the contents of the confession were true then it should have set the alarm bells ringing in the Staffordshire police headquarters because it cast considerably more than a reasonable doubt on Edalji's guilt. If Green, a yeoman trained to wield a sword, did maim his horse, which suffered similar wounds to the other animals, then a direct link was provided with all the other maimings. With the chief constable later claiming footprints were found on the 29th June and 18th August leading from the fields not only to the vicarage but also to Green's farm, perhaps Green, under suspicion, killed or participated in killing his own horse to deflect attention from himself, a hypothesis just as plausible as the argument put forward against George Edalji for allegedly accusing himself in the anonymous letters.

News of a confession for the Green maiming filtered its way into the public domain when the police revealed that the mystery had been solved and predicted no further maimings would occur. The police referred to the extraordinary circumstances preventing them from taking action against this unnamed maimer but declined to reveal the nature of those constraints. In justifying its decision for not taking action against the culprit, the police explained it away as a 'give and take' policy in which the maimer provided the names of three young men, accessories to the Green outrage, whom the police were now watching, in return for not being prosecuted. High on the list of accessories were Green, Hart and possibly Sharp. Captain Anson later admitted that the first two were suspected of involvement in the maimings,[258] and the third suspected of sending out anonymous letters. These suspicions should have removed George Edalji from any list of suspects because Jack Hart was a sworn enemy of Edalji as a result of Edalji's role in a libel case brought against him. However, the police made no effort to delve deeper into

---

[258] Capt Anson to Blackwell, 26 Aug 1907, HO File 989 Pt 1; Capt Anson, Notes on ACD letters, undated, HO File 989 Pt 2

the mire to establish whether the Green maiming could be linked to the other maimings or to the other suspects.

The objective in releasing the news of the confession was to massage public opinion by isolating the latest maiming from the offence for which Edalji was being brought to trial. Behind these silken words was a web of duplicity woven by the police in order to ensure the charge against George Edalji was not undermined, he was to remain the only and most unlikely of defendants – a clear illustration of the police's double standards when contrasting the way Green was treated, released without charge, with the treatment already meted out to George Edalji and which Edalji was due to face again during the next few days. Police duplicity did not go unnoticed and the scarcity of information released to the public on this maiming led one newspaper to accuse Captain Anson of showing more success in keeping secrets than in organising the investigation.[259]

---

[259] Despatch 16 Oct 1903; BME 17 Oct 1903

Chapter IX

A Staffordshire Euro-Asian in 'King' Hardy's Court

George Edalji was to spend four days in front of Sir Reginald Hardy at the Second Court of the Quarter Sessions with the press and the curious minded of Staffordshire watching on. The notoriety of the case attracted not only the 'masses' but also the 'ladies and gentlemen of the county' – simplified local press shorthand for the class character of British society. As the trial progressed, the 'welcoming' crowd gradually diminished although the audience was replenished by additional reporters from various parts of the country and by a large number of women, who turned to the light literature brought with them when the case failed "to retain its dramatic and sensationalist element." The Edaljis, in support of their much maligned son and brother, were in attendance, as were senior police officers with opposite motives. One absentee was T J Green, the father of Harry Green, who was barred from entering the court by the police.[260]

While the Grand Jury was considering whether or not George Edalji had a case to answer, the prosecution brought together its witnesses in a pre-trial conference. Among the crowd of witnesses was Elizabeth Foster, with a grudge against George Edalji still to satisfy, fuelling suspicion to onlookers that she had furnished the police with information about the anonymous letters, although what relevance it could possibly have to the present charges against George Edalji is not difficult to determine even in Sir Reginald Hardy's court, which became a veritable magnet for attracting inadmissible evidence into the proceedings. Nonetheless, if Elizabeth Foster had been ill served in 1888, she was to have her day in court albeit as an observer and, so it seemed, was Captain Anson to have his in the role of an *eminence gris*. Two other witnesses were Harry Green and Copestake, both subpoenaed to attend, no doubt to prevent the defence calling them since neither found their way into the witness box. Apparently at the gathering of witnesses, Green made it clear to the prosecution of his intention to tell the court he did not confess to killing his horse and when he left the room reserved for witnesses he went over to Reverend

---

[260] Despatch 21 Oct 1903; Yelverton to HO, 16 Dec 1903, Ho No 31, File 984; BME 21/22 Oct 1903; E & S 23 Oct 1903

Edalji to tell of his exchange of words with the prosecution.[261]

By midday, the grand jury had decided there was a case for George Edalji to answer on both counts, (i) maiming a horse under the Malicious Damages Act 1861, s 40, carrying a maximum sentence of 14 years, and (ii) threatening to murder Charles Robinson on or about the 11th July under the Offences Against the Persons Act 1861, s 16, which carried a maximum of 7 years imprisonment.[262]

Sir Reginald Hardy and four other members, including Vice-Admiral the Hon A C Littleton, made up the bench, with Mr Brough attending as adviser in matters of law and admissibility to compensate for the chair's deficiencies in these crucial areas – a procedural innovation to ensure the case was heard before a legal lightweight in the form of Sir Reginald. The consequence to George Edalji of administering justice in this novel way can be seen from the dual role performed by Mr Brough, who was also acting for one of his law practice clients in another court and was frequently absent from the Edalji trial in order to deal with matters in that other court.[263]

Prosecuting the Crown's case was Mr W J Disturnal, assisted by Mr H Harrison, instructed by A W Barnes of Lichfield. For the Defence was F S Vachel with W J Gandy, instructed by Litchfield Meek of Messrs Walters and Meek, who were fully aware of the Green affair, the issue having come to their attention by Green's visit to Walters and Meek. The jury was drawn from a wide area of Staffordshire – Stoke, in the North of the county, to Handsworth, now part of Birmingham, in the South, but excluding all persons living in the Cannock area.[264]

    (a) The Prosecution's Case

---

[261] Despatch 21 Feb 1907; BWP 7 Nov 1903; Yelverton to HO, 17 Dec 1903, HO No 33, File 984

[262] Mail 20 Oct 1903; Post, 21 Oct 1903

[263] Despatch 7 Mar 1907; Brough to Yelverton, HO No 23, File 984

[264] The details of the trial were taken from: Mail 20-23 Oct 1903; E & S 20-24 Oct 1903 and 23 Jan 1907; Post 21-24 Oct 1903; BME 21-24 Oct 1903; BWM 31 Oct 1903 and 23 Mar 1907; DT, 14, 17-19, 21 & 23 Jan 1907; PW, 6 Jun 1907; Gazette, 22-24 Oct 1903 and 18 Jan 1907; Despatch 22 & 23 Oct 1903; and 21 Jan 1907; Times 24 Oct 1903 and 14 Jan 1907; MG, 27 May 1905; CA 15 Dec 1907; LM 30 Oct 1903; Hardy's notes of the trial; Hardy to HO, 18 Dec 1903, England: HO Case of George Edalji – memos and papers, Bp 2/4 (19) p 3; Yelverton to HO, 22 Jan 1904, HO No 60, File 985; Hardy to HO, 27 May 1907, HO No 215, File 986; B Brough to A E Clarke, HO No 40 File 984

Prosecuting counsel, Disturnal, described by the press as a genial advocate, in his hour-long opening address acknowledged no direct connection could be made between the 17/18th August maiming and the previous offences or the anonymous letters, yet he continually referred to the series of similar outrages in the district occurring since February and offered the jury the prospect of testimony from an experienced handwriting expert, who would attest to George Edalji having written the anonymous letters in a disguised hand. Disturnal explained away his intention to present the court with inadmissible evidence, relying on the chair's inadequate grasp of legal matters, by impressing on the court that although Edalji faced only one charge of maiming, the jury would be unable to understand the anonymous letters without knowledge of the previous maimings. The letters were flagged up as important evidence containing as they did the names of people whom Edalji knew and which were sent out for the purpose of bringing Edalji into contact with the police in order for him to keep pace with the progress of police enquiries. They would also provide details of previous outrages and clearly showed Edalji to be preparing the commission of another outrage either by himself or in conjunction with someone else. Disturnal used the inadmissible anonymous letters to justify the inclusion of the inadmissible evidence concerning the previous maimings. Yet again, by trading on Sir Reginald's inadequacy, he had successfully introduced a means for linking the identity of the letter writer with that of the maimer without intending to offer any supportive evidence for that assumption. Disturnal did not mention, a failure not taken up by the defence, that the details contained in the letters relating to the previous maimings were available to anyone gathering information locally or who had read the local newspapers.

Exploiting the maiming of Green's horse and pre-empting the argument that as Edalji was in gaol he could not have had anything to do with it, Disturnal unfolded his own version of the horror story. He pointed to the anonymous letters, in which the perpetrator was depicted as acting in conjunction with others, and painted a portrait of a gang of conspirators committing the Green maiming to divert attention away from a gang member held in custody – a ploy previously attributed to Green during his conversations with Arrowsmith, brought to the attention of the police by Green's confidant, and the most likely source for the prosecutor's hypothesis. This alleged conspiracy was also put forward to explain Edalji's refusal to accept bail because he knew a maiming would take place if he stayed in custody.

Disingenuously connecting Edalji to the September outrage, Disturnal magnanimously advised jury members to suspend any judgement on this connection until they had heard the whole of the evidence. Judging from this line of attack it could be expected that the September maimer would be putting forward some devastating evidence to the jury but Disturnal knew that Green was not giving evidence. The Green maiming served the prosecution's purpose by placing in the jury's mind the idea of a gang and of a co-conspirator helping Edalji by killing another horse. The prosecution had turned the Green maiming from an impediment into an advantage.

Those in court must have held high expectations, hopefully or otherwise, of the prosecution bringing forward conclusive evidence to prove Edalj's guilt beyond a reasonable shadow of a doubt. Disturnal certainly set out his store on that premise but could he produce the goods to back up his trumpeted claims? The prosecution was in fact cobbling together a case against Edalji by linking him (a) to several outrages for which he had not been charged; (b) to a gang of maimers for which no supportive evidence was available; (c) to the September outrage as a prospective beneficiary of this unknown gang's actions, and (d) to a spate of anonymous letters that had no bearing on the charge. An intricate web of inadmissible evidence was being spun around the hapless Edalji, who had been told by his defence team there was no real case for him to answer.

The prosecution witnesses then arrived on stage. Ordinance maps of the Great Wyrley district were produced showing the distances to the vicarage from the various locations where witnesses claimed to have seen Edalji on his walkabout on the evening of the 17th August. William Cooper, the slaughterman, was again paraded to give evidence on the horse's wound in preference to the veterinary surgeon, a point taken up by defence counsel, who thought the prosecution should call the veterinary surgeon as his evidence would be of greater value. However, the prosecution relied on Cooper to describe the weapon capable of inflicting the type of wound found on the maimed horse. Cooper's description was of either a knife or a razor but certainly not a long weapon being used, although in cross examination he admitted to never having "seen a horse cut that way before" and was unable to give a time for the maiming because, in his own words, he was "not a vet." Cooper's own caveats had reduced his evidence to guesswork. The evidence of William Danbury, Frederick Gripton, William Thacker and David Hobson concerning Edalji's whereabouts on the 17th August did not vary from that given by them at the police court. The prosecution was firmly fixing in the mind of the jury that the maiming occurred between 9 pm and 9.30 pm on Edalji's walk back from Bridgtown.

The police witnesses called to the stand were Police Sergeants

Rowley, Robinson and Parsons, Inspector Campbell and Police Constable Cooper, although the two police constables, Weaver and Bradley, were again not called. In trying to smooth out inconsistencies and to get the police act together, certain parts of their evidence was omitted. Sergeant Robinson was not asked to repeat the evidence given at the police court where he had confirmed that several officers were on surveillance duty at the vicarage on the night of the 17/18th August and had spoken of the impossibility of Edalji being able to leave the vicarage during that night. Instead, he was asked solely about receiving anonymous letters. It was left to Inspector Campbell, who, at the police court had said one officer was watching the vicarage, and Sergeant Parsons, the officer compiling the duty roster, who claimed not to know the number of officers on watch when previously giving evidence. They stated that no one had watched the vicarage on that night – an unusual reversal of the evidence in the light of the police still seeking to show Edalji only had the opportunity to commit the offence between 9 pm and 9.30 pm on the 17th August. However, the change in this evidence could serve as a possible back-up should evidence be produced, as the police must surely have thought it might be, to show the horse was maimed during the morning of the 18th August.

Inspector Campbell mentioned the presence of a large amount of blood in the shed where the pony was standing, which threw considerable doubt on Edalji's jacket, showing only two minute spots of blood, being worn for the commission of the crime whatever time the offence took place. This evidence differed from Sergeant Parsons' contribution, in which he referred to a small amount of blood at the scene.

The attempt by the prosecution to place Edalji's boots at the scene of the crime was riddled throughout with contradictions in the police evidence. Constable Cooper's evidence was shown in a ludicrous light when he demonstrated how he pressed Edalji's boot into the soft ground with a heavy hand to make an impression. One juryman interrupted to say the weight distribution between a man making an impression when bringing the whole weight of his body on to his boot when walking was quite different from that made when pressing the boot with the hand.[265] The juryman was prevented from making a further point by the chair, who told him to direct any questions through the bench but did not give the juryman another opportunity to do that. The constable gave this

---

[265] He actually said, "When a man is fifteen stone weight he presses all his fifteen stone on one foot when walking and you can't get such a weight by pressing on the boot with the hand."

evidence in the wake of Inspector Campbell's evidence on the previous day, when in an unguarded moment, the inspector claimed that the track was so hard that to provide a cast of the footprint by cutting out a portion of the path with a footprint on it would have required a pickaxe to do so. The inspector, in another gaffe, had claimed the ground was so wet it was impossible to take a sod. The fields were also described as sandy rather than clay, yet Edalji's boots, according to the police, had clay on them. The footprint evidence was another piece of imagery spirited out of nowhere.

The evidence concerning the alleged hairs on Edalji's coat provided another bout of contradictions. Constable Cooper, having no recorded notes to which he could refer, claimed that Mrs Edalji said the hairs on the jacket might be from the gate, when she actually said it might be a thread. Interestingly, it was Edalji who suggested this possible way for the hair to be on his jacket when interviewed at his Birmingham office but Constable Cooper was not present at that interview. This gaffe could be attributed to pre-trial discussions between police witnesses and the constable probably confused his evidence with someone else's – Inspector Campbell's and/or Sergeant Parson's – an understandable but regrettable confusion since no one seemed inclined to take any notes. Constable Cooper also discounted the hairs being transferred to Edalji's clothes from the uniform of any police officer in contact with the slaughtered pony, leaving either the accidental transference of hairs to the coat when the hide and coat were being taken to the police surgeon or the deliberate placing of the hairs on the jacket by police officers. At a later date, the accidental transfer of the hairs was ruled out as a possibility. The police were being hung by their own petard but it was Edalji who would ultimately be at the end of the metaphorical rope.

The evidence relating to the state of Edalji's clothes when taken from Mrs Edalji; the existence of footprints or mud on the boots and trousers; two small bloodstains and hair on the jacket; the dampness of the jacket; the wet razors; and conversations with George Edalji had no independent witnesses to vouch for them, depending solely on the veracity of the police.

Disturnal, seeking to implicate Edalji in all the maimings, drew from Inspector Campbell a response that all the cattle were killed and injured in the same way, which gave Disturnal the opportunity to read out the complete list of outrages, excluding, of course, the Green maiming. Despite the procedural impropriety of the prosecution's action there was no record of Edalji's defence making an objection nor, not surprisingly, any intervention by the chair. But when Vachel, cross examined the inspector, he managed to bring in the Green maiming and get Inspector Campbell to admit that Harry Green had owned up to killing his own horse but could offer no information as to Green's whereabouts on the night of the 17/18th August, which he ought to have known having interrogated Green at Cannock police station.

The Green maiming was something of an Achilles heel to the prosecution and a hasty conference was obviously arranged between the prosecutor and witnesses after the inspector's admission because Constable Cooper's additions to his police court evidence were tailor-made to accommodate to the Green maiming. The constable's evidence, now containing references to Harry Green, was most opportune for a prosecutor determined to forge a link between Green and Edalji having already been forced to dispense with Green as a potential witness. When recounting his discussions with George Edalji, Constable Cooper managed to smuggle into his evidence a reference to Green. Edalji had allegedly mentioned that the maimer looked to have stopped killing cattle and taken to writing anonymous letters instead, prompting Cooper to remark, "Woe betide any man if he is caught by some farmers, for they are carrying guns." Conveniently for the prosecution, Edalji was alleged to have responded, "You don't mean that. Is Harry Green watched?" The likelihood of Edalji making this remark was fairly remote. If, as the police had claimed, Edalji wrote the anonymous letters to bring himself into contact with the police to find out what progress was being made and, as the prosecution was now claiming, to point the finger at Green, why was there no reference to Green in any of the letters? In an off the cuff response for failing to give this evidence at the police court, Constable Cooper claimed that Edalji's counsel had lodged an objection to this evidence. However, under cross-examination, when this was challenged as inaccurate, the constable could not come up with anything to explain why he failed to mention it at the earlier hearing. Constable Meredith was trotted out to present Edalji's reason for rejecting bail in such a way as to infer Edalji was expecting someone to maim another animal to cast doubt on his arrest – yet again the Green maiming proving to be a useful tool against Edalji. Disturnal also sought to conjure up a friendship between the two men and whilst being a duplicit tactic it no doubt registered in the jury's mind but the claim had no substance as one reporter, at a later date, was to show when he tried but failed to find any evidence of a friendship between the two men.[266]

Despite the attempt at conformity with police officers trying to

---

[266] Despatch 21 Jan 1907

corroborate each other's evidence, their presentation to the trial court contained significant differences from the evidence given at the committal stage. They introduced additional incriminating snippets of evidence plucked from nowhere to bolster those obviously weak areas of the case or omitted important evidence in Edalji's favour to strengthen the insipid case against him, adapted advantageously to fit in with the Green maiming. The trial resembled a shadow play involving police actors dumbly miming roles of 1890s vintage with stage directions orchestrated by Captain Anson.

The evidence of the police analyst, Dr Butter, followed the path laid down at the police court. However, in cross-examination, he admitted to being unable to express an opinion as to the age of the blood stains and they may well have resulted from Edalji having a nose bleed. All those in the court, including the jury, surely should have concluded how incredible it was for a horse to be disembowelled and the grass where the maiming took place to be covered with large quantities of blood, yet the stains on the clothes allegedly worn during the maiming might be attributable to an ancient nose bleed.

Wilfred Greatorex and Frederick Wootton made cameo appearances to give evidence on the anonymous letters. Predictably, they denied all knowledge of the letters, which added nothing of substance against Edalji. However, another 'independent' witness, Gurrin, who gave 'expert' opinion on the origin of these letters, provided the 'inadmissible ammunition' that proved fatal to Edalji's case. The possibility of Gurrin being a completely independent witness can be taken lightly since it was highly likely that Captain Anson brought his suspicions of George Edalji writing anonymous letters between 1892 and 1895 to the attention of Gurrin as he did with the barrister prosecuting the case against Edalji.[267] The prosecution placed a great deal of emphasis on Gurrin's testimony, inadmissible though it was since it had no bearing on the case against Edalji. Gurrin testified to all but three of the letters examined by him being written by George Edalji. The first letter sent out on the 30th June; the second postcard signed John L Sullivan; and in the third letter of the 7th July, the envelope bearing Wootton's name; were attributed to a writer other than George Edalji – a total of three missives not the work of Edalji and if he did not write them, who did? Neither the police nor the prosecution had

---

[267] Captain Anson to HO, sending the Brief, 30 Mar 1907, HO No 195, File 986; The Captain's predisposition to paint a prejudicial view of George Edalji was evident in many of his letters to prominent people sent after the trial..

shown any interest in this question and even though the police suspected Royden Sharp of sending out several obscene postcards on the 4th August and intended to arrest him, they chose not to make anything out of it. In fact, postcards written by the same person were sent to several people on the 4th August, yet only two were introduced at the trial, one addressed to George Edalji on the pretext that Edalji wrote it to divert suspicion from himself, the other one sent to the police. None of the others were ever publicly disclosed.

In the cross-examination, weaknesses in Gurrin's own analysis and in the art of handwriting analysis came under the spotlight. Gurrin admitted finding dissimilarities in the style of handwriting in the anonymous letters and in Edalji's handwriting but had made no record of the differences – a deficiency that limited the reliability of his analysis. However, Gurrin rejected the possibility of Edalji's handwriting being imitated by someone else without providing any reasons for drawing such a conclusion. If Edalji was the scheming individual put forward by the prosecution then he would hardly disguise his handwriting in such an inadequate way as to make authorship so easy to detect but if someone else wrote the letters then some similarity could be expected since the object was to incrimimate Edalji. Gurrin conceded that handwriting experts were not infallible and knew of cases where the expert's opinion was found to be erroneous - a significant concession on his part. Just over a year later, the chickens came home to roost for Mr Gurrin when Adolf Beck, imprisoned as a result of Gurrin's handwriting evidence, received a pardon and compensation when Gurrin's analysis was found to be seriously flawed.[268] Gurrin's evidence against Edalji raised more questions than it solved. Who wrote the first two missives and why did these scribes cease writing? Who collaborated with the writer by writing the postcript included in the letter of the 7th July? Did someone with a grudge take advantage of the first two letters to settle old scores with George or Reverend Edalji?

On completion of Gurrin's evidence, the prosecution sought court approval for the anonymous letters to be read out to the jury. An objection from defence counsel, somewhat belated since the damage

---

[268] Ludovic Kennedy, who investigated many miscarriages of justice, including those where handwriting evidence was submitted as evidence, made the point that "Handwriting is not a profession with firm ground rules. It is an empirical subjective activity with few yardsticks against which judgement can be measured. Handwriting experts often find themselves on opposite sides reaching contrary opinions." Kennedy, L [1985] The Airman and the Carpenter, Collins, London, p277

had already been done, was upheld by the chair, after consultation with Mr Brough, the acting legal adviser to the court. Shortly afterwards, biding its time, the prosecution took advantage of the temporary disappearance of Mr Brough, representing a client in another court, to have the letters attributed to Edalji read out beginning with the letter of the 7th July.

In yet another ploy, Disturnal introduced a copy of the 'Lover of Justice' letter and asked for the original to be produced by the defence, describing the letter as vital evidence against Edalji – a piece of demoniac gamesmanship because he knew the original was written by Loxton to assist Captain Anson in his attempt to entrap Edalji and he also knew that the letter would not be produced. Disturnal was being consistent with the view he expressed when asking Captain Anson to request the letter to divert suspicion away from it being a frame-up, made all the more necessary following an admission by Inspector Campbell, when giving evidence, that the original was not in Edalji's handwriting. Apparently, Barnes, the solicitor for the prosecution, sent a notice of disclosure for the 'Lover of Justice' letter to Edalji's solicitor but as the request was sent at such short notice, indicative of the prosecuting lawyers merely going through the motions, the defence argued it was too late to comply with the request. But why Edalji's counsel avoided submitting the letter is a mystery. If shown to Gurrin it would surely be marked out as different from the rest, a possibility not likely to harm George Edalji's case, unless Edalji's defence was planning to argue that all the letters were inadmissible – something it failed to do. Did Disturnal know that Edalji's defence doubted his innocence concerning the letters and had Disturnal contributed to that doubt?

A member of Edalji's defence team, Mr Hazell, MP for West Bromwich, in a conversation with the Home Secretary, Herbert Gladstone in 1907, told him that during the trial Vachell was approached by a member of the Edalji family, whom Hazell thought might be George Edalji's brother. This informant showed Vachell a letter offered as a specimen of George Edalji's handwriting for expert examination to prove the handwriting was different to the anonymous letters. The letter, reputedly found in one of George Edalji's drawers in the vicarage, turned out to be what was taken as an unposted anonymous letter and Vachell and Hazel decided to suppress it since it was most damaging to George Edalji's defence.[269] Hazell's revelation

---

[269] Hazell to Gladstone, 6 Jun 1907, HO File 988, The record of the conversation is marked Secret in the files

raised a number of issues: (i) As Hazell only assumed the donor's identity, it was almost certain that he did not actually meet him because Horace Edalji's appearance would be particularly noteworthy and if Hazel had been there when the letter was shown to Vachell, he would surely have been introduced to the donor, making it unnecessary for Hazell to speculate on his identity. It was more than likely the letter was brought to Hazell's attention by Vachell without Hazell actually seeing the donor; (ii) the letter was so easily found by Horace Edalji in the vicarage in October 1903, yet the police in August 1903 had carefully searched all over the vicarage looking for evidence, therefore, it was most unlikely for the police not to have found such an easily located letter;[270] (iii) surely the Reverend or Mrs Edalji would have come across the letter, especially if it was in one of George Edalji's drawers in a bedroom George Edalji occupied with his father, and in their desire to protect their son would certainly dispose of such damaging evidence; (iv) if Horace Edalji was seeking samples of his brother's writing and he found this letter, he would have read it and realising the implications, he would hardly present it to the defence for examination, unless Horace Edalji had an axe to grind against his brother. If this was his intention and he wanted to sabotage George Edalji's case he could not have chosen a better means of 'nobbling' the defence; (v) other letters written by George Edalji could have been taken as samples yet Horace Edalji took this one rather than ask his parents for assistance; (vi) was the story a fabrication on Hazell's part to deflect attention from the inadequate defence with which he was involved – this can be dismissed since why would he choose such a bizarre story for this purpose; (vii) the letter, several pages long and containing 'unmentionable' things and abusive remarks on scraps of paper, had been addressed to the Edalji's servant in 1895 and was very similar, if not the same letter, passed on by Reverend Edalji to the chief constable, which Captain Anson eventually sent to the Home Office with many other anonymous letters of the 1892 – 5 period after Edalji's conviction. If this was the letter passed on to Captain Anson in 1895, how did it come to the attention of the defence? The only possibilities were (a) it came from the chief constable not directly but through a third party, probably a member of the prosecution team and shown to the defence on the pretext that it came from Horace Edalji in order to undermine the defence's commitment to Edalji; (b) if Horace Edalji was the donor, how did he manage to get hold of a letter passed on to Captain Anson in 1895? Was he an intermediary acting on behalf of the chief constable against his

---

[270] Depositions 3/4 Sep 1903, HO File 990

brother? But why did he do that? Was it a grudge?; (viii) if it was not the letter sent to Captain Anson and was an unposted letter from 1895, how did it manage to avoid detection for eight years including the police search and come into Horace Edalji's possession?

In whatever way and for whatever motive the letter came to the attention of Edalji's defence it undoubtedly influenced the way the defence was conducted.

(b) The Defence's Case

The defence's turn to play a part in this well prepared charade on justice began on the third day but not before Sir Reginald Hardy had decided the court should sit until 10 pm to conclude the case. The haste shown by the chair in wanting to dispense with the trial was not matched by Edalji, who continued to display his laid back composure.

Mr Vachell, known for his ironical witticisms, thanked Mr Disturnal for the fair way he had conducted his case, perhaps Vachell's praise for his opponent's endeavour in getting so much inadmissible evidence presented to the jury was a demonstration of his noted ironical wit. In opening the defence, he succinctly weighed up the dilemma facing the police, who, recognising they were on trial in the district, needed to charge someone and without any evidence decided Edalji served that purpose. Inspector Campbell, it was noted, had obviously decided as early as 6.30 am on the 18th August that Edalji was their man when he despatched a constable to intercept Edalji on his way to Birmingham, yet all he had to go on was the knowledge of another horse being killed. With the sole objective of laying the guilt at Edalji's door, police officers looked at every piece of evidence with a jaundiced eye and forced facts into a pre-determined theory while rejecting anything not accommodating to this theory.

Vachell took the prosecution's evidence apart by showing its implausibility: a man mutilating a horse and getting on his jacket only a couple of small bloodstains that turned out to be the result of a bleeding nose or cut finger; and the so-called saliva and foam from the dying horse's mouth being nothing more than bread and milk stains. He rhetorically asked how could hair get on Edalji's jacket when he was not wearing it at the time he was supposed to have carried out the maiming. Taking the jury through Edalji's journey from Bridgtown to the vicarage, Vachell drew attention to several witnesses not called by the prosecution, who could provide evidence challenging the police's theory. He pressed home the point that even if the prosecution theory on the time of the maiming was correct, Edalji would have barely ten minutes to catch the horse, commit the outrage and return to his home. Vachell cast doubts on: (i) the so-called tracking of the footprints apparently discovered in places where only a couple of days before grass cutters and harvest reapers had been trampling over the ground; and (ii) Inspector Campbell's claim that a pick would have been required to cut out a piece of path with a footprint on it when it had rained all night.

Vachel brought out the sheer impossibility of George Edalji sending the 4th August anonymous postcards while *en route* to Aberystwyth when they were posted but failed to draw attention to the three pieces of correspondence not attributed to Edalji and the damage these unattributed letters could pose to the prosecution's case. The idea of Edalji writing letters to himself to bring him into contact with the police in order to find out what they were doing was discounted as far too subtle, a substantive point since it was the police who first went to see Edalji at the vicarage before Edalji received any letters himself even though Vachell failed to mention that point. Vachell rounded off by pointing out that even if Edalji was responsible for the letters, it did not show any culpability on his part for the maiming – not a particularly perceptive point since the author of the letters had threatened to kill Sergeant Robinson and if Edalji was guilty of that limb of the charge, whatever the sentence, Edalji's career as a solicitor would be over.

Vachell's attention came to rest on Harry Green. He wanted to know why he was not called to deny committing the other maimings after being subpoenaed by the prosecution for that purpose – a bit of window dressing by Vachell as Green was not on trial and the case was about the 18th August maiming. All that could be expected of Green was to give evidence about that particular maiming. However, by informing the jurors that Green lived at the end of the footpath to which the tracks had led it should have added further doubts in the minds of the jury as to Edalji's guilt. Vachell concluded by issuing a caveat to the jury not to accept the prosecution's evidence based entirely on police witnesses without independent corroboration, which in fact was a warning covering most of the prosecution's case.

With his opening address completed, Vachell examined Edalji, whose performance was described by one press observer as creating a favourable impression by the excellent manner displayed when giving evidence, speaking quietly, dispassionately and distinctly for two hours and forty minutes. Edalji's evidence covered the rumour implicating him in the maiming; his advert in the local press; the 'Greatorex' letters; the police visits to the vicarage during which he discussed the outrages; and the 'Lover of Justice' letter – some of which corresponded with police accounts. He covered his movements from his arrival at the vicarage from work on the 17th August until his arrest on the 18th August, including his journey to and from Bridgtown; described the clothes worn on that trip, that is, the blue serge coat, and the condition of the jacket worn at breakfast the following morning – the jacket taken by the police as evidence.

Edalji explained the meaning behind comments, which the police inferred had some deeper, incriminating meaning. His comment of not being surprised about the police questioning him over the maimings as he had warning of it, referred to warnings received from the rumours; the Osborne & Son letter with his name pencilled on the envelope enclosed within it; and the ''Lover of Justice'' letter. He denied saying to either of the officers "Is Harry Green watched?"; was unaware of anyone in contact with Green after his own committal; and his reference to 'risky work' meant hazardous for the police. His written comment to Greatorex "that when the truth is known you will find it is somebody in a very different position" referred not to the outrages but to the rumours in circulation linking Edalji to the anonymous letters. His decision to reject bail was for reasons of not being able to carry on his business with the trial hanging over him and the possibility of another outrage rebounding to his benefit.

Edalji denied having any connection with the maiming, nor did he know of anybody who was connected with it. Nor did he have any profound explanation for the police's forensic 'evidence', other than the stains getting on his jacket in many ways over several years; the hairs having attached themselves to the jacket when he leaned on the gates in the vicarage garden; and the boots probably becoming wet due to the state of the road to Bridgtown.

Disturnal, either unaware of the veterinary surgeon's findings or, if aware, playing a curious game, directed his cross examination towards (i) proving that the maiming was committed between 9 pm and 9.30 pm on the 17th August by asking questions about Edalji's trip to Bridgtown and (ii) connecting the author of the anonymous letters to the previous maimings – the latter point covering two areas of inadmissible evidence. Disturnal also wanted to know the origins of the sleeping arrangements at the vicarage, duly explained by George Edalji, but Disturnal criticised Edalji's explanation as a fabrication to provide him with an alibi. Why Disturnal pursued this line is difficult to assess since why would Edalji need an alibi to cover the night time when the whole of the prosecution's case was directed to a 9 pm to 9.30 pm maiming, unless Disturnal was trying to imply the family had unusual, if not weird and illegal, habits as later rumours circulating in the area definitely suggested. On the anonymous letters, Edalji explained that he was unable to express any opinion as to whether his handwriting was similar to the writing in the letters because the opportunity to examine them was never given to him. When asked about the 'Lover of Justice' letter, which seemed to preoccupy the prosecution to some degree, Edalji thought it was sent to get him out of the district in circumstances casting suspicion on him. Querying Edalji's apparent lack of interest as demonstrated by his failure to press Inspector Campbell to show him the whole of the 7th July letter and not just the postscript, Edalji recalled that the inspector told him the content like the postscript was nonsense.

The defence then brought into play those witnesses, Harry Loach, Fred Cope and Walter Whitehouse, whose evidence squeezed the time available for Edalji to have committed the crime on his 'walkabout', and Mr John Hands, the shoemaker, who had informed the police Edalji was wearing a blue coat, not an old jacket, when visiting his shop – four witnesses whom the police thought prudent to ignore after Constables Bradley and Weaver had taken statements from them on the 18th August. When cross-examined by Vachel on the previous day, Constable Cooper had claimed not to have asked Whitehouse, who reported seeing Edalji enter the vicarage no later than 9.30 pm, the time of his sighting of Edalji – a curious omission on the constable's part when time was crucial to the police case.

The police theory was now looking decidedly thin with regard to the time Edalji was alleged to have committed the crime and the relevance of the stains and hairs on Edalji's jacket, which he had not worn on his errand to Bridgtown. The next witness provided crucial evidence, which if the trial had been properly held at the Assizes would have blown the prosecution's case completely away, sending it back to the corridors of police power in Stafford where the pursuit of Edalji had undoubtedly originated and the case against him concocted. This was the evidence supplied by the veterinary surgeon, Robert M Lewis of Cannock, who testified that the wound could not have been inflicted more than six hours before he examined the horse at 8.30 am on the 18th August. Nor could the wound have been inflicted with a razor and could only be carried out with a curved and pointed weapon having concave sides attached to a handle to give the user a good grip. This evidence completely laid to waste the police theory placing Edalji at the scene of the crime between 9 pm to 9.30 pm. It also blew a hole in the police's view of Edalji using one of the rusty and blunt razors taken by the police from the vicarage. The concept of reasonable doubt must surely have penetrated the minds of the jury by the time Reverend

Edalji, looking ill, entered the witness box to provide an alibi for his son and to give his version of the police examination of the jacket and razors – evidence at variance with that given by the police. Given Reverend Edalji's dogmatism and his tendency to believe rigidly whatever became fixed in his mind, his claim to have woken up at 4 am and saw his son sleeping might well be an example of that dogmatism. However, even if his early morning stirring was a figment of his imagination or a paternal attempt to assist his son, it was irrelevant since George Edalji could not have left and re-entered the vicarage without being seen by the waiting police.

Mrs Edalji, Maud Edalji and Dora Earp, the servant, gave evidence of George Edalji's presence in the home at or shortly after 9.30 pm, further confirming it was not possible for George to have been in the vicinity of the field at 9.30 pm, which anyway, given the veterinary surgeon's evidence, had made the police theory irrelevant. Mrs Edalji, who wanted to give evidence on George Edalji's poor eyesight but was never asked by defence counsel to do so, was particularly conscious that any evidence she gave would be thought not to be true because she was his mother.

The length of time taken to present the defence's case meant there was little prospect of the case finishing that night and, as several jurymen would miss their trains home if the case carried on, it was adjourned at the close of the defence's evidence.

The additional day was no doubt welcome to the prosecution who had some serious thinking to do to retrieve a case seriously mauled and in all reasonableness should have expired at the conclusion of the defence's case. The prosecution's case based on a 9.30 pm killing had managed to amass the following 'evidence': (i) a not too wet jacket allegedly worn by Edalji when he took his Bridgtown walk but in fact not worn by him that (a) somehow had managed to attract a large quantity of hairs from the maimed horse onto it, and (b) at the time of the police examination of this jacket in the vicarage had prompted a dispute over whether or not the jacket had a hair or a thread/roving on it; (ii) horse's saliva on the same jacket that turned out to be oatmeal; (iii) miniscule blood stains on that jacket probably human blood of indeterminate age; (iv) a weapon, namely a razor, wet and stained, but rusty and blunt and incapable of carrying out the deed; (iv) muddy boots apparently matching the footprints claimed to have been found near the scene of the crime and near the vicarage, which were covered in slate grey clay apparently attaching itself to the boots in an area with sandy soil, (v) those same boots, muddy right up to the top, which was inconsistent with the mudless state of the jacket and trousers, although the police did claim in their evidence that the trousers were muddy on their morning visit to the vicarage but could not explain why they failed to take them away at that time as evidence. That was the sum total of the police's evidence.

What the prosecution needed was (i) a muddy, soaking wet jacket, (ii) trousers in a similar state, and (iii) a weapon capable of disembowelling the horse – none of which they had. Nor had the police provided any proof of footprints, which was not surprising since any footprints made at the time of the offence would more than likely have been washed away by the driving rain that fell during the night. The forensic evidence presented by the prosecution; the choice of witnesses whose stories fitted in with the police theory; and ignoring witnesses whose evidence did not conform to that theory; leads on to the assumption that the police, or the higher echelons of the police force, sought to railroad Edalji not because of the maimings but for other reasons concerning the Edaljis.

The prosecution's case looked moribund; however, they did have an incompetent chair of the bench to rely on and an unknown quantity in the Staffordshire jury.

(c) Defence versus Prosecution

Mr Vachell, who addressed the court for one and a half hours, began his final address by accusing the police of selectively presenting evidence to support its 9 pm to 9.30 pm maiming theory while deliberately ignoring evidence undermining that theory. He criticised the prosecution for failing to call witnesses who saw Edalji at places on his way back from Bridgtown that showed it was impossible for Edalji to have committed the maiming and that he had not worn the old jacket on that journey. Vachell pointed out the police's own admission that no injury had been inflicted on the horse at 11 pm and he reminded the court of the veterinary surgeon's evidence fixing the time of the maiming between 2.30 am and 8.30 am on the 18th August yet the prosecution had failed to call him and did not call any specialist witness to rebut the veterinary surgeon's evidence. Vachell was highlighting the 'pick and mix' character of the prosecution's case against Edalji.

With an inkling of what the prosecution might seek to do in order to get out of an almost irretrievable position, Vachell speculated that the prosecution might decide to claim that Edalji got up in the middle of the night and went to the field to commit the offence. Pre-empting that possibility, he drew the jury's attention to Reverend Edalji's testimony and to the absence of any evidence showing George Edalji had left the vicarage during the night. Vachell was emphasising that the whole of the prosecution's case was based on the crime being committed between 9 pm and 9.30 pm and if the jury found that the crime could not have been carried out during that time, which it surely must, the prosecution's case must inevitably fall.

Vachell then went through the limitations in the forensic evidence: the miniscule quantity of blood on the jacket; the hair on the coat resulting from some previous occasion; and the impossibility of the razor being the cause of such a wound. When it came to the letters, the jury was reminded that handwriting was a matter of opinion and time after time the opinion of handwriting experts had proven to be at fault. Nor should the jury read anything into Edalji refusing bail as it was simply a matter of wanting a retreat from prying eyes and pointing fingers.

The failure of the prosecution to provide a motive was another factor seized upon by Vachell and he speculated on the prosecution claiming the maiming to be an insane act and, yet again, pre-empting the likelihood of such a claim, reminded the jury that no medical officer had been called to testify on the state of Edalji's mental health.

Turning to the Green issue, counsel posed the possibility of the prosecution, whose case against Edalji was based on the outrage being the work of a single individual, offering up Green as not only an accomplice but also a member of a gang associated with Edalji. Once more pre-empting the prosecution, Vachell drew attention to the police patrolling the countryside for months without finding any evidence of a gang. Adopting the method of the prosecution, that is, speculating without offering evidence but probably with more justification, Vachell introduced the possibility of Green being the perpetrator of the 18th August maiming as Green had confessed to killing his own horse by ripping it open in the same way as the other animals were maimed. Concluding what was described as an elegant speech for the defence, Vachell asked the jury if it was prepared to find Edalji guilty on such flimsy evidence and on the crumpled and shattered theories of the police. Vachell answered his own question by saying the only possible verdict the jury could return was that Edalji did not commit such a fiendish offence. Vachell's address should have been enough to wrap up this limb of the charge in Edalji's favour.

When Disturnal took his final turn in the proceedings, he was undoubtedly aware of the weakness of the prosecution case and that its whole theory of a 9 pm to 9.30 pm maiming had been scuttled by the veterinary surgeon. Therefore, at this late stage in the proceedings, he needed something to retrieve the tattered remnants of his case and, using Sir Reginald's lack of judicial knowledge and experience in cases as serious as this, he chose an entirely novel way to fix the blame on Edalji. His major route forward was to direct the jury's attention to the anonymous letters, after all an expert had testified to the letters being in Edalji's handwriting whereas the defence decided not to commission its own expert to challenge the prosecution witnesses' claims. But how could Disturnal make an effective link between the maimings and the letter writer? Realistically he could not. Even discounting the inadmissibility of the letters, no evidence was contained in them to show the writer had anything to do with the maiming. The contents of the letters were either common knowledge in the locality or unsubstantiated claims having all the hallmarks of fantasy. However, it was on this 'peg' that Disturnal hung the prosecution's hat. Drowning in the depths of a lost cause, Disturnal surfed his way back into the case by riding on a wave of inadmissible evidence.

Addressing the court for one hour and forty minutes, Disturnal admitted to the jury that without the anonymous letters the case might have assumed a different light – in other words Disturnal was conceding that without the letters the other evidence could not sustain a case against Edalji. Directing the jury's attention away from the paucity of evidence on the maimings, he told them that the most important issue in the case was the identity of the letter writer and the most significant fact was that since Edalji's arrest no more letters in this disguised handwriting had been received – a false claim because the letters and postcards ceased two weeks before the arrest of Edalji at the time when the police expressed an intention in arresting Royden Sharp for sending out obscene postcards. The claim was also duplicitous because even if Disturnal was unaware of the intended arrest of Royden Sharp, he knew when the letters ceased. At the other end of the anonymous letters' 'time spectrum', he misled the jury with the claim that as soon as the rumours began to circulate about Edalji being arrested on the 2nd July and Edalji's advert being published in the paper on the 6th July, the anonymous letters began to arrive, the earliest being on the 7th July. This, too, was an erroneous and dishonest claim since the first letter was sent out on the 30th June followed a few days later by the John L Sullivan letter, which Gurrin had told the jury Edalji had not written. Disturnal referred to the supposed similarity of handwriting and inferred from Edalji's failure to press the inspector to show him the contents of the Osborne & Son letter that Edalji already knew those contents and he dragged up the old chestnut of Edalji writing the letters to get into communication with the police to find out how much they knew.

Disturnal used part of the contents of these letters to show the writer was in a gang and the Green maiming was an example of a member of the gang committing an outrage when another gang member, Edalji, was arrested in order to take the pressure off him. This was a curious comment since it claimed Edalji and Green were members of the same gang but no evidence was ever put forward to allow the prosecution to draw such a conclusion and if the prosecution was correct why was Green not in the dock alongside Edalji.

In itself, this 'evidence' should have been a non-starter, not only was it inadmissible but also the connection between the author and the maimer was entirely spurious, even Captain Anson – a self-acknowledged foe of the Edaljis, thought the author and maimer were different people. Pushing the boat out further, Disturnal, using his own layman's 'expertise', thought that not even Gurrin's analysis was required as it was obvious to any ordinary observer that a strong resemblance existed between Edalji's handwriting and the writing in the anonymous letters. In an interim conclusion, Disturnal offered the jury a choice upon which to base its verdict, either Edalji wrote the letters, which if he did was clear evidence to connect him with the outrage and the jury must convict him, or if the jury decided otherwise then the case against Edalji became a very different one. Interestingly, Disturnal did not say Edalji must be acquitted if they so decided on the second option.

Having redirected his case into this avenue out of the cul-de-sac into which it had been driven, Disturnal was still left with having to address the other evidence, going through the motions in a not particularly convincing manner. This 'evidence', weak in substance, was a side issue not now the centrepiece of the prosecution's case, which by necessity had been discarded. Disturnal described Edalji's refusal to delay his journey to Birmingham as the sign of a guilty man wanting to postpone an explanation for as long as possible – another doubtful proposition since Edalji thought it was concerned with the anonymous letters, not a particularly pressing issue.

Disturnal explained away the minimal amount of blood on Edalji's coat as resulting from the speed associated with inflicting a wound fourteen inches long with a razor while the horse was running away from the scene, overlooking the considerable quantity of blood on the grass where the horse was standing when attacked – evidence provided by one of the prosecution's police witnesses. To discredit the alibi evidence placing Edalji's return to the vicarage at sometime just before 9.30 pm, still pursuing the original police theory as to the time of the maiming, Disturnal referred to the contradictory evidence given by the Edaljis about their discussion with the police over the clothing and razor, reminding the jurors it was upon these witnesses that they had to rely for Edalji's alibi. The prosecution was implying that the Edaljis were lying about the clothing and razor, therefore, they must also be bearing false witness about the time Edalji returned to the vicarage – another spurious connection and equally irrelevant.

Having pursued in his closing submission the lame duck police theory as to the time of the maiming, even to the point of expressing no doubt as to the police being given the clothes Edalji wore on his late evening trip to Bridgtown and ignoring the evidence of Mr Hands, suddenly, at the eleventh hour just as Vachell had forecast, Disturnal discarded the police theory in its entirety in favour of an equally dubious theory. Without providing an iota of sworn testimony but with some creative illogicality, Disturnal offered the jury the prospect of Edalji's clothes not getting wet between 9 pm and 9.40 pm because he would not wear a wet jacket to sit around the house after returning to the vicarage from Bridgtown. So how did the jacket become damp, if in fact it was damp, the following morning? Disturnal's solution to this conundrum was to state that after midnight it had rained for several hours, which it did, and Edalji's jacket became wet and his boots muddy as a result of a trip he had made through the fields to perpetrate the crime after midnight. This really was an outrageous submission, one beyond the wit of Sir Reginald Hardy to handle, because everything in the prosecution's case was geared to a 9 pm to 9.30 pm maiming. With the original theory shot down in flames the prosecution turned its back on all its previous evidence presented to the court relying on a new theory for which no evidence had been introduced.

Quite improperly and without admonition from the chair, Disturnal plumped for a maiming in line with the veterinary surgeon's estimation of the time and chose to make this switch to a new 'theory' at a time that prevented the defence from countering this blatant piece of charlatanism. It was a clever, if disingenuous ploy, which boiled down to this. If George Edalji did not do the maiming when he was seen on the main road then he must have done it when he was not seen at all.

To bolster this change of direction, Disturnal thought it suspicious for Edalji not to provide an independent witness to prove he did not go out after 9.40 pm. However, the onus was on Disturnal to provide reliable evidence that Edalji did go out but he was unable to do so. Surely it would have been more suspicious if Edalji had called a witness, who had spent the whole of that rainy night on the vicarage doorstep in order to swear Edalji never ventured out. However, several people were sited around the vicarage who could do just that and had done so in their depositions and evidence at the committal proceedings – the police on watch at the vicarage who had said it was impossible for

George Edalji to have left the vicarage between 10 pm and 5 am without being seen but this evidence had been withheld from this court. One observer saw this change of timing as inflicting considerable damage on the defence – damage that could be laid at the feet of Sir Reginald Hardy for allowing the prosecution to pursue an entirely new line in its final address to the jury after providing no sworn supportive testimony. With little factual evidence to support his case now that he had switched the time of the maiming, Disturnal promoted the benefits of circumstantial evidence. He tried to do this in spite of the absence of any such evidence. All he had was a collection of unconnected, inassimilable suppositions not adding up to anything of real substance.

Disturnal conceded that Dr Lewis, the veterinary surgeon, should have been called to give evidence but made the excuse of not knowing of his existence or his evidence, admitting that had he known he would have called him. If Disturnal is to be believed, and there is no reason to doubt him given that he had to redirect his whole case following Dr Lewis's appearance, then it must have occurred to him after the third day of the trial that he had no case against Edalji because where was his evidence to connect Edalji with a post-midnight tour of the shrubs and hedgerows of Great Wyrley. However, having stated he would have called Dr Lewis, which could only be on the basis of Lewis's expert testimony, Disturnal set about discrediting Lewis's expert testimony regarding the type of weapon used in the maiming despite not having called any expert testimony himself and relying solely on his (Disturnal's) own layman's assessment. Applying his own 'expertise', Disturnal noted that Lewis did not think the wound could be inflicted by a razor unlike the horse slaughterer, who thought the wound was inflicted by some sharp, shallow instrument, and Disturnal pointed to the razor as being a sharp, shallow instrument. Disturnal then proclaimed the superiority of the evidence of a layman, the horse slaughterer, who had admitted never to have seen a wound of that kind inflicted on a horse, elevating it over the expertise of a professionally qualified witness often used in that professional capacity by the Staffordshire police. Disturnal's own view was of the injury being inflicted quickly with an extremely sharp instrument such as a razor, ignoring the fact that Edalji's razor was blunt, according to the police analyst, a prosecution witness. While rejecting Lewis's evidence on the weapon, Disturnal made no such challenge to the time of the maiming fixed by Lewis but had altered the police theory to accommodate to it. This was another example of the 'pick and mix' character of the prosecution's case.

Continuing this farce, which turned out as tragedy for Edalji,

Disturnal, contrary to his explicit claim when opening the case for the Crown that the crime was committed between 9 pm and 9.40 pm, which had been reported in all the newspapers, now denied ever having advanced that theory. In trying to cover for this untruth, he offered up the reason for presenting evidence about Edalji's return walk from Bridgtown on the 17th August as being solely for the purpose of showing that Edalji did not give the police a clear and full account of his movements on that night, and, unless Edalji was to be believed in preference to the police, the jury must also come to the same conclusion. In other words, Disturnal was saying that Edalji lied over his trip back from Bridgtown, therefore, he must be lying over the maiming of the horse and about everything else, while the police must be telling the truth. This was a patently mischievous conclusion since if Edalji did not side track into the field on his way back from Bridgtown to maim the horse and had gone straight home then his story was true give or take a few minutes. This was yet another example of the duplicity, not merely of the police but also from the prosecuting counsel. If Disturnal was to be believed, he had been in court for 3½ days arguing for a 9 pm – 9.30 pm maiming merely to attack Edalji's credibility as a witness by trying to show Edalji was not telling the truth about his trip back from Bridgtown! Incredible!!

Well into his stride, Disturnal even sought to discredit Reverend Edalji's evidence by referring to the extraordinary sleeping arrangements at the vicarage. Acknowledging it to be possibly a small matter, which it undoubtedly was, the prosecution inferred the arrangement had resulted from Reverend Edalji, aware of his son's nocturnal proclivities, wanting to keep an eye on him and to provide him with an alibi. Disturnal incorporated this 'piece of evidence' into his description of circumstantial evidence. Explaining to the jurors that circumstantial evidence was made up of small facts fitting into each other, Disturnal advised them that if the small facts were found to be proven they must come to the conclusion Edalji had something to do with the offence. A rather dubious 'lecture' on circumstantial evidence, one ordinarily left to the chair, because the step from unusual sleeping arrangements to horse maiming is an extremely large one and a *non sequitor* but why spoil a good case by cluttering it up with facts or truth or accurate explanations of law. Interestingly, all Disturnal could claim was that Edalji "had something to do with the offence" in a case that required 'guilt beyond a reasonable doubt' for a conviction.

Moving on to the reason for the August maiming, Disturnal dispensed with the need for any apparent motive by arguing that the mutilated animals belonged to so many different kinds of people, yet again improperly linking all the maimings together when Edalji was on trial for only the August maiming. However, Disturnal did offer a motive - not spite, nor mental derangement nor insanity, but a lust for blood, or an uncontrollable passion to kill something carried out by a person of diabolical cunning actuated by a desire for notoriety by outwitting the police. How a person with "uncontrollable passion for blood", an irresistible urge, could rationally desire notoriety is hard to fathom and would not such a desire conform to some form of mental derangement.

Disturnal turned to the September maiming and the confession of Harry Green, who was falsely described as a life long friend of George Edalji. Rejecting defence counsel's argument that Green should have been called as a witness, Disturnal claimed that putting Green in the witness box was against the public interest because Green was attainted and it was not appropriate for the prosecution to identify itself with a man like that. Of course, Disturnal would hardly be likely to provide the jury with the real reason for Green's non-appearance as a witness.

Disturnal linked Green to Edalji not as an accomplice in other maimings, thereby justifying the fact that Green was not standing alongside Edalji in the dock, but because Green, not realising it was a crime to mutilate his own animal, wanted to save Edalji by casting doubt on his guilt. Yet another inappropriate statement since Green had not given any evidence upon which the jury could form any opinion, bringing little credit to the prosecuting counsel but no doubt making an impression on the jury. Disturnal was, in fact, one member of the prosecuting team who did realise that Green's action was in fact a crime but that realisation brought scant consolation to Edalji. Disturnal's closing speech, like the contents of the anonymous letters, had a 'Boy's Own' flavour to it but would the jury be astute enough to see through the innuendoes, the speculative assumptions and the blatant change from the original theory.

(v) Sir Reginald 'Aids and Abets' the Prosecution

The chairman, who had allowed the prosecution a freedom of action that would have promptly been checked by a judge in the Assizes, began summing up at 12.45 pm, speaking for one hour and fifteen minutes. Newspaper reports on the contents of his summing-up were limited but from this limited reportage and Sir Reginald's own notes, the summing-up had the quality of a layman's simplicity daubed all over it, mirroring many aspects of Disturnal's final address. Almost a repeat performance of Disturnal's contribution, it was hardly a judicial appraisal of the points at issue but this was not surprising when the chair had not only allowed so much inadmissible evidence to enter the proceedings but also had placed no restriction on the prosecution counsel changing the most significant part of his case in his final address to the jury.

Contrary to the function of a judge to allay any prejudices that might reside in the minds of the jury, Sir Reginald failed to tell the jury to "disabuse their mind of feelings of prejudice engendered by rumour", standard directions in cases such as this invoking strong local passions.[271] Instead, going beyond the remit of the actual charge, he drew attention to the importance of catching the perpetrator of the outrages that had created a reign of terror in Great Wyrley and disgraced the fair name of the county, which drew critical comments from the Lord Chancellor shortly after the trial.[272] This type of statement was usually made after a guilty verdict had been returned and while the sentence was being passed.

The chair put it to the jury that the horse was injured and similar injuries had also been inflicted on other cattle in the same neighbourhood as referred to in the anonymous letters – an improper inclusion in the summing up because it directed the jury to take into consideration the other cattle maiming incidents and the anonymous letters as supportive of Edalji's guilt. He advised the jury to take the anonymous letters into consideration, pointing out that Gurrin, the expert, had said some were written by Edalji, adding, "Now if you agree with Mr Gurrin, you will find strong corroboration of the guilt of the prisoner, and for that purpose you can read the letters and understand the peculiarities I will put on paper for you," which more or less told the jury to convict Edalji because in what way could they disregard Gurrin's evidence since no alternative was offered to them.

Sir Reginald produced another gem when he dealt with the hair on the clothes. He asked the jury to contrast the anxiety of the police to see suspicious things with the anxiety of the parents not to see suspicious things. This was hardly an aid to the jury in assessing the variance in evidence between the police and the Edaljis. Another dubious point arose when Sir Reginald dismissed the veterinary surgeon's evidence because he thought Lewis of limited experience, yet he accepted without question the evidence of the horse slaughterer, who had admitted to his own lack of knowledge. He recognised faults in police

[271] Quote by Justice Bingham in the Whitaker-Walker case, Yelverton to HO, 22 Jan 1904, HO No 60 File 985

[272] Lord Chancellor's opinion, 30 Jan 1904, HO No 63, File 985

evidence concerning the footprints but put this down not so much to the inadequacy of the evidence itself but to the failure of the police to use the evidence as it should have been used. He later claimed to have put to the jury the issue of the police possibly perjuring themselves on the footprint evidence but such an important point as possible misconduct by the police was never reproduced in the press nor in Sir Reginald's own notes – omissions that cast doubts on Sir Reginald's memory and possibly his integrity.

Virtually paraphrasing the prosecution's line, he described Green as a 'tainted witness', who, having made a confession withdrew it, and he claimed it was impossible to call Green to ask him incriminating questions. Yet Sir Reginald did not question why Green was subpoenaed and listed as a witness in the first place. He did question one point the prosecution made when he trotted out the police claim, not referred to during the trial so picked up elsewhere, that Green was entitled to put an end to his own sick horse, which was not only irrelevant but also inaccurate. He made a couple of concessions to George Edalji – Edalji's remark that he was "expecting it for some time" was thought more consistent with innocence than guilt and he referred to the absence of a motive. Yet, although thinking it remarkable that no motive was revealed – there was "no spite, no legal mental insanity... only some diabolical cunning", Sir Reginald thought it impossible to determine why a man like Edalji should commit such a horrible act. He added that just as people commit suicide without any apparent motive, the cause for the maiming remained a matter of conjecture, making it clear to the jury there was no need to look for a motive.

Circumstantial evidence was explained to the jury as being like intertwined parallel threads such that if one thread snapped the others remained intact, hardly the most informed exposition of the concept. Sir Reginald also provided members of the jury with samples of Edalji's own handwriting and his (Sir Reginald's) own written summary of the peculiarities in the handwriting 'discovered' by Gurrin. Judging by the quality of Sir Reginald's notes of the proceedings, criticised a couple of months later as an "insufficient record of the trial" by Home Office officials,[273] any summary given to the jury would probably be extremely injurious to Edalji's case. The chair had clearly demonstrated an inclination not to question how police evidence was gathered and overstated the importance of the anonymous letters while overlooking their inadmissibility. All in all, the jury was left to decide Edalji's guilt

---

[273] HO Comment in HO No 35 File 984

or innocence, principally on inadmissible evidence and a less than competent summing up. Justice shrivelled at the touch of this member of the Staffordshire judiciary.

The jury took only fifty minutes to find Edalji guilty with a recommendation for mercy on account of his position, an unusual codicil to the case. The bench retired, re-emerging three minutes later to deliver the sentence.

The chair, claiming to have taken Edalji's professional position into account, although in what way is not clear, and referring to the disgrace inflicted on the county of Stafford and the district of Great Wyrley, concurred with the jury's verdict and imposed a sentence of seven years penal servitude, obviously not heeding the jury's recommendation.

Disturnal had conjured up a remarkable success, if not in terms of justice but in terms of how to win. He had prosecuted a man on a charge of maiming a horse between 9 pm and 9.40 pm on the 17th August whilst wearing a brown jacket when the defendant was actually strolling between Bridgtown and Great Wyrley wearing a blue coat. In the process of this prosecution he had a man convicted of maiming a horse after 2.30 am on the 18th August on a stormy rain sodden night whilst wearing a brown jacket – a jacket the man wore the following morning at breakfast, a jacket dry and free of any mud. Having achieved its objective, needless to say, the prosecution decided not to proceed with the second charge of threatening to murder Sergeant Robinson.

When Edalji heard the verdict and sentence, according to newspaper reports, he showed no outward sign of emotion although his face paled slightly. But going through Edalji's mind was the elaborately planned police conspiracy that had led to a monstrous injustice, which, optimistically, he believed would soon be righted. Mrs Edalji collapsed while Reverend Edalji was observed later in the hall of the courts shedding tears but soon regained his composure.

The Edaljis – Reverend, Mrs and Maud went off to the station to catch the train back to Great Wyrley. The proposed popular celebration by the people of Great Wyrley, certain of George Edalji's acquittal, had to be shelved. The Great Wyrley station was also the venue for another proposed celebration arranged by a number of young men set to welcome Harry Green's return. However, Green's friends had a fruitless wait because Green, no doubt wishing to avoid the wider public, left the train at Cannock. George Edalji also took a train ride to Stafford gaol to await a semi-permanent residence at another of His Majesty's prisons.

It had taken eight months for the police to manufacture a case against Edalji, weak though it was, but the jury needed only fifty minutes and the 'judiciary' barely three minutes to do the police's work, more accurately Captain Anson's, by removing George Edalji from Great Wyrley for seven years which, in effect, turned out to be a life sentence because George Edalji made only two fleeting visits to the area from then until his death.

Meanwhile, on the very same day, a hundred and fifty miles away from Stafford, Thomas Hemmings, on trial at the Old Bailey for shockingly mutilating a mare, was sentenced to twenty months but, of course; he did not have the jury's recommendation for mercy presented to the Court.[274]

---

[274] BME 24 Oct 1903

Chapter X

The First Hundred Days

(i)   The Media Reaction: Appearance over Substance[275]

The media paid some attention to the 'contents of the trial' – 'contents'
being a more appropriate way to describe what in other trials might be
referred to as evidence. Avoiding any reference to the prosecutor's last
ditch sleight of hand in his final address to the jury and ignoring the
reams of inadmissible evidence, a few column inches explaining how
the police 'got its result' managed to get into print. The Wolverhampton
Express and Star did recognise that the evidence, containing trivialities,
had tended towards an acquittal in English law or a 'not proven' verdict
under Scottish law, but decided overall that these trivialities produced
important links in the chain of evidence – the most damaging being the
handwriting (albeit inadmissible), the hairs on the clothes (debatable),
the wet clothes (highly dubious) and Edalji's presence in the locality at
the time of the crime on the 17th August (neglecting that the
prosecution dispensed with this theory at the eleventh hour). The
Birmingham Weekly Post thought the evidence not strong but
identified, as the crucial factor leaning towards a guilty verdict, the
maiming committed by Green to assist Edalji but overlooking that the
Green maiming was not relevant to the charge against Edalji, at least
not in the way it was presented to the jury. The Birmingham Gazette
accepted without question that Harry Green attempted to save a friend
by going as far as to maim his own horse. To the editor of the
Birmingham Post, the determining factor was the anonymous letters,
which once it was proven Edalji had written them was sufficient proof
of his guilt for the maimings – accepted unquestionably as if the
handwriting evidence was free from doubt or admissible or even
relevant to the charge.

  The media seemed more interested in making an exotic portrayal
of Edalji's appearance and in delving into his darkened psyche to

---

275 E & S 24 Oct 1903; BWP 31 Oct 1903; Gazette 4 Sep & 24 Oct 1903; Post
24 Oct & 7 Nov 1903; DM (Lon) 4 Sep & 21 Oct 1903; Mail 24 Oct 1903;
Outlook in BWP 7 Nov 1903; BME 24 & 25 Oct 1903; LM 30 Oct 1903;
Harding to Barnes, 12 Jan 1907 in Barnes to Gladstone, 28 Jan 1907, File
988; Northern Echo in WO 10 Oct 1903; DT 17 Jan 1907; BSE 25 Oct 1907

dredge up an 'unfathomable' motive for the crime, coming up with a compound of ethno-centric imagery and pseudo-psychological 'analysis'. These reports reflected an ethno-centric vision of the world that incorporated the multitudinous cultural variations east of Suez and compressed them into an undifferentiated mass.

George Edalji, possessing the features and characteristics of his Eastern father rather than his Western mother, was pictured as a man more at home wearing the flowing robes of a Parsee than in the light check summer suit in which he was attired. A description embracing populist imagery rather than reality since Edalji had spent his whole life in a Christian environment, having a father who embraced Christianity and was loyal to king and country, and a mother, who was a typical representative of the middle classes from the shires – a couple identifying more with the English establishment than most of the people living in South Staffordshire.

The Birmingham Gazette wanted to know why Edalji, who was of good social position, comfortable means, great legal talent, living in a refined atmosphere of a country vicarage, hating no man and hated by none, with enviable prospects and, so far as is known, of irreproachable past, had stolen out into the night to maim a horse. The answer it came up with was Edalji's desire to amuse himself not by causing agony to the horses but by baffling a few county policemen and terrifying a village. The source of this curious blend lay in Edalji's Eastern extraction and in his ability to project himself into other people's minds – a description produced by one reporter after reading the anonymous letters, whose "every word reeks of the blood and thunder reading of youth," without expanding on the connection between 'Boy's Own' adventures and Edalji's part-Indian origins, and ignoring that George Edalji, at almost 29 years of age, was beyond reading comics. Another portrayal of Edalji described him as an "intricate psychological freak" taking "a diabolical pleasure in contemplating the agony of a helpless dumb animal under torture (and) delight (in) pitting his individual cunning against the army of police." Edalji's alleged psychological pathology apparently spawned a similar freak in Harry Green.

The images conjured up to connect George Edalji's eastern origins were tailored to suit the particular stereotypes or prejudices of the column writer or readers. One presumed Oriental trait attributed to Edalji was a reputation of being a lover of mystery offered up to explain his anonymous letter writings. The Birmingham Gazette argued that crimes committed by Europeans had their origins in egoism, which sought its outlet in notoriety, whereas the Eastern mind was vain and couched in mystery and satisfied to keep its secret – an explanation at variance with the one offered by Disturnal, who thought Edalji's motive was the search for notoriety. The Lichfield Mercury reported that when the sentence was announced George Edalji went "into a hypnotic trance...then literally and visibly relaxing into resignation...the Oriental's acceptance of fate." The London Daily Mail had initially, at the police court, described Edalji as a typical Parsee without the nervousness of the pure bred Indian, while the mingling of Parsee and English parentage produced a man of wonderful nerve and coolness. Following the trial, having little doubt as to his guilt for the outrages and coarse anonymous letters sent out over a period of twelve years, the paper shared Captain Anson's attachment to the Lombroso theory of criminal types, depicting Edalji as a "degenerate of the worst type, whose jaw and mouth are those of a man of very debased life."

A contributor to the magazine 'Outlook' blended 'Orientalism' with an innovative form of 'anthropological psychology'. Identifying the Parsee name of Edalji as of 'Hindoo' origin and referring to the shedding of blood as one of Hinduism's principal rites, he analysed the maimings as "a fearful case of heredity – a force so strong as to make this man, educated, refined, trained as a prosaic Englishman, break through more than a century of civilisation and go back in spirit to his ancestors to do as they did." He asked if "this unhappy man became for a few hours paganised and returned to the Orient?" The Express and Star offered the fanciful notion of Edalji being 'activated' by feelings originally born in the breast of a Parsee ancestor, which the law of heredity had transmitted to the present generation. Hereditary factors apparently outweighed the Christian, English and educated environment within which Edalji was reared causing him to descend to the "depths of fiendish cruelty such as only a barbarian might rival." The Birmingham Daily Mail described Edalji's action as "a throwback to mediaeval cruelty (and) prehistoric bestiality with an admixture of some of the cunning that Rudyard Kipling attributed to the fanciful inhabitants of the jungle."[276]

Even the jury's recommendation to mercy was considered 'Kiplingesque' with its demonstration of the mercifulness associated

---

[276] This prejudicial view of Asians was nothing new. As mentioned above, adventurers and wanderers offered up descriptions to an eager British public, especially in the wake of the Indian uprising of 1857. John Lang, who wandered through India, referred to one of the leaders of that uprising as having eyes that "were expressive and full of cunning like those of most Asiatics." Lang, J, [1859] Wanderings in India and Other Sketches of Life in Indostan, London, pp410/11

with the 'White Man's Burden' and making adequate accommodation for it. The paternalistic twelve 'White Men', or more specifically Englishmen, had generously taken into account the barbaric behaviour associated with those unfortunate not to have been born English. Judging by the determination to prosecute Edalji and the sentence handed down to him, both Captain Anson and Sir Reginald Hardy had 'unburdened' themselves of any such generosity.

At a later date, one contributor, an ex-Indian civil servant, Harding, showing signs of the not unusual *pukka Sahib* distaste for those of European and Asian parentage, claimed, "Eurasians are something very peculiar in temper and habits combining often the vices of both races and the virtues of neither" – yet another example to add to the racist lexicon. Harding diagnosed Edalji as harbouring a grudge against someone and had introduced his own name into the anonymous letters to direct suspicion from himself but was eventually caught in the trap he laid for another. Harding turned the motive on its head by blaming Edalji for seeking to satisfy an alleged grudge rather than considering Edalji might be the victim of someone else's grudge - inverting the situation by placing the blame on the victim. Apologists of racism tried to dismiss Edalji's 'burden' as no more than a phenomenon peculiar to the individual victim's psyche rather than examining its cause and effect within the structures and ideology of society – an approach still prevalent today but not as widespread as it was in the early-twentieth century.

(ii)   The Edaljis Fight Back[277]

Edalji's conviction may have given pleasure to the police and members of the aristocracy and gentry circulating in the orbit of the chief constable but outside those hallowed circles serious doubts were entertained about the type of justice meted out to Edalji. In less than two weeks, three factors came into play to convert 'serious doubts' amongst a few into grave concerns amongst the many. Firstly, the verdict itself and the procedural irregularities drew numerous people into a campaign in support of Edalji, who were not run of the mill followers jumping on to any bandwagon: in Great Wyrley an 'Edalji party' came into existence; in the Birmingham district a committee of

[277] Post 4,5,6 & 16 Nov 1903; BWP 31 Oct & 7 Nov 1903; CA 12 Dec 1903; BME 28 Oct, 16 & 28 Nov 1903; J B Stone Collection, pp 165/6; BWM 21 Nov 1903; LM 13 Nov 1903; Mail 3 Nov 1907; Yelverton to HO, Nov 1903 to Mar 1904, HO Files 984/5; E & S 24 Aug 1903

lawyers was formed; and nationally prominent people spoke out in favour of Edalji. Secondly, a week after Edalji's conviction, Harry Green was escorted to Southampton by Staffordshire police officers and put on a ship bound for South Africa, and, two days after embarking, Green's second confession was published in the press. Thirdly, eleven days after George Edalji began to taste his 'dose of penal servitude' and four days after Harry Green disappeared from the scene, another horse was disembowelled with injuries similar to those inflicted on previous victims.

The campaign launched to draw attention to this serious miscarriage of justice was headed by prominent people: Sir George Lewis, the distinguished KC/MP, involved in several cases of note, amongst them the Mrs Crawford, Parnell, Dilke and the Hatton Garden Diamond cases, wrote to the Home Secretary convinced of Edalji's innocence, a view concurred with by many distinguished members of the Bar; Mr Jasper Moore, the MP for Ludlow and friend of Mary Stoneham, visited Mrs Edalji to outline a plan of campaign he intended to launch in Parliament. Unfortunately, that campaign received a severe setback when Moore died unexpectedly; the Member of Parliament for the Lichfield division, Courtenay-Warner, was firmly behind moves for Edalji's release from prison; and J B Stone, MP for Birmingham East Division, to whom Edalji had sent a begging letter in 1902, also made enquiries but seemed to do little afterwards.

By far the most significant intervention came from Mr Yelverton, ex-chief justice of the Bahamas, a zealous reformer although never quite achieving professional success as a barrister, thought of by some as a crank and others as unconventional, and like his future co-campaigner, Sir Arthur Conan Doyle, a convinced believer in the supernatural. A careful scrutiny of the evidence was enough to convince him that Edalji was the victim of a serious miscarriage of justice. He criticised Sir Reginald Hardy for allowing inadmissible evidence to be introduced at the trial contrary to the rules of evidence and was amazed at the jury for not acquitting Edalji when presented with such a "wretchedly weak" case. Just as the prosecution had secured Edalji's conviction through inadmissible anonymous letters, Yelverton believed the route to exonerate Edalji lay in refuting his alleged authorship of those letters. As no Criminal Court of Appeal existed at the time, Yelverton's, and Edalji's, only way forward involved petitioning for a pardon under the royal prerogative whose gatekeeper, the Home Secretary, was to show considerable reluctance to set the record straight or to question the dubious practices employed by the Staffordshire police. As the leading light in the early campaign, Yelverton came into serious conflict with Captain Anson, the first of many bitter confrontations the captain would engage in with anyone giving support to Edalji or questioning the veracity of the police or casting the slightest doubt on the verdict – a series of conflicts exposing the flawed character of the person behind the prosecution of Edalji.

Yelverton's intervention came as a breath of fresh air to the dank atmosphere that had pervaded the Edaljis for a considerable period of time. Reverend Edalji, who had shown his own brand of resilience when confronted with adversity during his twenty eight years sojourn as the vicar of Great Wyrley, continued to show that his resolve had not diminished because over the coming years, as he did in the 1890s, Reverend Edalji waged a relentless, selfless action on behalf of his son. Having great faith in English justice, the reverend began to fight back temporally and spiritually. On the one hand, he took the lawful and constitutional way to present the case to the public and, on the other, taking the opportunity of the medium at his disposal - the pulpit, he promoted his son's case in the belief that justice and truth would ultimately triumph. The trial had made St Mark's Church, Great Wyrley, the Mecca for large audiences of worshippers, sightseers or the just plain curious, who crowded into the aisles, the sides and the rear of the church. The reverend used the Sunday church services to inform the large congregation of Yelverton's campaign and read out many letters of sympathy received by the family. His sermons served as his own personal 'jawbone of an ox' cutting down the Philistines and he urged everyone "to commend (themselves) to God, as Daniel did when God saved him and proved his innocence..." Needless to say, the use of this approach did not always commend itself to some of his parishioners, including its most vocal critic, W H Brookes.

Nor did George's defence team escape the reverend's ire. He criticised them publicly for overlooking important evidence, particularly Sergeant Robinson's admission that the police were watching the vicarage on the night of 17/18th August, bringing from Litchfield Meek, Edalji's solicitor, a rebuttal in that police officers swore at the Quarter Sessions that the vicarage was not being watched on that night.[278] Litchfield Meek seemed as selective in his memory as were several police officers, ignoring Sergeant Robinson's and Inspector Campbell's evidence at the police court reported fully in the Cannock Advertiser on the 5th September 1903 and stated in the police depositions,[279] which Meek must have seen. If Meek had failed to

---

[278] Post 5, 6 & 7 Nov 1903
[279] Depositions of 3/4 September, in HO File 990

notice this evidence it was indicative of a somewhat shoddy approach in his instructions to Mr Vachell.

Not to be left out of the campaign, Mrs Edalji made her contribution by taking up the pen to write in a genteel, almost apologetic vein, to many prominent people asking them to use their influence to secure her son's release.

(iii) Great Wyrley Parish Hit by a New Atrocity[280]

With the literal tide carrying away Harry Green after his police-escorted departure from the United Kingdom, the metaphoric tide began to turn once more against the Staffordshire police when Great Wyrley was rocked by a repeat performance of the terror visited upon the locality on many occasions since February. On the 3rd November, two horses belonging to Mr Stanley were maimed with cuts indistinguishable from the other maimings as even Captain Anson was prepared to admit. Perhaps someone was after that alleged wager made in a public house but not the version naming George Edalji as the hopeful beneficiary. People in the locality, including two who had themselves lost animals, came to the conclusion that Edalji was innocent of all the previous maimings and one in particular, Mrs Green, mother of Harry, thought "the poor lad (Edalji) who is at Stafford" might now be released. The ordinary folk of Great Wyrley appeared to have more faith in the fair mindedness of the authorities than either previous or later events would warrant.

Several possible lines of enquiry for the police to pursue opened up to them: (a) a gang of at least three members, which had previously included both Green and Edalji; (b) a gang, which had included either (i) Green or (ii) Edalji but not both; (c) an individual or gang independent of Green and Edalji; (d) a 'copy cat' criminal; or (e) an Edalji sympathiser unconnected with any of the previous maimings. Whatever alternative combinations the police intended to follow, sections of the press poured cold water on their ability to discover the culprit(s) citing the existing police theory of pinning the previous offences on Edalji as likely to hamper any investigation. Seriously doubting the ability of the county police to offer a way forward – trapped as the police were in a dogmatic belief in Edalji's guilt, the

---

[280] BWP 7 Nov 1903; Gazette 7 Nov 1903; Mail 3 & 9 Nov 1903; LM 6 Nov 1903; BME 5 & 9 Nov 1903; Observations on the Truth Article by Bettany, 9 May 1905, England, HO Case of George Edalji – memos and papers, Bp 2/4 (19) App VII, p 55

press suggested that Captain Anson called in Scotland Yard detectives led by a Sherlock Holmes figure to investigate the new maiming - a prophetic suggestion in the light of what was on the horizon.

Little hope could attach itself to the appeals from the press because Captain Anson did not look favourably on deductive reasoning, the intellectual arm of criminal investigation, nor was he inclined to entertain any Scotland Yard investigation that threatened to exonerate Edalji. The captain, wrapped firmly in the belief that he and his men should be beyond criticism, must have been less than enamoured with the suggestion to bring in Scotland Yard to investigate the maiming and in raising the possibility that the police had caged the wrong man.

The police theories covering the February to August series of maimings and the specific Green maiming now had the appearance, like the maimed horses, of having been well and truly gutted. With the pillars holding up the case against Edalji crumbling and the police completely at a loss over the latest maiming as both Edalji and Green were out of the way, senior police officers were forced into adopting an entirely new theory. Rejecting the possibility of a gang carrying out the atrocities when pursuing the case against Edalji, except in implying a gang might be involved during the trial to secure Edalji's conviction, the police now changed tack. The police claimed that for some time, whatever 'time' actually represented since it was only just over a week since Edalji's conviction, it had been in possession of information pointing to the existence of a gang. In line with this new 'theory', if police guesswork warranted the description of the term 'theory', Captain Anson put out a statement to the effect that numerous people were in the frame for the offence.[281] The police began to test the viability of this 'theory' with Captains Anson and Longden making the journey to Great Wyrley almost daily to keep in touch with developments.

Captain Anson, who privately subscribed to the 'theory' of a gang, including Green but excluding Edalji, in the series of maimings, as his later communications with Yelverton and the Home Office clearly revealed, was not about to do anything if it brought any relief to George Edalji. Whatever leads the police might have or any approach for the police to adopt or any theories that came to mind, one essential criterion that had to be satisfied was for the police to be able to connect it to Edalji, which, as the press noted, restricted any police investigation. With this kind of dogmatism it was little wonder that the police were incapable of re-visiting the whole series of maimings, all the police

---

[281] Capt Anson to Simpson, 31 Dec 1903, HO No 44 File 984

would do was to treat each new maiming in abstraction from the others. With Edalji in prison and Green on the open sea bound for South Africa, did the police honestly believe that another perpetrator, having no connection with the other maimings, committed this one by inflicting a similar wound with a similar weapon?

Unable to pin the crime on anyone within the framework of his new gang 'theory,' an inevitability since he refused to even consider Edalji's innocence, and at a complete loss, the captain anchored himself to an entirely new 'theory'. This 'theory' isolated the maiming from any previous incident – although basing the motive on the same grounds as the Green maiming. Captain Anson's new animal killer was the horses' owner, Stanley, whom he alleged was in financial difficulties and killed the horses to make a profit on the transaction. Financial consideration was a common theme put forward by Captain Anson as a motive explaining any incident and a financial dimension featured in many of the slurs he made against people who came into conflict with him on matters relating to the case against Edalji. These slurs were more often than not voiced without the knowledge of the victim who was, therefore, in no position to challenge them.

Edalji happened to be Captain Anson's personal Achilles heel and with the captain's feet bound so tight for protection he was unable to do anything other than shuffle along the never ending road to avoid an accurate and just solution.

(iv) Local Recriminations[282]

The Reverend's pounding of the pulpit on behalf of his son; Yelverton's critical intervention on behalf of Edalji and Captain Anson's dismissive arrogance towards Harry Green, fuelled the increasing resentment against the police. The local populace had not been exactly hostile to the police but during the investigation into the Stanley maimings, the police lost their support because when questioned people felt police officers were not so much interested in collecting information as in trying to incriminate anyone to whom they spoke.

When Harry Green's complaint of police intimidation to get him

---

[282] BWP 7 & 28 Nov 1903; Post 5 Nov 1903; Mail 24 & 26 Nov 1903; CA 7 & 28 Nov 1903; Brookes to Mail and reply, 23 & 25 Nov 1903, in Capt Anson to Blackwell, 25 Mar 1907, File 989 Pt 2; CA 12 Dec 1903; SA 12 Dec 1903; Affidavits, TJ, SE & CM Green, 15 Dec 1903 in HO No 31 File 984

to sign a confession prior to Edalji's trial became public knowledge, Captain Anson tried to explain away Green's confessions as two statements, an initial statement and a signed amplified one – apparently 'statement' was an *Ansonian* euphemism for confession. In attempting to bolster the reliability of his explanation of Green's 'statements' and to justify police inaction over the killing of Green's horse, Captain Anson revealed that Green admitted his guilt to Mr Benton in whose field the animal was kept. The captain held up the Green-Benton conversation as the answer to any accusation of police malpractice. Released on the 5th November, the chief constable's attempt at justification fooled few people; instead it opened up another storm of criticism seriously undermining his credibility and honesty. The captain's tendency to gloss over the truth, so very evident in his private communications, and his absolute disregard for 'facts', was exposed by his foray into the public domain when it became all too obvious that the police had not checked out the contents of Green's 'confession' with Mr Benton. On this 5th November, additional fireworks to those normally reserved for Guy Fawkes were set off when the 'first rocket was fired' at Captain Anson's damp squib explanation. Mr Benton, Chair of the local Vigilante Committee, publicly denied Green had confessed to him about killing the horse and he criticised the police for failing to draw his attention to Green's claim, which Benson could reasonably expect to have his attention drawn to it for confirmation. The failure to inform Benton could be attributed to the fact that the police never expected to disclose this confession to the public and Captain Anson had made a *faut pas*, maybe an arrogant *faut pas*, by indiscreetly naming Benton when trying to defend himself. If Green had not spoken to Benton, and it was obvious he had not, why had the police found it necessary to include Benton's name in the confession dictated to Green by Superintendent Bishop. A reasonable conclusion to be drawn was that the police wanted substantiation from a third party included in the confession to show to someone else, notably the prosecuting counsel in the Edalji case to set Disturnal's mind at rest should any bombshells be dropped at the trial by Edalji's defence. If this was the reason, it was somewhat short-sighted since if Benton's name had been mentioned in the court, he would surely have volunteered evidence to discredit the confession. But this was par for the course as the police had shown itself on numerous occasions to suffer from acute myopia.

The Green family, in jumping to Harry Green's defence, turned on Captain Anson's informant, Arrowsmith, after the shop manager publicly denied being paid to keep his conversations with Harry Green secret. Their spokesperson, Green's brother-in-law, Mr Peake, had not got his act together because he erred when claiming that the Green-Arrowsmith conversations took place after Green's confessions to the police and not before. Peake was also in error in claiming that Harry Green did not have a ticket for South Africa before the trial took place as Green bought a ticket to sail for South Africa on the 10th October and, when his ticket was taken from him by the police before Edalji's trial began, had approached a solicitor with a view to retrieving it. Mr T J Green's response was clear cut and to the point when making it clear that Harry Green would have denied any knowledge of the maiming if called as a witness at the trial.

In an interview with a Birmingham Daily Mail reporter, Captain Anson, very much on the defensive, put some spin on the issue, by refusing to recognise the confession as anything other than an autographed statement and he denied extorting the 'statement' from Green. The captain 'gilded the lily' by claiming it would be impossible for the police to coerce a man into writing an untrue statement – words of comfort falling on deaf ears for numerous people in the twentieth century who have found themselves subject to this type of coercion.[283] Not wanting to publish Green's second confession in full, Captain Anson explained that the abridged version published in the Birmingham Daily Mail covered the whole ground and he had no intention of hawking it about the country for inspection.

South Staffordshire was not all doom and gloom for Captain Anson, who was able to find a willing ally in the Edalji's perennial opponent, W H Brookes, the same W H Brookes, who had played an underhand game against Reverend and George Edalji since the 1880s. W H Brookes' bile was rekindled when Yelverton resurrected the 1892 anonymous letters in an article in the Birmingham Daily Mail in which Brookes was alluded to but not mentioned by name. Brookes was further aggrieved when his rejoinder was rejected on legal grounds by the paper. In Brookes' unpublished rejoinder, he wrote of events surrounding the 1892 anonymous letters and of his role in halting their flow, which Brookes knew to be untrue as he was visited months later by Morgan, a suspect for the anonymous letters sent out in 1893. As in the 1880s, Brookes criticised Reverend Edalji for forgetting he was a Minister of the Gospel and for turning the House of God, St Mark's Church, into a theatre where the Edalji drama or farce was performed for curiosity mongers from all parts of the country. Brookes also denounced the reverend for dragging the church through the mud to

---

[283] To name but a few recent examples, the Guildford Four, the Birmingham Six, the Bridgwater Four and the 'Bakewell Tart' murder

attract sympathy from uninformed people in order to get them to sign the petition.

When notified of this rejection, Brookes immediately contacted Captain Anson for assistance and an article on the same subject reached the columns of the Staffordshire Advertiser and the Cannock Advertiser under the nomenclature of a police spokesman

Mr Brookes' less than charitable response to the burden laid on the shoulders of the reverend and his family illustrated his deeply held hostility towards the Edaljis despite a common interest the families shared ten years before when anonymous letters were floating around the parish abusing the members of both families. The reverend had few people in the parish on whom he could rely and Brookes' melodramatic performance combined with Captain Anson's role in stoking up trouble for the Edaljis merely confirmed the isolation under which the reverend and his family had suffered for all those years.

(v)   Captain Anson Answers Back[284]

The spectre of George Edalji, now confined in Lewes gaol, rose from the funeral pyre of another dead horse in the knackers' yard to haunt the chief constable. Assailed on many sides - a feature destined to haunt him at the national level for several years, Captain Anson showed how low was his regard for the intelligence of the residents of South Staffordshire, and elsewhere for that matter, believing he could feed them any kind of story. He went into battle on several fronts against the campaign to free Edalji, which had received added impetus from: the latest maiming; the anonymous letters again bombarding the district; and the grave doubts widely voiced about Edalji's conviction. Like a late twentieth-century spin doctor, Captain Anson dredged up anything to use as ammunition however unsavoury and misguided the content.

The captain's opening gambit was to try to influence Reverend

---

[284] CA 12 & 19 Dec 1903; BWP 19 Jan 1907; Despatch 7 Feb 1907; BME 27/28 Nov 1903; Capt Anson to Yelverton, 8 Nov 1903 in F E Smith, Hansard, 18 Jul 1907 v 178 cols 1013/4; Post 1 Dec 1903; Yelverton to Stone, 19 Nov 1903, J B Stone Collection; SA 5 Dec 1903; Churton Collins in an undated, unpublished letter to the DT sent between 1903 and 1907 in Capt Anson to Blackwell, 24 Mar 1907, File 989 Pt 2; HO comment, 22 Feb 1911, HO No 315, File 987; Churton Collins, Gazette 6 Feb 1907; Capt Anson to HO, confidentially, 10 Nov 1903, HO No 5, File 984; Report from the Chief Constable on the George Edalji case, 22 Dec 1903, England, HO Case of George Edalji – memos and papers, Bp 2/4 (19) App II pp35 -37

Edalji into not pursuing his son's case – a forlorn hope as he must have known judging by the reverend's determination to protect his son during the events of 1892 to 1895. In the captain's second move, he made a discreditable attempt to 'nip in the bud' any potentially dynamic movement to assist Edalji. Having been sent numerous testimonials as to Edalji's good character, Captain Anson, in a letter to Yelverton dated the 8th November, rejected what he described as Yelverton's "attempt to prove that George Edalji could not…have been guilty of writing offensive and abominable letters", and falsely accused Reverend Edalji of being only too "well aware of his (George's) proclivities in the direction of anonymous writing, and several other people have personal knowledge on the same subject." These 'several other people', who were to remain as equally anonymous as the anonymous letter writer(s), were rather dubious sources who allegedly gave information to the police about the incident of the stolen key in 1892. Captain Anson's bilious response had no effect on Yelverton, long experienced in law and in protests for legal reform, who dismissed the captain's letter as bad taste preferring to rely on his (Yelverton's) own satisfactory enquiries into Edalji's character. The captain's letter was more than bad taste, it was vindictive and lacking in substance, a measure of the depths to which Captain Anson was prepared to sink in order that Edalji would continue to taste "his dose of penal servitude." Yelverton, quite perceptively, suspected Captain Anson of sending letters of a similar kind to the Home Secretary in an attempt to prejudice Edalji's petition for a pardon. Yelverton, advised by Sir George Lewis, put pressure on Captain Anson by asking for the names of anyone prepared to substantiate the claim that Edalji had written the anonymous letters. Asking for substantiation from Captain Anson was one way of aggravating the captain and attracting his wrath and, needless to say, Yelverton's request brought no positive response. Instead, Captain Anson gave an interview to the Birmingham Daily Mail on the Great Wyrley outrages, which, following the usual line adopted by the captain, was a long way from the truth. Yelverton hit back by accusing Captain Anson of misusing his position and rejected the captain's overambitious and unrealistic claim in the paper of having solved the Edalji case, a claim also contested by Sir George Lewis; by the President of the Law Society; and by 10,000 other people, including clergymen, magistrates, solicitors – all of whom signed the petition denouncing the trial as a 'Miscarriage of Justice'. As a retort to Captain Anson's public declaration in the press, Yelverton announced his intention of publishing recent letters sent by the chief constable to himself and also the captain's dismissive letters sent to the Reverend and Mrs Edalji in 1895. The purpose behind the publication of these documents was to illustrate Captain Anson's attitude towards the family during the previous anonymous letter campaign that had the Edaljis as its target. The captain's second assault on the Edalji campaign had been repelled suggesting that he or his Edwardian 'spin doctors' needed to catch up on their homework.

Captain Anson's third line of attack was even more discreditable, publicly refuting "that (Edalji) was a promising young solicitor with bright prospects" and that "at the time of his arrest he was being pressed on all sides for debts incurred through gambling and other transactions and which he had no prospect of paying" – a disingenuous and irrelevant attack on Edalji published in several newspapers. This particular smear tactic coincided with the news, sufficient to raise an air of optimism in the Edalji camp, of the Incorporated Law Society suspending the hearing for Edalji's removal from the solicitor's roll. This was welcome news to the Edaljis since it suggested that the principals of the Law Society considered the conviction might be quashed because as a solicitor serving time in prison George Edalji would have no chance of staying on the rolls.

Captain Anson's third prong of attack seemed not to halt the forward march of the Edalji campaign. The first of Edalji's several petitions was submitted to the Home Office on the 8th December 1903, containing 10,000 signatures, including 1,000 solicitors, with testimonials from people who knew, or knew of George Edalji; or who were critical of the evidence at the trial and of the verdict, including two members of the Royal College of Veterinary Surgeons, Mr E Sewell and Mr R Lewis, who criticised the prosecution's failure to call a veterinary specialist to testify as to the probable cause and extent of the injury.

Under increasing pressure, Captain Anson continued to hit out in what was a concerted effort on his part to publicly discredit Edalji and to undermine the campaign seeking a free pardon for him. The Staffordshire Advertiser published an article that looked like a handout from Staffordshire police headquarters with the watermark of Captain Anson indelibly printed through it. The article began by articulating the Anson-Brookes position, condemning 'pulpit campaigning' as the improper use of the pulpit in discussing the rights and wrongs of criminal cases – although the 'handout' did not take into account the possibility that other people might argue that the injustices in society were suitable topics for discussion in a Christian environment. The author identified two groups of people but unlike other commentators, who saw the groups divided on the issue of either Edalji's guilt or innocence, this writer saw the groups separated into (i) those who 'screen the miscreants' and sympathise with Edalji and (ii) those who seek to maintain law and order and uphold the police.

True to form, the letter writing of ten years before found its way into the article and, surfacing yet again, the unsubstantiated claim of the police collecting evidence to implicate George Edalji in writing those letters, which in reality the police never did but why spoil a good story by providing facts. An unknown double life George Edalji was allegedly leading was said to have been uncovered – a life of feigned simplicity in the vicarage and of rash speculation on the stock exchange as if this had anything to do with cattle maiming. Then came *the coup de main*. Edalji, following his arrest, had apparently accused the police of stealing two £100 notes forming part of £214 entrusted to Edalji for investment. The chief constable ordered enquiries to be made and he claimed Edalji had cashed the notes at the Bank of England in Birmingham. However, as was usual, the captain provided no evidence to support his claim of embezzlement, which given his obvious malice towards George Edalji, he would certainly have produced if evidence was to hand as he did with other non-illegal financial activities Edalji was allegedly mixed up in: notices were served in November 1902 for £340 owed to stockbrokers after gambling on the stock exchange, which other people might reasonably describe as investment or playing the stock market; for £44.12s to a bill discounter; and in early 1903 for £7 borrowed from a money lender. Apparently, these financial difficulties were the motive for Edalji's involvement in the maimings and the police were in the process of tracking down Edalji's accomplices (note: not associates) in these financial dealings. To supplement the article, the editor declared the paper's firm support for the sentence passed on Edalji and praised Captain Anson, Superintendent Bishop and Inspector Campbell for their actions while the vicar and his family were demeaned as ridiculous. This 'article' was undoubtedly a contribution from Captain Anson as will be seen later when examining the numerous letters he sent to the Home Office. A week later, the Cannock Advertiser, reproduced the same article.[285]

The police spokesperson had plummeted to new depths. To introduce embezzlement and financial recklessness as a motive for maimings when no one had been able to find any motive for the crimes and when Edalji's indebtedness was the result of misplaced loyalty in standing surety for a colleague who absconded leaving Edalji with the debt, showed a duplicity on the part of the police matched only by

---

[285] SA 5 Dec 1903; CA 12 Dec 1903

similarly outrageous claims made in confidential reports to the Home Office by Captain Anson. One other claim made by the police worth a mention, was that Edalji was acting either in a gang carrying out maimings or with 'accomplices' engaging in financial dealings, yet no other gang member or financial 'accomplice' was ever identified by the police, other than mentioning that the 'accomplices' met in a Birmingham pub – only George Edalji was unearthed. To make these crass and irrelevant allegations public at a time when Edalji was seeking a Home Office review of the case was both duplicitous and malicious.

Reverend Edalji, out of the pulpit and into the press, reprimanded Captain Anson for bringing George Edalji's private financial affairs into the public domain but the reverend took the opportunity to explain that George Edalji's total liabilities when arrested were under £100 and were not gambling debts. Battling on despite his sixty years, he similarly rejected Captain Anson's claim that George Edalji had accused the police of stealing the £100 notes and he gave a detailed account of what was reported to have happened on the 19th August when the police visited George Edalji's office in search of a weapon and any other evidence to incriminate him. Reverend Edalji also revealed his conversation with Inspector Campbell on the 4th September when the reverend, thinking the police may have taken the money missing from the cash box for safe keeping, asked the inspector if the police had taken it but the inspector claimed the police had not done so. The client whose money had disappeared from Edalji's office responded to the article in the Cannock Advertiser, by writing in support of George Edalji and making it clear he had no doubts whatsoever about George Edalji's integrity.[286] But even if George Edalji was a thief and embezzler and that seemed highly unlikely since the cash was to be handed to the client on the 20th August – only two days on from George's arrest – it did not make him a horse maimer nor

---

[286] J Hawkins, CA 19 Dec 1903

an anonymous letter writer.[287]

Other rumours of a particularly distasteful type focussing on purported immorality in the Edalji family were circulating far beyond the parish boundaries. A particular allegation concerning an unlawful relationship between the Reverend and George Edalji was being put about as the reason behind the unusual sleeping arrangements at the vicarage. In fact, an attempt was made by a member of the academic

---

[287] An interesting story arose from the police trip to Edalji's Birmingham office on the 19th August. According to the housekeeper, after the police left Edalji's office, she and her husband went into the office and found the window smashed and the sash cords cut, the place disarranged and Edalji's cash box open and empty. The following day, Mrs Edalji went to the office to retrieve the cash box only to be told it was empty. On the 21st August, at Stafford jail, Mrs Edalji, unaware of the full contents of the box told George about it being opened. George told her it contained £220 in banknotes, which Edalji had been prevented from paying to a client on the 20th August because of his arrest, and containing some postal orders and stamps. The matter was referred to the reverend, who thought the police may have taken it for safekeeping. When the reverend asked Inspector Campbell in September if he had taken the money, the inspector claimed not to have done. Mrs Edalji repaid the money to the client. Where did the money go? Whoever took the money had to have a key to the cash box as no mention was made of the cash box being forced open. The police had taken a key from Edalji on the 18th August. If George Edalji had misused the money, the cash box would have been empty when the police arrived in his office on the 19th August and surely they would have taken the empty cashbox with them as evidence. Captain Anson claimed that Edalji had cashed them at the Bank of England but provided not a scrap of evidence in support of that claim. If neither Edalji nor the police took the money, who did? Could the housekeeper and/or her husband have taken the cash box before the police arrived, then after the police left returned the empty box and disarranged the office to give the impression of burglars but if so the police would surely have queried the disappearance of the cash box when they searched the office. Moreover, the housekeeper would need a key, which she was unlikely to have. It was also unlikely for the police to have searched the office and left behind an untouched cash box so that rules out the housekeeper and her husband. Could the police have taken it for themselves and left the room in disarray with the sash cords slashed to give the impression of a break in? And what happened to the stamps and postal orders? Captain Anson was quiet on them. Rev Edalji to HO, 12 Dec 1903, HO No 28 File 984; Rev Edalji, CA 19 Dec 1903

staff at Birmingham University, using these very rumours, to dissuade his fellow academic, Professor Churton Collins, from becoming involved in the Edalji campaign. Collins believed the police were behind the accusation of sodomy made against Reverend Edalji and he raised this with Superintendent Barrett, who claimed never to have heard the faintest suggestion of immorality made against the Edalji family. Although the source of the rumour was never directly traced to anyone in particular, they coincided with Captain Anson's efforts to prevent support for Edalji gaining ground. The captain's overall responses to the Edalji campaign and the type of slurs he made against the Edaljis, gives some weight to the view that he might have engineered these rumours since he was aware of the accusations of homosexuality made against Reverend Edalji in the 1895 anonymous letters. Just over three years later, this issue would come back with a vengeance when Sir Arthur Conan Doyle located the source of these rumours to the corridors of power in the Staffordshire County Constabulary.

With the Edalji campaign gaining strength, Captain Anson lost no time in contacting Home Office officials, who were also in contact with the other two members of the Quarter Session's Holy Trinity - Disturnal and Hardy. In a confidential memo to the Home Office, Captain Anson, although previously of the opinion that Edalji was not involved in the maimings, changed his mind and accused Edalji of responsibility for the killings in collaboration with others and that Edalji should have been tried for conspiracy instead of the simple maiming offence. Of course, Captain Anson, failed to explain the basis for this conclusion or why he did not run Edalji's fellow felons to earth. All he could offer was his difficulty in "get(ting) to the bottom of things... owing to the Oriental birth of the convict and of his family" – another ethno-centric allusion to explain away the captain's failings. Nor did he bother to explain why, during the Green fiasco, he was satisfied with putting only Edalji behind bars. But, of course, as far as Captain Anson was concerned, Green committed no crime and had only maimed his own horse for the compensation available from the Yeomanry for any horse sustaining injuries during military training, which, considering Green's horse had suffered no injury in training, was surely fraud. The claim made in Green's statement of confessing his guilt to Benton was admitted as being untrue and, magnanimously, the captain signalled his readiness to dispense with Green's statement (confession) because Green was extremely untruthful. Needless to say, this the captain never did. The captain's principal contribution in this memo was his assessment of Edalji being convicted entirely on the anonymous letters of which he had not the slightest doubt Edalji had written – an acceptance of Edalji being sent down solely on inadmissible evidence. Predictably, he made it clear that other strong 'evidence' not produced at the trial was available and went on to raise his 'pet hobby horses', the issue of the 1892 to 1895 letters and of his own suspicions as to the identity of the author – a theme Captain Anson was to perennially harp upon over the next four years. Nor did he waste the opportunity to raise the slur of Edalji misappropriating £214 belonging to a client and, incredibly, claimed that Edalji's arrest "was a perfect godsend to him" by taking him out of the way of his creditors. If nothing else, the chief constable of Staffordshire portrayed himself as a mean and vindictive character, which eventually filtered through to officials in the Home Office.

(vi) The Unusual Correspondence of Horace Edalji!

In the face of Yelverton's assault on police practices and prejudices; the revelations emerging from the Green confessions; and three weeks of intense defensive activity by Captain Anson, fortuitously for the police, in mid-November, a lowly police constable came up with 'startling' evidence, albeit hearsay, from a resident of Great Wyrley, Chris Hatton, son of J T Hatton, an old protagonist of the reverend. Hatton junior revealed to Police Constable Cooper, a police witness at the Edalji trial, the contents of conversations and correspondence between himself and Horace Edalji, from mid-November onwards.[288] It was truly amazing how the 'evidence' now appeared to flow so freely and unabated to the police. If such diligence and perseverance from the police and 'openness' from the local population had been evident between February and August 1903, the mystery of the Great Wyrley slasher would surely have been laid to rest quite easily and the police and prosecution would not have had to rely on the dubious 'evidence' presented at Edalji's trial.

Horace Edalji was obviously not full of Christian spirit towards his elder brother George, soon to spend his first Christmas at the expense of His Majesty's Government and, from the contents of these letters, Horace did not intend to allow his ageing parents the opportunity to spend an enjoyable Christmas, if that were possible in the circumstances. For reasons best known to himself, Horace poured out his heart to Chris Hatton from his Shropshire domicile in an exceptionally hostile manner towards his brother, his parents and those

---

[288] PC Cooper to Supt Bishop, 18 Dec 1903, HO No 124, File 985

supporting his brother. Horace allegedly revealed that George was the author of the 1892 – 5 anonymous letters but, when urged by Hatton to inform his father, displayed a marked reluctance to follow this advice, excusing himself on the grounds that his parents were likely to claim the police had bribed him (Horace) and were also likely to disown him. If this was Horace's expectation, his parents must already have harboured an exceptionally low opinion of their second son. Horace also criticised Yelverton for resurrecting the 'ancient letters' from 1892 – 5, a similar complaint to the one made by Mr W H Brookes to the Birmingham Daily Mail a week later.

At the beginning of December, Constable Cooper again met Chris Hatton and was told that Horace Edalji had decided to risk all and tell his father but as Yelverton was visiting the vicarage at the time, he thought it best to defer making known George's guilt until after he had left. On the 11th December 1903, Chris Hatton let Constable Cooper know that Horace, displaying a perverse hostility to Yelverton, had written to his parents about George's letter writing and advised his father to tell Yelverton to leave the police alone because the more Yelverton agitated the more would come out about George. As a consequence of Horace's 'familial diligence', an allegedly highly critical thirteen page letter was sent to him by Mrs Edalji admonishing him for not telling them in the 1890s about George's involvement in the anonymous letters.[289]

Horace, apparently sick of the whole affair having contributed £50 to George's defence and being pressed for more, ridiculed Jasper Moore, the recently deceased Ludlow MP and friend of Mrs Edalji's sister, for believing George to be not guilty and for 'identifying' the Great Wyrley maimer as the brother of Courtenay Warner, MP for Lichfield, whom Moore was also said to have believed was involved in the Whitechapel murders. An unlikely but propitious tale implicating a relation of Courtenay Warner, who had 'coincidentally' recently come out in support of George Edalji. Incidentally, this 'revelation' about Moore did not figure, as was claimed, in any alleged letter from Horace Edalji to Hatton and, coming so soon after Moore's death, Captain Anson, as he did on other occasions, had used this post-mortem ploy to attribute statements to people that were impossible to verify.

Horace's ill feeling towards his brother went as far as refusing to collect any signatures for a petition for George's release sent to him by

---

[289] This did not square with the number mentioned in a typed copy of Horace Edalji's alleged letter which mentioned 32 pages. The Captain could not even get this right.

his father. However, Chris Hatton, for some unknown reason, took the petition from Horace and gave it to his own clerk, who then managed to get thirty signatures – an act of generosity on Chris Hatton's part displaying considerable ambiguity.

A few days later, on the 15th December 1903, Constable Cooper, demonstrating yet again his devotion to duty, asked Chris Hatton to obtain a copy of Horace's letter to Reverend Edalji. Chris Hatton, thinking it might take some time, claimed to be in possession of other letters saying practically the same thing but if he meant letters from Horace to his father none were ever released to the police. During this *tête-à-tête*, Hatton also disclosed that Horace provided a motive for the killing, which no one previously had been able to do, namely, if George killed the horses (GW: note the plural) it would be for money or to buy influence. Adding grist to the mill, Chris Hatton made his own contribution towards the belief in George's guilt by mentioning an incident of a cow being killed in Much Wenlock, where George Edalji's grandmother and his aunt lived. Hatton was visiting the village at the same time as George but he was unsure whether George had returned to Great Wyrley before the maiming occurred. Horace Edalji, through Hatton, referred to "a strange visit to London" undertaken by George in February 1903 shortly after the first horse maiming. What this was supposed to prove is difficult to comprehend as it was hardly mysterious, it was a business trip, and in no way connected George to the February maiming. After all when the other maimings occurred, there were no stories of George making 'strange' journeys out of Great Wyrley.

Horace asked Hatton if the pulpit references had ceased – a 'Brookes-Anson' concern, and his final sentence in this letter was "Lets hear any news." It is not clear why Horace asked for the latest news, he seemed to be the one who knew everything and was keen to share it with anyone.[290]

---

[290] The contents of Horace Edalji's letters were: What an awful mess Yelverton is making of George's case. No idea he was going to introduce ancient letters. Yelverton's latest. He says if George is not released by the time of the Ludlow election he is going to come here and speak!! The Home Secretary won't stand threats so I am afraid Yelverton has quite spoilt his case…Did you see in the papers the late Jasper More had been to see me "to arrange for a campaign in parliament." Sounds comical doesn't it? The fact is that Jasper More telegraphed me twice the week before he died to meet him at the Craven Arms. I told him just how the case stood…He was keen on that sort of thing but the "campaign" is only in the imagination of someone in London…I hear that George says he was "never better in his life." Wants to stay I should think. Horace Edalji,

In a final missive, Yelverton was alleged to have written to Horace informing him that George was likely to be released that week but why would Yelverton write to Horace about this when he appeared not to have written with similar news to Reverend Edalji,[291] who, if such welcome news had reached him, would have heralded it from the pulpit. But no such news was ever proclaimed at St Mark's. Surprisingly, these

---

28 Broad St, Ludlow, to C Hatton, 1 Dec 1903, HO File 989 Pt 1 Have written to the mater telling her what I know about George and the 1892 – 6 letters. I have asked her to have this agitation against the chief constable stopped and pointed out how serious it is. I don't know what my people will think but I believe I have done my duty in telling them. Yelverton wants jolly well sitting on and I will see if I can do it. Horace Edalji to C Hatton, 6 Dec 1903, HO File 989 Pt 1

My people awfully wild for telling them. Had 32 pages of it from mater. She says the Governor won't believe it and she takes up an inconsistent position. I am a liar and that I should have told them before. I cannot make them see it's to George's interest that the agitation against the police should be stopped. I wish the last outrage could be cleared up. There might be some chance at getting at the truth. The petition has been sent up I understand several days ago. Have the pulpit references ceased? What a treat it will be when Wyrley really has peace again. I have never been able to see that the evidence against George was anything like strong enough to convict him. If however he did the outrages I think he must have done it for money considering what desperate financial straits he was in. There was a bankruptcy petition against him at the end of last January but he got over it. It is quite possible someone got a hold over him which might explain subsequent proceedings. He paid a mysterious visit to London about the end of February and was away about a week. He never said a word about what he did except that he had business, which was no doubt true. I don't know whether the police have ever thought there may be someone at the back of him. If he really did the outrages I cannot see that he can have done them except for money. Only sensation, madness or money could be at the bottom of it. I don't think he was mad. So it must have been for money or else he was innocent. What do you think of my theory? I shan't be very welcome at home I am afraid. I have always been very sorry for the pater and mater though, and they cannot see how they have been deceived. I don't know when I shall come over to Wyrley again. I hope your toothache is better. I did not see Connie that evening in Birmingham. Weather is abominable here. Let's hear any news. Horace Edalji to C Hatton, 13 Dec 1903 in Capt Anson to Troup, 2 May 1905, HO File 989 Pt 1

[291] Horace Edalji to Hatton, 17 Dec 1903, in Anson to Troup, 2 May 1905, HO File 989 Pt 1

latter points in Horace's alleged letters were not disclosed by Captain Anson until eighteen months later and only conjured up when the captain's back was further against the wall.

The contents of the Hatton-Edalji conversations and the Horace Edalji 'letters' were very much a pro-Anson treatise with a few personal details thrown in at the end in what seemed like an attempt to give the letter the appearance of being written between two friends. The contents could not have been more favourable to Captain Anson and the particular line he was pursuing than if he had written them himself. Like manna from heaven for the captain, all this information, including criticism of people who had come out in support of George Edalji, emerged at a time when he was coming under increasing attack and was very much on the defensive from Yelverton's campaign.

In a letter to the Home Office in December 1903, Captain Anson mentioned Horace Edalji having told his parents about George Edalji writing the anonymous letters in 1892,[292] giving the impression that the parents were given this information by Horace way back in 1892 and not in December 1903 as recorded in the alleged Horace Edalji-Chris Hatton correspondence. Captain Anson's manner of presentation almost indicted the Reverend and Mrs Edalji as accessories to the 1892 letters. However, the captain failed to divulge any of the more important information in Horace's letters; he merely mentioned having the letters in his possession. It was much later, when the captain was under increasing attack in the wake of the 'Truth' weekly newspaper publishing a series of critical reviews of the Edalji case in early 1905, that the Cooper-Hatton conversations were revealed to the Home Office and the alleged letters produced, not originals but typewritten 'copies'. Given that Captain Anson was not loath to disclose matters unfavourable to the Edaljis, having been extremely cavalier in his attitude to their feelings in the past, or slow in showing any reluctance to stoop to any depths to discredit the family, why did he not make these additional revelations available to either the Home Office or the public in December 1903? It could not be to protect Horace Edalji because his family had, allegedly, already cut him off.

This series of letters when combined with the 1895 anonymous letter allegedly presented by Horace Edalji to Vachell, the Defence barrister, gives the impression, at first glance, of providing the necessary credibility to indict George Edalji as the unknown scribe. However, having already pointed out the difficulty in accepting the version of how Horace came into possession of the 1895 letter, could

---

[292] Capt Anson to Simpson, 22 Dec 1903, HO 39 File 984

these pro-police and anti-George Edalji campaign letters have been written by Horace Edalji to scupper George's campaign. If Horace was the actual source of these revelations and acting independently from any other party, why did he send these 'open-heart' letters to Chris Hatton? Was it a sense of justice that encouraged him to put the finger on his brother? Was it a sense of Christian duty to expose his brother's sins? Was he the 'Abel' to George's 'Cain' unless it was vice versa and, as in a biblical precedent, Cain (Horace) metaphorically slaughtered Abel (George) for reasons known only to Cain. Horace Edalji, an employee of the Inland Revenue, working and living in Ludlow, Shropshire, was a relatively 'grey' insignificant figure, a bit player in the whole Edalji saga, who had been mentioned but once in passing during the previous fifteen years and never once in an anonymous letter when the other members of the Edalji family were subject to vile accusations and constantly being vilified.

These alleged revelations from a member of the Edalji family and, as such, not seemingly influenced by the Staffordshire chief constable, coincided with the police supremo attempting to debunk every prominent person associated with the Edalji campaign who, in one way or another criticised, challenged, accused or disagreed with Captain Anson. In these letters, Moore, Yelverton and Warner were the victims. It seems incredible that Horace Edalji, and earlier Harry Green, were prepared to pour out their hearts on extremely personal matters to people like Arrowsmith, who was paid by the police for services rendered, and Chris Hatton, who passed on Horace's *cris de ceour* to the police – highly fortuitous information passing to Captain Anson, who then relayed them to the Home Office at a time when the captain was trying to establish a defence for his actions.

What was also highly dubious, was the claim attributed to Horace of having discovered George to be the anonymous letter writer in 1892 after which the letters ceased, a claim already made by three other people. In the depositions prepared for the trial, Captain Anson, basing himself on the report produced by Sergeant Upton in December 1892, claimed that the letters stopped in 1892 after George Edalji was discovered to be the writer; a similar claim was also made by Mr W H Brookes, 'the sour-faced' grocer; as did James Morgan, the 'infidel'. In the not too distant future, an unknown correspondent residing in the South Staffordshire area would also make the same claim in a letter to a Birmingham newspaper. Interestingly, all these would-be saviours of Great Wyrley, who claimed to have curbed the pen or pencil of George Edalji, achieved this objective around the same time but none of the claimants ever took the trouble to explain why the anonymous letters continued to bombard the Edaljis for a further three years, a fact that Captain Anson knew only too well, after all it was he who sent out those dismissive letters to the Reverend and Mrs Edalji in late 1895.

(vii) The Anonymous Letters Re-commence:

The gradual development of the Edalji campaign and the malicious attempt by the Staffordshire constabulary to halt its progress triggered off another bout of anonymous letters. Between September and December 1903, the majority of these letters were signed by Captain W H Darby and brought threats to fire ricks, and "to slice up 10 wenches before Christmas and 10 after", to be carried out by a gang operating in the district. The police regarded them as red herrings because the handwriting was different to the July/August 1903 letters. One letter came from a 'Lover of Justice', which Captain Anson knew to be a hoax.[293] A few other letters came from a different source or sources. These letters: mentioned the "funny father and son sleeping in the same room – trying to take the guilt off one locked safe" (4th November 1903); accused Benton of killing his horse at the instigation of Reverend Edalji to clear George Edalji (12th September 1903, London); and claimed that Greatorex knew the identity of the maimer (5th November, J Smith). The author(s) also threatened to shoot Police Constable Weaver, do Will Kingston's horse next and identified Fred Wooton (Wootton) as unsuccessfully trying to maim Bungay's horse in May. A more illuminating letter was sent to Constable Weaver, on watch at the field on the night of the 17th August, but, according to the author, actually playing crib in the Wyrley engine house at the time of the deed. The writer also said he "owed that darkie a grudge, (as) he got me into a hell of a row once and I have not forgot him for it" – a reference, perhaps, to George Edalji's part in the Hart libel case in 1901; or to Elizabeth Foster in 1889; or to some local toughs, Joseph Gladwin and William Walker, who assaulted him in 1901; or to the daubings on the wall giving offence to Loxton in 1901.[294] Other letters with a touch of humour seeping into them were sent out offering advice although the 'comics' were no doubt serious about their suggestions for catching the maimer and the anonymous scribe. One contributor suggested that two men disguised themselves in animal hide, a ruse apparently employed successfully in Germany. Another writer

---

[293] The Darby letters were also hoaxes because 30 years later, they were found to have been sent by a serial letter writer, Enoch Knowles.
[294] CA 12 Dec 1903; BWP 3 Oct and 7 Nov 1903; HO Papers, File 990

suggested concealing officers in post boxes in the West Midlands area and when letters to Green or anyone else dropped into the box, the officer should leave the box to follow the mailer – a suggestion improving the employment prospects for police officers of extremely short stature and with laser-sharp eyesight. This last suggestion must surely top the list of hare-brained schemes, although another letter supplying motives for the maimings and containing prejudicial comments against a large number of groups of people came a close second.[295]

(viii)   The Home Office Response

The initial reaction of Home Office officials to the mounting pressure for and against Edalji was to contact Sir Reginald Hardy for his views. Sir Reginald's contribution came from the less than adequate notes he had taken during the trial and a more recent reappraisal of the case from memory. The results of his efforts, formal and informal, showed him to be an extremely naïve or imperceptive man, or inept in the magisterial task assigned to him or a man to whom dissembling came easy or inflicted with all of these faults.[296] Home Office officials described Sir Reginald's notes as of little use.

The prosecutor, Disturnal, was another whom the Home Office contacted and in an interview with officials, expressed his belief that Edalji was given a fair trial with ample evidence put to the jury to justify a conviction, although he did admit that the evidence regarding the footmarks and the blood stains was not worth much. However, as far as he was concerned, the evidence stood because Edalji offered no explanation as to how the blood got on his clothes, conveniently

---

[295] T Evans of Worcester to Jos Greensill, provided these motives: (i) spite – neighbour, discharged servants, Irish Land League labourers, unsuccessful farmer or businessmen; (ii) homicidal maniac – South African Yeoman lunatic, religious mania, enteric malaria; (iii) Hooliganism – Dick Turpin, gamblers, pigeon flyers etc; (iv) Anarchy – Walsall socialist, Liberal or Unionist free traders or protectionists; (v) Dishonest trade – horse dealers, slaughterers, butchers – illegal gain; (vi) Sect mania – Parsee, Jew, Moslem, Zulu – witchery. God of light symbolised in New Moon; (vii) Medical – vivisectionist, medical student, veterinary surgeon. 3 Oct 1903, File 989 Pt 1; See also, Dr H Strousberg to Staffordshire police, 14 Nov 1903; E J Gore, Yost of Coventry, 27 Oct 1903, both in File 989 Pt 1

[296] Sir Reg Hardy to HO, 18 Dec 1903, England, HO Case of George Edalji – memos and papers, Bp 2/4 (19) p3

overlooking that it was not Edalji's responsibility to establish the source of the bloodstains but for the prosecution to prove it came from the maimed animal, which it was unable to do as even its own analyst believed them to be human. Disturnal also agreed that other parts of the evidence were obscure – none more obscure, although Disturnal did not admit to it, than the evidence convicting Edalji of maiming the horse after 2.30 am without putting forward a shred of evidence to implicate Edalji in a crime committed after that time. Mr Brough's presence as adviser to the chair on technical points was acknowledged as irregular but Disturnal claimed this caused no injustice to Edalji. As a sop he pointed to Brough advising the bench to reject the admission of the anonymous letters, yet, conveniently omitted to inform the officials this was only a momentary rejection because the chair allowed the letters into evidence as soon as Brough left the court to deal with another case elsewhere. Disturnal was disingenuous about Edalji having a fair trial, considering he changed his argument regarding the time of the offence after the defence completed its final speech to the jury; had placed great stress on the significance of the inadmissible anonymous letters; and, without calling Green, used the Green maiming against Edalji by implying Green did it to assist a fellow gang member.[297]

Home Office officials accepted that the Edalji family had contested the assertion by the police of hair being on the coat, however, it was thought highly improbable for police officers, after their attention was expressly drawn to the absence of hair on the coat, to put them on afterwards – but they did not venture an opinion as to how the hairs actually ended up on the coat. They hit the nail on the head as to why the police had not been specific about the time of the maiming, albeit in reverse and perverse logic, namely, the police had left the question of time open so if Edalji established a satisfactory alibi from 10 pm to 5.30 am, they could fall back on the earlier time of 8 pm to 9.30 pm. In other words, if it were shown that Edalji could not have committed the crime at the actual time of the offence, the police would be able to concoct another story to get him convicted anyway.

The papers on the case, including the representations from Captain Anson, Sir Reginald Hardy, Disturnal and Edalji's petition were despatched to the Lord Chancellor for his views although Home Office officials had already made up their minds on what action to take – none.[298]

[297] Chalmers and Troupe interview with Disturnal, 21 Dec 1903, HO Paper 40a, England: HO Case of George Edalji – memos and papers, Bp 2/4 (19) pp3/4

[298] HO to Lord Chancellor, 23 Jan 1904, HO No 63, File 985

The Lord Chancellor placed little reliance on the evidence used to convict Edalji, recognising: the impossibility of determining the date of the bloodstains; the absence of casts or photographs of the footprints; the contradictory evidence of Inspector Campbell and Sergeant Parsons concerning the hairs on the razor; and the whole of the evidence covering the clothes, blood and hairs, footprints and weapons coming as it did from the police with no independent corroboration. He subjected many of the assumptions presented by the police and readily accepted by Sir Reginald Hardy and his colleagues at the Quarter Sessions to a vigorous critique.[299] He dismissed the interpretations made by the police of the contents of their conversations with Edalji prior to the maimings and described the questions Edalji put to the police as the type any ordinary person interested in the outrages might ask. He thought the prosecution's attempt to draw inferences from the smiles Edalji made during these conversations as rather childish and the remark "Is Harry Green watched" may have been merely "chaff" or an allusion to some current rumour. Nor did he attach any significance to Edalji saying he "didn't wear those clothes," since Inspector Campbell had just described the clothes with stains on them and a man generally knows which of his clothes were old or stained and which were not. Edalji's explanation for the hairs on his clothes was thought feeble but the Lord Chancellor doubted if any better explanation could be given. Nor could Edalji's remark "I am not surprised at this" made to a police officer in Birmingham be considered strange if it was remembered Edalji received anonymous letters about the outrages and had placed an advert in the papers to find the source of the rumours made about him.

The Lord Chancellor also thought a number of the points could be interpreted in two ways. The remark "Is this the only charge against me," could be that of a guilty man afraid in case other outrages might be brought against him, or merely the cautious remark of a solicitor who wished to know the utmost he had to face. The reason George Edalji gave for refusing bail, quoted prejudicially against him by the prosecutor, was thought not an unnatural thing for Edalji to say and do if he were innocent but it could also be explained to Edalji's detriment. When Edalji said "Where's your evidence, you've got no evidence", he might mean "I've been so very careful in my depositions I'm sure you can't have any evidence" or it might be the remark of an innocent man, a lawyer, who felt that there could not be anything to connect him with the crime. Similarly, Edalji's readiness to give an account of his

---

[299] Lord Chancellor's opinion, 30 Jan 1904, England: HO Case of George Edalji – memos and papers, Bp 2/4 (19) pp4/5,

movements might be the act of a guilty man anxious to establish his alibi or that of an innocent man eager to put himself in the clear. He detected prejudice against Edalji in the initial actions of the senior police officer, who, after the maiming was reported to him, proceeded immediately to the vicarage with a strong conviction of Edalji's guilt and removed his clothes, boots and some razors, while searching for a weapon. He rejected police accounts for the small amount of blood on Edalji's jacket, and thought the evidence of hairs on the coat was dubious because the police witness admitted that Edalji's father had disputed their existence, yet that same police witness did not investigate the objection in the presence of others. He held back from the logical step of accusing the police of fabricating the 'hairs' evidence and accepted that the police might have wished to keep the jacket undisturbed to retain the position of the hairs but still thought it unfortunate for the police officer not to go further to verify his initial observation. In the matter of the footprints, the court had placed reliance not upon *bona fide* evidence but upon a police officer's judgement – no plaster impressions, no photographs, no measurements, and considering the police description of the ground after raining all night, the Lord Chancellor found it impossible to conclude that the police evidence was at all satisfactory.

The accusation against Edalji of writing the anonymous letters to divert suspicion from himself on to some of the people mentioned in the letters was thought wildly improbable and the fact that one of these letters, the letter of the 15th July, had Edalji's name and address on it imperfectly erased by the writer reduced the accusation to an absurdity. The Lord Chancellor's assessment of the evidence had also reduced the conclusions already reached by Home Office officials to an absurdity because it was on the basis of these anonymous letters that the officials concluded Edalji was guilty.

The Lord Chancellor had no doubts that the Edalji family gave the police every assistance, affording them every facility in their search, acting quite openly and straightforwardly and not like people seeking to screen a guilty person or even knowing him to be guilty. The cleaning of the trousers, denied by Mrs Edalji, was more foolish than suspicious – the natural desire of a mother to remove evidence, and it in no way indicated she knew her son to be guilty. Sir Reginald Hardy also came under fire for not thinking of the effect on the jury of telling them "it was difficult to overestimate the importance of detecting the perpetrators, which had created a reign of terror in Great Wyrley, and disgraced the fair name of the county." Only one point was unfavourable to Edalji and that was Reverend Edalji's sudden recollection at the trial of his attack of lumbago not mentioned in his deposition; and the sleeping arrangements were thought to suggest the father knew he ought to keep his eye on his son. The Lord Chancellor obviously knew nothing of the long-term nature of the sleeping arrangements, nor did he seem to be aware of the police being even more guilty of introducing new 'recollections' at the trial stage that did not figure in their depositions nor at the police court.

The rigorous examination carried out by the Lord Chancellor and his observations were soundly in Edalji's favour – it stripped the prosecution's case to virtually nothing, yet, ambiguously, his recommendation leaned towards maintaining the *status quo*. His final comment was that the conviction was unsatisfactory but not so unsatisfactory for him to advise the Home Secretary to recommend a free pardon. The Lord Chancellor suggested, following a precedent set fifty years previously, trying Edalji on the second indictment of threatening to murder a police officer. In the case cited, R v Mellish and Douglas, 1851, Mellish was tried on a second indictment, acquitted and subsequently pardoned. The Lord Chancellor was offering the Home Office a way out without exposing the Staffordshire police and judiciary to ridicule.

With this 'Pontius Pilate' style of justice, the case went back to the Home Office, whose officials met other government law officers to deliberate on the Lord Chancellor's observations. With the overwhelming probability of a miscarriage of justice and a police conspiracy against Edalji, Home Office officials refused to travel the extra distance to formally accept that probability. They dismissed the opportunity to redress Edalji's grievance by claiming that even if police evidence was faked, the existence of the anonymous letters could not be explained away by assuming the police wrote them as this would reduce the theory of a police conspiracy to an absurdity. Not yet aware of Captain Anson's attempt to entrap Edalji through the 'Lover of Justice' letter, they ignored the possibility that the scribe might be someone other than the police but in collaboration with them. The inadmissible vehicle used to secure Edalji's conviction, namely, the anonymous letters, were accepted as being written by Edalji and also as admissible, therefore, enabling them to uphold the conviction as reliable. What was an equally incredible declaration was the opinion that the jury might not have been competent but an incompetent jury did not matter because its verdict matched the conclusions they (the officials) had arrived at. Highly questionable ways of running a judicial system – no need for a jury, incompetent or otherwise, merely refer cases to Home Office officials for judgement using inadmissible evidence![300] The law officers concurred with Home Office officials in agreeing that justice was done when Edalji was convicted and their unanimous opinion that no jury would consider the letter to Sergeant Robinson as a serious threat to murder him conveniently maintained the *status quo*.

The Attorney-General,[301] when rejecting the Lord Chancellor's suggestion for a trial on the second indictment, advised the officials that any such trial would revolve around the authorship of the anonymous letters and this evidence was inadmissible. However, this assessment can be challenged since although the letters were inadmissible for the maiming charge they could be admitted into evidence on the "threatening to kill" charge, or at least that particular letter could, as the threat was made in an anonymous letter, which the handwriting expert attributed to Edalji.[302] Assessing the trial evidence as weak, he, nevertheless, felt the circumstantial evidence pointed to Edalji unless the police officers and the police analyst deliberately perjured themselves, which he ruled out as a possibility. But why he ruled it out when it was known to those in the Home Office that the police were not averse to manufacturing evidence in cases like Edaljis can only be put down to the bureaucratic philosophy of 'protecting their own'.[303] The Attorney-General did recommend an inquiry into the circumstances that allowed Green to leave the country but, needless to say, this was not taken up by Home Office officials. The most the law officers could come up with was (i) to submit the anonymous letters to a fresh handwriting expert if a reliable expert could be found; (ii) to find out if Edalji had the opportunity to obtain paper with an Osborne and Son heading; and (iii) to contact Horace Edalji to make a statement as to his brother's connection with the previous anonymous letters, which even if true, like items (i) and (ii), had nothing to do with the case against

---

[300] HO Comment on Yelverton to HO, 9 Jan 1904, HO No 49, File 984; HO Note for DPP, 15 Jan 1904, HO No 63, File 985

[301] Points under Consideration by the Attorney-General, England: HO Case of George Edalji – memos and papers, Bp 2/4 (19) App V pp42-5

[302] PRPS, Memo for Consideration of Home Secr: In G E T Edalji (undated) HO No 127, File 985

[303] The Home Office comment was "It cannot be denied that if the police ever manufacture evidence, and the Home Office know that this has been done, this is exactly the case in which a zealous officer would be tempted to do so..." Summary of Depositions, 5 Dec 1903, HO No 21 File 984

Edalji.[304] In fact, Horace Edalji's alleged statements were looked on with considerable scepticism by the officers, who referred to them as "the gossip reaching the chief constable" and related only to previous years, having nothing to do with the present case.[305] Home Office officials, not keen to follow these particular avenues, not wanting to delve into the issues at all, apprehensive, perhaps, of what might come to the surface, did go some way to meeting these suggestions. Their initial attempt to get another handwriting expert was unsuccessful as the institutions approached for advice all used the services of Gurrin and the other experts mentioned were thought third rate. As to the second suggestion, the Home Office sought help from Captain Anson, hardly an objective source or disinterested party, to find out if Edalji had access to Osborne & Son envelopes. The captain dutifully reported back that Osborne & Son was a well known stationers in Birmingham supplying items to its customers in envelopes – which in reality meant that an innumerable amount of people had access to those envelopes. Taking every opportunity to let his prejudices ooze out, Captain Anson, without ever having secured a single item of substantive evidence, alleged that writing on envelopes or wrappers addressed to himself was an old trick of Edalji. Further extending his brief, the captain added that 'God-Satan' was the 'Good and Evil' of Persian theology put into other words – another *Ansonian* cultural gem whose origin is unknown.[306]

Captain Anson was also entrusted with the third task of finding if Horace Edalji was willing to make a statement and the captain was instructed to give an assurance to Horace that he was under no obligation to comply. Captain Anson, never in direct contact with Horace Edalji, was reluctant to take up this task arguing that any statement coming via himself "would be looked upon as suspicious by the Edalji party," but his alternative suggestion for Home Office officials to meet Horace was rejected on the grounds that if the officials interviewed him, they could hardly refuse to interview the dozen or so people Yelverton wanted to be given a voice.

The Home Office utilised the usual bureaucratic way of dealing with those problems reflecting on the integrity of the police and judiciary by referring them back to the police, the very body of people impugned by Edalji's petition. The subsequent decision of the Home

[304] Chalmers, Report of a meeting of the Home Secretary, Attorney-General, Solicitor-General, Lord Desart, England: HO Case of George Edalji – memos and papers, Bp 2/4 (19) pp5/6,
[305] Ibid p7
[306] Capt Anson to Simpson, Mar 1904, HO No 76 File 984

Office, relying on police evidence, was arrived at using the contents of a dossier withheld from Edalji and his representatives.[307] Its enquiries were naught but an empty farce with the prosecutor investigating the prosecutor's actions[308] and none of the claims made in these contributions saw the outside of Home Office circles for critical analysis except when Captain Anson occasionally and opportunistically chose to make them public. Justice also shrivelled at officialdom's touch.

In the following three years, the Edalji case occupied more and more of the time available to his supporters; to Captain Anson; and to Home Office officials; as well as drawing new participants into play. The more the issues were delved into the more questions were raised about Edalji's arrest, trial and conviction, which increasingly took on the appearance of a police 'fit-up', with serious doubts raised about the reliability of the conviction. In spite of the doubts and reservations surrounding the case, Home Office officials continued to maintain that Edalji was guilty. At the same time, the heat generated by Edalji's supporters took its toll on Captain Anson, who appeared to lose touch with reality as he concocted the most bizarre claims and irrationally attacked anyone daring to offer even the slightest doubt as to Edalji's guilt.

---

[307] Truth 16 Jan 1907
[308] CA 21 Oct 1905

Chapter XI

From the Farrington Affair to the 'Truth'

Home Office officials had accepted, or more accurately were disinclined to contest, the claim made by Captain Anson that the police had got its man and like 'true' bureaucrats were prepared to sit back and let the storm of discontent blow itself out. However, an increasing number of people in South Staffordshire did not share Captain Anson's confidence that the maimer was safely secreted away in one of His Majesty's prisons. Great Wyrley remained in a state of unease long after the Edalji conviction. One South Staffordshire newspaper, the Cannock Advertiser, noted that "Nothing in the history of crime in this county is on a parallel with these despicable deeds...the occurrences are still mysteries" and to confirm its doubts pointed to the large scale police presence consisting of one superintendent, one inspector and forty officers still searching the district for the perpetrator(s) where prior to the outrages only one constable was stationed there.[309] When any animal suffered any kind of injury the immediate response from the victim's owner, supported by local opinion, was to question whether or not it was the work of the maimer. The police often responded by refusing to provide the services of a publicly-financed veterinary surgeon to examine any maimed animal and, predictably, categorised all injuries as accidental, obviously not wishing to pursue any avenue that might eventually lead to the exoneration of George Edalji. However, the police could not fob off the owner or the local populace when two sheep belonging to Mrs Badger, who lost a horse a year before in similar circumstances, met their death on the 24th March 1904 and were discovered at 5.45 am the following morning by Sam Brough, an employee of Mrs Badger.

(i)   Farrington[310]

The veritable dynamic duo of South Staffordshire, Inspector Campbell and Police Constable Cooper, made a few enquiries, which led them to Great Wyrley Colliery at 2.30 pm to arrest a married

---

[309] CA 2 Jan 1904
[310] Details of the case came mainly from: CA 26 Mar, 2 & 9 April 1904; DT 23 Jan 1907; BWP 2 & 9 Apr 1904; Truth 23 Feb 1905

middle-aged miner, Thomas Farrington, a stall man at the colliery, with previous convictions for disorderly conduct. When they arrived at the colliery, the police claimed to have found Reverend Edalji 'hanging about'[311] but when this claim was brought to the reverend's attention years later he denied having been there when Farrington was arrested.

Captain Anson lost no time in reporting the latest maiming to the Home Office worried, no doubt, lest this maiming raised yet more doubts about Edalji's guilt. The captain need not have feared on this score since those in government circles were not prepared to come out into the open and broadcast the opinions expressed by legal experts attached to the Home Office, who were already having serious doubts about Edalji's guilt. Constantly in touch with Home Office officials, Captain Anson continued to prime the pump against Edalji by claiming that the latest maiming was Farrington's first attempt, seeking, as before in the Green and Stanley maimings, to isolate this maiming from previous offences. The captain played his card despite knowing of Farrington's presence in the vicinity of the first two maimings in the previous year and suspected of committing those maimings by the owners of those animals. Captain Anson informed the officials of the pending magistrates hearing, forecasting that Farrington would be committed to the Quarter Sessions rather than to the Assizes. He ingratiatingly asked if the Home Secretary had any views on the venue to be used – a view the captain promised would be given every attention by our magistrates (my emphasis). Not wishing to be drawn surreptitiously into Captain Anson's dubious orbit, Simpson, head of the criminal department at the Home Office, through whom he directed the offer, declined to express any opinion on the suitability of either the Assizes or the Quarter Sessions.[312] Captain Anson, as did Reverend Edalji during the education issue, exhibited a strong appetite for putting his head on the chopping block or it might be, in the captain's case, a form of arrogance derived from a feeling of 'class superiority', which

<hr>

[311] Capt Anson to HO, 12 Dec 1904, England: HO Case of George Edalji – memos and papers, Bp 2/4 (19) App IV p39

[312] Correspondence between Capt Anson and Simpson (HO) 25, 29, 30 & 31 Mar 1904, HO No 87 File 985; Simpson was to receive a severe mauling from a committee enquiring into the case of Adolf Beck for the role played by the Home Office in a serious miscarriage of justice publicly exposed in November 1904. According to one source, the severe criticism made against Simpson by the Beck Committee tended, over the years, to sour him. Scott, Sir H R [1959] Your Obedient Servant, Andre Deutsch, London, pp 61-2

left him oblivious to any errors on his part. Wasting no time in offering up less than credible conclusions for the maimings, Captain Anson threw into the melting pot the idea of Reverend Edalji being aware that the maiming was to be carried out and, scraping the pusillanimous and vindictive barrel, accused another of his protagonists, Yelverton, of course not to his face, of complicity in the maiming.

Unconvincingly, he sought to justify his accusation against Edalji's campaigner-in-chief by referring to a letter written by Yelverton, the day before the maiming, criticising the Staffordshire police for incompetence, which the captain rather ridiculously interpreted as being written in anticipation of the maiming. Another hypothesis put forward by the police, whose only spokesperson happened to be the chief constable, was of Farrington, who was one-eyed – a strike against him in Captain Anson's lexicon of criminal types based on physical appearance, being persuaded or bribed to commit the crime in order to counteract the cessation of outrages with the reverend providing the pieces of silver.[313] Little real thought lay behind these accusations because if Reverend Edalji had incited Farrington, bribed or otherwise, to maim animals, he would hardly turn up at the colliery to meet Farrington on the day the crime was discovered. If the reverend was in fact there, it was probably in the hope of hearing some form of admission from Farrington of committing the other maimings. Another alternative conjured up by the chief constable was of the maimings, now over a year old, being the work of more than one person with Edalji as one of the participants – a worn out hypothesis reflecting his own determination not to budge an inch on the Edalji conviction. Captain Anson's duplicity verged on the incredulous and every time he was put under pressure, in trying to squirm out of it, he merely dug a deeper pit in which to flounder.

Farrington was arraigned at the Cannock police court and remanded without bail. Two days later, the committal proceedings were held at Penkridge police court before Lord Hatherton and Mr Wolverson, making a lie of the claim, made several months earlier, that Lord Hatherton could not hear the Edalji case because of the interests he held in the locality. Mr Barnes was again called upon to prosecute and Mr Wilcock appeared for Farrington, who was committed for trial at the Quarter Sessions at Stafford, bailed at £20 with two sureties of £10, quite a contrast to the treatment meted out to George Edalji. Captain Anson's influence over the local magistrates, implied in his remarks to Home Office officials, appeared to be sustained as the plea

---

[313] Fidelitis, ex-Cannock resident, Woking, DT 23 Jan 1907

by Mr Wilcock for a committal to the Assizes was refused by the magistrates.

The case was heard within a week hardly giving time for an adequate defence to be prepared with Lord Hatherton in the chair. His lordship, who had committed Farrington for trial, was now to be the trial chairperson. Disturnal was the prosecutor and Mr B C Brough, *aide-de-camp* of Sir Reginald Hardy at the Edalji trial, represented Farrington, who entered a plea of not guilty. The evidence offered up by the prosecution and defence produced the following picture of events leading up to Farringon's arrest.

On the day of the maimings, Farrington spent time in a Cannock pub until 2 pm and then moved on to the Royal Exchange public house at Bridgtown drinking with a friend, Mr Hardy, until 8 pm or 8.30 pm. When leaving Hardy, Farrington mentioned some business he had to attend to and of his intention to go home afterwards. He was later seen at 9.10 pm in Badger's field by John Morgan, an old resident of the district, although at the police court Morgan was less specific about the time claiming to have seen Farrington climbing over a gate leading out of Badger's field between 8.45 and 9.15 pm. Sam Brough, the employee, who later found the dead sheep, said he left the field at 8.50 pm and the sheep were uninjured, therefore, if his claim was correct, Farrington had between no time at all to maim the sheep or up to 25 minutes to do so.

Farrington did not deny entering the field before going on to the Swan Inn, kept by Mr H Badger, arriving there at 9.30 pm and leaving in a sober condition at 10 pm. Interestingly, having allegedly slit the throats of two of Badger's sheep before going on to the pub nothing was said by the bar owners about any blood on Farrington's clothes – all Mr Badger said was that Farrington was an inoffensive man and seemed upset whereas Mrs Badger thought Farrington appeared not to be flurried. Farrington then went home but instead of going into his house chose to go into the outside water closet staying there until about 2 am before settling down in the pig sty where he lay until the 'bull' (siren) blew for work. When the bull sounded, he went into the house to change into his work clothes.

After being tipped off about Farrington, Police Constable Cooper went to Farrington's home to collect the clothing Farrington had worn the previous night. When the clothes were examined at 1 pm, the buttons on the trousers, minus a missing one, matched a trouser button stamped "our own make" discovered by Sergeant Parsons in the shed where the sheep were slaughtered. Farrington initially denied going to the field or that the button was his but when charged at the colliery allegedly said "All right. Well I can't help it." On the way to Great Wyrley police station, when passing Badger's field, Farrington referred to it as the field he had been in the night before and it happened to be the one where the shed stood in which the animals were maimed. Farrington allegedly commented that "This is a nice thing. Badger says someone has killed some of his sheep last night," but Sergeant Parsons warned him to "Be careful what you say you are in custody now" – if the caution was given, it was one lesson the police had learned from the Edalji case!

Some disagreement had arisen at the police court over the number of people involved in the killings. Mr Stokes, a local butcher, believed two men committed the crime since one man could not have held the sheep and struck at the same time. He offered the scenario of one of the sheep being killed by someone skilled in slaughtering and the other killed by an unskilled man – as if they had taken turns. He also thought it impossible for blood not to be found on the clothes, especially on those of an unskilled man. The prosecution challenged this evidence by calling Superintendent Bishop, a one-time apprentice butcher, who said the killings were the work of one unskilled man. Typical of the way evidence was weighed up in South Staffordshire – a one-time apprentice butcher versus a practising butcher. However, at the trial, the prosecution dispensed with the ex-butcher's apprentice-cum-senior police officer to call a veterinary surgeon, Mr Forsythe, another novel experience for the prosecution. Forsythe said it was the work of possibly one unskilled man, who killed the animals in an unscientific manner. Interesting to see how the police/prosecution showed no hesitation in calling a veterinary surgeon when his evidence was favourable to the police.

The police analyst, Dr Butter had found several strands of cloth on Farrington's trousers as did Forsythe, and also examined a coat, vest and boots, finding wool and excrement on the boots, which he believed was from the sheep. However, there was no mention of blood on the clothes. What the veterinary surgeon did not comment upon was the time of the maiming – a curious omission. All that was offered on the time was of a maiming committed sometime after 8.50 pm and when it began to snow between 11 pm and 12 midnight – a cut off point determined by the absence of footprints in the snow.

As for the forensic evidence: the button was from a type of trousers worn in their thousands in the district; the strands of wool were likely to have become attached to the clothes of anyone like Farrington in contact with shepherds or may even have come from the lamb kept as a pet in the Swan Inn; and the excreta found on Farrington's boots assumed to be from sheep was just as likely to have come from the floor of the pigsty where Farrington had slept that night.

The evidence against Farrington was circumstantial – what else, consisting of a trouser button, one in common use, found in the shed where the sheep were killed; some excrement on his trousers, not surprising since he slept in the pig pen that night; and some fibres of wool on his trousers, which was not entirely unusual for someone who might come into contact with sheep farmers in the many public houses frequented by Farrington.[314] Nor was there any apparent motive for the slaughter of this animal.

Lord Hatherton directed the jurors to be satisfied beyond a reasonable doubt of Farrington's guilt and unless they were he should be acquitted, quite a difference from the 'balance of probabilities' direction given by Sir Reginald Hardy in the Edalji case. The jury took 40 minutes to find Farrington guilty, slightly less than the jury took to convict Edalji, on the evidence of one trouser button in common usage, a bit of fluff and some excreta. In the absence of a plea for mercy by the jury, Farrington received a three-year sentence, less than half the punishment awarded to Edalji, who had a jury recommendation for leniency. The continuation of the maimings for several months after Edalji's arrest could only be reconciled with Edalji's guilt if he was a member of a gang but no evidence was ever provided in support of that hypothesis and if Farrington was also a gang member a connection would have to be shown between Farrington and Edalji – a ridiculous suggestion as pointed out by the 'Truth' magazine when it took up Edalji's case in early 1905.[315]

Captain Anson, expecting the Farrington case to provide fresh grounds for Edalji's supporters, was able to rely on aristocratic help on that score, in the personage of Lord Hatherton, who came to the aid of the Staffordshire Constabulary by asserting that Farrington's crime was different from the others previously tried[316] – a view conveniently shared by Captain Anson and Sir Reginald Hardy. Despite his lordship's comments, the Farrington affair, as had the Green and Stanley maimings, cast long shadows of doubt over Edalji's conviction. However, the news of another outrage and Farrington's conviction did not push the Home Office into reviewing Edalji's case and his petition for a pardon was rejected, accompanied by the belated action of the

---

[314] Capt Anson and Simpson (HO) 24 Mar 1904, HO No 87 File 985; CA 26 Mar, 2 & 9 Apr 1904
[315] Truth 23 Feb 1905
[316] CA 9 Apr 1904

Incorporated Law Society in striking Edalji off the solicitor's roll. George Edalji was not only in prison, he was serving a veritable life sentence as his career was in ashes.

Reverend Edalji, realism budding as his faith in English justice withered, came to the conclusion that a complete review of his son's case was not undertaken because the Staffordshire police would be disgraced. When on two occasions he wrote to the Home Secretary in May 1904 asking for details of any contribution made by the chief constable in response to George's petition, the Home Secretary let it be known that it was contrary to usual practice to disclose strictly confidential police reports sent to the Home Office.[317] The use of 'confidentially' to keep Captain Anson's communications under wraps was not confined solely to Home Office dealings with the reverend because nine months later when the Edalji issue was again brought into prominence, the Home Office extended its tentacles of bureaucratic manipulation into the House of Commons to thwart an attempt by Captain Norton, MP for Newington, to allow George Edalji's representatives to have access to all prosecution documents and reports sent to the Home Office.[318]

(ii) George Edalji's Eyes

Following Farrington's confinement, further evidence surfaced during 1904 to cast even greater doubts on Edalji being the maimer. The doubts centred on the state of George Edalji's vision. Although several requests for George's eyes to be tested were ignored by the Home Office, Edalji's sight impairment was taken into account by officials at Lewes gaol and, as a result, he was assigned to 'half tasks at cell labour', ironically, picking coir for horse nose bags. When transferred to Portland gaol, his eyes were tested as part of the medical examination given to each prisoner and found to be very seriously impaired.[319] On account of his astigmatism and myopia, he was not allowed to use the stairs and the prison doctor placed him in a medical ward.[320]

A proposal from the Lord Chief Justice, who was not without sympathy for Edalji, was acted upon and the Home Office despatched Major Clayton, Secretary to the Prison Committee, to ask Edalji if he

---

[317] Edalji, Rev S [1905] Miscarriage of Justice: The Case of George Edalji, United Press Association, London, p57;Times 2 Jun 1904
[318] Hansard, 21 Mar 1905, vol 143 col 650
[319] Medical Officer, Portland Prison to HO, 9 Mar 1904, HO No 98 File 985
[320] DT 15 Jan 1907

wanted any enquiries to be made on his behalf. Edalji requested an examination of his eyes and an inquiry into the possibility of Farrington committing the 1903 maimings.[321] The inquiry into the Farrington affair was a non-starter as far as the Home Office was concerned but Mr Akers-Douglas, the Home Secretary, agreed to an eye examination. The examination, of greater significance than the ones carried out at the prisons, was performed by Dr Riesen Russell, chief surgeon to the Metropolitan Police.[322] The results of the examination, never released on the grounds of confidentiality, confirmed Edalji's extreme short-sightedness and his abnormal difficulty in walking in the dark, especially on unfamiliar routes or if obstacles were in his path. However, Dr Russell thought that in places known to Edalji he should have no reason for not being able to find his way around.[323] As the route Edalji was alleged to have taken contained numerous obstacles and was unfamiliar to him, on this prognosis it would have been extremely unlikely, perhaps impossible, for him to successfully negotiate the route to the scene of the maiming and back to the vicarage especially on a storm-ridden night with numerous police on watch.

Dr Russell's findings exposed the metaphoric myopia suffered by Home Office officials, who, whilst recognising the implications of the specialist's findings, tried to minimise them by describing them as not sufficient to rule out Edalji as the maimer, yet this is exactly what the findings should have done if the officials had taken the trouble to consider the route Edalji would have had to take – a task undertaken two years later by Sir Arthur Conan Doyle. The officials manoeuvred around the findings by conjuring up the theory of Edalji having someone to keep watch, schoolboy accomplices acting as observers, consequently, his short-sightedness would not count as an impediment and as it was very dark it made no difference anyway.[324] These officials had completely overlooked the fact that it poured down with rain for most of the night and could it realistically be contemplated that anyone participating in a maiming would go on the mission with Edalji. The accomplice would have to lead Edalji past the police lines outside the vicarage, through police patrols and numerous obstacles *en route* before returning with him through these same police lines to the vicarage. Home Office officials gave little thought to the reality of the situation

---

[321] HO meeting with LCJ, 7 Nov 1904, HO No 102 File 985

[322] HO memo, 20 Dec 1904, HO No 105 File 985

[323] Riesen Russell's exam, 2 Feb 1905, HO No 109 File 985

[324] HO Comment, Mar 1904, HO No 98, File 985; HO Comment, 18 Dec 1903, HO No 35 File 984

and more to saving the reputation of the second son of the Earl of Lichfield.

The issue of Edalji's eyesight drove Captain Anson into some extremely banal and subjective reasoning. Throwing out scientific opinion in favour of the so-called lay opinion of some inhabitants of Great Wyrley, the captain offered his prognosis of Edalji not being short-sighted and able to see at night better than in the daytime. Digging into his memory, Captain Anson recounted that he noticed how, when it got dark in court, Edalji's eyes "came out with a strange sort of glow like a cat's eyes" and the captain adopted the unsupportable position of comparing his own physical condition with Edalji's in an attempt to show no miscarriage of justice occurred. Captain Anson, claiming to have eyesight as good most people, said that he would be surprised if Edalji was unable to see at night as well as himself (Anson) and, with even more blatant subjectivity, he reckoned the route to the scene of the maiming could be travelled almost blindfolded by anyone like Edalji, who had lived on the spot all his life. The captain went even further by suggesting that "no one could have done it more easily than the convict (Edalji) unless he has really some defect of vision."[325] As the then well-known ophthalmologist, Kenneth Scott, made known a couple of years later, it was illogically dogmatic to attribute the vision of one individual to another.[326] In the light of Captain Anson's ill-thought out contribution, which flew in the face of objective reasoning, could anyone take him really seriously. Apparently the Home Office did or gave the appearance of doing so.

(iii) Gurrin's 'Myopia' Under the Microscope[327]

Well away from the Edalji case but having important links with it, evidence pointing to Edalji's responsibility for writing the anonymous letters was seriously undermined by revelations surfacing from another miscarriage of justice case. A new scandal was brewing destined to

---

[325] Capt Anson to HO, 12 Dec 1904, England: HO Case of George Edalji – memos and papers, Bp 2/4 (19) App IV p40

[326] K Scott, DT 21 Jan 1907

[327] Report of the Committee of Inquiry into the case of Adolf Beck, PP 1905, Cd 2315 LXII; HO No 101 File 985; Gurrin to Inspector Kane, 18 July 1904 in The Strange Story of Adolf Beck, Stationery Office, 1999; Times 20 May, 28 June, 4 and 18 Aug 1904; CA 3 Sep 1904; Peller J, [1982] The Home Office 1848 – 1914: From Clerks to Bureaucrats, Heinemann, London.

bring the professional competence of Gurrin, the handwriting expert in the Edalji trial, into serious doubt when an innocent man went to prison as a result of Gurrin's negligent conclusions.

Almost thirty years before, in 1877, John Smith was imprisoned for robbing women of the "unfortunate class" by a series of confidence tricks. Just under twenty years later, in 1896, Smith committed similar crimes but it was Adolf Beck, in a case of mistaken identity, who was arrested for the offences. Gurrin was the handwriting specialist set the task of establishing if the handwriting in the 1896 letters, actually written by Smith, were in Beck's handwriting. Gurrin examined numerous letters, cheques, telegram forms and other documents actually written by Beck and compared them to letters sent to the women as part of the confidence trick. Gurrin had no doubt it was Beck's hand behind the pen performing the confidence tricks and he swore on oath that they were all written by the same hand. As a result, Beck was imprisoned for the offences.

Gurrin claimed that the characteristics of the writing were those of a Scandanavian, which Beck happened to be and of which Gurrin was fully aware before he carried out the analysis of Beck's handwriting. In April 1904, Beck was again arrested and found guilty for similar crimes again committed by Smith. However, shortly afterwards, John Smith, alias William Thomas, was apprehended committing further crimes and it came to light that he was guilty of all the offences. The factor that conclusively determined Beck's innocence was that Smith, who was Jewish, was examined in prison in 1879 and found to be circumcised whereas Beck, examined in 1898, was not. When this information was passed on to the Home Office in 1898, officials contacted the judge at the 1896 trial, Sir Forest Fulton, who, coincidentally, was the prosecutor in the original case against John Smith in 1877. The judge decided that there should be no interference with Beck's sentence. Home Office officials went along with the judge's suggestion, thereby, abdicating their responsibility to Beck and instead of taking action to pardon him chose not to redress an obvious miscarriage of justice on the grounds of maintaining good relations with the judiciary.

In July 1904, when the saga surrounding Beck became public knowledge and he was confronted with indisputable evidence of Beck's innocence, Gurrin made a declaration acknowledging he had erred in identifying Beck as the scribe. The declaration was, "I gave my evidence that to the best of my belief the handwriting in the incriminating documents of 1896 was Beck's. I have already admitted frankly I was wrong. I very deeply regret the error."

A commission set up to inquire into the trial of Adolf Beck, found

Gurrin to be seriously in error. Apparently, Sir Forest Fulton, at the 1896 Beck trial, despite ruling as inadmissible an alibi witness for Beck, did warn the jury against relying on handwriting evidence and at Beck's 1904 trial Judge Grantham instructed the jury to disregard the handwriting evidence altogether.

Gurrin had been prepared to see what he, and his employers, wanted to see when condemning Beck and there was no reason for his 'methodology' and motives to be any more skilful or honourable when applied to Edalji's handwriting but the tarnished Gurrin made no such admission that he may have erred when it came to Edalji. However, Home Office officials fully recognised a new difficulty had arisen in the case against Edalji now "that Gurrin should be so discredited by the mistake in the Beck case". Not surprisingly, they ducked the issues raised by the Beck handwriting fiasco and these 'difficulties' were accommodated by the claim that the jury in the Edalji trial had made a careful comparison of the handwriting evidence and anyone accustomed to studying handwriting would be convinced the letters were written by Edalji.[328] Yet another bureaucratic cop out by officials since they were now proposing, following the discrediting of the handwriting 'expert', that no expert opinion was necessary to conclude Edalji wrote the letters. These officials declined to explain how the jury 'made a careful comparison' since the jury was only out for fifty minutes, hardly sufficient time for twelve jurors to give careful consideration to the handwriting or to any of the other evidence for that matter.

The Edalji campaign took advantage of the opportunity presented by the discrediting of Gurrin and brought together Mrs Edalji, Adolf Beck and several other speakers on the same platform at a hall in London. Beck spoke of the injustices he had suffered and called for the creation of a Criminal Court of Appeal and a resolution was passed calling for a public inquiry into the prosecutions of George Edalji and ex-Constable Rolls.[329]

(iv) In Memoriam

---

[328] HO Comment, 24 Oct 1904, HO No 101, File 985

[329] CA 11 Feb 1905; William James Rolls, a constable in the Metropolitan Police, was sentenced to five years penal servitude for 'wilful and corrupt perjury after arresting a Mr Wheelerbreed for allegedly frequenting a place for the purpose of committing a felony.' The evidence against Rolls was thought to have grave discrepancies but Rolls was sentenced as a deterrent for others. Times 18 & 19 Sept, & 22 Oct 1902

While rallying calls were breathing life into the Edalji case close to the halls of power, back in Heath Hayes not far from Great Wyrley another possible, and less renown, victim of the 1888 anonymous letter writer, Elizabeth Foster, now Smith, breathed her last, dying on the 19th February 1905 at the early age of 34 years. Elizabeth Foster, too, considered a grave injustice had been done to her and on her deathbed asked her husband Arthur G Smith to clear her name. In the light of events over the previous eighteen months, she had intended doing something herself but was prevented by her illness and her ignorance of procedures. Mr Smith, with the help of several influential persons and the sympathy of many people in the area, intended to present a petition to the Home Secretary seeking to have the conviction set aside.[330] No record exists as to whether or not Mr Smith carried out his wife's dying wish. The feelings held by Elizabeth Foster/Smith of the events of 1888/9 raised a point of law later to be picked up and used by the Home Office. A statement made by a dying person is considered in law to be equivalent to a sworn oath and is admissible as hearsay evidence, therefore, considerable weight could be attached to it, although in itself it did not prove George Edalji's guilt of the offence for which she was convicted nor did it have any relevance to the maiming charge and conviction against him.

(V) 'Truth' Will Out

As Elizabeth Foster lay in her bed dying, the Edalji campaign, still milking the Gurrin debacle, had another important breakthrough when the campaigning weekly newspaper 'Truth', owned by the 'maverick' Member of Parliament, Labouchere, gave the Edalji case pride of place in weekly features for several editions.[331] The attention of Voules, the Editor of 'Truth', had been drawn to the Edalji case by someone unconnected with either the Edaljis or the police, who had initially believed Edalji to be guilty and the police free from blame but after making enquiries, his own researches dissipated his previous predispositions and drew him to the conclusion that Edalji had been wronged. Voules, initially reluctant to get involved because public interest in the case had evaporated, decided to give it a run, no doubt influenced by the revelations in the Beck case, and his intervention threw the case back into the public domain.

'Truth' parodied the image of Edalji, a lawyer, allegedly amusing

[330] CA 4 & 11 Mar 1905
[331] See Truth 12 Jan to 23 Mar 1905

himself by killing cattle and allied with a gang of ruffians, who were so bound together that they committed a fresh crime to get him off – an implausible scenario given that neither Edalji nor his family were popular and even Captain Anson had admitted that George Edalji had no real friends or associates. 'Truth', describing it as a more flagrant miscarriage of justice than the one delivered to Beck, provided an overview of the many discrepancies in the case, making the point that a conviction upon such evidence would have been impossible before a judge of the High Court. The decision of the prosecuting counsel not to call Green, although defensible by the rules of legal practice, was seen as a ploy for withholding evidence that would have thrown suspicion on another man confessing to a similar crime – a ploy not dissimilar to the one adopted by the prosecution during the Beck trial.

'Truth' located part of the problem in the prejudice directed against Reverend Edalji because of his nationality – racism in today's vocabulary, and in Captain Anson's prejudicial attitude towards George Edalji when promising him a "dose of penal servitude." 'Truth' attributed this prejudice to the spirit motivating the police investigation. There were a number of minor errors in 'Truth's' report, journalistic license, but that did not detract from the overall contribution it made to redress the injustice surrounding the conviction.

The thrust of the 'Truth' article had its effect on Captain Anson, who appeared to be seriously losing the plot, seeing in Labouchere a new enemy for him to debunk. However, Labouchere, wearing a hat of a decidedly different colour, did not share 'Truth' magazine's strong support for Edalji. Accepting the evidence against Edalji to be legally weak and the chair at the Quarter Sessions as not up to the mark, Labouchere still believed Edalji might be guilty and may well have been proven guilty if the local police had not put in questionable evidence. However, the maverick MP thought a stronger case could be made out against Reverend Edalji.[332]

Captain Anson, showing himself to be obsessed with the Edaljis especially George, paraded his malice as if it were a virtue by hunting among the wreckage of the police case to grab at any irrelevant debris to feed his prejudices. He was always ready to discredit George Edalji

[332] Labby (Labouchere) to Akers-Douglas, From Hotel Belle Vue, Caddenabia, 2 Sep 1905, HO No 134, File 986; Labouchere, described as an incorrigibly flippant raconteur, a Little Englander despite his Huguenot descent, was the model for George Elliot's 'Grandcourt'. Ecott T H S [1898] Personal Forces of the Period, Hurst and Blackett, London, pp18 and 190

at every opportunity and never as keen as when someone stepped forward to condemn the Edalji conviction as did 'Truth' magazine. Not merely satisfied with raking up the old issue of the bankruptcy proceedings taken against Edalji in 1903, which was resolved at the time, Captain Anson went as far as to accuse George Edalji of committing perjury when making out affidavits in relation to those proceedings. The captain, keen to pursue these old issues, offered to scour county court judgements to supply particulars of this perjury to enable Home Office officials to respond to the 'Truth' articles.[333] He also resurrected the dubious claim of George Edalji embezzling £200, adding, more in spite than for clarification, that Edalji had not a penny and was making nothing from his solicitor's practice. Introducing a 'psychological' analysis of George Edalji hating his father for being Black, the chief constable spuriously linked this pseudo-psychology with his statement on Edalji's finances to claim that in 1903 George Edalji was in such a desperate financial situation and not caring what happened to himself, may have wanted to bring disgrace on his father by committing serious offences.[334]

Captain Anson's proposed rummaging through Edalji's private life and the purpose behind it was not appreciated by Lord Desart, the Director of Public Prosecutions, who was asked to comment on the captain's proposal of dredging the county court judgements to find any 'dirt' on Edalji. An element of distaste can be detected in Lord Desart's comment to the Home Office, when he stated, "I fail to see how the allegations, if true, could have any bearing on Edalji's guilt or innocence and it seems very undesirable that the DPP, either on his own account or at the desire of the chief constable, should engage himself in looking for matters of prejudice against Edalji, if, as it seems to me, they have no bearing on the only matter which can be under consideration by the authorities."[335] Consequently, Captain Anson's determination to prejudice Edalji's campaign with unsavoury items sluiced out from his so-called informants was turned down out of hand by the DPP.[336]

With his obsession knowing few boundaries, the captain turned on Maud Edalji by accusing her of writing an anonymous letter posted in Stafford to the police in November 1903, containing the term, "Many thanks for what you have done for my brother', or words to that effect."

---

[333] Capt Anson to DPP, 6 Feb 1905, HO No 118, File 985
[334] Capt Anson to HO, 7 Mar 1905, File 989 Pt 1
[335] Lord Desart to HO, 7 Mar 1905, Ho No 118, File 985
[336] DPP to Capt Anson, ibid

The ground ploughed by the captain in order to attribute the letter to Maud Edalji was the term, 'my brother', and the fact that the Edalji family were alleged to be in Stafford visiting George Edalji in prison on the day it was posted. For Captain Anson, this letter threw light on the Edalji family's tendency for self-incrimination, and while claiming not to have bothered with it at the time, he decided in the light of the publication of the 'Truth' articles to find the time to compare Maud Edalji's signature, a specimen Captain Anson almost certainly obtained in 1892, with the 1903 anonymous letter, expressing his confidence that the letter would be found to be in her handwriting. Captain Anson's suspicion, to say the least, was unconvincing since it was based purely on the signature of a ten years old girl written eleven years before. The captain considered trying to confirm his suspicions of Maud Edalji by getting a sample of her handwriting by seeking the assistance of the allegedly ever acquiescent Chris Hatton in this venture.

Rather egocentrically, the captain thought the anonymous letter allegedly attributed to Maud was an attempt to annoy him and he suspected that some other letters sent to the police were written by her. However, he conceded that he only had her signature for comparison and, contrary to the earlier confidence expressed in the same letter, admitted to not being able to rely on that. This concession would lead any reasonable person to seriously question their own suspicions, yet not for Captain Anson, who confided to the Home Office that it was indifferent to him whether or not she wrote them. Considering that George Edalji was sentenced to seven years penal servitude on the basis of his alleged authorship of the anonymous letters, this senior officer's comments betrayed not only an irresponsible attitude but one steeped in prejudice if he suspected someone else of writing the letters but was not concerned whether his suspicions were true or not. Captain Anson had by now declared that he did not think George Edalji wrote the letters nor killed the horse, yet he stood firmly behind the prosecution of Edalji and worked hard to prevent him getting a free pardon. Perhaps his admitted indifference as to who was responsible told a lot about Captain Anson's attitude to the 'Hindoo' parson and his off-springs. Yet again, with this kind of reasoning could anyone really take Captain Anson seriously? Apparently, the Home Office continued to do so, or more accurately, continued to pay lip service to it.[337]

Captain Anson used the 'Truth' article to disclose the contents of the alleged Horace Edalji-Chris Hatton correspondence but was reluctant for the letters to be used officially. In fact, Horace Edalji's

[337] Capt Anson to HO, 7 Mar 1905, File 989 Pt 1

letters sent to the Home Office were copies typed up on the Staffordshire police's own typewriter, hardly conclusive of Horace Edalji writing any of them. The captain also admitted responsibility for the 'Lover of Justice' letter and, in trying to implicate George Edalji for allegedly copying some of the contents of the 'Lover of Justice' letter in the follow-up 'Greatorex' letter, claimed that no one in his (Anson's) office knew Loxton had written it, and the only people who could have seen the letter were those to whom it was shown by George Edalji. Captain Anson justified his accusations by expressions used in these two letters that were different to all the other letters but why would Edalji, if he had been the scribe of the other letters and knowing that the 'Lover of Justice' letter did not come from his own pen, write a letter immediately afterwards aping several key phrases and, in doing so, advertise himself as the scribe.

Captain Anson remained silent on other people who saw the letter, Loxton, Inspector Campbell and himself, who were equally in a position to copy the contents from the 'Lover of Justice' letter to the 'Greatorex' letter. It was more than likely that Anson and Loxton were involved in the 'Greatorex' letters in order to pin them on to Edalji. The Home Office accepted that a connection existed between the 'Lover of Justice' letter and the following 'Greatorex' letter and arrived at the conclusion that either George Edalji wrote it or the police took part in a conspiracy against Edalji. Captain Anson, whose memory appeared quite deficient at times, further condemned himself because, on the one hand, in trying to prove Edalji wrote the Greatorex letters he was claiming Edalji had no confidante and, on the other, was claiming that Edalji was in cahoots with a gang of accomplices conspiring to maim cattle; to write anonymous letters; and to 'gamble' in dubious financial ventures. Contradictions came easy to Captain Anson when trying to ensure the blame stayed fixed on Edalji.[338]

The 'Truth' article, by firmly locating the Edalji case in the public domain, pushed Home Office officials on to the defensive, and not altogether impressed with Captain Anson's performance, these officials sought a contribution from Scotland Yard. This was provided by a senior officer, MacNaughton, who believing the maimer was a sexual maniac, offered up the inspired observation, right out of Captain Anson's criminal directory, that if physiognomy accounted for anything, Edalji had the face of such an individual. The allegation against Edalji of writing letters to himself so he could discuss the case with the police was thought of a similar genre to the motives of Dr Neil

---

[338] Capt Anson to HO, 2 May 1907, and HO Comment, HO File 988

Cream, described by MacNaughton as a sexual maniac, who was hanged in 1892 for poisoning prostitutes.[339] This contribution, the best that the Yard could offer, was hardly likely to quell the concerns raised by the 'Truth' article.

The Home Office, smarting under the Beck Committee's criticisms found it necessary to have the issues raised by 'Truth' examined in an attempt to dismiss the possibility of a miscarriage of justice in the Edalji case. The Beck case and the 'Truth' articles had pushed Edalji's case back into the public limelight but this created additional reasons for obstructing any possible revelations of police, judicial and civil service incompetence. The Lord Chancellor's analysis was available but, despite its conclusion being favourable to the Home Office's position, it was hardly suitable for the Home Office's purpose because the contents had in fact demolished the police's case against George Edalji. To retrieve the situation, not for public consumption but for the enquiring minds of one or two Members of Parliament, a piece of creative writing was necessary. The person chosen to provide this was a clerk in the Home Office called Bettany, who entered the fray to defend the various interests under threat of exposure. Bettany's contribution was a complete whitewash of the police utilising much of the material from Captain Anson's initial response to the Edalji campaign in late 1903. Bettany went through the motions of examining a range of issues but in the course of his examination separated himself from reason and analytical ability. The Edalji case, like the Beck case and other miscarriages of justice, certainly brought out the worst in people.[340]

Culling from the grossly inadequate notes of Hardy, Bettany compared the anxiety of the police to catch the criminal with the greater anxiety of the Edalji family to protect one of its members, and there seemed little doubt to Bettany that the Edaljis had the stronger motive. This was a curious way of determining George Edalji's guilt based not on the evidence against him of which there was little of merit as the Lord Chancellor confirmed but on who was the most likely to lie about

---

[339] Dr Cream frequently wrote to prominent people accusing them of the murders and took the opportunity from police enquiries to discuss the case with the police. MacNaughton believed history repeated itself with Edalji. MacNaughton to Troupe, 18 Jan 1905, HO No 105, File 985

[340] Observation on articles in 'Truth', by Bettany, 9 May 1905, England: HO Case of George Edalji – memos and papers, Bp 2/5 (19)) App VII, pp 47 – 54, based on Anson's letters to the Home Office and the Home Secretary, 2 and 4 May 1905, HO No 124, File 985

the existence of hair on a coat Edalji could not have worn even if he had carried out the maiming. Bettany used the police depositions and the evidence at the police court but was highly selective in his choice. He dismissed George Edalji's movements from 8 pm to 9.30 pm as of no importance – an accurate assessment of irrelevant evidence but overlooked the fact that the whole of the prosecution's case was based on this presumption. Bettany rejected the insinuations against the police of putting hairs on the coat or deliberately packing the hide and the clothes together as not being supported by the depositions – as if he expected the police to make such an admission in those depositions. He claimed that if the police were culpable they would have had to place the hairs in the exact spots exhibiting a surprising level of intelligence – perhaps, but not a surprising level of duplicity for the police, since Home Office officials admitted that this particular practice of planting evidence was not without precedent amongst the nation's constabulary.[341] The kind of attitude residing amongst the police and Home Office officials was an example of what Edalji was up against and it made a mockery of British justice. Nor did Bettany question why it was necessary for the police surgeon, Dr Butter, to examine the jacket on two occasions, the 18th and 21st August 1903 respectively.

Reverend Edalji's failure to mention his attack of lumbago at the police court was picked upon but no mention was made of the police omitting evidence at the earlier hearing on which they later relied at the trial. He also claimed that Reverend Edalji was unable to remember if his son left the room during the night of the maiming but nowhere in any newspaper report, deposition or Hardy's trial notes was any reference made to the reverend saying he was unsure whether or not George Edalji went out of the room, the reverend was always reported as claiming George did not leave. Bettany discounted the significance of the sightseers in the immediate vicinity of the maiming, pointing out that Police Constable Cooper found tracks going to the field near the vicarage between 6.20 and 7am and pointed them out at 7 am to Inspector Campbell and Sergeant Parsons. This was wrong as Constable Cooper did not follow the tracks until his third visit at 4 pm[342] accompanied by Sergeant Parsons when the area had been contaminated both by sightseers and workers – and perhaps Mr Bettany was unfamiliar with workers starting work in the early hours of the day and

[341]HO Summary of deposition in Edalji's petition, 5 Dec 1903, HO No 21 File 984

[342] Depositions of Committal Proceedings App I: England, HO Case of George Edalji – memos and papers, Bp 2/4 (19) p14

actually walking to work!

Bettany accepted Captain Anson's description of Green being an untruthful person, yet did not doubt the veracity of Green's confession. He also accepted the captain's claim that Green, seeking compensation from the Government, maimed the horse for fear of being found out – a claim Captain Anson had already retracted as untrue but the captain changed his mind so often that Bettany could be excused for not keeping up with it. Another of Captain Anson's points readily accepted was his claim that the maiming was done so quickly there would be little trace of blood, ignoring both police evidence of the grass near the maiming being heavily blood stained and the view of a veterinary specialist.[343] Bettany threw out the evidence of Lewis, the veterinary surgeon, as to the type of weapon required to commit such a wound and accepted there was no watch on the vicarage on the 17/18th August ignoring the statements made in the depositions or the evidence at the police court, sources he was only too ready to quote concerning the evidence of the police surgeon and police officers on matters relating to the state of George Edalji's clothes.

Like so many other people, Bettany claimed to see a striking resemblance between the 1903 anonymous letters and George Edalji's handwriting, needlessly and opportunistically venturing as far back as the 1892 – 5 letters. Without any real knowledge of the issues surrounding the reverend's tenure at the vicarage, he came out in support of the police by accepting the chief constable's 'expertise' in handwriting and his unsubstantiated claims against George Edalji concerning events during 1892 – 5. Betttany also accepted Elizabeth Foster's innocence in 1888/9 due to the servant girl's protests at the time of her death but whilst her deathbed protest had strong evidential weight, that did not prove Edalji wrote those anonymous letters or any of the subsequent ones.

Bettany linked together what he described as several insignificant but recurring details about Captain Anson's conjectures and Horace Edalji's 'discovery' of his brother's involvement in the anonymous letters of 1892 – 5. He arrived at the conclusion that George Edalji was responsible for all the series of anonymous letters – a conclusion having nothing to do with the case at issue. Given Captain's Anson's manipulation of 'evidence' and Bettany's gullibility, it was little wonder Bettany concluded George Edalji possessed the ability to

---

[343] Capt Anson to HO, 22 Dec 1903, HO No 39 File 984; Ins Campbell, Original Depositions, 3/4 Sep 1903, HO File 990; Edward Sewell, MRCVS, sworn declaration, Despatch 14 Mar 1907

sustain a disguised hand and adapt his literary style to the character he represented in the letters. Yet Bettany, like others before and after him, failed to take into account that if the letters were so easily identifiable by a lay person then George Edalji could hardly have disguised his handwriting nor adapted his style. The straw-grasping exercise behind the Bettany-Anson hypothesis was illustrated by the assertion that "If a boy could imitate the handwriting of his nurse (sic – servant) at 12 years, it is not unreasonable to suppose that he was so proficient at 17 as to be able to simulate the writing of a man, while the writing of a schoolboy hand at 27 must have been mere child's play."

Bettany's 'examination' identified Edalji as both maimer and scribe since, to him, the two acts were on a par with each other – the same mental twist displaying itself in the extraordinary anonymous letters was also seen capable of committing the aimless maiming of cattle. This "blood lust or creation of sensation" was confirmed for Bettany by the Neil Cream case, which he claimed offered a remarkable parallel. To complete the round up of innuendo, distortion and 'Boy's Own'/'Penny Dreadful' speculation, was the allegation that the reverend's "extraordinary meekness and inaction…and his lame submission to the insinuations of the chief constable, (was) accounted for on the grounds of either pusillanimity or knowledge of his son's guilt." Captain Anson had obviously not shown nor mentioned to Bettany the protestations of George Edalji's innocence made by Reverend Edalji and, for that matter, Mrs Edalji, on many occasions between 1892 and 1895 and from 1903 onwards.

The fruits of Bettany's labours were as equally improbable as Captain Anson's submissions and looked to be straight out of the captain's exercise book. Bettany's appraisal was more an example of 'washing one's hands' rather than having the South Staffordshire police, the judiciary and Home Office bureaucrats getting their 'finger's burned' yet again. In protecting their own, Home Office officials arrived at the unsupportable conclusion, contrary to the view of most informed persons, that it was unfair to accuse the police of harbouring a bias against Edalji.

Bettany's contribution should be placed in the context of the repercussions arising from the revelations in the Beck case and what was described as the "undue proportion of the blame" directed at Home Office officials.[344] This defensive response from the Home Secretary, Akers-Douglas, did not alter the fact that the Beck Committee had

[344] Cabinet Paper by Akers-Douglas, 7 Dec 1904, CAB 37/73, 1904; Hansard, 21 Mar 1905, vol 143 cols 688-701

shown that not only was Gurrin's contribution worthless but also the Home Office had failed in its role as "the reviewing authority to detect the flaws and redress the wrong."[345]

Bettany's defence of those involved was in stark contrast to two other contributions, the one from the Lord Chief Justice and another carried out by an unnamed contributor probably associated with the Personal Rights Protection Society, an organisation comprising chiefly of barristers, sent to the Home Office in May 1905.[346] This unnamed researcher, who produced a comprehensive insight into the case, thought Edalji's defence counsel was inadequately prepared and had presented an equally inadequate case to the court. He argued that the two indictments against George Edalji should have been tried separately with the anonymous letters used in the charge of 'threatening to kill' but not for the maiming charge. In his view, the letters could only be admissible for the charge of maiming if they had amounted to a confession and the authorship proven but these letters contained neither confession nor any allusion to the particular outrage for which Edalji was charged. In fact, the allegations in the letters related to other outrages either previously committed or contemplated but not committed, showing the writer had no knowledge of any conspiracy to maim. The failure of Edalji's counsel to make this point and the wrongful admission of the letters on the maiming charge led to a grave injustice to Edalji because the letters contributed as much as anything to his conviction as confirmed by the prosecution's final summary and Sir Reginald Hardy's summing up. Overall, there was no evidence to connect Edalji with a single outrage prior to the 18th August outside of the allegations made by the letter writer who did not know all he pretended to know. The researcher held back from suggesting a police conspiracy to procure the conviction of an innocent man but recognised that the police held a preconceived view of Edalji being secretly addicted to anonymous letter writing.

There can be little doubt that the evidence collected by the police was distorted by these preconceptions, undoubtedly emanating from Captain Anson, who as early as 1892 developed an unfavourable opinion of Edalji and who again, following Yelverton's petition,

---

345 Report of the Committee of Inquiry into the case of Adolph Beck, PP 1905, Cd 2315 LXII

346 This undated report was filed at the PRO amongst documents dated May 1905. This analysis is unsigned but is likely to be the report from the PRPS, Memo for Consideration of Home Sec: In Re: G E T Edalji (undated) HO No 127, File 985

showed a strong and unreasoning animus towards Edalji, which would inevitably find its way to police officers engaged in preparing the case, especially when professionally interested in procuring a conviction.

Then out of the blue, against all expectations and despite deciding there were insufficient grounds for interfering in the sentence, the Home Secretary made a complete *volte face* by announcing that if George Edalji's conduct in prison remained good he would be released on license upon completion of three years, that is, in October 1906. The Home Office tried to dumb down Akers-Douglas about-turn by claiming it was not because the Home Secretary thought the sentence wrong.[347] However, the Home Secretary, coincidentally representing the constituency which housed the college where the Reverend Edalji studied thirty five years before, had independently arrived at the conclusion that the conviction was a bad one after seeing the Edalji trial papers.[348] No doubt influenced by the fall out from the Beck Committee's findings, the Home Secretary did not wish to 'rock the Home Office boat' by making this reason public. The reverend was not appeased by the announcement as he wanted his son to be released unconditionally and without delay, dismissing any notion that this concession had accomplished his objective of complete exoneration for his son.[349]

A bizarre story was discovered by the PRPS researcher. During the spate of anonymous letters descending on Great Wyrley in the first half of 1904, two letters connected with each other went to the vicarage. One sent to Reverend Edalji, on the 19th March 1904 postmarked Chiswick, purportedly written by a servant on behalf of her mistress, the other to Mrs Edalji, on the 10th June 1904 postmarked Brentford, signed 'Idena-de-le-Moyle', claiming to be the mistress referred to in the previous letter, giving her address as 19 Brook Road, South Brentford. The alleged purpose of the letters was to get George Edalji out of trouble; however, the Edaljis took no notice of them. Later enquiries discovered that in March and June 1904, Mr and Mrs Davey resided at the South Brentford address but subsequently moved to Chiswick. When Mrs Davey was contacted by the researcher she gave an extraordinary account. In June 1904, a young lady giving her name as 'Idena-de-le-Moyle' lived at 19 Brook Road for a few days as a lodger. She told Mrs Davey of the trouble she was in over her sweetheart, who was in prison. An elderly gentleman arrived in a

---

[347] See HO, 23 Aug and 2 Sep 1905, HO No 134, File 986
[348] E & S 16 Jan 1907
[349] Times 13 Oct 1905

221

carriage and took her away in tears. Afterwards, a gentleman with the complexion of a 'Hindoo' and a foreign accent, calling himself Hanson, inquired after her. On hearing she had left, he asked to use her room to write some letters. Mrs Davey saw no more of him until April 1905 when he went to her new address in Chiswick and asked to use the address to receive letters. She gave him a room without her husband's knowledge and he called there once or twice but never received any letters before finally disappearing. Significantly, the letter sent to Mrs Edalji in June 1904 bore a coronet and monogram with the printer's address, Henningham and Hollis, West London. On the 4th April 1905, a letter signed P S Hanson was sent to the printer from Mrs Davey's Chiswick address ordering 100 of these envelopes. The handwriting was the same as in the letter from Idena-de-le-Moyle to Mrs Edalji. The envelopes were of a type supplied to a titled lady many years before and for that reason Hanson's order was not fulfilled. Mrs Davey denied any knowledge of the Edalji family or the maiming case other than what was in the newspaper during the trial. However, Mr Davey suggested that his wife's mind was wandering as he could not support anything she said.

The researcher thought the letters sent to the Edaljis were curious but leaned in favour of the husband's explanation. He found it difficult to understand, assuming Mrs Davey suffered from delusions, why she would send letters to the Edaljis six and nine months after George Edalji's trial or why she ordered more envelopes. He answered his own question by suggesting this was proof of how anonymous letter writing was stimulated by particular circumstances and how letters circulating in and around Great Wyrley over the last sixteen years were inadequately dealt with at Edalji's trial.

All kinds of scenarios come to mind over this 'discovery' especially the use of the name Hanson (Anson), 'Hindoo' gentleman (Reverend Edalji), boyfriend in prison (George Edalji). However, the researcher probably hit the nail on the head by accepting that Mrs Davey might be responsible. Any other explanation would have to solve the riddle of how the letters to Mrs Edalji and to the envelope manufacturer were in the same handwriting – one written from Mrs Davey's Brentford address by 'Idena-de-le-Moyle', the other from the Chiswick address by Hanson, who for whatever reason had decided to track Mrs Davey to her new address merely to order more envelopes.

(vi) The Education Issue Re-emerges[350]

The struggle for justice appeared to stimulate an untapped source of energy in Reverend Edalji because he took on the National Board of Education when the education issues of the 1880s were resurrected by the Staffordshire County Council, in which some of the Edalji's protagonists were members, Lord Hatherton, as Chair; Sir Reginald Hardy, as Vice-Chair; and Mr Albert Stanley of the Miners' Federation.

The reverend made an application to use the Cheslyn Hay school premises as a higher education institution for moral and social improvement. However, the Staffordshire County Council decided to oppose this scheme using as its *raison d'etre* the need to satisfy the increasing demands for school accommodation. Interestingly, the local education authority had made no moves to remedy the deficiency in the provision of school accommodation until the reverend sought to make use of the premises. The council's decision to raise old but still unresolved issues 'coincided' with the reverend's campaign to free his son, during which the two leading lights on the Staffordshire County Council, Lord Hatherton and Sir Reginald Hardy, had been openly criticised. Therefore, a cynic might argue that the Council's response was an attempt to put additional pressure on Reverend Edalji at a time when the campaign for a pardon for George Edalji was gaining ground.

The council wanted Reverend Edalji to relinquish control of the school in Cheslyn Hay, which the UDSB had failed to achieve some 20 years before, and Lord Hatherton, with a vested pecuniary interest in the issue, played a significant role as an *eminence gris* acting as a go-between for the Staffordshire County Council in its dealings with the National Board of Education.

When the reverend went ahead and published his scheme in June

---

[350] Report of Public Inquiry, 16 Nov 1906, Attorney-General v Edalji, 1871-1909; Graham Balfour, 17 Jan 1908; Correspondence between Rev Edalji and the Board of Education, 20 Mar, 9 Jun, 5 & 15 Oct, 1, 5, 7, 8 & 10 Nov 1906; Yarde to Board of Education, July 1906; Rev Edalji, affidavit, 24 Feb 1908; Swinfen Eady, J to Attorney-General at the trial, in Report of Public Inquiry, 16 Nov 1906, Attorney-General v Edalji, 1871-1909; pp 2, 49, 56 and 58; G Blule, 13 Dec 1907; all in HO File TS 18/251

1906, objections came from Great Wyrley Parish Council;[351] the UDSB; the Local Education Authority (LEA); and Lord Hatherton - a formidable array of opponents. With so many objections, the Board of Education set up a public inquiry, which was boycotted by Reverend Edalji.

Mr Coore, of the Board of Education, not without some sympathy for Reverend Edalji but seeing him as a difficult man continually pursuing a policy of procrastination and evasion, assessed the reverend's motives as inspired by the belief he could frustrate the public inquiry rather than by a conviction that the LEA's proposal was bad. Another official applying a still enduring imperial ethnocentrism described the reverend as "an Oriental" and somewhat slippery, as "you never know when you have him." Another example of how the reverend's personal qualities and the racism of the era formed an unholy alliance.

The public inquiry, arranged for the 16th November 1906, shortly after George Edalji was released from prison, was attended chiefly by small traders, artisans and workmen. Although in favour of the public inquiry, Lord Hatherton, with three fingers in the pie, was unable to attend or chose not to do so.[352] There was a noticeable absence of Anglicans in the meeting because of Reverend Edalji's advice for them not to attend. The reverend was convinced that the board had made up its mind, a reflection of his previous dealings with the education authorities, and the inquiry was merely to rubber-stamp that decision but in refusing to attend, and advising his flock to do likewise, the reverend gave his opponents the opportunity to denounce his scheme unopposed. G Pearson, acting on behalf of Cheslyn Hay Parish Council, did just that, arguing that the reverend's proposals were likely to create disputes where none existed as religious feeling in Cheslyn Hay was weak. However, Pearson's opposition, as with Albert Stanley's, should

[351] The motive of the Great Wyrley ratepayers was financial as the rate contribution from Great Wyrley was considerably higher than Cheslyn Hay. Cheslyn Hay's rateable value was £8900 and Great Wyrley's £14944. Cheslyn Hay was a small industrial village employing a considerable portion of the population from outside the parish, whereas Great Wyrley's population was largely scattered and involved in agriculture. Source: Graham Balfour, Director of Education, Staffordshire LEA, 17 May 1907, Attorney-General v Reverend Edalji in HO File TS 18/251

[352] Lord Hatherton's three stakes in the issue were as: (i) as Chair of the Staffordshire County Council and ex-officio member of Education Committee (ii) a resident in that part of the county and (iii) son of the donor with an interest in the reversion.

be assessed in relation to their membership of the Methodist New Connexion, neither likely to favour the re-opening of an Anglican institute by an Anglican minister not disposed to non-conformism. One member of the reverend's congregation breaking ranks to attend, Mr Brookes, continuing to exhibit his deep rooted antagonism towards the reverend, accused Mr Edalji of not being reliable, noticeably not referring to him as Reverend – a social nomenclature also employed by Captain Anson when referring to Reverend Edalji.

The audience was unanimous in its opposition to the reverend's proposals, which Mr Coore interpreted as being representative of the local population, another exaggerated claim as the audience was comprised primarily of dissenters, a point acknowledged later when the organisers were criticised for not attempting to feel out the opinion of the Church of England members.

The board of education, having its own agenda for the school, was concerned about the school property reverting to Lord Hatherton, whilst His Lordship, oblivious to the game the education authorities were playing, seemed keen for Reverend Edalji to be taken to court although not prepared to take any active part himself. To enhance its case, the board of education tampered with Pearson's sworn affidavit, produced for a Court of Chancery hearing, by inserting into paragraphs left blank by Pearson the erroneous claims that: (i) Pearson had canvassed the opinions of the poor and had reflected their views; and (ii) the attendance at the public inquiry was large and representative. The reverend appeared to be as vulnerable as was George Edalji in another arena to those who fabricated evidence to further their cause and, like his son, fell victim to it by eventually losing the case in 1909.

Chapter XII

Picking Up the Gauntlet

George Edalji took leave of His Majesty's prison service on the 19th October 1906 with a gratuity of £2/9/10d (£2.49p) in his pocket and a requirement to report to the police every month by letter until the expiry of his sentence a further four years hence. Upon release from Pentonville prison, he went straight to a London branch of the Church Army,[353] to be met by his mother before beating a hasty retreat to his mother's lodgings in London to avoid being cornered by the national press. The authorities misled the public into thinking Edalji's release would be from Stafford gaol to prevent crowds gathering at Pentonville and so avert any demonstration of popular support for Edalji as well as denying the press the opportunity to champion his cause. This was one Home Office decision welcomed by the Edaljis, who wanted George not to be put under pressure by well-wishers or the press until ready to pick up the gauntlet in his own time.

During the previous three years, Edalji spent three weeks at Stafford gaol, nine months at Lewes prison as a 'Star class' inmate and two years and two months at Portland prison, remaining there until two days before his release. Edalji's transfer from Stafford gaol in 1903 was put down to the influence of his representatives, who wanted to get him away from the area but it was more likely a precaution by the prison authorities to move him away from the incipient 'Free Edalji' movement. Mrs Edalji and her sister, Miss Stoneham, occasionally visited him at Portland, rewarded for their long sojourn from the Midlands with a twenty minutes visit. The reverend never made the trip but received regular letters from his son. [354]

When George Edalji eventually made a statement to the press he made no complaints about Portland Prison, in fact, he spoke of the prison officials as "kindness itself," unlike the severe regime experienced at Lewes.[355] Edalji's praise of prison officials brought out a brand of scornful humour, or pettiness, which occasionally shone through the less than humane darkened corridors of Whitehall. One Home Office official, responding to Edalji's remarks, said that his

---

[353] Mrs C Edalji to HO, 17 Sep 1906, HO No 156 File 986

[354] Mrs C Edalji to Voules, 18 Aug 1905, HO No 134 File 986; Gazette 5 Oct 1906

[355] DC 20 Oct 1906; BWP 27 Oct 1906

praise "might be useful if it were necessary to advertise for voluntary inmates."[356] Indifference, duplicity and now sarcasm were Home Office substitutes for concern for justice.

Shortly before leaving Portland, Edalji, eager to fight for complete exoneration, wrote to his father outlining his programme for proving his innocence: (i) publish a pamphlet on the case; (ii) enlist the support of the public; and (iii) return to Great Wyrley. To Reverend Edalji, who had already made a contribution in a book about the case,[357] the issue was not just about George but embraced a wider concept - public liberty and justice, the particular had become the general, so often the case when individual circumstances are transformed into an understanding of the wider socio-political milieu. However, to one Birmingham newspaper, the Birmingham Gazette and Express, the reverend's determination to pursue his son's case was situated within the experiences of colonial subjects confronted with the reality of so-called British imperial protectiveness. The paper described Reverend Edalji as one of those "natives of the Far East" who were taught that English "law can do no wrong", but when the law inflicted an unjustified personal blow asked "What of your boasted fairness?"[358]

Apprehensive for the safety of his son as long as Captain Anson remained chief constable, Reverend Edalji, instead of encouraging George to return to Great Wyrley as was George's intention, provided funds for him to remain in lodgings in London.[359] George did make a brief visit to Great Wyrley on the 22nd October accompanied by a legal friend and stayed there for a few hours before returning to London where he intended to remain for about six months.[360] In fact, apart from attending his father's funeral in 1918, George Edalji never went back to Great Wyrley again. Captain Anson, whose racism was so easily perceived by his remarks way back in 1889 when he queried the presence of the 'Hindoo' Parson in a working class area of South Staffordshire, had, albeit 18 years later, achieved partial success in resolving the inference behind his earlier question, that is, to deal with the unexpected and undesired presence of the Edaljis in the area by seeking their removal.

Trying to tie up loose ends, George Edalji followed three

---

[356] HO official's comment, HO No 158 File 986

[357] Rev S Edalji, Miscarriage of Justice: The Case of George Edalji, 1905, United Press Association, London

[358] Gazette 5 Oct 1906

[359] M Edalji to the Home Secretary, 8 Feb 1956, HO File 45/24635

[360] Gazette 10 Jan 1907

suggestions put to him by Mr Voules, the editor of 'Truth' magazine and an Edalji campaigner. Firstly, he despatched a letter to Captain Anson seeking permission to photograph the anonymous letters held by the Staffordshire police. After receiving approval he travelled to Stafford with a photographer to accomplish his objective.[361] Secondly, having had plenty of time to mull over the evidence while serving his time and with copies of some of the letters now in his possession, George noted that the author of the 7th July 'Greatorex' letter mentioned the Stanley and Quibell boys and in the following letter of the 10th July, referred to the police going to see Stanley and Quibell, indicating that he knew the police had called on the Stanley's and Quibell's between the 7th and 10th July 1903. Wanting to know the details of the visit, Edalji wrote to Albert Stanley, now MP for Staffordshire North West and a member of the Staffordshire Joint Standing Committee that had come out strongly in support of the chief constable, asking if the police had called about the anonymous letters and if he knew how the author of the subsequent 'Greatorex' letter came to be aware of the visit. Edalji believed that Stanley senior may have put the poison down for him (Edalji) during that visit. Stanley, well versed in the bureaucratic tradition, declined to give out any information on the matter and handed Edalji's letter to Captain Anson. Apparently, Stanley was none too happy about this letter and told the Captain that if Edalji came within arms length he would not be able to keep his hands off him, prompting Captain Anson, when reporting this incident to the Home Office, to say that he wished Stanley could be afforded that chance – another example of Captain Anson's petty, spiteful, prep' school attitude.[362] Local figures like Stanley in 1906, Brookes in 1892 and 1903 and J T Hatton in 1903 expressed their prejudice towards the Edaljis in the vindictive manner they displayed towards George Edalji, whose own politeness was well known. Thirdly, Edalji's eyesight was tested by two specialists, Sir W Collins, who was unaware of Edalji's identity, and T J Bokenham, who knew of George's background. Both specialists arrived at the same conclusions, namely, Edalji's myopia was such that without the use of glasses, which he never wore, he would find it difficult to see clearly any objects more than a few feet off. Another specialist, Phillip Brooks, thought it improbable for George to be able to carry out such a risky venture as cattle maiming. Another stated George would be unable to distinguish

---

[361] Truth 30 Jan 1907
[362] G Edalji and A Stanley correspondence, 23 and 27 Nov 1906, in Capt Anson to Simpson, 24 Jan 1907, HO File 989 Pt 2

between a bush, a haystack or a pony beyond a distance of a few yards. Yet another believed it would be "impossible for him or anyone else in similar circumstances, to have raced so quickly across an intricate piece of country in order to commit the crime even in broadest daylight, and practically impossible after dark." Nor was there any mileage in anyone arguing that Edalji's eyesight in 1906 was different to 1903 since no evidence of progressive myopia causing any deterioration was observable. Of eleven opthalmic surgeons assessing the potential success of someone with George Edalji's eye condition overcoming the difficulties raised by the terrain, six thought it impossible, three thought it presented great difficulty, one thought it highly improbable and only one thought it possible.[363]

As with its own specialist's report, the Home Office threw cold water on the views of these opthalmists by dismissing them in a cavalier manner,[364] and placing reliance on alternative viewpoints of a general rather than a particular character in relation to the crime. One such alternative contributor argued that Edalji's sight defect lent no support to his innocence because even with a high degree of myopia and without using glasses, Edalji may have learned to guide himself around the area and darkness would make no difference. The example he used to support his hypothesis was of blind men daily travelling backwards and forwards to a school for the blind in Birmingham without hindrance.[365] However, this example performed every day was a far cry from the one off journey George Edalji would have had to make in atrocious weather conditions. Another contributor thought that if Edalji was wearing glasses, he would be in a better position than a man with natural sight,[366] obviously unaware that Edalji did not wear glasses as none were any use to him, which even the police knew,[367] and glasses would be of little assistance to Edalji when it was pouring down with rain as it was on the night of the maiming.

Despite the Home Office trying to dampen things down, changes

---

[363] Truth 16 Jan 1907; K Scott, DT 21 Jan 1907; Courlander, DT 15 Jan 1907; DT 11 Jan 1907; ACD to HO, 25 Jan 1907, HO File 989 Pt 1; ACD to HO, 8 Jan 1907, HO No 165 File 986

[364] HO Comment, 28 Dec 1906, HO No 165 File 986

[365] Priestley Smith, Professor of Opthalmology at Birmingham Un and President of the Opthalmologist Society to HO, 2 Feb 1907, HO No 175 File 986

[366] S Stevenson, Editor of Opthalmoscope to Medical Press and Circular, 14 Jan 1907, HO File 988

[367] DT 15 Jan 1907; Capt Anson to ACD, 28 Dec 1906, HO File 989 Pt 2

were beginning to take place and would soon alter in a most dramatic and dynamic way. Mr Yelverton, since October 1903, and Mr Voules, since January 1905, the leading lights in the campaign to redress this miscarriage of justice, were soon to be joined by Sir Arthur Conan Doyle, who brought with him his skill as a publicist. Conan Doyle's entrance on to the stage followed on from an approach made by George Edalji, an admirer of Sherlock Holmes detective novels, who sent the crime fiction author some press cuttings on his case published in the 'Umpire' newspaper.[368] Edalji's decision to contact Conan Doyle was a pointer in the direction of innocence because if he was not innocent would he seek a wholesale investigation of the case by Conan Doyle, to whom Edalji attributed considerable skills as a great detective having read his books while in prison? Would Edalji also have kept the issue alive for two-thirds of the rest of his life and urge others to do so if he was not innocent?

After acquainting himself with some of the background details, Conan Doyle arranged to meet Edalji at the Grand Hotel, Charing Cross. On first impressions Doyle thought Edalji to be an unlikely suspect for a maiming. As a qualified oculist, Doyle doubted the possibility of Edalji committing the crime after observing Edalji, without his knowledge, holding a newspaper askant and reading it close to his eyes, which indicated a high degree of myopia with a marked astigmatism. Observing Edalji's physical condition, which gave him a vacant bulged eyed, staring appearance, which together with his dark skin, must have made him appear a very strange man to an English villager, Doyle claimed to have identified a reason for Edalji becoming the scapegoat for a maiming because any strange event would likely to be associated with him. Unknown to Conan Doyle at the time, he had succeeded in placing Edalji's 'unusual appearance' within Captain Anson's 'Lombroso' manual where particular physical characteristics equated with criminal tendencies.

After subjecting Edalji to a bout of searching questioning, Doyle's interest was aroused and he meticulously examined every available record and document dealing with the case and other related matters. He then contacted Captain Anson to arrange a visit, following this up with another letter expressing an interest in writing an account of the case

---

[368] Despatch 12 Jan 1907; Conan Doyle claimed in 1924 to have come across the Edalji case while reading the 'Umpire' but in 1907 Doyle mentioned Edalji had written to him enclosing details of the case. Doyle, Sir Arthur Conan [1924] Memories and Adventures, Hodder & Stoughton, London, p216

dealing with facts not introduced at the trial. He also mentioned a certain uneasiness about the verdict, which the public might need to be assured was just and proper.[369] When Conan Doyle penned his second letter to the captain, having completed a detailed examination of the evidence, he had already made up his mind. He wrote to the Home Office on the same day seeking justice for Edalji and criticising the officials and the police for perpetrating "such an incredibly stupid injustice."[370] Conan Doyle was also in contact with Reverend Edalji arranging to meet him and any resident who might want to clarify points of evidence given at the trial. He also intended visiting the field where the maiming took place.

The chief constable upon receiving Conan Doyle's initial communication, his vanity no doubt massaged by "what Sherlock Holmes might have to say about a real life case" [371] and in embracing a new ally, offered Doyle every assistance in writing an account of the end of the Edalji case.[372] (Anson's emphasis) As an indication of how he would deal with Doyle, Captain Anson made an *aide memoire* of three points written down on the letter Doyle sent to him – a portent of how the captain would try to use Doyle's interest to discredit the Edalji family. The first point (a) merely mentioned the captain's willingness to look up any particular point raised by Doyle. It was the other two points that showed his real intent, which was to tell Doyle about (b) the "Lying of Reverend Edalji in the witness box (that) no doubt influenced the jury against him" and (c) that "He had his son to sleep with him."[373]

Captain Anson offered Doyle "any amount of information for your own satisfaction if it would go no further than yourself"[374] (Anson's emphasis) and he assured Doyle that the public had no need of reassurance about the verdict. Perhaps the captain saw Doyle's visit as an opportunity in the midst of considerable campaigning by Yelverton, who had the gall to question his veracity and competence, to have the world famous author putting to the sword all those supporters of the re-emergent Edalji 'party'. Captain Anson's self-centred vision of the world seemed to cushion him from any fear of Conan Doyle finding anything remiss and, ever the gentleman to people of note, offered Doyle the hospitality of his home during his visit, suggesting the 4th or

369 ACD to Capt Anson 24 Nov and 21 Dec 1906, HO File 989 Pt 2
370 ACD to HO 21 Dec 1906, HO File 989 Pt 2
371 Expressed in Capt Anson to ACD 28 Dec 1906, HO File 989 Pt 2
372 Capt Anson to ACD 22 Dec 1906, HO File 989 Pt 2
373 Written on ACD to Capt Anson 24 Nov 1906, HO File 989 Pt 2
374 Capt Anson to ACD 22 Dec 1906, HO File 989 Pt 2

5th January. Captain Anson was heading for a rude awakening where his crude intrigues were outdone by Conan Doyle's own scheming, which laid the foundation for bitter acrimony between the two men lasting for many years. The Staffordshire spin doctor was outwitted by the weaver of detective fiction.

Under the pretext of providing some confidential information not for publication but merely given to satisfy Doyle about the case,[375] Captain Anson wasted no time in smearing the Edaljis as the second and third point of his *aide memoire* clearly signified, especially as the third point, in essence, should have provided an alibi for George. However, it was quite obvious that the captain did not intend to use it as such because that would help Edalji. This 'not for publication information,' as Doyle's later responses made clear, contained an accusation of sodomy involving the Reverend and George Edalji. The captain's choice of words included "The father had his son to sleep in his room for many years with the door locked. That is not disputed. The reason had not been given."[376] Doyle queried the meaning behind this comment although he was not unaware of the implications arising from the wording as he had been informed of rumours of sodomy circulating in the area after Edalji's conviction. Captain Anson responded immediately to explain that the father had good reason to keep his eye on his son and he revealed that the reverend "had the boy to sleep with him" in 1895 adding "I presume he had good reason."[377] Doyle was under no illusions as to the meaning behind the captain's reference to the Edalji's sleeping arrangements and raised it with the Home Office a couple of weeks later.[378]

Captain Anson had set the pattern for the type of information Doyle was to receive 'for his ears only' and he sought to debunk another pillar in Doyle's argument, although the captain had overlooked Doyle's expertise as an opthalmist. The captain claimed that the Home Office specialist who examined Edalji's eyes found nothing particularly wrong with them and he (Anson) was in no doubt of Edalji's ability to find his way blindfolded to the scene of the crime. Of course, unlike Conan Doyle, the captain was completely unaware of the examinations

---

[375] Correspondence between Capt Anson and ACD 25 to 28 Dec 1906, HO File 989 Pt 2

[376] Capt Anson to ACD 25 Dec 1906, quoted in Blackwell to ACD 27 Mar 1907, HO File 989 Pt 1

[377] Correspondence between ACD and Capt Anson 27 & 28 Dec 1906, HO File 989 Pt 2

[378] See Chapter XIII section iv

carried out by two opthalmic surgeons on Edalji's eyes, within the previous two months, which had produced results decidedly in Edalji's favour. The chief constable went into the 'annoyances' caused by George Edalji in the 1890s and of his warnings to Reverend Edalji in 1895 about his son's culpability. Surprisingly, the revelations bearing upon George Edalji's guilt allegedly coming from Horace Edalji to Captain Anson via Chris Hatton, Police Constable Cooper, Inspector Campbell and Superintendent Barrett were never disclosed to Conan Doyle. This omission, given the captain's determination to crush George Edalji and the Edalji campaign, placed some doubt on the veracity of the alleged exposé leaked by Chris Hatton. Perhaps, the captain's omission was due to the likelihood of Conan Doyle approaching both Horace Edalji and Chris Hatton personally for confirmation of their conversations.

Doyle travelled incognito to Great Wyrley on the 3rd January 1907 and met several residents and then went on to see Captain Anson. He assessed Captain Anson's written and oral account and examined the information provided by Reverend Edalji and Great Wyrley residents in the light of his own documentary research and more than tentative conclusions. He acknowledged having being confronted with a number of issues that placed questions marks against Edalji's innocence but when he had followed up the queries, the answers he discovered established that Edalji was the victim of a grave miscarriage of justice. He was not slow to recognise the difficulties in getting the case reopened in the absence of a Criminal Court of Appeal but if he could encourage the authorities to give proper consideration to the evidence it might lead to an acquittal and Edalji's restoration to his profession.

Doyle saw the setting up of a tribunal to examine the evidence and the way the police carried out the investigation as a way forward.[379] With this in mind, he got in touch with the Home Office, referring to his enquiries and the proposed article he intended to publish on the case. He received the standard Home Office reply, used so often that it must have been indelibly pre-printed on its stationery albeit with a few stylistic variations. The Home Office noted that an enquiry had already been carried out, which cast no doubts on the jury's verdict, and as Edalji was now a free man the case was at an end. This 'enquiry' must have been the Home Office's response to the 'Truth' articles where Bettany's observations had resembled a handout from Captain Anson and Sir Reginald Hardy, and not the Lord Chancellor's appraisal that had cast considerable doubts on all aspects of the evidence presented at the trial.

---

[379] Gazette 10 & 14 Jan 1907; ACD to HO, 7 Feb 1907, HO File 989 Pt 1

Despite the bureaucratic brush off, Conan Doyle's criticism of the officials and the police for their part in an "incredibly stupid injustice," raised fears amongst Home Office officials that "hot agitation will be stirred up over the case" and in an attempt to avert this Doyle was invited into the inner sanctum of the Home Office to discuss the case.[380] In fact, the Permanent Under-Secretary of State to the Home Secretary, Sir Mackenzie Chalmers, wrote to the previous Home Secretary, Akers-Douglas and Lord Dunedin, the Lord Advocate, seeking their assistance in order to strengthen the Home Office's position in the light of the forthcoming articles to be written by Conan Doyle in what was described as the 'Sherlock Holmes' style. Although recognising some unsatisfactory features of the case, the Home Office wanted to be able to say with Akers-Douglas' and Lord Dunedin's support that there were no grounds for interfering with the verdict.[381]

Being told by Home Office officials that the matter was closed made little impression on Doyle, who had every intention of securing access to the "tribunal that never errs", the Great British public, by using the Daily Telegraph, whose editor had agreed to publish an article containing the results of Doyle's enquiry into the Edalji affair with a "No copyright" notice to allow other papers, especially in the Midlands, to publish the article in full.

Conan Doyle completed his article for the Daily Telegraph and just prior to advertising its proposed publication, he wrote to Captain Anson on the 5th January confirming his intention to take up the cudgel on Edalji's behalf. Whilst expressing regret for taking such a severe view of the Staffordshire police, he justified his actions by pointing out that he was honour bound to do justice to his enquiries. Doyle disclosed the results of Edalji's recent eye tests showing Edalji to be so blind he could not tell one man from another at three yards. He added to the captain's discomfort by describing the extremely difficult route Edalji would have had to follow to carry out the maiming and chided Captain Anson by saying that if he had taken the trouble to walk it himself he would never have claimed it to be easy. Rejecting the captain's accusations of Reverend and Maud Edalji being liars, Doyle wrote of the truthfulness of the Edaljis; of the vicar's own Christian charity which was as great as his veracity; and of the debt owed to this ill-used

[380] Correspondence between ACD and HO, 17, 20, 21 and 23 Dec 1906, HO File 989 Pt 2

[381] Sir Mackenzie Chalmers to Akers-Douglas, 5 Jan 1907, in Akers-Douglas, E A, [1961] The Political Life and Times of Aretas, Akers-Douglas, First Viscount Chilston, RKP, London

family. Captain Anson was reprimanded for some of his private comments made to Doyle concerning the reasons put forward for Reverend and George Edalji sharing the same room. Doyle could see nothing suspicious in these arrangements nor in the reverend keeping his bedroom door locked as many people did. Doyle cautioned him that "if similar reports have gone to the Home Office and stand in the way of justice, then the Edaljs must find some public way of showing how baseless they are. In this they have my sympathy." In his discussions with Doyle, Captain Anson had obviously made inferences of sodomy involving the Reverend and George Edalji as indicated by the references in the captain's *aide memoire* written on Doyle's first letter and by Doyle's reprimand and caveat in this letter. In mid-January 1907 Doyle raised these inferences with the Home Office in a more direct way. As a parting shot, Doyle mentioned the considerable amount of evidence he had collected about the maimings and the anonymous letters and he pointed to other culprits whom he would identify when Edalji's innocence was established.[382]

Captain Anson must have been apopleptic when reading this letter since he could not abide any criticism of himself or any praiseworthy comments about the Edaljis, an almost obsessive characteristic that was to increase out of all proportion over the coming years. Obviously chagrined by the turn of events, experiencing a deep sense of betrayal, the captain lost no time in writing a severe criticism of Doyle to Simpson at the Home Office in a letter dated the 6th January 1907. Despite later claiming that Doyle's letter of the 5th January was not received by him until the 8th January, the tone of Captain Anson's letter to Simpson suggested he had received Doyle's letter on the 6th January because prior to taking up the pen to Simpson there had been nothing to sour Doyle's relationship with the captain. Captain Anson's description of Doyle as Sherlock Holmes, the self appointed Court of Criminal Appeal who viewed himself as "L'etat c'est moi" and "so vastly superior to us" was confirmation of the captain's recently acquired antagonism towards Doyle. In this letter Captain Anson began the twisting and turning in all directions that became a feature of his contributions on all matters concerning the Edalji case. Previously convinced without question of George Edalji's authorship of the 1903 anonymous letters, Captain Anson changed tack by claiming that his own suspicions had always rested on Maud Edalji as the author of some of the letters with George Edalji posting them. Flailing in the wind, the captain had inadvertently disposed of the prosecution's star witness,

---

[382] ACD to Capt Anson, 5 Jan 1907, HO File 989 Pt 2

Gurrin, who testified to George Edalji being the author of all the post-7th July anonymous letters.[383]

In another curious twist, Captain Anson received an extremely bizarre communication that began another series of pseudonymous letters written by 'Martin Molton', the 'Nark' and 'Lew Is'.[384] The Martin Molton letters contained a considerable amount of information concerning the accusations made against George Edalji by Captain Anson to Home Office officials. The attempt by this scribe to discredit Edalji, initially arriving at a time just prior to the publication of Conan Doyle's analysis of the Edalji case in the Daily Telegraph, was played out for several weeks. The 'Nark's' letters over a shorter period of time went to both Conan Doyle and Royden Sharp of 1892 'rick-firing' fame. The 'Lew Is' missive, only one, was written by a religious fanatic in California. Investigations were undertaken by Conan Doyle over many months to try to link the 'Lew Is' missive to the 'God-Satan' era, while Captain Anson made similar investigations with the opposite objective in mind.

In the main arena, several avenues opened up. While these avenues offered opportunities to place Edalji's conviction into perspective, albeit raising more questions than answers, one factor emerging from this was the bitter acrimony developing between Captain Anson and Sir Arthur Conan Doyle, which in many ways took over centre stage and became the principal issue between the two men.

[383] Capt Anson to Simpson, 6 Jan 1907, HO File 989 Pt 2
[384] The 'Molton' and 'Nark' letters will be dealt with in Chapter XIV and the 'Lew Is' in Chapter XVII

Chapter XIII

'Telegraphing' the Message

(i)   The Article[385]

Sir Arthur Conan Doyle's overall findings from his investigation into the Edalji case were published in a two part article in the Daily Telegraph on the 11th and 12th January 1907. After paying tribute to Yelverton, friends and supporters of Edalji, and 'Truth' magazine, whose "excellent series" of articles had kept the flame of Edalji's innocence alive and to whom "Edalji will owe so much when the hour of triumph comes,"[386] Conan Doyle went into the historical background of the situation in Great Wyrley. He systematically sifted through the evidence presented to the jury as well as dealing with other issues raised in discussions with Captain Anson and other contributors.

Doyle gave short shrift to the prosecution's case for failing to provide a single item of evidence able to withstand detailed examination, ultimately arriving at the conclusion that Edalji's arrest and conviction were the result of a pre-conceived campaign conducted against him by the Staffordshire police.[387] The main forensic evidence was quite easily explained away as part of this campaign, whose principals were forced into grasping for any straw to achieve their ends. The horse hairs 'found' on Edalji's jacket, similar in colour, length and structure, were underbelly hairs and not the type of side hairs - longer, darker and harsher, that would get on the maimer's clothes when

---

385 DT 9, 11 and 12 Jan 1907

386 Years later, Doyle claimed nothing practicable was done for Edalji until he had served three years in prison, amplifying his own contribution. This was a rather unfair and narrow view since the considerable campaigning carried out by Yelverton and others provided fertile ground upon which Doyle could spread the seeds of his own very significant contribution. Doyle, Sir Arthur Conan [1924] Memories and Adventures, Hodder & Stoughton, London, p216

387 F E Smith, later to become Lord Birkenhead and hold the post of Lord Chancellor, who was soon to rally to Edalji's cause, stated in Parliament with regard to the Edalji case, "Those who have conducted prosecutions on police evidence know the appalling risks which arise when the police approach a case with a preconceived notion of the guilt of the accused." F E Smith, Hansard, 18 Jul 1907, Vol 178 c1010

leaning against a horse to do the deed. The presence of hairs on Edalji's clothes was diplomatically put down to the inadvertent transfer of hairs from the hide to the jacket when carried together in the same bag, although it was pointed out that if the hairs had attached themselves in this way they would not have congregated solely on the cuffs and breast of the jacket. By adding the comment that "the incident leaves an unpleasant impression on the mind," Doyle implied the transfer was not entirely accidental. As for the blood stains, Doyle was of the opinion that even the most skilful of operators could not rip up a horse on a dark night and have only two 'threepenny bit' spots of blood to show for it, and the boots and footprint evidence were attributed the description of being absurd. Doyle's *coup de grace* was the 'eyesight' evidence from which he showed the utter implausibility of someone with such defective vision being able to avoid the police watch on the vicarage and fields as well as negotiating all the obstacles, man-made and natural, while on his way to and from the scene of the maimings. As Doyle put it, that such a man could scour the fields at night assaulting cattle while avoiding the watching police, could only be seen as ludicrous to anyone with an understanding of myopia.

Doyle was hardly endearing himself to the Staffordshire police and he twisted the knife in a little further when attacking the police for not prosecuting Green for killing his own horse; for subpoenaing Green to prevent Edalji's Defence calling him; and for conniving in Green's flight from the country, which had they not done so would have ended the miscarriage of justice perpetrated against Edalji. Conan Doyle condemned the police's theory of a gang with a membership including Edalji and Farrington as illogical. The former was shy and nervous, a professional man, a vicar's son, a teetotaller and non-smoker; and the latter was a rude illiterate miner, a loafer at public houses. He dangled in front of the reader the prospect of Farrington committing the August 1903 maiming because after Farrington's conviction in March 1904 the outrages ceased. Yet Doyle drew back from accusing Farrington of responsibility for the August offence, merely posing it as a possibility to show that as strong a case could be made against Farrington as against George Edalji.

When addressing the anonymous letters, Doyle thought that the whole series of letters descending on the area since 1888 were inspired by one person even if that person did not actually write them.[388] His opinion was based on the similarity of phrasing; the audacity and

---

[388] Doyle's attempt to pin the anonymous letters and maimings on others is dealt with in Chapter XIV & Appendix I

violence of language; and the attention given to the Edalji family in the letters. Any differences in the handwriting were not thought significant because the author boasted of his ability to change his handwriting and to imitate George Edalji's writing.

Casting his net widely, Doyle trawled in Edalji's defence team, whose presentation of the case was thought not as strong as it should have been, blaming the deficiency not so much on Edalji's counsel but on lack of information – an overgenerous coyness on Doyle's part neglecting several errors of judgement committed by Edalji's legal representatives.

Overall, the blame for Edalji's conviction was put down to: (i) Captain Anson for allowing his 'unconscious' prejudice towards George Edalji to filter down to the whole Staffordshire police force; (ii) the errors committed by the handwriting expert, Gurrin, whose evidence in the Beck trial had, by his own admission, caused an innocent man to go to prison; and (iii) the gross stupidity of the jury.

With a touch of drama rather than realism, Doyle likened the actions of the Staffordshire police to the clique of French officers, who went from excess to excess in trying to cover up the initial mistakes in the Dreyfus case. Other parallels were drawn: Edalji a Parsee, Dreyfus a Jew; both with promising careers blighted; both suffering expulsion from a profession; and both cases decided by forged handwriting – Esterhazy in the Dreyfus case and an anonymous scribe in Edalji's. Doyle could have mentioned one other connection – Gurrin, who had assisted French handwriting 'experts' in the Dreyfus case.

The path along which Doyle trekked was paved with the belief that only an appeal to public opinion would put an end to this "dark stain on the administrative annals of this country" and his solution for redressing this miscarriage of justice was the setting up of an independent committee to: (a) consider the complete reorganisation of the Staffordshire constabulary; (b) investigate the procedural irregularities during the trial at the Quarter Sessions; and (c) identify and punish those Home Office officials responsible for failing to take action over Edalji's petition for a pardon. An appeal doomed to failure bearing in mind that in the corridors of power in any institution bureaucrats tend to look after their own.

(ii) The Public Response

Doyle's article was applauded in many quarters. 'Truth' magazine, whilst seeking to claim parity with Doyle for championing Edalji's case, recognised that Doyle's analysis would carry considerable weight with a large section of the public but realistically thought it was "no use to suppose the walls of London will fall down from a few blasts of the journalistic trumpet." The Daily Chronicle provided a dramatic flourish by describing the article as "the Sherlock touch which made Sir Arthur's statement of the case so piquant."[389]

Edalji's case became linked to both the Beck and Rolls cases as typifying the way convicted people were subjected to undue bias; how secret dossiers were used against them; and enquiries refused when the convictions were challenged. The Law Journal, an organ of the legal profession, believed Doyle's line of reasoning and the Home Office's unexplained early release of Edalji raised serious doubts about the proper administration of justice and public unease over the case could only be satisfied by a Beck-style enquiry. The Times' legal correspondent thought Conan Doyle's points, even if not entirely convincing, merited careful consideration: the problems concerning Edalji's eyesight; the harassment of the Edalji family; police prejudice against George Edalji; the likelihood of Edalji, if he had been the maimer, being caught on that night when the police were surrounding the vicarage - all these points were thought to contain some measure of value. Edalji's alibi for the night, the prosecution's change of the time of the maiming and the unreliability of police evidence with regard to the stains, hairs, razor and boots also merited attention. Gurrin's evidence in the wake of the Beck inquiry could not be relied on and the prosecution's attempt to use the contents of the anonymous letters to support the case against Edalji were insufficient to provide a connection to any other link in the chain of evidence. Furthermore, the three similar crimes committed in the same district after Edalji's committal raised grave doubts about Edalji's guilt and the release of Edalji long before completing the full term of his sentence was an obvious result of those doubts. Although stating it was premature to say this was "another Beck case or a kind of squalid Dreyfus case", he thought the whole matter merited a full public inquiry without delay and was a clear illustration of the advantages of having a Criminal Court of Appeal. The Police Review, the organ of British constabulary, (i) pointed the finger at Home Office officials and accused them of cajoling two Home Secretaries, described as "the flabby mouthpieces of paid officials," into compliance; (ii) called on the chief constable to justify his actions for the serious errors of judgement on his part; and (iii) demanded a 'fresh eye' to counter the secret influence of one man's report (Captain Anson's) determining the fate of an innocent victim. Another police

---

[389] Truth 16 Jan 1907; DN 14 Jan 1907; DC 18 May 1907

journal, the 'Police Chronicle' called for a full-scale public inquiry carried out by a committee having similar powers to the Beck commission.[390]

The Edalji case had become a *cause celebre* for those seeking to make changes in the judicial system of England and Wales. Lawyers offered to appear free of charge on Edalji's behalf at any future enquiry and others offered to contribute to any fund set up to assist the Edalji campaign. Yelverton took advantage of this publicity to form a Support Committee,[391] attracting numerous people keen to join, and a Campaign Fund Committee sponsored by the Daily Telegraph.[392] The members of these committees were no soap box orators or anti-police brigadiers fabricating complaints against the police but representatives of middle class society with no particular axe to grind about the police or the higher reaches of the constabulary.

While Conan Doyle's contribution attracted considerable accord not all were enamoured of it. The Birmingham Gazette, not convinced of the impartiality of the article, believed more was at stake than the verdict on Edalji as other reputations were under threat. However, the paper still thought it necessary for a public inquiry to establish either Edalji's innocence or guilt and it appealed for the establishment of a Criminal Court of Appeal. While the author of this article was hedging his bets, a hornets' nest of claim and counterclaim was opening up and the attacks directed at Doyle's article showed the considerable weight the article actually carried. More strident opponents, setting their face against a reinvestigation of the case, were not without allies and the assault on the integrity of the police and the claims of a police conspiracy drew a number of spokesmen to the police's defence.[393] One Great Wyrley resident, claiming to reflect the opinion of many, accused Conan Doyle of trying "to blacken the name of a poor dead servant

---

[390] Law Times 26 Jan & 16 Feb 1907; Police Chronicle (Organ of the Police Mutual Assistance Association) 2 and 16 Feb 1907; Police Review (Organ of British Constabulary) 11, 18 and 25 Jan, and 22 Mar 1907; Law Jnl, Vol 42 No 2140, 19 Jan 1907 p29; The Humanitarian League, MG 25 May 1905; Times 29 Jan 1907

[391] The Support Committee consisted of the Hon John Gordon, Sir William Bull, Dr Waldo, Dr Bastian, Prof Churton Collins, Prof Faraday Franklin, Rev Horniman and Yelverton.

[392] The Fund Committee consisted of Jerome K Jerome, Voules, Sir George Lewis, Conan Doyle, J Hall Richardson (Daily Telegraph) and Churton Collins. Gazette 19 Jan 1907; SS 9 Feb 1907; DT 11 Feb 1907; EN 18 May 1907

[393] Gazette 15, 18 & 21 Jan 1907

girl", Elizabeth Foster; of accusing the police and all prosecution witnesses of perjury; and of accepting no evidence as reliable except that favouring the Edalji family. Another contributor refuted the claim that the Edaljis suffered persecution and blamed Reverend Edalji for the difficulties created over twenty years before, obviously referring to the Education issue. He referred to a Mr Brook (sic) threatening to thrash the author of the 1892 letters at Walsall Station and also claimed Elizabeth Foster was illiterate.[394] This letter reflected the type of people the Edaljis had been up against for over twenty years. The writer apparently knew of Brookes' clash with the youthful George Edalji in 1892/3 and, contrary to his claim, Elizabeth Foster, although not well educated, was not illiterate. An ex-resident of the Cannock area, to be described later by George Edalji as a "tool of a certain gentleman at Stafford,"[395] wrote in support of Captain Anson to 'disclose' that the police believed Farrington was bribed in 1904 to commit a maiming because the outrages had ceased, adding that Reverend Edalji was seen in conversation with Farrington either directly before or after the outrage in March 1904. The writer's uncertainty of the time of the reverend's presence in Farrington's company indicated that he had been told of this alleged 'sighting' by someone else and had obviously forgotten what was told to him. Nonetheless, not knowing exactly what went on at the scene of the arrest, he implied that the reverend had bribed Farrington, which brought in its wake a prompt denial from Reverend Edalji.[396]

Another correspondent lauded Captain Anson as a member of a revered Staffordshire family, "esteemed by publicans and sinners for his willingness to inquire into any wrong which may be brought to his notice." This same correspondent queried why, if George Edalji was the village scapegoat, the police did not raid the vicarage earlier in the series of outrages.[397] Perhaps, if this correspondent had known that Edalji was only suspected after a local Justice of the Peace, a protagonist of Reverend Edalji, had mentioned his name to the police, the idea of Edalji being a scapegoat might not be too difficult for him to accept. The chair of the Staffordshire Standing Joint Committee, Colonel Wilkinson, 'neutrally' declaring to have nothing to say on the Edalji case, made it perfectly clear where his sympathies lay. The

---

[394] Correspondent, Gazette 21 Jan 1907; J E, Calf Heath, Gazette 21 Feb 1907

[395] DT 24 Jan 1907

[396] Fidelitis, posted at Woking, DT, 23 Jan 1907; Rev Edalji, DT 24 Jan 1907

[397] Correspondent, DT 24 Jan 1907

Colonel, displaying a touch of Captain Anson's literary style, expressed his disagreement with the conclusions drawn by both 'Sherlock Holmes' and Mr Yelverton but failed to elaborate on the reasons for his dissent. Nor did he expect the Joint Committee to take action on the allegations against the police at the present time, which in a sense meant at no time at all because he went on to claim that the impeachment of the police system rested with the Home Office[398] –a claim lacking in substance as the Home Office was not in a position to discipline the police – all it could do was to withhold a certificate of efficiency from the Staffordshire police.[399] Did anyone in the Staffordshire administration know the extent of the responsibilities they held?

Staffordshire officials also jumped to the defence of the judiciary for holding the trial at the Second Court of the Quarter Sessions. The assistant magistrate's clerk, Mr Horton, justified the decision on two grounds. Firstly, the sessions were due to be held at an earlier date than the Assizes. Secondly, the case was a 'session's case', and if sent to the Assizes without any reason being assigned, the judge would have wanted to know the reason for such an unusual and unnecessary step. He tried to justify these claims by referring to the Farrington case and the absence of any suggestion that his trial should be at the Assizes.[400] Horton had overlooked that Lord Hatherton refused the request made by Farrington's lawyer for the trial to be committed to the Assizes and Horton's 'legal' view flew in the face of the opinions of eminent lawyers and legal scholars, including advisers to the new Home Secretary, Herbert Gladstone.[401] The reasons given by Horton conformed with the observations made by Captain Anson to the Home Office on the venue to be used in these cases. Only one person seemed to be writing the script for these Staffordshire players to act out.

The owner of 'Truth', Labouchere, seemed afflicted with the same subjectivity engulfing Captain Anson as he too dismissed the eyesight evidence. The reason for Labouchere's cavalier dismissal of the evidence was based on his own shortsightedness. Despite this failing, he claimed to be able to see his way when the light was indistinct, going as far as to say that if he knew the country, he could find his way across fields, night and day, and feel for a place to wound a horse – a kind of machismo on Labouchere's part defying science and logic.

[398] Gazette 15 Jan1907

[399] Blackwell to Troupe, 3 Feb 1911, HO No 314 File 987

[400] Mr Horton, asst magistrate's clerk, Gazette 21 Jan 1907

[401] Mallett, Sir Chas [1932] Herbert Gladstone, a memoir, Hutchinson, London, pp215/6

Notwithstanding this bravado, Labouchere took an unusual position between the two major conflicting parties – a view not shared by the staff at 'Truth'. Unable to detect any evidence to convict George Edalji or to support a theory of a gang with members writing anonymous letters and killing animals, Labouchere replaced George Edalji with an unlikely substitute, none other than 'Edalji père,' arriving at this conclusion by accepting that the evidence tending to prove George Edalji's guilt also applied to the father – a curious conclusion since he was of the view there was no evidence at all to convict George Edalji.

Labouchere further speculated on George Edalji actually suspecting his own father but could not reveal this even in his own defence. As for the anonymous letters, Labouchere, too, 'observing' an Oriental mode of phrasing contained within them, attributed the style to the father – another gem to add to the growing collection of solutions.[402] Labouchere wrote to Doyle about the possible guilt of Reverend Edalji but Doyle chose to ignore it, no doubt treating it with the ridicule it deserved. Notwithstanding the implausibility of this Labouchere scenario, after the trial in 1903 the police were bombarded with letters accusing both George Edalji and Reverend Edalji of being the maimers. If these letter writers and Labouchere were correct, they conjure up a vision of a short-sighted, lumbago-ridden, sixty-year old vicar and his myopic astigmatic solicitor son traversing the rain sodden countryside in search of animals to dispense with. Not the most convincing of submissions.

(iii) The Home Office Response

Home Office officials had thought it would be a shrewd move to meet Conan Doyle when he first contacted them about the Edalji case and when Doyle's articles were published it became even more expedient for them to discuss the case with him. Gladstone admitted to his predecessor at the Home Office, Akers-Douglas, that the resurgence of the pseudonymous letters of Martin Molton and the foment in the public mind made it necessary for him to submit all the papers to the Lord Chief Justice, who had advised him to hold an inquiry.[403] The Home Secretary had arranged a meeting at the Home Office on the 15th January consisting of Conan Doyle, now the Edalji Committee's go-

---

[402] Labouchere to Gladstone, 25 Jan 1907, HO File 988

[403] Gladstone to Akers-Douglas, 8 Feb 1907 in Akers-Douglas, E A [1961] The Political Life and Times of Aretas, Akers-Douglas, First Viscount Chilston, RKP, London

between with the Home Office; Herbert Gladstone, the Home Secretary; Sir Mackenzie Chalmers, Permanent Under-Secretary; and Mr Blackwell, Legal Assistant Under-Secretary.[404] Three items dominated the discussion. The first item covered the granting of a free pardon to Edalji and the setting up of a commission to enquire into what Doyle considered to be a grave miscarriage of justice. The second item was an expose of Captain Anson's prejudicial and malicious attitude towards the Edaljis and the influence his attitude had on Edalji's arrest and conviction – an attitude freely displayed by the captain during his discussions and correspondence with Conan Doyle.[405] Doyle's revelations should not have caused too much of a surprise to the *ensemble* or to anyone else who had seen Captain Anson's letters on the case. The third item concerned Conan Doyle's conviction that a strong *prima facie* case could be made against two local men both with links to the butchery trade, Royden Sharp and John E Hart, which attracted an offer from the Home Office of all possible assistance from the CID to pursue these suspicions.[406]

When Doyle came out of the meeting, he announced to the waiting reporters that his meeting with the Home Secretary went well and was confident that the Home Office would clear up the matter.[407] This was an overly optimistic view as the Home Office, wishing to sweep the affair under the table, was playing the bureaucratic game of giving the impression of seeking an equitable solution in response to the needs of justice whilst proceeding in another direction to protect the interests of paid officials whether residing in Staffordshire or in London.

At this early stage, at least on the surface, Yelverton and Conan Doyle, still working in absolute unison, were confident that a public inquiry was on the agenda.[408] However, within a few days, Conan Doyle realised that the impression given of a full-scale public inquiry being on the cards, in line with the precedent set in the Beck case, was only a smokescreen to hide the preparation for a more limited inquiry to be shunted in to deal only indirectly with the issues at stake.[409] Doyle, already playing both ends against the middle and adopting a single-minded approach of personally seeking Edalji's exoneration, took the first step in dissociating himself from the Edalji Support Committee. In

---

[404] Gazette 16 Jan 1907

[405] See section (iv) of this Chapter

[406] ACD to HO, 18 Jan 1907, HO File 989 Pt 1

[407] DT 16 Jan 1907

[408] Gazette 15 Jan & 11 Feb 1907

[409] ACD to HO, 18 Jan 1907, HO File 989 Pt 1

January, detecting that Home Office officials distrusted Yelverton, he lost no time in advising the Home Office he intended to have nothing more to do with the Edalji Support Committee and he asked the Home Office to give him something in the way of a settlement to dampen down rather than encourage public agitation and distrust of public institutions.[410] Just as public interest in the case was really stirring, with Edalji's friends organising meetings and agitating for funds, Doyle became a restraining influence by playing a lone game and making moves to operate independently and outside of Edalji's present supporters. Within two weeks, Doyle announced that Gladstone was to appoint a special committee with full powers to investigate both the prosecution's conduct and the methods used by the Staffordshire county police to secure Edalji's conviction with a leading member of the Bar to appear on Edalji's behalf.[411]

In the corridors of power where resided the self-styled arbiters of unjust verdicts, the *ex-officio* views of some officials were not in unison with the rearguard action waged by more senior officials in support of establishment figures. Blackwell, who followed a line quite different from the one canvassed by Captain Anson and swallowed, if not digested, by other Home Office officials, thought: (i) the Home Office could assume Elizabeth Foster was guilty of writing the 1888/9 anonymous letters; (ii) the conclusion that George Edalji was the culprit in the 'Walsall Grammar School key' incident was idiotic; (iii) Captain Anson's attempt to get Edalji to confess by writing the 'Lover of Justice' letter was, similarly, idiotic; (iv) the police charges against Edalji when he was 17 years old cast suspicion on their handling of the maiming case; (v) the police discussions with Edalji should not have been allowed to count against him in the slightest degree; (vi) and police prejudice against Edalji should be viewed in the "darkest light".[412] Notwithstanding this censure of police practices, the Home Office did not budge an inch and accepted: (i) Edalji was possibly insane, despite one specialist in the employ of the Home Office finding no evidence of such a state of mind; (ii) the 1888/9 anonymous letters in a childish handwriting were written by either Elizabeth Foster or George Edalji, despite Sergeant Upton, with no axe to grind at the time, finding evidence pointing to Elizabeth Foster, (iii) the 1903 anonymous letters were prime evidence against Edalji, despite their inadmissibility due to being unconnected to the charge and the 'expert' linking them to

[410] ACD to HO, 25 Jan & 7 Feb 1907, HO File 989 Pt 1
[411] Gazette 11 Feb 07
[412] Blackwell's comment on G Edalji, Jan 1907; HO File 988

Edalji subsequently discredited; (iv) Gurrin's belief that the Martin Molton letters were a trap set for him (Gurrin), so that if he identified the writing as Edalji's, the person copying Edalji's handwriting on Edalji's behalf would come forward to claim authorship.[413] Not a very convincing contribution from the handwriting 'expert', who exhibited a considerable lack of confidence in his own handwriting ability – an anxiety about his own competence that Captain Anson later shared.[414]

Gladstone was in somewhat of a cleft stick as the remission of the sentence was a virtual admission that something was amiss. Moreover, he was advised that the evidence at the trial was unsatisfactory and so important a case as this should have been tried by a judge at Assizes.[415] Gladstone began to have doubts but 'guarded' by a group of reticent Home Office officials, he turned to Akers-Douglas to confide his doubts and misgivings – doubts considerably strengthened by the latest anonymous letters and Conan Doyle's theory as to who was the guilty party. Contrary to Blackwell's opinion, Gladstone tried to downgrade the significance of the Edalji miscarriage of justice by stating "Our opinions may be right or wrong but there is no question about any omission or blunder as in the Beck case."[416] Gladstone showed a considerable reluctance to set up an inquiry and later went on to disavow ever contemplating a Beck-style commission or 'investigate the conduct of the officials concerned', which was undoubtedly true as far as he and Home Office officials were concerned, but it flew in the face of what others thought was on offer or of what was required. Gladstone tried to massage his actions with the usual diversionary tactics common to officialdom in claiming that the extraordinary complexity of the case was the problem and not the failure of anyone to give it adequate consideration. Gladstone was disingenuous and was seen to be so later when, despite having the Beck case as precedence, he changed the original reasons for not having a public inquiry by claiming not to have the power to do so.[417] This did not come as a surprise to Voules, of 'Truth', and Kempster, of the Police Review, two leading

---

[413] Home Office comments on Lord Chancellor's report, 2 Feb 1907, HO No 174a, File 986

[414] Capt Anson to HO, 15 Sep 1907, HO File 989 Pt 1

[415] Mallett, Sir Chas [1932] Herbert Gladstone, a memoir, Hutchinson, London, pp215/6

[416] Gladstone to Akers-Douglas, 8 Feb 1907 in Akers-Douglas, E A [1961] The Political Life and Times of Aretas, Akers-Douglas, First Viscount Chilston, RKP, London

[417] Gazette 15 Jan & 14 Mar 1907; Times 14 May 1907; Truth 24 July 1907

lights in calling for a Commission of Enquiry to be heard in public, who from the beginning had taken a pessimistic view of any good springing from any Committee of Inquiry set up by the Home Office.[418]

Loyalty and *esprit de corps* amongst Home Office officials and the Staffordshire police and judiciary seemed to be the reason for Gladstone's duplicity as well might have been his nepotic lack of enthusiasm in seeing his cousin, Sir Reginald Hardy, the chair of the bench at the Quarter Sessions, or his friend, Captain Anson, roasted over an open spit. Gladstone's position may also have received an inadvertent boost from Conan Doyle. By this time, the middle of March, disagreements between the views of the majority in the Edalji Support Committee and Conan Doyle were reaching breaking point and a split occurred when Edalji, increasingly influenced by Doyle, dissociated himself from Yelverton. In letting the Home Office know that Yelverton was not now acting for him in anyway, (Edalji's emphasis) Edalji left himself vulnerable to any plots hatched up by Home Office officials.[419] Acting on Doyle's advice and against that of the Support Committee, Edalji believed that redress might be obtained through his own personal efforts, and as a result, he submitted a statement to the Home Office practically approving Gladstone's secret enquiry.[420] Yelverton thought it an unfortunate decision on Edalji's part but not one for him to criticise and the Support Committee members, not wishing to do anything that appeared to be at odds with Edalji's interests, did not press for a public inquiry or agitate for compensation.[421] Edalji gave signs later of regretting his decision to put all his eggs in one basket. There was no doubt that Edalji obtained more from the Home Office than would have been possible if Doyle had not taken up his case but less than what was possible if Edalji, under the influence of Doyle, had not distanced himself from the Support Group and the public clamour it was capable of provoking.

Gladstone was able to achieve his clandestine objective, albeit

[418] DT 11 Mar 1907

[419] G Edalji to HO, 2 Mar 1907, HO No 293, File 987. A consequence of this split later brought an unusual accusation from Yelverton – see Chapter XVII

[420] M Harley, a later contributor to the Edalji case, certainly had this the wrong way round when he claimed George Edalji exerted considerable influence over Conan Doyle. Harley, M, Whodunnit & The Wyrley Maimings: Mr X Stands Accused, CA 11 Nov 1983

[421] Yelverton, EN and ES 18 May 1907; Letter to Temple Committee by Yelverton, Despatch 24 May 1907

temporarily, by empanelling a committee chaired by Sir Robert Romer, ex-Lord Justice of Appeal between 1899 and 1906, with Sir Arthur Wilson and J Lloyd Wharton as the other members, holding a brief to carry out an inquiry of a far inferior status with functions limited to determining whether or not Edalji should receive a pardon and was "in no sense an inquiry into Home Office action."

The Home Office wanted the committee to sit in secret and act as 'judge and jury' on the question of Edalji's guilt or innocence using documents held by the Home Office and excluding a great deal of evidence in the possession of Edalji's representatives.[422] Contrary to what Gladstone later claimed, the committee's esteemed chair, Sir Robert Romer, expected an inquiry different in type to the one Gladstone eventually convened. Sir Robert thought the inquiry should be held in public according to the ordinary rules of procedure governing criminal trials, with the committee having the power to call witnesses, who would be examined and cross-examined by counsel acting on behalf of the defence and the prosecution. When it became apparent that the committee had an extremely limited remit, Sir Robert withdrew from the inquiry.[423] The other members of the committee, while agreeing with Sir Robert's terms of reference for the inquiry, did not withdraw but agreed to examine the material in the Home Office's possession and to give their advice. The Home Secretary accepted Sir Robert's withdrawal, no doubt gladly since it scotched any possibility of a public inquiry on the scale suggested by Edalji's supporters and by many prominent legal practitioners. He was replaced by Sir A de Rutzen, chief magistrate of London, who conveniently happened to be Captain Anson's cousin, and who, four years earlier, thought the forging of documents by the police to effect an arrest was an acceptable police practice.[424]

Gladstone and his Home Office advisers, seriously concerned about the prospect of Edalji being cleared of the crime because it would raise the spectre of the police concocting evidence, were determined to influence the findings by insisting on the police being fully heard at the inquiry but making no such arrangements for Edalji or his representatives to present evidence.[425] Edalji was to be re-tried in camera on a secret official dossier, a similar format relied on by successive Home Secretaries to refuse him a pardon.

---

[422] Romer to Gladstone, 15 & 16 Feb 1907, HO File 988

[423] Times 2 Mar 1907; LM 8 Mar 1907

[424] See above, Chapter V

[425] HO Comment, 15 Mar 1907, HO No 187, File 986

The Police Review described Sir Robert Romer's withdrawal as due to his not being prepared to hold himself responsible for what was thought of as 'a hole and corner' inquiry, nor did it think Sir Robert would have retained any respect if he had assumed the role of a puppet pretending to administer justice.

The Review accused the Home Secretary of seeking to prevent the exposure of misconduct on the part of Crown officials and it was less than pleased about the police and Gurrin being able to submit evidence in defence of themselves but barring Edalji from so doing. Nor did the brief given to the Committee of Inquiry impress the legal profession. The Law Journal favoured a Beck-style commission not a committee to act as judge and jury without the power to call witnesses.[426] Bishops, Deans, Professors, Archdeacons and academic staff at Birmingham University and Trinity College, Dublin were other unheeded voices calling on the Home Secretary not to abandon the original intention to hold a public inquiry.[427]

(iv) The Sodomy Controversy

The second item on Conan Doyle's agenda, when he met the Home Secretary on the 15th January, dealt with certain insinuations made by Captain Anson about the Edaljis far beyond the domains of the case. Having already drawn the Home Office's attention to rumours accusing George Edalji of lacking professional integrity and the Edalji family of sexual immorality – rumours springing from a common source and allegedly spread by Captain Anson, Doyle let it be known that the captain had more than implied that Reverend Edalji and his son slept in the same room with the door locked for the purpose of sodomy.[428]

Before taking up the Edalji case, Conan Doyle was warned of rumours accusing Reverend Edalji of practising sodomy that were circulating in late 1903 when the campaign to release George Edalji was getting under way.[429] Churton Collins, with his ear to the ground in the West Midlands, had accused the chief constable and the local police of fabricating the rumours and had raised the issue with Superintendent

---

[426] Police Review 8 & 22 Mar 1907; Law Jnl, Vol 42 No 2147, 9 Mar 1907 p160

[427] Times 14 and 22 Mar 1907

[428] ACD to HO, 10 Jan 1907, HO No 169 File 986; Blackwell to Troup, 3 Feb 1911, HO No 314 File 987

[429] ACD to Blackwell, 23 Mar 1907, HO 989 Pt 1

Barrett, who referred the matter to Captain Anson, who in turn denied ever having heard of any such allegation.[430]

Conan Doyle paid little heed to the captain's protestations of ignorance because Captain Anson's knowledge of the rumours appeared to be confirmed by an inference in one of his (Captain Anson's) letters to Doyle when he mentioned that "The father had his son to sleep in his room for many years with the door locked. That is not disputed. The reason had not been given."[431] Conan Doyle latched on to this in his reply of the 27th December 1906 and probingly noted "I fear I did not quite follow the point why the father sleeping in the same room and locking the door (as nervous people have a habit of doing) told against the accused. At first sight it would seem that he could not get out without his father's knowledge – it is hard to believe that the father connived at such excursions. But perhaps I have not quite seen the bearing of the fact." Captain Anson responded the next day by expressing a belief that the "father had some very good reason for keeping control over his son's movements at night. It is probable (though not certain) that George Edalji could not get out without his father knowing. If the jury had believed the father, they would not have convicted the son." This seemed to put the captain's comment into a different mould moving from "The reasons had not been given" to "control over his son's movements at night" but, as he often did when trying to extricate himself from a difficult situation, Captain Anson put himself back into the mire because further in this letter, when delving into the past, he reverted to his previous position by adding, "I think before that time (1895) he had the boy to sleep with him. I presume he had good reason." This addendum changed the captain's explanation from the reverend keeping an eye on George Edalji because he suspected him of committing the maimings to some entirely different motive. Doyle may well have hit the nail on the head when pointing out that Captain Anson's reply on the 28th December seemed an afterthought from a man who thought he might have gone too far, a characteristic noticeable in some of the captain's letters to the Home Office and remarked upon by Home Office and law officials. Doyle's nitpicking appeared to be confirmed by the note made on Doyle's initial letter to the captain prior to his visit to see him, where Captain Anson had noted, "The father had the son to sleep with him", as one of three

---

[430] Collins in an undated, unpublished letter to the DT sent between 1903 and 1907 in HO comment, 22 Feb 1911, HO No 315 File 987; Capt Anson to Blackwell, 24 Mar 1907, HO File 989 Pt 1;
[431] ACD to Blackwell, 23 Mar 1907, HO File 989 Pt 1

significant points to deal with when he met Conan Doyle. If Captain Anson had meant they slept in the same room in order for the reverend to keep an eye on George, was this information so important in relation to all the other points at issue that it would figure as one of three significant items on the captain's *aide-memoire*.

Doyle was under no illusions about Captain Anson's insinuations and viewed the captain's denials as trying to retrieve a tasteless situation into which he had placed himself and he warned Captain Anson of the risk he ran should he repeat his insinuations to others as "the Edaljis must find some public way of showing how baseless they are."[432] Doyle also advised the Home Office that he had not shown the Anson letters to the Edalji family because they might wish to take proceedings against Captain Anson for the statements he had made. He also informed the Home office of the warning he had received when taking up the case and the captain's letter appeared to be corroboration and he forecast that "No man would have read it in another way." [433] Nor was Doyle alone in arriving at this interpretation – several people to whom he showed Captain Anson's letters shared the same impression as Doyle.[434]

When Captain Anson's comment on his *aide-memoire* and his remark in the letter of the 25th and the reference to 1895 in the 28th December letter are read together a reasonable inference can be drawn that the captain had deliberately introduced the sleeping arrangements in order to imply sodomy was practised in the Edalji household to discredit the family in Doyle's eyes. Interestingly, Doyle's threat to expose Captain Anson came immediately after his visit to the captain's residence and this might suggest that some rather distasteful comments were made about the Edaljis during the "for his ears only" discussion, which Doyle was honour bound not to reveal. Given his record on the Edaljis it was most unlikely for Captain Anson, who maliciously, and often underhandedly, did his level best to discredit the Edalji family, not to have taken the opportunity to make these allegations to Doyle bearing in mind that the sleeping arrangements figured so significantly in his *aide memoire*. The Home Office was fully informed in writing of Doyle's discourse with Captain Anson on this particular issue and, in mid-March, officials told the captain that Doyle had raised the issue of sodomy when he met with Home Office officials. Captain Anson denied ever having made "suggestions of immorality in the Edalji family," but

[432] ACD to Capt Anson 5 Jan 1907, HO File 989 Pt 1
[433] ACD to HO 23 Mar 1907 HO File 989 Pt 1
[434] Ibid

in his reply he revealed, coincidentally, that less than a month before on the 13th February 1907, completely out of the blue, an acquaintance of Captain Anson's allegedly told him of a report circulating in London that Mr (Reverend) Edalji kept the door shut for reasons of sodomy. The captain thought it extraordinary that such a rumour was current in London and believed it was deliberately spread as nothing had been heard locally.[435] Fortuitous circumstances seemed to fall in the captain's lap from unidentified sources when the occasion necessitated it – a means of deflecting attention away from himself!

As for his remarks, he tried to pass them off as perfectly legitimate since he was only repeating the prosecution's comments about Mr Edalji locking the door to prevent his son venturing out at night.[436] Taking great exception to Doyle's allegations, he accused him of behaving "like a contemptible brute" for corresponding in terms of friendliness after having gone much further into the case than he pretended when contacting him on the 21st December to arrange a meeting. Rejecting Churton Collins' allegations of rumours of sodomy originating in the Staffordshire police in 1903 as unfounded, he claimed that enquiries in the district picked up nothing about immorality and he denied ever suggesting, suspecting or hearing of any immorality in the Edalji household. He also produced the extraordinary claim that any suggestion of immorality would favour George Edalji because it would explain why the bedroom door was locked. [437]

Captain Anson's claimed ignorance of rumours against the Reverend was less than honest and merely clouded the issue because raised in the previous anonymous letters were allegations: (i) of sexual immorality between Mrs Edalji and Mr W H Brookes (1892 and 1895); (ii) of homosexual activity between Reverend Edalji and a youth in Liverpool (1895);[438] and (iii) of sexual immorality between George Edalji and Miss Quibell (1903); all of these allegations were known to Captain Anson because the letters found their way into his possession. The captain also overplayed his innocence of the Edalji's sleeping arrangements since he had known as far back as 1892 that George

---

[435] Capt Anson to Blackwell 20 Mar 1907, HO File 989 Pt 1

[436] Capt Anson to Blackwell 20 Mar 1907 & Blackwell to ACD 19 Mar 1907, HO File 989 Pt 1

[437] Capt Anson to Blackwell 24 Mar 1906, HO File 989 Pt 1

[438] The original letter accusing Reverend Edalji of homosexual conduct in Liverpool was in the possession of the Staffordshire police as late as September 1993. See Dr J Ward, [1993] The Story of George Edalji, Paper to the Police History Society, p 10, at Wm Salt Library, Stafford

Edalji and Reverend Edalji shared the same room[439] and that the arrangement had nothing to do with any alleged nocturnal wanderings by George Edalji.

Blackwell, seeking to rescue Captain Anson from an unsavoury situation, was convinced Doyle deliberately placed a wrongful construction on the captain's words to prejudice him in the eyes of the Home Secretary in order to further his own aims, conveniently overlooking his own appraisal of Captain Anson's attempts to prejudicially discredit George Edalji. Nor was there any reason for Conan Doyle to fabricate an issue like this or to misrepresent it in order to discredit Captain Anson and the role he played in the conviction of George Edalji as so many other factors were available for him to do just that.[440] When Captain Anson's aggrieved denial was brought to Conan Doyle's attention, Doyle accepted the captain's explanation, at least at the formal level, and expressed regret for conveying a mistaken interpretation. This appeared to be no more than a matter of form because in his letter to Blackwell he asked why the captain did not give the explanation made in the 28th December letter in the letter sent on the 25th December, adding that Captain Anson's later explanation was an afterthought from a man who had gone too far.[441] Doyle had touched a raw nerve with Captain Anson because the captain never forgot this and dragged it up again out of the blue four years later.[442]

(v) Captain Anson's Response

The disclosures in the 'sodomy issue' and the fallout from the Doyle articles prompted a reaction from Captain Anson, who kept up a constant barrage of correspondence with the Home Office in defence of his actions and, in the process, never missed an opportunity to smear the Edaljis. Twisting and contorting in his own defence, the captain, digging deeper into a hitherto undisclosed past, continued to undermine

---

[439] The sleeping arrangements were mentioned in Sergeant Upton's 1892 report.

[440] Capt Anson to ACD, 28 Dec 1906, HO File 989 Pt 2; ACD to Blackwell, 23 & 29 Mar 1907, HO File 989 Pt 1; Blackwell to Troup, 3 Feb 1911, HO No 314 File 987; Capt Anson to Blackwell, 20, 22 & 24 Mar 1907, and 14 April 1907, HO 989 Pt 1; Capt Anson's remarks on ACD letter, 24 Nov 1906, HO File 989 Pt 2

[441] ACD to Blackwell 29 Mar 1907, HO File 989 Pt 1

[442] Blackwell to Troup, 3 Feb 1911, HO No 314 File 987; Blackwell to ACD, 18, 19 & 27 Mar 1907, HO File 989 Pt 1

the substance of the case against Edalji. Previously writing of his belief that Edalji wanted to be locked up but may not have killed the horse himself, Captain Anson confirmed this view a couple of months later when claiming not to have shared the local police view that Edalji was the maimer. Yet only a few sentences further on in the same letter he thought George Edalji was too sharp to be caught out as the maimer unless caught red-handed.[443]

On the 20th March 1907, Captain Anson admitted that following reports of George Edalji's 'prowling' around the district in mid-June 1903, a moderate surveillance of his movements and of the vicarage was put in place. If the watch on the vicarage did begin in or around mid-June 1903, how did Edalji manage to leave and re-enter the vicarage on the 29th June 1903 to maim Blewitt's horse, especially as the captain agreed that Edalji was never seen leaving the vicarage late at night. In another letter on the 30th March 1907, which included the 'Brief for the Prosecution' in the Edalji trial,[444] it was admitted that between the 6th and the 18th August 1903, the police kept a nightly watch on the fields and the vicarage, confirming that the vicarage was under surveillance on the night of the maiming.

Yet in the 20th March letter, the captain had written of his decision to end the watch on the vicarage prior to the 18th August. It was difficult to believe anything Captain Anson said about the period of observation as three different versions had now been given.

Skirting around the police's failure to detect Edalji leaving the vicarage, Captain Anson offered an incredible solution of how easy it was for Edalji to slip unnoticed past the police observers, based on his own experience of entering the field where the maiming took place without the police seeing him. However, the captain failed to disclose when this experiment in elusiveness took place and under what circumstances. The captain constantly demonstrated a tendency of assessing evidence only in accordance with the way it was experienced by himself - gratuitous subjectivity, everything reduced to the personal. Another 'solution' thrown up by Captain Anson, realising the virtual impossibility of Edalji committing the crime between 5 am and 5.40 am on the 18th August, was of Edalji committing the offence after the police went home at 3.15 am, yet another error because the police did not go off duty until 5 am.

Captain Anson also denied exercising any influence over the local

443 Capt Anson to Simpson, 20 Jan 1907, HO 989 Pt 2; Capt Anson to HO, 20 Mar 107, HO No 192 File 986
444 Capt Anson to HO, 20 & 30 Mar 1907, HO No 192 & 195 File 986

police against the Edaljis as the officers dealing with the Edalji family were different in 1903 to those in 1895 and could not know of the Anson/Edalji communications of 1895, unless George Edalji told them, which he thought unlikely. The only contact between the police and the Edalji family was in 1901 when they assisted George Edalji in identifying some men who had assaulted him. The captain lacked an understanding of 'folk lore' or 'cultural transmission' operating within institutions and communities through which information is communicated from one 'generation' to another – in this situation a 'generation' barely eight years apart. He also threw up a novel reason for the dispute about the hairs on the coat and Reverend Edalji's claim of not seeing them. His explanation was that the hairs were very short and not at all noticeable on a casual inspection, overlooking that the Reverend, Mrs and Maud Edalji, according to police officers present at the time, made a careful examination of the coat. The captain also ignored that when the coat reached Dr Butter twenty-nine hairs were on the coat; hardly not noticeable if the hairs had in fact been there when the coat was inspected by the Edaljis. Captain Anson's attempt to debunk the credibility of the veterinary surgeon was argued on the grounds of the cut inflicted on the horse not being deep nor the bowels exposed.[445] He dismissed the wound as relatively insignificant, so insignificant that if the animal had any monetary value its life would have been saved – yet again the captain introduced financial factors to explain all things. For an aristocrat Captain Anson was extremely bourgeois in his interpretation of people's behaviour. He disclaimed any involvement in constructing the police theory concerning the time of the offence or taking any active part in the prosecution, an unlikely claim since he was undoubtedly the hand behind the 'pen' producing the brief for the prosecution.

Captain Anson was very generous in his appreciation of Vachell, Edalji's defence lawyer, and readily jumped to his defence as a far more learned and capable lawyer than Yelverton, who had criticised the handling of Edalji's defence. Yet in the next sentence, probably not recognising another contradiction, he slighted the defence for not presenting any expert evidence on the anonymous letters nor on George Edalji's eyesight, which he thought a serious omission on the part of the defence. When discussing possible suspects, he claimed that when the maimings began the investigations focussed on anyone with a known grudge against the owners but no suspicion fell on Edalji or anyone

---

[445] Captain Anson overlooked that the pony's bowels were hanging out when found.

else. It was only after several maimings that the police directed attention to any person of 'roving or eccentric habits'. In mid June 1903, Inspector Campbell was informed by various people of Edalji's suspicious late-night habit of 'prowling' the district and the inspector thought there might be something in the 'sightings'. This piece of information did not square with a previous claim made by the police that George Edalji only came under suspicion after the Blewitt maiming on the 29th June 1903 after a tip off from a local Justice of the Peace with a grudge against George Edalji and his family. Several observers claimed to have seen Edalji 'prowling' the area: (i) John England Hart, a butcher, who had a grudge against George Edalji, and at the time of the alleged sighting was breaking in a colt for a local gentleman, proof of Hart's ability to handle horses – another quality required by the maimer; (ii) William Thacker, a witness against Edalji at the trial whose evidence was contradicted by another witness, had fortuitously included in his statement a comment about George Edalji's eyesight not being seriously impaired – an interesting medical observation from the village ironmonger and a very convenient observation for 1903 bearing in mind the revelations to be made public about the serious deficiencies in Edalji's eyesight four years later when Captain Anson decided to make known these sightings. Two other observers, Police Constable Knight and Mr Herbert Hughes, allegedly saw Edalji in mid-July and early August 1903 when the police were patrolling the area and watching the vicarage. These 'several people coming forward,' later to be described by Captain Anson as 'shoals of people,' were being used in yet another malicious attempt to claim, contrary to specialist analysis, that the issue of George Edalji's short-sightedness was a red herring and he had no problem with his eyesight. The captain also failed to mention to the Home Office that no one ever saw Edalji post an anonymous letter nor maim an animal nor was Edalji ever seen coming out of the vicarage during the night nor on the roads, lanes or fields where animals were maimed, the only person seen in the vicinity of a maiming, twice in fact, was Farrington sentenced in 1904 for killing two sheep.

All the statements alleging George Edalji was seen 'prowling' were signed within two days of each other, the 14th and 16th February 1907, at the height of the public uproar following the Daily Telegraph article, and between four to six years after the sightings occurred and nowhere near a place of any maiming.[446] Significantly, in a letter Captain Anson sent to the Home Office in December 1903 denouncing as 'indisputably false' a defence claim that Edalji did not go out at night, he made no mention of the availability of this wealth of evidence now paraded before the Home Office.[447] The captain had certainly engaged himself in a veritable flurry of activity to secure these statements in the wake of Doyle's attacks on him, reflecting a desperate need to defend himself based on recollections of events four to six years earlier.

---

[446] Ernest Albert Roberts claimed that while driving a vehicle he passed Edalji several times between 11 pm and midnight and, one occasion, about four miles from the vicarage. This was very late on a very dark night, yet he picked George Edalji out and took the trouble to mention it to his workmates. (Statement: 14 Feb 1907) PC J A Knight claimed to have seen Edalji on several occasions around 10 pm about 4½ miles from the vicarage and on the last occasion, a month before his arrest, George Edalji was seen carrying a book under his arm, which the constable took the trouble of mentioning to the landlord of a pub. (Statement: 16 Feb 1907) This sighting would be in mid-July when police officers were watching the vicarage and Edalji's movements, yet no one saw Edalji going into the vicarage later that night, at least 1½ hours later and, as Captain Anson himself admitted, no one ever saw him leave or enter the vicarage. John E Hart, the butcher, whom Captain Anson thought was involved in the 'Green' and other maimings and who harboured a grudge against Edalji, saw Edalji at 11 pm about 2 miles from the vicarage on the night of the fire at Norton Canes walking at a leisurely pace. (Statement: 16 Feb 1907) In early August 1903, Herbert Hughes, general dealer, Bridgtown, saw Edalji at 9.15pm, 3 miles from the vicarage. (Statement: 16 Feb 1907) This was another night when the police were patrolling the area and watching the vicarage, yet they 'failed' to see George Edalji. In the Summer of 1902, William Thacker, ironmonger, later a prosecution witness, met George Edalji 4½ miles from the vicarage, and also mentioned Edalji was short-sighted and had met him frequently in the dark but Edalji never appeared to have any difficulty in getting about. (Statement: 16 Feb 1907)
[447] Capt Anson to Simpson, 31 Dec 1903, HO No 44 File 984

Chapter XIV

New Letters – Old Stories: New 'Experts' – Old Ideas

Martin Molton and the Nark

Three days after Conan Doyle had visited Great Wyrley,[448] with storm clouds gathering over Captain Anson in the wake of Doyle's oral 'notification of intent' to intervene on the side of George Edalji, a new twist corkscrewed its way into the chief constable's office in Stafford. A bizarre letter, the first in a new clutch of pseudonymous letters signed by 'Martin Molton', arrived on the 6th January. This signalled a resurgence of the persecution of George Edalji by someone displaying an intimate knowledge of the Edalji case.[449]

Martin Molton's letter was composed of 'information' stretching back to the 1888/9 letters and despite admitting an inability to prove George Edalji wrote them, Molton was certain of Edalji's involvement in the anonymous letters written by one of Edalji's relatives in 1893. For Molton to be correct either Reverend Edalji, Mrs Edalji, Horace aged thirteen or Maud aged ten was responsible, a view not far distant from the one held by the chief constable. George was also identified as the culprit putting the key on the vicarage step after receiving it from a boy called Collings, who was the thief. Sergeant Upton's version of the 'leaflet incident' was discarded as "not consistent with the truth" as George put the leaflet on the step only after the sergeant temporarily left his post. The scribe also claimed to be the detective working for Henry Slater, who made "a useless visit to Great Wyrley 14 years ago (for) a divorce it was said Mrs Edalji wanted." Molton was also aware of Edalji losing money in 1901 through a fraud committed by a solicitor named Phillips, who was struck off the law list, and of the story of Edalji wagering fifty guineas at Christmas 1902 to rip up six horses, six cows and six sheep before the end of 1903, with "men on the turf", "three thorough scamps, two of them having done time for card sharping and all three for riding without tickets." Unlike the chief constable, the author blamed Edalji for the maimings but not for the anonymous letters, reasoning that Edalji could not possibly know the

---

[448] ACD to HO, 7 Feb 1907, HO File 989 Pt 1

[449] Martin Molton to Anson, 5 Jan 1907, NW London, 5.15pm, MM Letters, England: HO Case of George Edalji – memos and papers, Bp 2/4 (19) pp57/8

contents of these letters unless he was in contact with the Stanley and Quibell boys, which the scribe claimed he (Edalji) was not. Reverend Edalji's decision to lock the bedroom door, keeping the key under his pillow, ensured that no maimings took place between the 29th June and the 18th August, however, despite the reverend's vigilance, George slipped out of the vicarage at 5.15 am on the 18th August and, using a route from the reverend's garden across Green's fields and not over the tram road, went on to maim the horse. Reverend Edalji, guessing what George had been up to, lied in order to provide him with an alibi. This new hypothesis meant that the myopic George Edalji had less than twenty-five minutes to complete the journey, avoid workers on the way to work, find and pacify the horse and do the deadly deed – extremely fortuitous for Edalji to find an animal to kill on the first morning out after so long a layoff.

Two other maimings were specifically marked out as George Edalji's work, those carried out on the 1st February and the 29th June 1903, which were two maimings Captain Anson claimed to have some information suggesting Edalji was involved. Snippets of other 'information' were offered up: Superintendent Bishop was held responsible for putting the hairs on Edalji's coat but overdid it; a good case against Edalji was spoiled by manipulating the time of the maiming; police officers were blamed for failing to find an old top coat, reeking with blood, used by Edalji for his crimes – a coat hanging in the Rectory as late as September 1905 and probably still there; Harry Green had killed his own horse in what was a put up job and retracted his confession through a 'dummy' lawyer named Hallam, paid for by George Edalji; the Stanley maiming in November 1903 was in Green's interest and the Farrington maiming was merely a drunken imitation. Martin Molton did not waste the opportunity to have a 'dig' at Judge Yelverton, George Edalji and his friends for their tightfistedness in not offering to buy his services.

Martin Molton appeared only interested in money-making, £50 for himself and expenses for 24 witnesses, which, in itself, may have been merely a subterfuge to direct attention away from the real purpose of sabotaging Edalji's campaign. In conclusion, he advised Captain Anson, if he was interested in acquiring further information, to place an advert headed 'Rats and Mice, Jupiter' in the London Daily Mail early the following week as "certain things are about to happen." Martin Molton's concluding point suggested he had knowledge of events likely to unfold within a few days and the most significant future event was Doyle's soon to be published but not yet advertised Daily Telegraph article.

The author had discounted the tram road as the route taken by the maimer, Edalji – a pre-publication rebuttal of one of the arguments in support of Edalji's innocence figuring in Doyle's article. Whoever wrote this letter had an inkling of the proposed article and was aware of or suspected what would be Doyle's argument – a lead to someone attached either to the Edaljis or to Captain Anson, but what possible reason would any Edalji have to debunk Doyle's claim – Horace, maybe, if he was the Judas in the Edalji camp. But how could Horace know the basis of Doyle's case bearing in mind by this time, if he had betrayed his brother, his parents would hardly trust him with any information, unless Horace was tipped off through the Anson-Hatton network. If the Horace Edalji-Chris Hatton correspondence of December 1903 was genuine and was used as a two-way communication route to and from Captain Anson then all those involved – Horace Edalji, Chris Hatton, PC Cooper, Inspector Campbell, Superintendant Barrett, Captain Anson and maybe a few other policemen, would have access to that information. If the Horace Edalji-Chris Hatton communications were not genuine then only Captain Anson, and possibly other senior police officers, were in the know and the best person to use this information with a desire to do so was none other than Captain Anson. Noticeably, the Martin Molton letter contained the very issues that Captain Anson was always promoting - his suspicions about the 1888/9 and the 1892-5 anonymous letters; repeating details of George Edalji's financial circumstances procured from an informant of Captain Anson's in the debt collecting world; and criticism of Yelverton. The captain was also aware of a letter from a loan officer referring to an associate named 'Moulton'[450] – a letter George Edalji would know nothing about. George's involvement in the Phillips scandal was known to the police at Stafford gaol and to Captain Anson. George had written of his losses resulting from Phillips' deception and the captain held a copy of that letter at Stafford police headquarters, which he later drew to the attention of the Home Office as 'proof' of Edalji's responsibility for the Martin Molton letters[451] but it could equally indict Captain Anson. Martin Molton was familiar with the legal profession or friendly with lawyers as he knew about Phillips being struck off the solicitor's roll. It was also interesting that the Stanley and Quibell boys were mentioned as potential scribes bearing in mind Edalji

---

[450] "I have not got Moulton's papers yet," A E Toghill (loan office) headed W G Coulton, sol, Crown Buildings, 28 Aug 1903, HO File 989 Pt 2
[451] Capt Anson to Blackwell, 1 June 1907, HO File 989 Pt 1

had written to Stanley seeking information on a visit made by the police to the Stanley household in 1903, which was passed on to Captain Anson.

George Edalji, at the time of the Molton letter, was communicating with the press and other people, including Captain Anson, in his search for information and it was unlikely for him to write a letter of self-accusation in order to give an impression of innocence as argued by the prosecution over the 1903 letters. Moreover, it was inconceivable for George or any of his family living in Great Wyrley to make demands for any sum of money, a few days before George's case was to be published in a leading national newspaper by a famed writer of crime fiction when he was seeking a free pardon and compensation for an unjust conviction. Putting responsibility for the Martin Molton letter on Edalji appeared to be nothing short of ridiculous - an utterly pointless venture on Edalji's part, attributing to him a 'death wish' of gross proportions. Nor was it likely for Doyle to be behind it since he had nothing to gain from such a duplicitous venture.

Captain Anson reacted to the Molton letter by immediately contacting Simpson at the Home Office and, true to form, claimed to recognise Martin Molton's handwriting as that of George Edalji.[452] Having accused Edalji of sending the letter, the captain again showed his inconsistency, in the very same letter, undermining this accusation by implying that Maud Edalji might be the Martin Molton scribe. The reasoning behind this amazing feat of deduction was Captain Anson's belief that Maud Edalji wrote some of the 1903 anonymous letters, which made her just as likely, therefore, to have written the Martin Molton letter. In fact, the captain was more explicit about Maud Edalji's involvement at a later date when he wrote that the Martin Molton letters "may be her actual writing without being her composition."[453] Yet as he had previously made known, the only example of Maud Edalji's writing for comparison purposes was a specimen text and signature almost certainly of 1892 vintage when she was but ten years old![454] The very next day, the 7th January, in another letter to Simpson, the captain again changed his mind and accused George Edalji of being Martin Molton. Plunging the hatchet deeper into Edalji, Captain Anson moved from handwriting analysis to psychiatry by diagnosing Edalji as having a mind diseased "with a mania for creating mysteries" with the Martin Molton letters the latest in this line. Preparing the ground for what he

---

[452] Capt Anson to Simpson, 6 Jan 1907, HO File 989 Pt 2

[453] Capt Anson to Simpson, 10 Sept 1907, HO File 989 Pt 2

[454] Capt Anson to HO, 7 Mar 1905, HO File 989 Pt 1

now realised was about to be launched by Doyle,[455] the captain asked Simpson not to disclose the Martin Molton letter to Doyle because he "thinks his own astuteness so vastly superior to ours that he will be able to show at once some other person wrote the anonymous letters and someone else killed the cattle."[456] An indication, perhaps, that Captain Anson thought that too or even knew it and feared that Conan Doyle was not far from confirming it.

The Home Office put the matter into the hands of MacNaughton of Scotland Yard, who placed the required advert in the Daily Mail on the 10th January. The next day, Captain Anson received another letter asking for £2 in postal orders to be sent to Martin Molton, c/o GPO London, followed by a third letter on the same day telling the captain not to enclose a letter with the money.[457] On MacNaughton's advice, Captain Anson was instructed to send £2 on the 14th January and MacNaughton placed another advert in the Daily Mail on the 15th to say the money awaited collection. A detective was then assigned to the GPO to arrest anyone calling for the letter on a charge of obtaining money by menaces. Captain Anson advanced the view that Martin Molton was trying to trap him into paying money for information "to crush George Edalji!", something of a 'red herring' really since payment of this kind was not unknown or unexpected and if it led to a conviction was hardly likely to be thought discreditable. The captain, flagging up the possibility of a trap being set by Edalji, asked MacNaughton to detain any person asking for the letter on suspicion of conspiracy to injure.[458] This may well have been a ploy to distract attention from a trap he might be constructing for Edalji as Conan Doyle suspected was the purpose behind the Molton letter.[459]

Martin Molton then wrote to Edalji at his London address, posting the letter in Birmingham, instructing Edalji to go to the GPO on Wednesday evening, the 16th January, to collect a registered letter addressed to him (Martin Molton) sent by a friend containing the proof of who maimed the pony, which he would pick up from Edalji on Thursday, the 17th, and pass on any information concerning the identity

[455] Capt Anson to Simpson, 7 Jan 1907, HO File 989 Pt 2

[456] Capt Anson to Simpson, 6 Jan 1907, HO File 989 Pt 2

[457] MM to Capt Anson, p/m WC London, 2am, 11 Jan 1907, England: HO Case of George Edalji – memos and papers, Bp 2/4 (19) p59

[458] Capt Anson to MacNaughton, 13 and 14 Jan 1907, HO File 990; MM Letters, England: HO Case of George Edalji – memos and papers, Bp 2/4 (19) pp58/9

[459] ACD to HO, 27 Jan 1907, HO File 989 Pt 1

of the maimer to Edalji. Edalji was advised to destroy this letter, together with the instructions to call at the GPO, "for fear it should fall into wrong hands."[460] In another letter sent to Captain Anson,[461] posted in London, Martin Molton signalled his intention to pick up the cash from the GPO on 17th January. The scene was now set for Edalji to ask for a letter addressed to Martin Molton containing money extorted from the police. The following day, detectives would be at the GPO in wait for Molton to pick up the money only to be told it had already been collected by George Edalji with his signature on the post office receipt. With the letter instructing him to carry out Martin Molton's wishes now destroyed, Edalji would be in deep trouble. Quite an ingenious scheme if the purpose was to entrap Edalji and subsequent events pointed to this possibility. However, Edalji showed the letter to Yelverton and Doyle and following their advice Edalji sent off a reply to Molton but this was returned through the dead letter office. On further advice from Yelverton and Doyle, Edalji waited for Martin Molton's visit on the 17th and when he failed to turn up it was decided that Edalji and Yelverton would go to the GPO on Saturday, the 19th January.

When they arrived and asked for the letter, the post office clerk asked if either of them was Martin Molton. Yelverton introduced himself and also George Edalji, who produced the letter instructing him to collect the registered letter, wisely not having destroyed it. The clerk declined to release the registered letter as neither man had sufficient authority and advised them to apply to the Post Master General. Outside the post office, Police Sergeant McPherson, tipped off by the clerk, asked Edalji if he had gone to collect a letter for Martin Molton. Yelverton, the law man, explained that they had "not asked for a letter but about a letter." The detective asked for Yelverton's authority and the letter sent to Edalji was produced, with that the detective appeared satisfied and left.[462] The detective's report back pushed MacNaughton into despatching Chief Inspector Arrow to get the letter sent to Edalji on the pretext of using it to identify Martin Molton, who was now wanted on a criminal charge, but in reality to compare the handwriting, which meant passing the letter on to Gurrin, whom MacNaughton had already suggested using to analyse the handwriting – the Beck debacle obviously making little impression on Scotland Yard.

---

[460] Birmingham postmark, Sunday, 9.15 am, 13th Jan 1907, in Gazette 21 Jan 1907

[461] p/m NW London 4.15pm, 15 Jan 1907, MM Letters, England: HO Case of George Edalji – memos and papers, Bp 2/4 (19) p59

[462] Gazette 21 Jan 1907

Yelverton made a bloomer that ended any possibility of catching Martin Molton red-handed if any such possibility really existed given that the whole Molton-inspired exercise appeared to be for the purpose of compromising Edalji. In reporting the incident to the Observer on the 20th January, Yelverton was rash enough to disclose all the details and, after such an advertisement, MacNaughton decided to withdraw the watch on the GPO. There was little likelihood of the scribe calling for the letter anyway,[463] since why would he risk arrest after getting Edalji to ask for the letter although his main objective in getting Edalji arrested went unrewarded.

With Molton's plan unfulfilled, Edalji received a letter on the 22nd January 1907 from an unknown author calling himself 'one who knows'.[464] The contents and the handwriting linked this letter to the first Martin Molton letter sent to Captain Anson. The writer admitted sending the letter to Edalji posted in Birmingham on the 13th January, which linked together all the pseudonymous letters sent out since the beginning of the new year. Presenting himself as an old man whose handwriting had changed over the years, he wanted to own up for his misdeeds as he was about to leave for Melbourne. He admitted writing the 1892 to 1895 anonymous letters, which he claimed was easy for Edalji to ascertain because of his use of the Greek 'E' to be found in some of the letters. However, he disclaimed responsibility for the 1903 letters as he was absent from Staffordshire during 1903 and 1904. The motive behind the letters was his hatred for all foreigners – one of the features of the letters at various times, suggesting that xenophobia was a component part in the writer's thinking. In the same vein as Loxton when he had written on behalf of Captain Anson in the 'Lover of Justice' letter, an anti-foreigner reference was placed in the text but since jingoistic dislike of foreigners was prevalent in this era, a xenophobic dimension in the previous letters did not necessarily identify the guilty party but it did provide a hint of where they may have originated from.

'One who knows' had recently discovered that young Greatorex had killed Green's horse, a fact known to Greatorex's father, and Edalji should advise the police to arrest Greatorex. The author's confidence in the police doing the 'right thing' was matched by his dislike of Doyle, whom he accused of being "only a novel writer for the gutter press."

---

[463] Blackwell note, 21 Jan 1907, HO File 990

[464] p/m Birmingham 11.30pm, 21 Jan 1907; MM Letters, England: HO Case of George Edalji - memos and papers, Bp 2/4 (19)) p62; AL to G Edalji, Mecklenbergh St, date obscured, HO File 990

This disparaging comment about Doyle displayed shades of the hostility of Captain Anson towards those who either crossed or disagreed with him and was wholly consistent with the captain's contemptuous remark made about the author of detective novels, "Remember Sherlock Holmes said 'I am the last Court of Appeal. L'etat c'est moi.'"[465] Apologising for the "cruel injury" inflicted on Reverend Edalji and for the "wickedness" shown in writing to Captain Anson after George Edalji's articles had appeared in the Umpire, the conversion to justice of 'one who knows' was 'Road-to-Damascus' style since his original letter to Captain Anson blaming George Edalji was sent only sixteen days before.

The Home Office decided to bring in its own 'lay expert' to analyse the Martin Molton letters – an official, Blackwell.[466] Blackwell applied the usual 'pre-discrediting of Beck' method of comparing any handwriting style with the 'Greatorex' letters and taking it for granted, if the handwriting matched, Edalji must be the scribe. Acting as if the Beck case never happened, Blackwell concluded that the Martin Molton letters were written in the same hand as the 'Greatorex' letters, plumping for Edalji as Martin Molton.[467] Blackwell also prognosticated on the motive for Edalji's renewed venture into anonymous letter writing, which led him into an avenue that should have exonerated Edalji. The first letter of the 5th January 1907 was seen as an attempt by Edalji to induce Captain Anson into raiding the vicarage in search of a coat to make a fool of him and if a raid on the vicarage had been undertaken Martin Molton's/George Edalji's objective would be satisfied without the need of a written response compromising Captain Anson. In sending the second letter of the 11th January 1907, Edalji was looking to obtain proof of Captain Anson's readiness to buy evidence from a scoundrel prepared to sell to either side but to expose the captain for involvement in the shady transaction of buying evidence depended either on the captain including a note in his own handwriting when sending the £2 or the postal orders being traceable to him. However, this assessment carried little weight, as Blackwell acknowledged, since Martin Molton asked the captain not to include a covering letter. The intention behind the third letter of the 15th January 1907 was to demonstrate that Edalji's enemy, responsible for the 1903 letters, was still hounding him since would anyone believe Edalji wrote

[465] Capt Anson to Simpson, 6 Jan 1907, File 989 Pt 2

[466] Blackwell notes, 3 Feb 1907, England: HO Case of George Edalji - memos and papers, Bp 2/4 (19)) pp70/1

[467] Blackwell/HO to ACD, 23 Nov 1907, HO No 300 File 987

to himself at this particular juncture.

Blackwell thought it would not be too difficult for Edalji to have gone on a return trip to Birmingham to post the letters on the 5th and 11th January or had an accomplice to post them for him; or to send one to himself on the 13th January in order to explain his conduct at the GPO when asking for the letter with the money in it and to enable him to deny any responsibility for the first two Martin Molton letters. However, this was problematic since the 13th January letter was sent without the writer knowing until the advert appeared in the Daily Mail on the 15th January that money would be sent to the GPO. To get around this problem Blackwell thought Edalji could have sent the letter to Birmingham to be reposted on the 13th January in anticipation of the advert appearing. Yet even Blackwell admitted that Edalji's conduct upon receiving the letter from Martin Molton was compatible with innocence unless he was involved in a very devious game. It was on this apparent innocence that Blackwell thought it implausible for Edalji to send the Martin Molton letters but, if Edalji was not the scribe, why did Blackwell think Martin Molton's and 'Greatorex's' handwriting were the same? Could it be that they were the same and it had nothing to do with Edalji?

Blackwell also found it difficult to accept that on the 5th January 1907, only a week before Doyle's articles were due to appear, Edalji would despatch a letter describing himself as guilty, although it might be argued this was what he did in 1903 but to Blackwell that would be arguing in a circle. Blackwell addressed the possibility of someone else being behind the Martin Molton letters, and went on to make out a case against Doyle's suspect, Royden Sharp referred to as X, writing in an 'illiterate' hand but adopting some of Edalji's handwriting characteristics. Blackwell's deductive approach was shown to be somewhat better than his handwriting analytical skills.

The scenario Blackwell constructed, was of Sharp writing as Martin Molton to Captain Anson on the 5th and 11th January and in anticipation of the advert being placed in the Daily Mail wrote to Edalji on the 13th January, advising him to go to the GPO to collect the awaiting letter containing the postal orders. Sharp might reasonably suppose that Captain Anson, believing Edalji to be the author, would arrange for his arrest or identification when turning up to collect the letter. This process would clinch Edalji's connection with the previous Martin Molton letters. Could it realistically be argued that Royden Sharp, considered by Captain Anson to be less than basically equipped intellectually, was able to construct such an elaborate plot single-handed? After working through this sequence of events, Blackwell doubted Sharp's guilt and recognised that Sharp would have had to keep apace with the changes in Edalji's handwriting – the old nutmeg that stumped whatever Blackwell tried to do.

Unlike Blackwell, who failed to consider the possibility of the Martin Molton letters being part of a Captain Anson conspiracy, or if he did had decided not to entertain it, Conan Doyle believed the Martin Molton letters were part of an ingenious scheme thought up by someone with a legal mind and carried out by the police to sabotage George Edalji's campaign for a free pardon. Doyle fixed his mind on Royden Sharp as the hidden hand behind the Martin Molton signature. Doyle had been pointed in that direction by two local men, Arrowsmith, the police informant in the Green maiming, and Beaumont, a miner. Doyle believed Sharp to have had the means, motive and opportunity to commit the Martin Molton deception as well as having the same handwriting as the writing in the letters. The fictional detective writer was curious as to who with legal knowledge would assist Sharp in the venture.[468] Doyle's curiosity may have been well founded as Captain Anson had carried out a similar deception in 1903 with the assistance of Loxton, the lawyer. A connection also existed between Captain Anson and Sharp, since Sharp was working for the chief constable as an informant. Whether or not Sharp was the maimer or the scribe for the initial 1903 letters, he had a vested interest as Doyle was trying to get him convicted on both counts. This was a new Holy, or Unholy, Trinity of interests, each with a perceived or real axe to grind against George Edalji or his supporters.

George Edalji was more specific, suspecting the hand of Captain Anson to be behind the Martin Molton letters and believing that the captain knew he (Edalji) suspected him of complicity. In fact, Edalji was on the score sheet with this prediction since Captain Anson did believe Edalji suspected him and the captain reported this to the Home Office.[469] 'Experts' and lay people were quick to identify the handwriting in the Martin Molton and 'Greatorex' letters as the same, and if they were, Blackwell's proposition fitted more easily with the facts if Loxton or another party was writing the letters under the direction of Captain Anson.

If Captain Anson was responsible for more than the 'Lover of Justice' letter and the follow up 'Greatorex' letter in 1903, and included the Martin Molton letters, then a similarity in handwriting could be

---

[468] ACD to HO, 27 Jan 1907, HO File 989 Pt 1; Capt Anson to Simpson, 10 Sep 1907, HO File 989 Pt 2

[469] G Edalji, DT, in Capt Anson to Simpson, 24 Jan 1907, HO File 989 Pt 2

expected between all these letters, which could be blamed on George Edalji, since he was identified as the author of those previous letters on the dubious testimony of the discredited Gurrin. In fact, when admitting to Blackwell in 1907 that he was the initiator of the 'Lover of Justice' letter, Captain Anson saw nothing wrong in his deception since there was "no intrinsic harm in writing anonymous letters, which cannot harm the receiver," a view very similar to the one held by his relation, De Rutzen, when giving judgement on the actions of a detective-sergeant, who had forged a letter to effect an arrest. However, the captain claimed it was the only time he used this method and doubted he would do so again.[470]

A more realistic alternative solution was of Royden Sharp, in the pay of Captain Anson, travelling around the country as the post boy for an Anson/Loxton type conspiracy. Bearing in mind that the captain had previously used the ruse of sending anonymous letter(s) to Edalji in an attempt to entrap him, might this be another attempt by the captain to discredit Edalji and put a spoke in Doyle's campaign for a free pardon. After all, Captain Anson arranged some kind of a deal with Harry Green to Edalji's detriment. In fact, if the captain was behind the Martin Molton letters, as was quite possible, using information from Edalji's previous letters was an ideal way for him to fix the blame on Edalji. Like the Horace Edalji communications, the contents of the Martin Molton letters could not have been more in line with Captain Anson's own views and needs than if he had written the letters himself or had them written under his tutelage.

The Martin Molton affair had all the ingredients for such a scheme. Captain Anson was not without the relevant resources to keep abreast of changes in Edalji's handwriting. Captain Anson had samples of George Edalji's 1906 handwriting from letters Edalji wrote to the captain asking for permission to photograph a selection of anonymous letters and from Edalji's letter to Stanley, which had been passed on to the captain. If Captain Anson, or more likely an accomplice, wrote the Martin Molton letters, they knew the advert was to be placed in the newspaper and the money sent the GPO. The letter to Edalji accepting his innocence had the purpose, as did the 'Lover of Justice' letter in 1903, of putting Edalji off his guard and so encourage him to collect the letter from the GPO. If Edalji had destroyed the 13th January letter as instructed he would have been left way out on a limb. The captain's insistence on Scotland Yard arresting the person collecting the letter

---

[470] Capt Anson to Blackwell, 23 Apr 1907, HO File 989 Pt 1; De Reske on the case of Det-Sgt Ward, Times 19/20 Aug 1903

would accomplish his aim of completely discrediting Edalji, which he had laboured so hard to achieve in the wake of Edalji's conviction, by clinching Edalji's connection with the Martin Molton letters and for demanding money with menaces.

George Edalji and Captain Anson were not the only ones receiving pseudonymous letters, Royden Sharp and Conan Doyle were also recipients. The first letter sent to Sharp, posted on the 26th February and addressed from "The Borough, SE", came from 'a Scotland Yard officer' warning him of the case the Yard was building up against him, J E H (Hart), and WG (Greatorex or Greensill?) and everyone else. The writer knew of the hut across the canal although not disclosing its significance – probably the meeting place for 'the gang' mentioned later by one of Doyle's South Staffordshire informants. He also divulged that the 'Yard' had a copy of Green's letter together with Sharp's reply written on telegram forms and Sharp was criticised for not hiding an 'r' in his writing that looked like an 'x'. Informing him that no escape was possible as the ports were being watched, Sharp was advised to make a clean breast of it by writing to Conan Doyle either at his home or at the Grand Hotel, London. Sharp was also told that Inspector Campbell was reluctant to arrest him but as Edalji was expected to be pardoned it could mean ten years in prison for him. Several weeks later, another letter sent to Sharp from London on the 17th April bearing the same postmark and in the same handwriting as one simultaneously sent to Conan Doyle, told Sharp that "They can't arrest you yet until Edalji cleared. Someone preached on you, Hunt from Wyrley Bank. Doyle setting watch on you. Your wife has told out of spite."[471] Since Royden was not married and his brother Herbert was in the process of divorcing his wife, the scribe may have confused the two brothers.

When the letters to Sharp were referred to Blackwell, he was of the opinion that the letter of the 26th February was written by Doyle or someone with whom Doyle had discussed the case since it contained many points raised by Doyle – a not unreasonable observation but Blackwell was not so reasonable when he failed to associate Captain Anson with points of similarity in the Martin Molton letters. Blackwell also honed in on Doyle for constantly harping on the 'r' in Sharp's writing, which was written like an 'x', mentioned in the first letter to Sharp and he thought Doyle had probably discussed it with Edalji among others, perhaps, even one of the several pressmen Doyle had taken into his confidence.[472] In one of the letters eleven 'r's were

---

[471] Diary of Events – MM, HO File 988
[472] Ibid

written in the Sharp way and thirteen in the Edalji way but this attempt at deception did not identify either Sharp or Edalji as the culprit. If Doyle was seeking to entrap Sharp why choose George Edalji to copy Sharp's writing with the consequent risk of exposure when someone like Arrowsmith was available. There may be some mileage in the police and Home Office officials suspecting Doyle of colluding with Arrowsmith in these dubious practices as a means of accelerating the identification of Sharp as the guilty person – an approach little different to the misguided methods and objectives practised by Captain Anson and his acolytes in Staffordshire.

Doyle's suspicion of Royden Sharp had been primed during his visit to Great Wyrley at the beginning of the year and Sharp was one of the suspects mentioned to the Home Secretary in January 1907. By the time Conan Doyle received a pseudonymous letter, which he attributed to one of the Sharp brothers, he had already extended culpability for the second series of anonymous letters of 1892 to 1895 to the four Sharp brothers. This 'Sharp' letter, of the 17th April was signed 'A Nark', who stated that "We are narks of detectives and know Edalji killed the horse and write the letters. Edalji not the right sort nor is Greatorex who killed horses too. Gladstone has proof of his guilty deeds. I so worship Sherlock Holmes I would lose my life to save his neck."[473] (My emphasis)[474] Doyle had earlier received an anonymous letter from London, on the 3rd February, headed 'The Temple', in the 'same' handwriting as in the Martin Molton letter and coinciding with a visit Royden Sharp made to London with his brother, Herbert, between the 1st and 4th February for Herbert's divorce hearing.[475] The 17th April letters to both Sharp and Doyle coincided with another trip Sharp made to London, confirmed by Mr Hunt, a porter at Cannock station. However, the porter's disclosure did not meet with police approval and following a visit by Inspector Campbell, he retracted his statement.[476] Mr Hunt was firmly in the middle of two intractable forces as his retraction did not please another anonymous scribe, who, on the day after Inspector Campbell's visit, sent Mr Hunt a letter imploring him to

---

[473] ALs to ACD, 17 April 1907, in Ibid

[474] The words underlined all appeared in previous letters, the first of 1903 vintage and not attributed to Edalji, the second figured in the 'Lover of Justice' letter and the following 'Greatorex' letter, and the last two were not unlike references made about Upton in 1892/3.

[475] ACD to HO, 3 Feb 1907, HO File 989 Pt 1; Note, HO File 989 Pt 2

[476] ACD to HO, 24 & 26 Apr 1907; HO Comment, 7 May 1907, HO File 989 Pt 1

confirm that Sharp left Cannock for London on the 17th April in order to provide the only link missing in the chain of evidence necessary to prove Edalji's innocence. This letter was believed to have been sent by Arrowsmith, one of Doyle's informants in South Staffordshire.[477] Other letters sent to Sharp were also attributed to Arrowsmith acting on the inspiration of Conan Doyle.[478]

Several other letters went to Conan Doyle, including two on the 27th May posted in Birmingham and Bilston. The first was written on the underside of two envelopes, a feature of the 1892 and 1903 letters. The writer expressed extreme hatred for Wil and Anthony Greatorex with whom he claimed to have attended Walsall Grammar School, and the scribe also displayed hostility to that "bloody swine Alldus (sic)" who was sacked after the governors received letters about him. The author made no secret of the racist views he held when criticising the release of Edalji, whom he thought should have remained in prison "along with his dad and all black and yellow faced Jews." The other missive, to become known as the 'Bilston letter', was written on note paper used in licensed premises and came from someone in the Cannock area. The letter contained snippets of information, e.g. a caustic comment about burning down the vicarage made by a police constable in a Cannock barber's shop three weeks before Edalji's arrest and identifying Sharp as the only sailor in the area likely to be involved.[479]

Captain Anson, true to form, when shown the Bilston letter, accused George Edalji of authorship despite admitting not to have looked carefully at the handwriting. The accusation was based on the spelling of Sharp as Sharpe and the reference to Sharp's connection to the sea, hardly the most enlightening material on which to base such a firm conclusion. He conjured up an unsustainable reason for suspecting Edalji by claiming that "no notice would be taken of strangers (in Bilston) unless there was something strange about them."[480] Considering the captain had previously laid great stress, as did newspaper reports, on Edalji's 'weird' appearance, for Edalji to sneak unnoticed in and out of licensed premises in Bilston during the hype created by Doyle's articles was most unlikely, after all, according to Captain Anson, several people spotted him without any difficulty in the

[477] ACD to HO, 17 Nov 1907, and HO Comment, HO No 300 File 987

[478] Capt Anson to Blackwell, 16 Oct 1907, HO File 989 Pt 1

[479] AL to ACD, 27 May 1907, HO File 988; Bilston letter to ACD, 27 May 1907, HO File 990

[480] Capt Anson to Blackwell, 30/31 May, 1907 HO File 989 Pt 1

darkness of night in several places in the South Staffordshire area.

The chief constable deployed men to call on licensed premises in Bilston, Willenhall and Wolverhampton taking samples of paper supplied to patrons but none tallied with the paper on which the letter was written.[481] But what the captain sought to achieve by this canvassing for pub notepaper is difficult to comprehend because unless he sent his men into every licensed house in the West Midlands area or in London, where Edalji lived, or anywhere else Edalji was capable of visiting, his action was an exercise in futility. Contrary to Captain Anson's less than rational reaction to detect the 'Bilston scribe', Doyle quickly discovered the author but declined to disclose the sender's identity unless the Home Office guaranteed to keep it from the police.[482]

The posting of some of the letters coincided with a period from the 13th May onwards when Sharp was away from South Staffordshire – an absence acknowledged by Captain Anson. The captain claimed that despite Sharp leaving South Staffordshire with a ticket for London, he had travelled to a destination away from the capital, and the captain revealed that he had openly disclosed Sharp's destination as London to see if any anonymous letters came from there.[483] However, the captain's explanation to exclude the possibility of Sharp posting the letters from London looked too much like an attempt to disguise the purpose of Sharp's travels outside the Staffordshire area in the service of the chief constable.

After MacNaughton had refused Captain Anson's request to deploy Scotland Yard detectives in the early days of the Martin Molton letters to follow Edalji and report on his movements, Sharp had been put on the Staffordshire police's payroll, ostensibly as a 'nark' to catch unsuspecting pub landlords acting illegally. This was the captain's front story but Sharp, ignoring the chief constable's warning that if others found out about his employment he would have no further use for him, was indiscreet enough to make known the role he was performing with the Staffordshire police. On one occasion, Sharp mentioned being employed by the police and, on another occasion, he disclosed that he was hired at a weekly rate by the police to keep in touch with Edalji's movements. He went even further with an old schoolboy pal, Charles Harvey, confiding to him that the county council was paying him £3 per week to track down Edalji, showing Harvey a letter of authority signed

[481] Capt Anson to Blackwell, 6 June 1907, HO File 989 Pt 1

[482] ACD to HO, 1 & 5 Jun 1907, HO File 989 Pt 1

[483] Capt Anson to Blackwell, 23 Apr & 28 May 1907, HO File 989 Pt 1

by Captain Anson to confirm it.[484] At a later date, Captain Anson sought to justify employing Sharp, whom he described as slow witted, on the grounds that it was difficult to find men not likely to be suspected of being police informants.[485] When Blackwell found out about Captain Anson's arrangement with Sharp, he thought it prudent for the Captain to keep quiet about it because if it became known to Doyle, he might try to make something of it[486] – a caveat for Captain Anson not to court publicity. Of course, Captain Anson did not disclose to Blackwell that Sharp was bragging in South Staffordshire about his employment with the police.

To ensure that the real purpose of Sharp's employment was not suspected by the Home Office, the captain sent Blackwell several very neatly written letters allegedly sent from North Staffordshire by Sharp reporting on his work as a police informant snooping on pub landlords. However, considering Sharp's school academic record and later comments by the Home Office on his poor writing skills, if these letters were genuine, Sharp must have spent many moonlit hours developing such a fine handwriting style as was displayed in the originals of these letters held at the Public Record Office at Kew.

When Sharp's employment with the police inevitably came to Doyle's ears, he played it down in a letter to Captain Anson by giving the impression he thought Sharp's claims of working for the police were not true. Nonetheless, Doyle's letter prompted the captain to make a note in an exercise book denying that Sharp's employment was to watch Edalji and to claim that the objectives in employing Sharp were threefold. These objectives were: (i) to obtain a sample of Sharp's handwriting; (ii) to keep him under observation to assess his character and disposition; and (iii) to give Sharp confidence in himself and in the goodwill of the police because Sharp was receiving threatening letters that might have a serious effect on someone like him not having a

---

[484] Harvey passed this 'confidential' information on to Arrowsmith, the same Arrowsmith who sold information to the police about Harry Green in 1903 and who was now working for Doyle. On hearing how much Sharp was being paid, Arrowsmith offered his services to Captain Anson. The information on Sharp was more than likely to be genuine given that Arrowsmith would need to impress Captain Anson with how much he knew and how useful he could be to him. Arrowsmith to Capt Anson, 19 Sep 1907, HO File 989 Pt 2

[485] Capt Anson to Blackwell, 9 Aug 1907, ACD to Capt Anson, 4 Sep 1907, in HO File 989 Pts 1 & 2

[486] Blackwell to Capt Anson, 8 Aug 1907, HO File 989 Pt 1

strong intellect.[487]

Captain Anson's reasons for employing Sharp were somewhat elaborate. Surely, easier ways existed for obtaining samples of Sharp's handwriting than employing someone of his 'character', all Captain Anson needed to do was follow the precedent set with Harry Green, bring him down to the police station and dictate something for him to write out. However, not even this was necessary because Greatorex senior, Sharp's uncle, had supplied samples of Royden Sharp's 1897 and 1907 handwriting to both Conan Doyle and Captain Anson. As for Sharp's character, Captain Anson had already pronounced on the dissolute type of person Sharp was thought to be, so why the need to reassess it at that time and in such an unusual way. His final justification for employing Sharp also seemed extremely generous putting the captain in the role of an Edwardian social worker and therapeutic counsellor assisting the rehabilitation of the fallen. The role Sharp played was obviously more than the captain was prepared to admit to anyone.

Captain Anson was forced by undisclosed circumstances to express some concern to Home Office officials about Sharp imitating others by sending out anonymous letters, described by the captain as the sort of prank someone like Sharp would be tempted to play on the public just to keep it up – sounding a little like Harry Green's statement in his confession of "keeping the game going". He was so concerned about this susceptibility on Sharp's part for letter writing that he arranged for Superintendent Barrett to caution Sharp as to his conduct. Captain Anson was apprehensive, understandably so, about what he described as one single harmless postcard genuinely traced to Sharp being pounced upon as proof of Sharp's guilt[488] – a clear indication that Sharp was sending out anonymous missives, as he was suspected of doing in 1903 and for which he was nearly arrested, but the captain was trying to pass it off as a 'copy cat' response just in case Doyle tracked it down. Captain Anson protesteth too much about Sharp's innocence.

Captain Anson also supporteth too much Edalji's guilt. Much later when having failed to nail Edalji to the Martin Molton cross, the captain raised the spectre of the letters originating in the vicarage.[489] Unable to find anything substantive against George Edalji, he turned to someone just as vulnerable but still one of the Edalji clan. The captain, repeating

[487] ACD to Capt Anson, 4 Sep 1907, Anson's notes on ACD letters, undated, HO File 989 Pt 2
[488] Capt Anson to Blackwell, 20 Sep 1907, HO file 989 Pt 1
[489] Capt Anson to Blackwell, 18 Sep 1907, 989 Pt 1

earlier claims, thought the contents of the letters had a familiar flavour, lighting on Maud Edalji and accusing her of writing the letters for someone else – Maud was George Edalji's 'front man'.[490] The captain appeared to want it all ways. Interestingly, Captain Anson admitted to Doyle that, "No doubt several persons have at different times been mixed up with writing forged and anonymous letters in the Wyrley district and the more done to clear it up the better."[491]

The Martin Molton and other letters became another battle ground between Captain Anson and Conan Doyle with a sub-plot consisting of George Edalji v Royden Sharp. The sub-plot may have been the means for Anson or Doyle to gain advantage in the main battle, with Conan Doyle seeking to expose Sharp's culpability in order to exonerate Edalji and the captain defending Sharp in order to confirm Edalji's guilt and to further discredit the parson's son. The Home Office, as to be expected, threw its weight behind Captain Anson.

(v) The Experts

When George Edalji was released from prison, the handwriting skills that Gurrin was reputed to possess had been exposed as seriously flawed and his reputation questioned, if not brought into complete disrepute. Notwithstanding the mauling Gurrin received at the hands of the Beck Commission, and the Home Office acknowledging that Gurrin was now discredited, that did not deter the Home Office from using him again. Gurrin was drawn once more into the orbit of the Edalji case to examine the Martin Molton letters, albeit not without some reservations on the part of Blackwell, who recognised that Gurrin had already committed himself by identifying Edalji as the author of the 1903 letters and allowances for that should be taken into account when accepting Gurrin's conclusions. Even Captain Anson came to doubt if Gurrin was up to the task.[492] A notable lack of confidence in the man who played a significant part in securing George Edalji's conviction but it never seemed to enter the captain's head, or if it did it was never expressed, to question Gurrin's competency in analysing the 1903 letters. Gurrin was again used by the Home Office in the expectation that he would try to salvage some of his reputation by showing consistency in his analysis,

---

[490] Capt Anson to Simpson, 10 Sep 1907, HO File 989 Pt 2

[491] Capt Anson to ACD, 11 Oct 1907, HO No 297 File 987

[492] Blackwell papers, England: HO Case of George Edalji – memos and papers, Bp 2/4 (19)) p 71; Capt Anson to HO, 15 Sep 1907, HO File 989 Pt 1; HO Comment, HO No 101 File 985

in other words, they were confident Gurrin could be relied upon to support the allegations of Captain Anson and Home Office officials that George Edalji was Martin Molton.

Gurrin was given photographs of the first Martin Molton letter; the 'Greatorex' letter of the 15 July 1903; specimens of Edalji's writing submitted at the 1903 trial; the 1904 petition; three letters written between October and December 1906, probably the letters Edalji sent to Captain Anson and Albert Stanley; and the handwriting of three of the Sharp brothers. Despite photographs of letters being thought an unsuitable method for analysing handwriting according to Gobert, a French expert, who was to examine some of the letters later on,[493] Gurrin was prepared to use them. On the basis of the photographic 'evidence', he came to the opinion that Walter Sharp's handwriting could be discounted; the differences with Royden Sharp's handwriting were material ones; and only two similarities existed between Frank Sharp's writing and Martin Molton's; but Edalji's writing was strikingly similar. Gurrin tried to hedge his bets by noting several points to be not at all like Edalji's handwriting. The dissimilar points included the way the letter 'r' was written, thought very similar to the 'r' used by Royden Sharp. However, as it was written in an apparently laborious way, Gurrin decided Edalji was responsible as he thought it unlikely for the unscholarly Royden Sharp to laboriously write every 'r' in that way – not a particularly convincing argument since Sharp could have feigned writing in a laborious way. Not only that, it seemed to escape Gurrin's notice that other people might also be prepared to take their time to write in the way described. While concluding that the similarities far outnumbered the discrepancies in the samples and that as a rule he would not hesitate to say Edalji wrote the Martin Molton letter, Gurrin thought that as the Edalji case was exceptional, without disclosing why, he felt only two choices were open to him – either George Edalji wrote the letter, his favoured theory, or someone else was imitating Edalji's handwriting in a most skilful way. Gurrin leaned heavily against Edalji but had given himself an escape route lest he erred again, which was not unexpected bearing in mind his record on the Beck case.

Despite his 'favoured theory', Gurrin admitted to not having made an exhaustive examination of the Martin Molton letter because its

---

[493] Blackwell papers, England: HO case of George Edalji – memos and papers, Bp 2/4 (19) p65

length prevented him from carrying out a thorough analysis[494] – an unconvincing reason that undermined any conclusion he drew on the letter's authorship and throwing considerable doubt on his 'analysis' of the 1903 anonymous letters, some of which were also lengthy. In an attempt to cover his back, Gurrin expressed the belief that the Martin Molton letters were written as a trap set for him (Gurrin), so that if he identified the writing as Edalji's, the person copying Edalji's handwriting on Edalji's behalf would come forward and claim authorship.[495] This, too, threw considerable doubt on Gurrin's analysis since if Gurrin was of the view that it was likely someone had copied Edalji's writing, how could he favour a hypothesis identifying Edalji as the scribe. Gurrin was another one painting himself into a corner.[496]

Gurrin also backtracked on the value of his evidence given at the Edalji trial, experiencing a lack of confidence in his skills following the Beck debacle, by noting that the police had received a number of letters not written by Edalji, demonstrating that others were participating in this activity.[497] Was Gurrin just spinning a line in an attempt to salvage some of his discredited standing or, if the Martin Molton letters did resemble Edalji's handwriting, was someone copying it from recent samples of his writing in the possession of the chief constable at Stafford?

Appreciating that an analysis by Gurrin played right into the hands of Edalji's supporters in the light of Beck, Home Office officials decided to find another opinion, not necessarily for the purpose of giving Edalji a fair hearing – their prevailing attitude was confirmation of not being prepared to do that, but to get someone to support Gurrin. On the 18th January 1907, a sample of photographs was sent via the British Ambassador in Paris to Monsieur Gobert, a French handwriting

---

[494] Gurrin to HO, 8 Mar 1907, HO File 990; Diary of Events – MM, HO File 988; England: HO Case of George Edalji – memos and papers, Bp 2/4 (19)) p63/4

[495] HO comment, 2 Feb 1907, HO No 174a File 986

[496] Albert S Osborn, a handwriting 'expert', who was soon to come to Gurrin's assistance although in a less than convincing manner, writing later on handwriting expertise said "evidence on this subject by a competent witness…is often…of very great force and, in fact, reaches that degree of proof that is properly described as moral certainty." Gurrin's conclusion hardly merited consideration for that category of moral, or even scientific, certainty. Osborn, Albert S, Proof of Handwriting, Illinois Law Review, Vol VI, No 5, Dec 1911

[497] Simpson, England: HO Case of George Edalji - memos and papers, Bp 2/4 (19)) p69

expert.[498] According to Gobert, a strict professional rule to work only with originals was always observed in France when analyzing handwriting because "photographs were liable to error and did not assist verification," a rule from which Gobert never departed. However, on this particular occasion, he threw French convention aside and with the photographic samples sent to him came to the conclusion that the 'Greatorex letter of the 15th July' and the Martin Molton letter were in Edalji's handwriting, a somewhat dubious conclusion given the significant caveat made when introducing his analysis.[499]

Gobert, a colleague of Gurrin as both were retained as experts by the French authorities,[500] was aware of Gurrin's extremely harmful errors in the Beck case, and, like two Americans who were later to intervene, Gobert's analyses, based on photographic copies of dubious quality, may have sought to retrieve the reputation of a colleague from the ignominy of a second strike against him and a profession from further disrepute. The 'closing of ranks philosophy' applied not only to bureaucrats and police officers, it was equally applicable to professional bodies, and handwriting 'experts' appeared to be no exception. Nonetheless, when Gobert's opinion reached the Home Office it was unreservedly accepted by the amateur handwriting sleuth, Blackwell, who despite his previous reservations about Edalji being behind the Martin Molton letters decided to go along with Gobert and Gurrin.

A transatlantic intervention took place when an American handwriting 'expert', W J Kinsley, contacted Gurrin after reading a series of articles on the Edalji case published in a US newspaper, 'The Sun'. Kinsley, and his partner, Osborn, of New York, expressed their irritation at the newspaper articles, which had described Gurrin's opinions as that of "a so-called 'expert' in handwriting." These two Americans with a definite 'axe to grind' offered their services free of charge to examine photographic copies of samples of Edalji's handwriting and the anonymous letters. Their minds were already made up on their conclusions, despite asserting they were uncommitted, because they wrote "we both feel that your skill and experience are such that you could not be mistaken in the matter and we desire to refute, in case we agree with you, the aspersions cast upon you and your

---

[498] England: HO Case of George Edalji - memos and papers, Bp 2/4 (19)) p60
[499] M Gobert - Analysis of Handwriting, 28 Jan 1907, England: HO Case of George Edalji - memos and papers, Bp 2/4 (19)) p65/6
[500] HO comment, HO No 295 File 987

work."[501] There was little doubt on which side of the fence they sat as it seemed their interest was to remove the stigma they felt had attached itself to their vocation. This self-interest did not go unnoticed by one Home Office official, who, hitting the nail on the head, thought Kinsley and Osborn were anxious to endorse Gurrin's opinion to repel attacks made on handwriting experts in general.[502] Initially reluctant to allow photos of the handwriting to be sent to these 'experts' but reassured by a report from the British Ambassador to the USA as to their 'experts' reliability,[503] the Home Office granted permission and the photos were sent but with the condition the photos could not be published.

---

[501] Kinsley to Gurrin,18 May 1907, HO No 291 File 987

[502] HO Comment, 29 May 1907, HO No 291 File 987; Osborn was a campaigner to get handwriting expertise accepted in all US courts as a scientific contribution in civil and criminal cases. He attacked medical experts and "charlatans amongst (handwriting) specialists…who ought to be in jail with the lawyers who discover and defend them." Described as a windbag, by Ludovic Kennedy, he sought the election of handwriting experts to serve the courts for a 10 year period with removal for inefficiency to be decided by a majority vote. Osborn, Albert S, Scientific Investigation of Documents, Legal Intellingencer, Vol 68 No 30; Osborn, Albert S, Proposed Reform in Use of Expert Testimony, Fair Play, Vol 1 No 1 Jan 1912

In 1935, Osborn gave handwriting evidence in the Lindberg child kidnapping and murder case, in what Ludovic Kennedy described as, the framing of Bruno Richard Hauptman, sent to the electric chair for the crime. Initially Osborn, after comparing samples of Hauptman's handwriting copied from the original ransom notes when being interrogated, found numerous dissimilarities. Samples of Hauptman's ordinary handwriting taken from his home showed no similarity with the ransom notes. Osborn doubted that Hauptman wrote the ransom notes. A few days later when told by the police that several thousand dollars of the ransom money had been found in Hauptman's house, Osborn rang the police to say Hauptman was the author of the ransom notes. Osborn's about-turn brought exclamations of disbelief from several police officers involved in the case. Fifty years later, Gunter Haas, a British handwriting expert, examined the handwriting evidence and could find no writing on the ransom note that could be considered to have been written by Hauptman. Arthur S Osborn had, on several other occasions, either in criminal or civil cases, been in error when providing his 'expertise' on handwriting Kennedy, L [1985] The Airman and the Carpenter, Collins, London, pp 181, 183, 201, 224, 277, 417; Times 12 – 15 Jan 1935

[503] W Maycock to Simpson, 12 Jun 1907, HO No 291 File 987

Kinsley, already certain that Gurrin had correctly identified Edalji as the scribe without examining a scrap of evidence, produced a report somewhat limited in content, devoid of any record showing dissimilarities and similarities in handwriting style that might reasonably be expected in expert analysis. In fact, his method did not differ from Gurrin's, circa 1903, since Gurrin readily admitted at the Edalji trial that he failed to make a record of dissimilarities between Edalji's writing and the handwriting in the anonymous letters. Despite the lack of scientific evidence, Kinsley came to the conclusion that anyone with good eyesight, approaching the case in an unprejudiced manner, should have no difficulty in identifying Edalji as the writer – an approach to the letters absent in Kinsley himself. With a touch of bravado or machismo, Kinsley promised that if he could have a few minutes with Doyle, Doyle would quit providing the US newspapers with that kind of material. Kinsley's 'analysis' was promptly despatched by Gurrin to the Home Office, whose officials accepted this insipid contribution as confirmation of the opinions of Gurrin and Gobert, ignoring the caveat of self-interest made by one Home Office official.[504]

Another 'dazzling' analysis of the photographs of the letters came from Kinsley's partner, Osborn, who, unlike Gobert, recommended the use of enlarged photographs, charts and blackboards as a contribution to the advancement of handwriting analysis. Osborn's contribution, consisting solely of the words "The photos establish conclusively the connection of George Edalji with the anonymous letters," arrived to buttress the slowly recovering reputation of Gurrin, at least in Home Office circles, whose officials again accepted this feeble contribution without question.[505] Such was the transatlantic contribution to the art or science of handwriting analysis.

The 'expert' evidence, canvassed or volunteered, had not in any substantive way brought the anonymous letters to Edalji's door. Despite the amount of trouble Home Office officials had undertaken to get back up for Gurrin's results, they recognised the inadequacy of these attempts. A singular lack of confidence was shown in expert opinion but this did not cast any doubts on their 'conclusions'. The officials decided it was unnecessary to use expert opinion to identify Edalji as Martin Molton since they believed too much importance was attached to finding similarities in handwriting styles. Judging by the quality of

---

[504] Kinsley to Gurrin, 3 Sep 1907, Gurrin to HO, 12 Sept 1907, in HO No 291 File 987
[505] Osborne to Gurrin, 10 Jan 1908 and HO Comment, HO No 303 File 987

'expert' opinion, the officials might have a point, although being right on that point did not in any way support the Home Office's view as to the identity of the author. The Home Office trotted out a layman handwriting 'expert', Simpson, to dip his toes in the fetid waters of the Gurrin-examined letters and he drew the conclusion, also from photographs, that the letters were in Edalji's handwriting but that Edalji was not acting alone. [506]

Anyone prepared to give an opinion on the Martin Molton letters was roped in and given some form of credence. Arthur Barnes, the prosecuting solicitor at Edalji's trial took the trouble to make a contribution. Barnes suggested that the letters be brought to the attention of the Wilson Committee[507] as he thought they were the work of Edalji – an assessment based on his memory as he had not seen the letters since the trial! A namesake of the prosecuting solicitor, a man of the cloth turned handwriting 'expert', Reverend Barnes, was also drawn in to give an opinion and he latched on to a similarity of style between Reverend Edalji and some of the letters, especially 'Yours in Satan', written according to Barnes by a clerical hand. He decided that the author of the 1892 to 1895 letters was not a young man, ruling out George Edalji, but someone who "unhappily breathes the atmosphere of a vicarage", possesses the skills for personating others, a man of education and imagination, who had read 'Carey's Danton', probably a clergyman of a certain period when the term 'Yours in Satan' as a parody of 'Yours in Christ' was regularly used. Reverend Barnes was more than implying that Reverend Edalji, a student of theology at the time the parody was in use, was the anonymous scribe basing his opinion principally on the strength of Reverend Edalji's letter published in the Times in 1895, interpreted by Barnes as a sign of someone desiring notoriety.[508] Yet another teleological explanation! Reverend Barnes' speculation might in some way apply to another of his clerical colleagues, Reverend Quibell, close to the ILP socialists, whose son was mentioned in the anonymous letters and who was aware of the police interviewing his son, a point referred to in the 'Greatorex' letter - but no one would seriously accuse Reverend Quibell on the basis of this hypothesis.

Conan Doyle also delved into the area of handwriting analysis

---

[506] Simpson, England: HO Case of George Edalji - memos and papers, Bp 2/4 (19)) p 69;

[507] The Wilson Committee will be discussed in the next chapter

[508] Barnes to HO, 22 Apr 1907, No 299, Re: AL 17 Mar 1893; Thomas Barnes, Hilderstone Vic, Stone, to Gladstone, 28 Jan 1907, HO File 988

without success and introduced his own specialist into the furore surrounding the handwriting issue. Doyle's choice was Dr Lindsay Johnson, described as a handwriting expert, who claimed to have approached the task independently of Doyle's theories. Johnson examined some of the 1892 to 1895 anonymous letters, a photograph of the Martin Molton letter, parts of the two anonymous letters sent to Doyle, the 'Greatorex' letter and specimens of Royden and Walter Sharp's handwriting. Dr Johnson's methodology, on a par with Gurrin's and others trotted out by the Home Office, was to enlarge photographs where even pulse beats could be detected. The 'Greatorex' author was said to write at 13 words per minute, inferring the author was addicted to drink, whereas George Edalji wrote much more rapidly an indication of him being a temperate man. Johnson recognised that the style, spelling, punctuation, formation of letters in Royden Sharp's letters were in varying degrees different from the anonymous letters but amazingly, and without any explanation, came to the conclusion the handwriting in the anonymous letters matched Royden Sharp's.[509]

Dr Johnson's analysis was less than inspiring and fitted well with his persona. Johnson, who claimed to have assisted Maitre Labori to unravel the Dreyfus injustice, was something of a dreamer, inflating his own self-importance, since no one in France had heard of him. However, as Labore never delivered his defence in the Dreyfus case, Johnson would never have been called to Paris to give evidence. Perhaps, this was the reason Johnson was unknown to French officials. Years later in South Africa, Johnson claimed responsibility for the liberation of Edalji and of running the real criminal to earth near Liverpool. This report on his contribution to unmasking the 'Great Wyrley Maimer', written as an epitaph to Conan Doyle, inspired about as much confidence as his handwriting analysis.[510]

To interested observers, an acceptable handwriting analysis was very much dependent on who was making the analysis and whether or not the opinion supported a particular protagonist. Inevitably, nothing conclusive came from the assessments, not surprising really since no one appeared to know much about handwriting – the 'experts' were woefully inadequate and any lay person seemed to be able to claim a competence, equal or superior to 'expert' opinion. Both sides in the dispute agreed that the writing in the Martin Molton letter and the 1903

[509] HO Comments on Lindsay Johnson Report, 14 June 1907, HO No 250, File 986

[510] Johnson, Dr Lindsay, The Late Sir Arthur Conan Doyle, A Reminiscence, Natal Mercury, Durban, 16 July 1930

letters were in the same hand but differed on who owned that hand, the Home Office and Captain Anson claiming it to be George Edalji, Johnson believing it belonged to Royden Sharp and Conan Doyle went through the whole male membership of the Sharp family, with no one thinking it might come from an alternative source – an Anson/Loxton-type connection. That so many people share the same errors does not make any of those errors to be truths.[511] When Yelverton asked to examine the anonymous letters, the officials commented that "any conclusions would inevitably be coloured by the general opinions of the case held by the person who examined them"[512] – this applied to experts just as much as lay persons since most 'experts' had a particular axe to grind.

It was interesting in the light of these comments and those made by the judge in the Beck case, who thought handwriting analysis of little value, how much reverence was paid by Home Office officials to anyone, 'expert' or layperson, making a contribution to the handwriting debate but only if they concluded Edalji was responsible – a veritable flock of sheep bleating the same tune. With such a harmonious melody wafting along the corridors of Whitehall would the Wilson Committee continue to sing from the same Home Office song sheet?

511 Fromm, E [1956] The Sane Society, RKP, London
512 HO Comment, 11 Dec 1903, HO No 26 File 984

Chapter XV

The Wilson Compromise

(i)   The Inquiry[513]

When the Wilson Committee was initially set up, the ubiquitous Captain Anson, as to be expected, offered his services to clear up certain 'facts' on the broader issues not entered into at the trial – an endeavour on the captain's part to 'gild the lily' by offering the committee's esteemed members the spin-doctored 'Ansonian version' of the history of the Edaljis in Great Wyrley. Captain Anson was determined to make sure the committee did not confine itself, as it should do, to matters relating to the charges against Edalji. The chief constable also indulged in a fishing expedition by offering to investigate any new information presented to the committee. Despite the keenness of Home Office officials for Captain Anson to be involved, the committee, most appropriately, declined his offer, at least at the official level. The captain's actions in this regard bore a marked resemblance to the accusation made by the prosecution against George Edalji at his trial, of keeping in contact with the authorities to find out what they knew.

Conan Doyle suspected that the captain would make insinuations to the committee about the father and son's alleged sodomy and other smears against the integrity of George Edalji but Home Office officials denied any such allegations were ever submitted to them for onward transmission to the committee.[514] Of course, Captain Anson did not need the Home Office to act as his messenger as he had an informal route to the committee through his kinsman and it was most likely for the captain to avail himself of De Rutzen's ear to present his jaundiced account of events, as he did to everyone who had some jurisdiction or bearing on the issues.

The first difficulty encountered by the committee, was to assess the trial proceedings in the absence of a complete record. There was

---

513 Committee of Inquiry into the case of G E T Edalji, (Wilson Committee) Home Office, May 1907, London.
514 Capt Anson to HO, 14 Mar 1907, and HO Comment, 15 Mar 1907, HO No 187, File 986; Correspondence between ACD and Blackwell, 17 & 18 Mar 1907, HO File 989 Pt 1

only an incomplete newspaper report; the deposition notes taken before the committal procedures; and Sir Reginald Hardy's fragmentary notes, described by Home Office officials in 1903/4 as of "no use", "barely legible" and containing serious errors of witness identification.[515] The Home Office also supplied 'secret' dossiers from the police; Edalji's articles from Pearson's Weekly; Doyle's Daily Telegraph article; and his letters incriminating the Sharps. The letters prompted a condemnation of Doyle from the Home Office on the grounds that the Sharps were given no opportunity to rebut the charges laid against them. Doyle countered with similar accusations against the police and the Home Office for submitting secret reports against the Edaljis without giving them an opportunity to respond. Doyle's response had a measure of justification, since Gurrin was allowed to elaborate on his evidence given at the trial; another prosecution witness, without doubt a police officer, presented an expanded version of his original evidence; and the partisan, defensive, misleading and disingenuous correspondence of Captain Anson to Home Office officials was also included without George Edalji or his advisers having the opportunity of cross examination or rebuttal.[516] The committee also contacted Sir Reginald Hardy, who not unsurprisingly reported that he and his colleagues strongly believed the conviction to be sound.

This committee was a far cry from the expected Beck-type commission but it performed the functions for which it was set up and its report of the 23rd April conformed to those functions – a compromise solution letting the senior participants in the miscarriage of justice off the hook.

The report was critical of the haphazard and inconsistent way the police collected evidence: the mud on the trousers did not appear to be important to the police on the first visit to the vicarage; the value of the footprints was practically nothing; the claim that the razor was the weapon could not be reconciled with the evidence of the veterinary surgeon; and the stains found by Dr Butter were perfectly innocent. A more damning condemnation was made of the police, baffled and anxious, for conducting their investigations not for the purpose of finding the guilty party but to find evidence against Edalji, as shown by the continuous watch placed on the vicarage and police officers going

---

[515] HO comments on Sir Reginald Hardy's notes, 27 May 1907, HO No 215 File 986

[516] G Edalji to HO, HO Nos 176 and 182, HO File 986; Correspondence between ACD and Blackwell, 16 & 17 Mar 1907, HO File 989 Pt 1; Unnamed source, Truth 24 July 1907

straight to Edalji's house from the scene of the maiming. The prosecution's case was found to be seriously flawed, particularly the way the timing of the maiming was changed, and the committee did not accept the claim that the vicarage was not being watched during the night of the 17/18th August 1903. The deposition statements provided by Police Sergeant Robinson and Inspector Campbell were found to be inconsistent and contradicted the evidence given at the trial. The committee addressed the implications thrown up by the Green fiasco by pointing out that the prosecution's original case blaming Edalji for all the outrages was weakened when Green's horse was killed and its subsequent attempt to claim the maimings were the work of a gang, with Edalji a member, was put to the jury without any evidence of the existence of such a gang. Furthermore, if Green was in a position to connect Edalji to a gang, the prosecution should have taken the opportunity to call him as a witness. Nor could the committee accept that the killing of Green's horse was not a crime because anyone in good faith who wanted to kill an old and valueless horse did not go out at night and rip up its belly.

Having seriously undermined the police's evidence, criticised the prosecution's manoeuvring at the trial and rejected the possibility of a gang, the committee seemed reluctant to deal with the wealth of analytical data submitted by Conan Doyle on the condition of Edalji's eyesight from the ten eye specialists but it did refer to the report from the Home Office's oculist. Even though the committee's report made it clear how unlikely it was for Edalji to travel the prescribed route to the maiming, for reasons known to itself and despite having demolished the other evidence against Edalji, the committee thought the eyesight evidence was insufficient to establish the impossibility of Edalji committing the crime.

With so many deficiencies, perhaps conspiracies, practised by the Staffordshire police and prosecution service, whose highest officials could not be unaware of the evidential weakness presented at the trial, and the after-the-event complicity of Whitehall officials reluctant to recommend overturning an obvious miscarriage of justice, responsibility had to be lain at someone's door and who was more convenient for that purpose than the victim of those deficiencies and conspiracies. To deflect culpability from officers and officials, the committee latched on to the anonymous letters, as had Disturnal, the prosecutor at Edalji's trial.

Lacking any handwriting expertise and without calling any independent expert testimony, inviting only the discredited Gurrin to elaborate on his findings, the committee recognised the letters to have nothing like the evidentiary weight attributed to them by the prosecution and doubted if the jury would have convicted Edalji if not influenced by these letters. The committee skipped over the Martin Molton letters, deciding it was safer to express no opinion – a surprising 'cop-out' as the committee had formed an opinion on the other letters by comparing them, so why not use a similar method, albeit primitive, to make a similar observation? Or better still why not call in an independent, disinterested, handwriting expert? Instead, the committee fingered Edalji as "a wrongheaded and malicious man, indulging in a piece of impish mischief, pretending to know what he may know nothing of in order to puzzle the police and increase their difficulties" - an interesting paraphrasing of the term 'impish mischief', a term used by Captain Anson to describe the 1892 anonymous letters.

Mirroring Captain Anson's earlier view, the committee concluded that Edalji was not involved in the maimings, earning him an acquittal, but had brought the troubles on himself by writing the anonymous letters, which the committee used to deny him any compensation – a not untypical bureaucratic cop-out. Despite disagreeing with the jury's verdict on the maiming, the committee actually accepted the jury's alleged findings on the inadmissible letters – only alleged as there was no evidence before the committee to confirm that the letters determined the jury's verdict. This conclusion was a bizarre reversal of fortune for George Edalji. Initially convicted of cattle maiming but not of sending the anonymous letters, although the letters may have influenced the maiming verdict, George Edalji was exonerated of cattle maiming but found guilty of sending anonymous letters.[517]

The committee came down hard on the Cannock police but relatives of the Home Secretary – Sir Reginald Hardy, and of de Rutzen – Captain Anson, came out of the inquiry officially unblemished and in the clear as far as the committee was concerned. Home Office officials were completely exonerated, absolved from any dereliction of responsibility, in fact, complimented for the "careful and patient endeavours to ascertain the truth of this extraordinary case" and with such a commendation the officials did not warrant investigation.

(ii) Home Office Spin

The committee's attempt to steer a path between partially clearing Edalji while protecting the vested interests of officialdom, did not make the situation any easier for Gladstone, left with the decision of what

---

[517] Sir G Lewis, CA 25 May 1907

action to take. The task of assessing the committee's findings and massaging them for the Home Office to put on its best public face was given to Bettany.[518] Bettany had to find a way to skirt around the committee's findings that showed the evidence had left a reasonable doubt, which should have led to an acquittal instead of a conviction based on the balance of probabilities. Bettany tried to minimise the impact of the committee's view that the judge should have summed up for an acquittal by disclosing that two of the three members of the Wilson Committee thought Edalji guilty – an unfortunate and improper disclosure on his part bearing in mind the committee's criticism of the evidence, which it found to be of extremely poor quality, and in revealing that the 'secret' inquiry was not so secret if individual committee members were making known their individual views. Unless Bettany's assertion was merely his way of applying a spot of lubrication to assist the massaging of the facts.

Bettany argued that the committee successfully disposed of the eyesight problem and its silence on accusations that the police submitted fabricated evidence at the trial must imply they found not the slightest trace of misconduct or conspiracy. Bettany conjured up reasons for the committee's silence, citing the way the police investigated every suspicious character in the neighbourhood, including Sharp and Hart; and that the police had good grounds for suspecting Edalji, e.g., writing letters accusing himself of complicity in the former outrages. Of course, Bettany had conveniently overlooked the failure of the prosecution to link the letters in any way to the maimings and had ignored the caveat about accepting handwriting evidence in the second trial of Beck. He also applied his own version of selective bureaucratic amnesia by disregarding the discrediting of Gurrin by the Beck Commission. A much stronger counter-argument to Bettany's attempt at a cover-up could be found in the committee's very silence on the possibility of the police colluding in order to get Edalji convicted – a nettle the committee found too hard to grasp since it would fuel agitation for a full scale public inquiry, with the possibility of bringing discredit on the upper levels of the Staffordshire police and the lower level judiciary.

Bettany thought it absurd to condemn the police for acting on their suspicions when those suspicions provided sufficient evidence for a conviction but this assessment could not be squared with the committee's actual comment that "the evidence should have left in the jury's mind a reasonable doubt as to lead to an acquittal." Bettany

---

518 Bettany review, 8 July 1907, HO No 127 but filed out of sequence

opened himself up to further ridicule by saying "if the hairs on the coat had been spoken to by an independent witness the conviction would not have been considered unsatisfactory," which may have had some validity if it had happened that way but it did not. Bettany might just as well have said that if the police had caught George Edalji in the act of maiming the horse that evidence "would not have been considered unsatisfactory."

While accepting police evidence to have been "inconsistent and contradictory," Bettany put that down to a clerical error in one of the depositions relating to the watch on the vicarage. However, this so-called 'clerical error' was another doubtful Bettany-creation since this 'clerical error' was overlooked so many times prior to the trial, even by Captain Anson, who was involved in producing the indictment and the brief for the prosecution barrister. The statement in the deposition kept at the British Library was, "I gave general directions to one watching the vicarage that night..." which, in the depositions sent by Captain Anson to the Home Office in 1907 and kept at the PRO, somehow became, "I gave general directions. no one watching the vicarage that night..." The second version was a highly unlikely form of words and with the 't', in lower case, now looking not dissimilar to an 'n'. The imagination is not stretched to see how easy it would be to insert a full stop in the deposition *ex-poste facto*.[519] But even Bettany's 'clerical error' version did not explain the police's oral evidence, given at the police court, revealing details of a police watch on the vicarage reported in the press and not subject to a clerical error.

In trying to justify the contradiction between George Edalji being acquitted of the charge of maiming and refusing to grant him a free pardon, Bettany argued that if the committee had delivered its view within a few months of the conviction, Edalji would have been released without a free pardon or compensation. This conclusion has no logic whatsoever – the granting of a free pardon depends on the innocence or otherwise of the claimant and the time factor when a miscarriage of justice is recognised is only relevant to the amount of compensation to be paid.

Betraying the real motive for his commission, namely to defend officials and the police and not to address the issues of justice and compensation, Bettany suggested that the Home Office could best defend its position by emphasising Edalji's "innocence not being

---

[519] Capt Anson to HO, undated but post-April 1907, and Depositions 3/4 Sep 1903 in England: HO Case of George Edalji – memos and papers, Bp 2/4 (19) p15 and HO No 201 File 986;

established" because if critics were allowed to assume without contradiction that Edalji's innocence was proven and the miscarriage of justice only partially remedied, withholding compensation would be difficult.

In 1903/4, Home Office officials chose to adopt a cavalier acceptance of Captain Anson's many destructive slurs in his letters. This they did to avoid any serious consideration of Edalji's grievances. In 1907, Bettany's similarly destructive and unjustifiable contribution played the same role in underwriting the position Home Office officials advised Gladstone to follow, which, needless to say, the Home Secretary obediently did.

(iii) The Court of Public Opinion

When the Wilson Committee Report was released, a spokesperson for the Edalji Support Committee, Yelverton, put some of the blame for failing to get any compensation on George Edalji through isolating himself from his own support committee. The committee decided to distance itself from what it saw as a fiasco created by the Home Office in cooperation with Edalji's adviser, Conan Doyle. Edalji, perhaps less enamoured of Doyle after the outcome of the enquiry, consulted the support committee to decide upon future action. The committee decided against recognising the findings of the Wilson Committee believing that if the findings were allowed to stand any man could be unjustly imprisoned, removed from his profession and disgraced without receiving any compensation. However, the split between Conan Doyle and the support committee raised question marks about the effect of any further pressure for a public inquiry.[520]

Despite these differences, Doyle, thinking that the Wilson Committee had reached a wretched decision favouring an "impeached officialdom," also believed that the case should be pursued until the injustice was removed. The outcome of the inquiry did not come as a complete surprise to Doyle because in the second week of April information was passed to him that the police, unable to sustain its position of Edalji committing the maimings, were maintaining that Edalji wrote the anonymous letters and was responsible for the misfortune that befell him. It was not the first time that the police/prosecution had changed position at a late stage when their evidence was shown to be of little value. Doyle was under no illusions

---

[520] EN 18 May 1907; ES 18 May 1907; DT 20 May 1907; Tribune 30 May 1907; MG 30 May 1907

that the Wilson Committee had failed to give due consideration to his evidence, a conclusion confirmed to him by the committee's acceptance of an opinion by some unnamed doctor concerning Edalji's eyesight while the opinions of ten experts submitted by Doyle were disregarded.[521] In fact, the unnamed doctor, Risien, had also found it unlikely for George Edalji to be able to carry out the crime, a part of his findings that the committee chose to ignore.

The Wilson's Committee's ambiguous findings found little support in the national or provincial press or the professional journals, either in the leader or correspondence columns. Having deliberated in secret, the committee aroused widespread criticism because the public was unaware of the type of evidence submitted; if witnesses from the trial, including police witnesses, appeared before the committee; or if police reports or statements, confidential or otherwise, were inspected by the committee.[522] The Spectator thought that to acquit a man of a crime but to hint that if all the circumstances were known to the public it would agree that he should be punished while, at the same time, remaining silent on these so-called circumstances, was thoroughly unsatisfactory, unjustifiable, unjust and ridiculous. Putting the committee's decision into its own words it said, "It seems after all he didn't do it, but he's a precious shady sort of customer all the same," which was a conclusion "well enough for the inn parlour" but not for the state in a matter concerning criminal jurisdiction. Taking a leaf out of Lewis Carroll, the Spectator believed that "outside the realms of wonderland no such report could have been put on paper." A similar sardonic comment came from a correspondent, who appraised the committee's verdict as: "It would have been safer not to convict him, but he did it, or had a hand in it, and we'll be hanged if we compensate him." One newspaper leader described the committee's decision as finding Edalji, "Not guilty, but don't do it again" and another thought it too far-fetched to say Edalji "brought the troubles on himself." A professional journal viewed as unfortunate the refusal of compensation or even legitimate expenses incurred in the defence of what must now be regarded as an unfounded charge of an exceptionally odious nature.[523]

[521] DT 23 & 27 May 1907; Doyle, Sir Arthur Conan [1924] Memories and Adventures, Hodder & Stoughton, London, p216; Gazette 23 May 1907

[522] Truth 19 June 1907

[523] Spectator 25 May, 1 June & 31 Aug 1907; Aberdeen Free Press in Police Review 6 Sep 1907; DC 18 May 1907; Law Jnl, Vol 42, No 2158, 25 May 1907 p338;

'Truth' wanted to know why the committee failed to call for an investigation of the Staffordshire constabulary but did not think it so strange considering that Herbert Gladstone, a cousin of Sir Reginald Hardy and a personal friend of Captain Anson, had appointed De Rutzen, a relative of Captain Anson, to sit on the committee. One judge looked on the committee's report as one of the most important documents of modern times dealing with police conduct towards accused persons and the way the state dealt with someone convicted in error. Accepting the committee's finding of police prejudice, this judge considered the report had raised the question of policing practises in Staffordshire where the action of police officers had flagrantly disregarded one of the first principles of English criminal law, namely, every man is innocent until proven guilty. Nor could Captain Anson, with his inconsistent statements, be acquitted of unjustifiable prejudice against Edalji. Extending his comments beyond Staffordshire, he warned that when innocent men, like Beck and Edalji, were deprived of their liberty it was a threat to the whole police force's reputation for efficiency and integrity.

The Police Review, while noting that Captain Anson had been very quiet on the need for a public enquiry until the Staffordshire police were criticised, pointed to Gurrin, Home Office officials, Akers-Douglas and Gladstone, who hung together for their own defence, as those who should carry the can and not the local police. Captain Anson's name should have been added to that list and for the very same reason had the Review seen his letters to the Home Office. With the police theories in ruins, the Edalji case had shaken confidence in the authorities because an innocent man had been convicted.[524] Reflecting the public outcry, the Criminal Law and Prison Reform Department of the Humanitarian League sent a resolution to Gladstone (i) stating it could not accept the committee's report and repeated its demand for a public inquiry, and (ii) calling on the government to ensure that in future accurate reports are taken at criminal trials.[525]

Some albeit very limited defence of the police found its way into the correspondence columns of the Police Review, although the editor made it known he disagreed with the contents.[526] A leader in the Daily

---

[524] Gazette 18 May 1907; Police Review, 31 May, 23 Aug and 6 Sep 1907; Truth 29 May & 19 June 1907; Judge Parry, MG 21 May 1905; Spectator, Manchester City News and Westminster Gazette in Police Review, 6 Sep 1907
[525] Times 27 May 1907
[526] Police Review 7 June 1907

News praised the Wilson Committee for an unprejudiced and careful survey of a complicated and mysterious affair and claimed that the police's failure was intellectual rather than moral but even so it still criticised the police for not realising that with the continuation of the maimings while Edalji was in prison they might have made a mistake.[527]

With the Staffordshire police again under attack and calls for a public inquiry reverberating in many different quarters, the police's defensive mechanism sprang into action. A highly placed official of the Staffordshire constabulary was quoted[528] as being supremely disappointed with the way the inquiry was conducted and resentful of "the unfair attack on the police." He expected the police to have had the opportunity to give oral evidence and complained of being condemned unheard. This official thought a public inquiry might have thrown a different light on the case as the Wilson Committee's report was distorted. The same old chestnuts were resurrected in an attempt to create a diversion, since no police officer really wanted a public inquiry as Captain Anson's machinations behind the scenes well away from public scrutiny were a testament. This unknown spokesperson, who appeared to have the ear and, possibly, the mouth of the chief constable was creating yet another public smokescreen.

The chief constable of Staffordshire, officially, put his name in print and as in the previous unattributed contribution, rehashed the now discredited arguments against Edalji. Captain Anson denied that the police held a negative attitude towards Edalji, who did not enter the frame as a suspect until some months after the first outrage. The captain explained why the police changed its story about watching the vicarage, between the committal proceedings and the trial, which, reading between the lines, suggested that had they stuck to the original story an arrest would not have taken place, let alone a conviction. Linking together two of his claims, Captain Anson maintained that, "the watch was abandoned sometime before the 18th August because it was found impossible to make absolutely certain that no one could come in or out of the house without being observed" and it became "obvious that if a further offence had occurred while the watching was going on and Edalji had been known not to have left the vicarage he would have been absolutely cleared of complicity."

Having condemned the committee's criticisms of the police with his own misrepresentations, Captain Anson, as to be expected,

[527] DN 18 May 1907
[528] Gazette 20 May 1907

concurred with its decision that Edalji had written the anonymous letters but, as he had a longstanding obsession with this, his view should not have come as a surprise to anyone. Like the 'anonymous' police contributor, Captain Anson regretted there had been no public enquiry, a somewhat hypocritical response since the captain had done everything he could to forestall such an eventuality by trading on his knowledge that the Home Office would not allow senior Staffordshire police officers to be subject to public exposure. As the principal bulwark against a proper investigation of Edalji's case, Captain Anson had the nerve to suggest that no one was prepared to go deep enough into the case to understand how matters really stood.[529]

This letter provided yet another example of Captain Anson's ability to sculpture the truth into another shape when it suited him and was naught but a new version of an old song composed with all the same old rhetorical lyrics. Captain Anson's sally into the press did not promote his cause but he could always rely on the Home Office to pull his chestnuts from the fire. However, the committee's exoneration of the bureaucrats was something of a Pyrrhic victory. The protective stance taken by the Home Office to safeguard the interests of the bureaucrats was not accepted outside the corridors of power and did not halt the attacks made on their handling of the affair, now conducted by the Conservative opposition in the House of Commons.

(iv) Westminster Chimes for Edalji

The Liberal Party had returned to office during the period of George Edalji's incarceration in a landslide victory over the Conservatives on the issue of free trade versus protection. The 'free traders', now in office, seemed to be just as protective as the previous incumbents when it came to the interests of the bureaucracy. The reverend's expectation of a more responsive approach from the Liberals to his son's difficulties was misplaced. Disappointment awaited him as the new Home Secretary, Herbert Gladstone, stalled in the same dogmatic way as his Conservative predecessor and the same bureaucratic brick wall was erected against George Edalji, albeit this model was cemented with a touch of nepotism.

Gladstone played the committee's report two ways.[530] Firstly, in protecting Captain Anson; the Staffordshire judiciary, particularly Sir Reginald Hardy; and Home Office officials; he disclosed the principles

529 Ibid, 23 May 1907
530 H Gladstone, Hansard, 3 June 1907, Vol 175 col 306; DT 18 May 1907

for advising the grant of a free pardon, which he claimed only applied when a prisoner's innocence was established to the Home Secretary's satisfaction. Secondly, in order not to fly in the face of overwhelming public concern over Edalji's conviction, Gladstone was forced to concede the Edalji case to be exceptional, but he was not prepared to go as far as declaring Edalji innocent. In fact, he diverted attention from the miscarriage of justice into an inadvertent consequence of the conviction – Edalji's removal from the solicitor's rolls was not part of the sentence and could now be redressed, a hypocritical stance on Gladstone's part because under normal circumstances he must have known readmission to the rolls would be most unlikely with an accusation of sending a letter threatening to kill a police officer indirectly confirmed by the committee. However, the Master of the Rolls, in the not too distant future, made a decision that threw sand into the faces of the Wilson Committee, the Home Secretary and Home Office officials.

After consulting Wilson on the advice to be given to the king for exercising the royal prerogative, Gladstone, in a paltry "grudging and ungracious fashion", used Edalji's ruined career as a means for recommending a free pardon without compensation, whilst protecting his own relative, his friend and government bureaucrats.[531] Not giving compensation was a means for Gladstone to thwart any possibility of complete exoneration for Edalji. As one judge put it, the Home Office appeared to be more interested in money than justice.[532] Officialdom, vindictively, was to have its last ounce of flesh. Obtaining a free pardon was the only means to officially admit that Edalji should never have been convicted but even this was tarnished by Gladstone and the Wilson Committee.[533]

Understandably, the Edaljis held mixed feelings and an appreciative response from them was not on the cards. Mrs Edalji's attitude to the pardon, eventually granted on 15 May 1907, was joy mingled with disappointment and she announced the intention of continuing the campaign. Reverend Edalji, barbed tongue in cheek, commented on the "diplomacy and statecraft" of the Wilson Committee's decision after his son had been imprisoned on false charges concocted by the Staffordshire police and ably assisted by the Home Office to keep him in prison for three years. Selecting a suitable comparison, Reverend Edalji made the point that the treatment meted

[531] DT 20 May 1907
[532] Judge Parry, MG 21 May 1907
[533] Truth 22 May 1907

out to his son would not have happened to the son of an English squire or nobleman – an interesting comparison choosing these types of social status for his example, since major protagonists of the Edalji family included respectively J T Hatton, known as 'squire', and Captain Anson and Lord Hatherton, of noble birth. Friends in Great Wyrley rejoiced in George Edalji's innocence being recognised, despite feeling their work only half done until compensation was granted to him. A pardon was less than sufficient for George Edalji, expecting at least an apology; out of pocket expenses to be refunded to campaign contributors; and compensation for his suffering. He felt yet again a scapegoat, this time to shield Captain Anson and the Staffordshire Constabulary for failing to catch the maimer and he was determined to push for a full apology and compensation.[534] He wanted redress for his suffering even if it took years, and over the years he was true to his word as was his sister, Maud, fifty years later.

The elected members, representing the majority of the male population, consistently raised the Edalji case in the House of Commons, applying considerable pressure for compensation for imprisonment, personal suffering and the ruination of Edalji's promising career.[535] However, Gladstone and Home Office officials refused parliamentarians the privilege of viewing the papers held at the Home Office upon which the Wilson Committee based its decision on public interest grounds. Then as now 'public interest' was masqueraded to all and sundry as a means to protect a cocktail of personal interests.[536]

Gladstone, also showing signs of that temporary debilitating ailment suffered by front bench spokespersons – short-term memory loss, disavowed knowing of any comparable cases for compensation, but others outside the Home Office were quick to discover several precedents, including the recently exonerated Beck. A few days later, Gladstone, memory restored, admitted to twelve cases of compensation being recommended by the Home Office in the last twenty years for persons convicted unsatisfactorily. The 'get-out' proviso for Gladstone was that compensation was given only in rare and exceptional cases

---

[534] DC 18 May 1907; Gazette 29 Apr 1907; DT 20 May 1907; G Edalji to HO, 13 Jun 1907, HO No 249 File 986; Despatch, 18 May 1907

[535] Pike Pease, Darlington, and Sir Gilbert Parker, Gravesend, Hansard, 13 Mar 1907, Vol 171 col 19; 13 May 1907, vol 174 col 634; 25 Apr 1907, vol 173 col 274; and 28 May 1907, vol 174 col 1473; Gazette, 30 May 1907

[536] Hansard, 17, 18 & 24 June 1907, vol 176 cols 160, 328 & 885/6

when a defendant's innocence was completely re-established.[537]

With the Liberal Party disappointing one of its loyal supporters, Reverend Edalji, it was left to the Tories to give notice of their intention of raising the case during the debate on the Home Office estimates. Edalji's supporters successfully ensured that F E Smith, the future Lord Birkenhead, was given first place to reply in the debate. The Liberals, as political parties tend to do when criticized, interpreted this as a political attack on the government because the Tories had done nothing themselves for Edalji when in office, in itself a valid criticism.[538] Protecting Home Office officials and the police was more important than the search for justice – nothing particularly novel in that.

When the Home Office estimates came up for debate, several topics occupied the House until past 10 pm, leaving less than an hour to debate the Edalji case. Just as Gladstone used the Commons to protect officialdom and the police, F E Smith, used the Commons to denounce Edalji's conviction. Illuminating the House with the background history, F E Smith provided a reasonable account of the Edalji case, covering many of the abuses experienced by the Edaljis after their arrival in Great Wyrley. Smith found it not too difficult to determine what kind of representations were made by the chief constable to the Wilson Committee – hardly likely to lead to a fair consideration of the case. He, too, pointed out the ambiguity of the Home Secretary binding himself to a finding on which the jury was not competent to pronounce - the anonymous letters, while overruling the jury's decision on a matter within their competence – the maimings.[539] After Smith's speech, Gladstone offered the lame excuse of the case having already been tried before a jury – which returned a unanimous verdict; had been seen by two Lord Chancellors; other law officers of the present government; and every kind of expert,[540] ignoring that the Wilson Committee overturned the jury's verdict; and some government legal experts produced an analysis exonerating Edalji albeit providing a conclusion whose intention appeared to be not 'to rock the boat'.

On the one hand, Gladstone defended the committee's assessment of the anonymous letters stating, disingenuously because he had already been advised as to their inadmissibility, that they formed part of the evidence and only after careful examination did the jury give their

---

[537] H Gladstone, Hansard, 3 & 6 June 1907, vol 175 cols 306 & 854; MG, 30 May 1905

[538] In folder titled "Tribune" in HO File 988

[539] F E Smith, Hansard, 18 July 1907, vol 178, cols 1004 - 1015

[540] H Gladstone, Hansard, 18 July 1907, vol 178 col 1015

verdict – a verdict on the maiming not on the anonymous letters. On the other hand, Gladstone defended the Staffordshire police against the Wilson Committee's findings, claiming they acted entirely in good faith throughout and there was no justification for the serious charges made against them.[541] Gladstone's 'pick and mix' response was part of a scheme to dismiss calls for a thorough investigation; punishment of the police; or exposure of the Home Office's handling of the case.

Insufficient time was left for a real debate on the issues and the parliamentary thrust was thwarted. Gladstone, however, concerned about the possible fall out from the committee's findings and quite willing to follow the dubious practices of his advisers and those, whom he sought to protect, improperly canvassed support from Sir Robert Romer, who had earlier withdrawn from the Committee of Inquiry unhappy with its terms of reference. Gladstone asked Sir Robert to write to *The Times* in support of the Wilson findings but Sir Robert, no intention of being drawn into the Home Secretary's machinations, declined this dubious invitation.[542]

Sir Reginald Hardy, whose brief supporting role at the Staffordshire Quarter Sessions in October 1903 had thrust him into the limelight, assailed from all directions and particularly smarting under the criticism thrown at him by the Wilson Committee and Members of Parliament, wanted to publish the correspondence between the Home Office and himself. However, when the Home Office put up no resistance to his proposal, Hardy's blustering evaporated and, thinking better of it, disappeared from view.[543]

With Sir Reginald Hardy throwing in the towel at least publicly, it was left to Captain Anson, made of sterner stuff, to line up politicians against Edalji. Trying to pull the strings behind the scenes, the captain, not averse to interfering in the so-called political neutrality of civil servants, suggested to Home Office officials that an approach be made to Albert Stanley, the new MP for North West Staffordshire, who, according to the captain, knew a lot about the people involved in the case. Captain Anson's dislike of Stanley's Liberal/Labour political opinion was of little significance when compared to his intense dislike of the Edaljis. The captain, drawing on other political contacts representing all sides of the political spectrum, encouraged Staveley-Hill, Conservative MP for Kingswinford, a Staffordshire magistrate and

---

[541] H Gladstone, Hansard, 3 June 1907, vol 175 col 305; 26 Aug 1907, vol 182 col 141;

[542] Sir R Romer to Gladstone, 5 Aug 1907, HO 989 Pt 2

[543] Sir Reg Hardy to HO, 26 Jun 1907, HO No 257 File 986

a captain in the Staffordshire Yeomanry, to contact the Home Office to express his belief that Edalji should not have been freed if there was doubt about his innocence and to raise a question in the House – duly arranged with Gladstone for him to do so.[544]

Staveley-Hill was initially inclined towards the argument put by F E Smith, a fellow Conservative, not through sympathy for the Edaljis but because a refusal to compensate George appeared inconsistent with a free pardon. However, Staveley-Hill eventually adopted a different line, no doubt after Captain Anson had given him the jaundiced presentation to which everyone else had been a recipient, and he offered to do all he could in defence of the chief constable.[545] The question put by Staveley-Hill was formulated by Home Office officials as was the Home Secretary's answer.[546] Staveley-Hill's plant question asked the Home Secretary if he was in a position "to say there is no ground for the grave charges made against the Staffordshire police in the Edalji case" bringing Gladstone's not unexpected response that there was no justification for the serious charges made against them.[547]

Whitehall did have a 'cuckoo in its nest' in the form of a political assistant, who wrote a statement for Gladstone attacking the Home Office and its system of dealing with petitions. Too hot for the Home Office to handle, its officials gave it the 'blue pencil' treatment by deleting parts and rewriting them. The original draft condemned the restrictions placed on the Wilson Committee, "hampered because it had no power to call witnesses"; was critical of the committee itself for "diverg(ing) from the question of Edalji's conviction, to consider the handwriting upon which they were not experts or authorities"; and yet, "All their findings, except one, proved absolute innocence of Edalji...Gladstone would no doubt have granted compensation but for their finding of Edalji contributing to his punishment...Gladstone bound by Home Office precedent (and the) Home Office(,) and (it was the) Home Office system (that was the) proper subject of attack."[548] The Home Office version finished up as Gladstone's statement to Parliament. No dissent was to be shown from the united front of ministers, Home Office officials, the Staffordshire police, judiciary and their machinery. It was a question of them hanging together or hanging separately, with apologies to Benjamin Franklin.

---

[544] Capt Anson to Blackwell, 26 Aug 1907, HO File 989 Pt 1

[545] Capt Anson to Blackwell, 22 & 25 Dec 1907, HO File 989 Pt 2

[546] HO No 276, File 987

[547] Hansard, 26 Aug 1907, vol 182 col 141

[548] In folder titled "Tribune" in HO File 988

(v) Trying to Turn Jack Hart:

Whilst Captain Anson was priming at least one sympathetic politician to turn his back on Edalji with questions set up for the Home Secretary to knock down, and Gladstone was trying unsuccessfully to rope in Sir Robert Romer to rally behind the establishment, Conan Doyle was bent on turning one of his suspects by roping in an accomplice and setting up Royden Sharp for the maimings. Conan Doyle may have twisted and turned over who was responsible for the handwriting and the maiming but Royden Sharp was not the only one he thought to be involved. Doyle believed a plot was hatched amongst the members of the local yeomanry, involving Harry Green, Fred Brookes, now in Manchester, Thomas and Grinsell, with Jack Hart co-opted into the scheme but did not explain how Sharp fitted in with the 'yeoman thesis'. Doyle expected all would turn king's evidence against Sharp if encouraged, however, it was to Hart that Doyle turned to perform this 'duty' with the unsupportable promise of a pardon from the Home Office and a reward from the Edalji Support Committee.[549]

Letters went from Doyle to Hart on the 6th and 9th June 1907 and the 25th July 1907, with this offer but Hart took no notice, convinced Doyle knew nothing definite. Not put off by Hart's silence, Doyle arranged for Mr Whitehouse, an insurance supervisor, to try to induce Hart to co-operate but Hart, reluctant to act, expressed considerable bitterness towards George Edalji because of the libel case at the Kings Bench that had caused him unnecessary expense. Doyle's offer was 'the stuff of detective fiction' because any promise of a pardon for financial consideration made a confession unreliable and valueless. Hart's testimony would also need corroboration to carry any weight in a court of justice and Sir Charles W Matthews and Lord Desart advised the Home Office, if Hart decided to collaborate in Doyle's scheme, to reject it as improper and immoral.[550]

Hart contacted the Staffordshire police about the offer, not something new for Hart since this intractable enemy of George Edalji had already given the police an eye witness account of Edalji, years before, allegedly 'prowling' around South Staffordshire. When told of

---

[549] ACD, quoted in Whittington-Egan R & M, 1985, Gray House Books, London, p123

[550] ACD to HO, 2 Aug 1907, HO No 271 and HO to Attorney-General, 1 Aug 1907, HO No 269 File 986/7; Capt Anson to Blackwell, 26 Aug 1907, HO File 989 Pt 1

Doyle's invitation, Captain Anson suggested Hart took up the offer but to tell Doyle he was unable to throw any light on the case. A curious direction from Captain Anson because if Hart really knew nothing what was there to throw light on. The captain's suggestion gave the impression that he wanted to conceal something that Hart knew about and was worried about what Doyle might find out or have what he might already know confirmed.

Hart travelled to London on the 16th August to be interviewed by Doyle in the company of Doyle's brother, and while he was there met other people, including his arch-foe, George Edalji. Hart wanted the terms of any deal well defined before saying anything and in all probability told Doyle nothing of substance. Hart denied knowing Sharp but admitted to being well acquainted with Harry Green, who was due shortly to return from South Africa – it looked as if Green went to South Africa to sit it out until things blew over and was coming back prematurely. Hart duly reported back to Captain Anson, who, believing Hart was not to be trusted, rejected Hart's version of telling Doyle nothing, which in a way implied that Hart had something to tell. The captain indicated what this might be in a letter to the Home Office in which he disclosed that he (Anson) "would not be a bit surprised to know that he (Hart) helped Green to kill his own horse, or anything of that sort. He is not a man to be treated as above suspicion." From then on, Hart completely avoided both the police and Doyle, and Doyle's attempt to incriminate Sharp through Hart bore no fruit.[551]

---

[551] ACD letters, undated, HO File 989 Pt 2; Capt Anson to Blackwell, 26 Aug 1907, HO File 989 Pt 1

Chapter XVI

Caricature Returns as Farce

(i)   The Maimings Return

While the fall-out from the Wilson Committee was descending on friend and foe alike; and the Doyle-Anson feud waged over the guilt or otherwise of the Sharps and the Edaljis,[552] animal bloodlettings returned to South Staffordshire. On the 20th August 1907, just passing the fourth anniversary of the 'Edalji maiming', a horse belonging to Mr Cartwright was discovered maimed by Joseph Wootton, an employee at nearby North Cannock colliery. Upon hearing of the crime, Superintendent Bishop and Inspector Campbell lost no time in getting to the scene but a cow in the field had blood on its horns so the incident was passed off as an accident. The owner was not convinced of a cow-perpetrated maiming as he thought the cow's horns too blunt to cause this kind of injury and, the veterinary surgeon, Mr Forsythe, although initially unsure, concluded that the wound was inflicted by someone with a blunt instrument. Despite Forsythe's informed analysis and Cartwright's experience, the police went along with its 'bovine' theory and chose to make no further inquiries. The maiming set alarm bells ringing amongst the villagers but despite their fears they went along with the police explanation.[553]

Superintendent Bishop's presence at the scene of this 'accident' was an indication of the pressure the Staffordshire police authorities were under following the Wilson Committee's criticism of their practices during the investigation of the 'Edalji' maiming, although this senior officer's contribution merely confirmed the police's predisposition to overrule expert evidence when that evidence did not suit its own interests. Evidence, as always, was tailored to fit a police hypothesis rather than forming the basis of any hypothesis.

Shortly afterwards, when two mares belonging to Captain Harrison, of Harrison's Colliery and a landowner in the area, were found by a farm labourer, John Smith, disembowelled in a field in the parish, the police could not dismiss this incident as an accident.[554] The

---

[552] See Appendix I

[553] Gazette 21, 22 and 28 Aug1907; DC 28 Aug 1907; DT 23 Aug 1907; PMG 22 Aug 1907; DE 20 Aug 1907

[554] DT 28 Aug 1907; Tribune 28 Aug 1907; MG 29 Aug 1907

maimings were carried out close to a factory manufacturing bill hooks and edge tools and within one mile of the railway station, as were all other maimings in the parish since February 1903. Police Constable Hodson was the first officer at the crime scene soon to be followed by a contingent of officers from Great Wyrley and Cannock, and joined shortly afterwards by Captain Anson and Chief Superintendent Bishop in a hurried trip to the area. The big guns may have been there to aid Inspector Campbell but their presence might also have been to 'vet' the situation so no benefits accrued to Edalji or no greater detriment was incurred by the Staffordshire police.[555]

Corliss and Forsythe, two veterinary surgeons, who examined the injuries, described them as similar to those on Stanley's horse in November 1903 - wounds that were long but not deep, inflicted by a sharp instrument and carried out with the same degree of skill and stealth as in the other outrages. But unlike those maimings, the Harrison, as well as the recent Cartwright, horses were cut vertically bolstering the view that the Cartwright maiming might not be an accident. Both horses were seen unharmed at midnight and also at 5 am with the time of the outrages fixed by both veterinary surgeons at around 3 am. Characteristically, the police decided the incident was committed at 11 pm, basing its decision on a cyclist seeing a man by the field at that time.[556]

The police were without a clue, admitted Superintendent Bishop, but not everyone was as clueless. The general manager of Harrison's Colliery, Mr Williamson, believed the perpetrator "must have known his way about the country blindfolded and have been expert in dealing with horses (as) the mare was extremely difficult to catch even to persons to whom she was accustomed."

The police were not really entirely clueless because they did have several suspects in mind. The most favoured candidate was 'the not long out of prison' Farrington, whose tendency to go out late at night – another one 'prowling' the district – drew attention to him. Another feature promoting Farrington to number one spot, was his imprisonment in April 1904 for killing Badger's sheep, after which the maimings ceased only to recommence once he returned to the area. Captain Anson thought it possible Farrington killed the latest victims for a financial

[555] Gazette 28 Aug 1907; DN 30 Aug 1907
[556] Gazette 28, 30 & 31 Aug 1907; Police Chronicle 31 Aug 1907; DM (Lon) 31 Aug 1907

consideration arranged through Hart[557] but after searching Farrington's home and examining his clothes, found to be free from incriminating evidence, Farrington was freed from suspicion. Farrington was also able to rely on an alibi of sleeping in a room with a lad, who corroborated his story of going to bed early on the night of the maiming - an explanation the police did not dispute. The captain, in his communications with the Home Office,[558] did not hide his disdain for Farrington but, interestingly, the alibi provided for a man with convictions for a previous maiming, drunkenness and disorderly conduct was accepted without question in stark contrast to the attitude towards a similar alibi given for George Edalji by Reverend Edalji, a minister of religion and free from any criminal convictions. The Staffordshire police adopted curious standards in assessing the veracity of witnesses. Nor did the sleeping arrangement between a man and a boy spawn the kind of malicious comments made about the two Edalji males, although communal sleeping arrangements amongst the impoverished working classes were not unknown. In spite of apparently clearing Farrington, Captain Anson thought he was not above suspicion and placed a watch on him, believing he might give "himself into our hands."[559]

Jack Hart figured in the police enquiries and the inside information from Mr Williamson about the mare being difficult to catch should have endorsed suspicions of Hart's involvement given that he was a suspect in 1903, identified as such by Captain Anson in a letter to the Home Office only the day before this latest maiming, and he was competent in handling horses. Royden Sharp was also in the frame and several people in the area knew him to be out and about – 'prowling', when the outrage was committed, including Mrs Sharp, who reported that her son did not return home until the following morning. Captain Anson, never slow in defending Sharp, put Sharp's night out down to a nocturnal rendezvous with a young woman named Hall living outside Cannock or with her successor. Nor was Captain Anson unduly concerned about Sharp's early morning return arguing that a guilty man would make sure not to be seen travelling from the scene of an offence and accepted Sharp's nocturnal ramblings as unconnected with the cattle maiming. A valid enough point but George Edalji was prosecuted

---

[557] Capt Anson to Blackwell, 4 Sep & 1 Dec 1907, HO 989 Pt 1 & 2; Tribune 31 Aug 1907

[558] Capt Anson to Blackwell, 26 Aug 1907, HO File 989 Pt 1; DM (Lon) 31 Aug 1907

[559] Capt Anson to Blackwell, 9 Oct & 1 Dec 1907, HO File 989 Pt 1;

partly on the grounds of nocturnal ramblings while Captain Anson believed Edalji was not connected with any maiming. One more example of the double standards operating within the captain's repertoire of police practices. In the expectation of any further maimings fuelling the clamour against Sharp, Captain Anson 'encouraged' Sharp to leave the area, not going so far as to send him a 'Lover of Justice' letter, but Sharp declined the invitation prompting police surveillance on Sharp for his 'own protection'.[560] Captain Anson's unavailing defence of Sharp appeared curious. Was it due to Sharp's employment with the police or some other serious issue at the heart of this protective behaviour? Was it to prevent Sharp from exercising his proclivity for writing 'copy-cat' anonymous letters?[561] And who was this mysterious maimer expected to kill other animals to 'fuel the clamour against Sharp'?

Captain Anson, stuck in his own particular groove, went through the usual routine and brought into play his fall back position of there being more than one person involved in the outrages, more than likely a valid point, but this time the captain drew back from suggesting it was another remnant of the gang Edalji was allegedly linked to in 1903.[562]

One person the police could not pin the Harrison maiming on was George Edalji, far away from Great Wyrley on holiday in Yarmouth, unless he used Eastern mysticism to transport himself from Yarmouth to Great Wyrley in an earthly version of the transmigration of the soul. Captain Anson was well aware of Edalji's trip to Yarmouth and was informed of Edalji's return to London on the 30th August – an indication of someone keeping track on his movements and it was an interesting coincidence for a maiming to occur when Edalji went travelling outside of London. To compound this coincidence, an anonymous letter, apparently in the same handwriting as the 'Alldus,' letter, was sent not far from where Edalji was staying on holiday in Norfolk, telling Captain Anson to keep an eye on the 'Old father'.[563] One outcome of the maiming, no doubt much appreciated by the chief constable, was that George Edalji never returned to Great Wyrley.

Within Great Wyrley, fear began to embrace the populace in

[560] ACD to HO, 17 Nov 1907 and HO Comment, HO No 300 File 987; Capt Anson to ACD, 11 Oct 1907; HO No 297 File 987; Tribune 29 Aug 1907; Capt Anson to Blackwell, 1 Dec 1907, HO File 989 Pt 2

[561] Capt Anson to Blackwell, 20 Sep 1907, HO file 989 Pt 1

[562] DE 29 Aug 1907; Gazette 28 & 30 Aug 1907

[563] Gazette 28 Aug 1907: Capt Anson to Blackwell, 8 Sep 1907, HO File 989 Pt 1

expectation of a rerun of the 1903 horrors. As in 1903, farmers lost confidence in the police and refused to leave animals in the fields or they resorted to having farm hands guard the cattle with firearms, scythes, sticks and other weapons, made more necessary when the London brokers, in expectation of another wave of maimings, refused to insure cattle in the Great Wyrley area.[564] In spite of their apprehension of a new outbreak of maimings, local people showed a marked reluctance to co-operate with the police using George Edalji's experience in 1903 as a yardstick because when he showed an interest in the crimes it was used against him at the trial. One beneficiary of the maiming was Reverend Edalji with attendances at St Mark's Church booming to reach 1903 levels, attracting people from Birmingham and Stafford into the pews,[565] as the feeling grew of Edalji being innocent of the August 1903 maiming. With these increasing doubts about the Edalji conviction, Captain Anson, as intransigent as ever, would not entertain any possibility of the recent maimings pointing towards Edalji's innocence.[566]

The Harrison maiming came on the morning after Gladstone chose to exonerate his friend, the chief constable, and the Staffordshire police, from all charges arising out of the Edalji case, more a demonstration of loyalty than rational thought – thus was it ever.[567] Perhaps the maimer was tweaking the whiskers of the Home Secretary and, more specifically, Captain Anson as might well be the reason for the maimings in September and November 1903. Conan Doyle thought the culprit wanted to make Inspector Campbell look ridiculous but the inspector's superior officer, Superintendent Bishop, knew of no one in the district holding a grudge against the inspector,[568] overlooking the Edaljis, Farringtons and Greens for starters and could it be honestly claimed that an inspector of police would not incur the enmity of some of the local villains.

Concerned about the inevitable fallout from the latest maiming, Captain Anson, not usually an advocate of detective work let it be

---

[564] The Great Wyrley Parish Council appeared to be more concerned about the potential contaminating effect on the district's impressionable youth by the sale of photographs of the maimed horses. Gazette 30 Aug & 5 Sep1907; EN 6 Sep 1907

[565] MG 28 & 29 Aug 1907; DE 31 Aug and 3 Sep 1907; Gazette 30 Aug 1907; DM (Lon) 2 Sep 1907; DC 2 Sep 1907

[566] Capt Anson to Blackwell, 26 & 27 Aug 1907, HO File 989 Pt 1;

[567] DC 30 Aug & 2 Sep 1907; DM (Lon) 27 Aug 1907

[568] Tribune 29 & 30 Aug 1907

known that he was turning to Scotland Yard for assistance. He asked the Yard for a detective to be sent in the guise of a photographer or an unemployed person acting openly in the role of a sleuth while another detective operated incognito. Four belated years had passed by and now the captain was admitting that investigating cattle maimings was beyond the ability of the Staffordshire police and to accept, if not welcome, a Scotland Yard investigation. However, Captain Anson's purpose had more to do with image than in achieving anything concrete because the hidden agenda behind his scheme was to "shut the mouths of those clamouring for outside assistance" who had criticized him for being too pig-headed in not allowing others to help. His request for a Scotland Yard duo was for the official record only since Captain Anson, intending to ask for only one man, was covering his back or the back of his subordinates since he did not believe a Scotland Yard officer could make anything of the case. However, the Yard's failing would at least show the public that the police in Staffordshire were not as stupid as they were thought to be. Anyway it was grist for the mill, as Scotland Yard showed little enthusiasm for the task. The commissioner thought sending one officer without local knowledge would court disaster and the Yard did not have sufficient men to carry out an effective investigation. Gladstone, with his back to the wall, wanted Scotland Yard to cooperate with Captain Anson and to this end Detective Inspector Collins was despatched to South Staffordshire to assist with inquiries. Authorisation was also given for Captain Anson to offer a £200 reward and Captain Harrison added another £50 to that figure.[569]

The usual range of weird suggestions for solving the mystery swept the area. One contributor, seeking only the payment of expenses, offered to detect the maimer with a divining rod. A Dudley man, claiming it was "the work of an hypnotised ape", left Great Wyrley in a huff after the Zoological Society refused to give him data on the behaviour of the Simeon family of apes when under mesmeric influence. Another blamed the maimings on the gypsies, whom he believed used a big hook attached to a fishing rod to inflict injury on animals while passing in their caravans. One belief, attracting some supporters, attributed the maimings to an Eastern secret society, whose

[569] Gazette 30 Aug 1907; Capt Anson to Blackwell, 20 Sep 1907, HO File 989 Pt 1; Capt Anson to Simpson, 30/31 Aug 1907, HO No 281 File 987; Capt Anson to HO, 28 Aug 1907, HO No 297 File 987; Commissioner of Scotland Yard, Bullock to Simpson, 28 Aug 1907, HO 277 File 987; Gladstone to Chalmers, 28 Aug 1907, HO No 277 File 987; DC 7 Sep 1907; Tribune 2 Sep 1907; DT 2 Sep 1907

members were tormenting the Edaljis by maiming animals. Several amateur detectives, wanting to put their theories to the test, moved into the Cannock area.[570]

With all these people and ideas milling around there was to be no let up for the police. When injuries were inflicted on another horse, belonging to Mr Atkins, the grocer whose address was used in a letter sent by Martin Molton earlier in the year, the police adopted their usual stance of putting the injury down to an accident inflicted by another horse in the field. This conclusion was arrived at despite the veterinary surgeon, Mr Watson, finding no evidence of kicking, identifying the injury as a deliberate act carried out by someone armed with a billhook or a carved knife attached to a long handle. Captain Anson, always alert to the need to find excuses and showing no respect for the integrity of professionals, accused Watson of being induced by the Daily Mail, for a money consideration – a sweetener, into signing a statement that the Walsall case was not an accident. Two workmen, Horobin and Cooper, appearing to corroborate the police version, gave statements claiming to have seen the horses kicking out at each other at 6.10 am, but both statements were so similar in style and content that it looked as if they were written out for them to sign. Shortly afterwards, both men were seen to be fighting and later declined to discuss the maiming with Superintendent Salt.[571] Whatever cause the police attributed to the injuries received by these horses it did not alter the fact that a maimer was abroad in the locality.

(ii) The 'Edaljiite' Morgan: Another Scapegoat

History repeating itself as farce seems appropriate to describe a rerun of the Edalji case. Yelverton had perceptively forecast an arrest would be made and, as happened with Edalji, a scapegoat would be provided to satisfy the public.[572] Sure enough, despite the presence of more likely candidates, the police honed in on a suspect after the manager of a public house in Wolverhampton belatedly told a police constable about the extreme anger of one of his customers when various theories about the 1903 Great Wyrley outrages were raised with this customer around eighteen months before. The suspect's 'crime' was to speak up in favour of George Edalji and this defence of Edalji travelled

---

[570] Gazette 5 Sep 1907

[571] DE 2 Sep 1907; Tribune 3 Sep 1907; Capt Anson to Blackwell, 8 Sep 1907, HO File 989 Pt 1; DC 2 Sep 1907

[572] Tribune 28 Aug 1907

from the police constable to his inspector then along the lines of authority to the chief constable of Wolverhampton and on to Captain Anson, who arranged for the Cannock police to send a cap and a pipe stem said to have been found near the scene of the crime to the Wolverhampton police.[573] Going much further than any of the captain's previous responses towards anyone showing any sympathy for George Edalji, this suspect was not merely smeared but was made to suffer.

After ten days of behaving like an elephant simulating a tiger, the police captured a dormouse. On the 5th September, the Wolverhampton police swooped to arrest a twenty-two year old butcher's assistant, Francis Hollis Morgan, employed in Horsley Fields, Wolverhampton, just as he was leaving work at 7.30 pm and, as they did with Farrington, the police lost no time in hauling him before the courts. Morgan, described by Captain Anson as an ardent 'Edaljiite', was a native of Great Wyrley, who often spent his weekends there. When arrested, he claimed to have visited the Bloxwich 'wake' (a fair) with a friend, Albert Whitehouse of Cheslyn Hay, on the 26th August although not completely certain of the date. Following the wake, he returned to his mother's home in Great Wyrley by 11.30 pm, getting up at 5.30 am to cycle to Wolverhampton. After questioning Morgan, three police officers went to his lodgings in Wolverhampton and found a broken pipe stem. A cap, supplied by the Cannock police, allegedly found near the scene of the crime, was shown to May Holding, working at the lodging house, who thought it similar to one Morgan used to wear before he bought a new one.[574]

Morgan's arrest was the signal for a series of anonymous postcards to circulate in the area. 'The Captain of the Wyrley Gang', a signatory of the 1903 post-trial letters, despatched several letters to Wolverhampton, posted in many different places in England, threatening harm to Mary Holding, Lewis (police inspector), Burnett (chief constable) and Thornton (Morgan's landlady) in the event of Morgan being convicted. Captain Anson, using another variant of his handwriting analytical techniques – the method of 'analysis from memory', identified the same handwriting in the May Holding letter as the same as in the 'Greatorex' letter threatening Sergeant Robinson. Another letter went to Mr Atkins, following the maiming of his

[573] Gazette 6 Sep 1907
[574] Capt Anson to Blackwell, 6 Sep 1907, HO File 989 Pt 1; PMG 6 Sep 1907; DE 6 and 7 Sep 1907; Gazette 6 & 7 Sep 1907

horse.[575]

Morgan, unrepresented when the case came before the Wolverhampton magistrates' court, was charged with feloniously, unlawfully and maliciously killing a horse. The evidence mustered against Morgan consisted of: (i) a cap found in the field where the animal was killed and identified as belonging to Morgan; (ii) a broken piece of pipe found at the scene of the maiming and claimed to correspond with a piece of pipe in Morgan's possession; (iii) familiarity with the parish and surrounding areas; (iv) staying in Great Wyrley on the weekend of the maiming; (v) an angry defence of George Edalji when the maimings were discussed in a public house; and (vi) taking a knife to Great Wyrley and sharpening it a few days before the outrage – a knife that had yet to be located.[576]

Morgan pleaded not guilty and was remanded to appear at Penkridge police court on the following Monday. An ex-Sunday school scholar of Reverend Edalji, Morgan was a studious lad attending evening classes and providing for his mother and her children. Described, as was George Edalji, as timid and shy, Morgan was not one of life's sturdiest characters, spending most of his time crying in his cell.[577]

The police seemed as determined as ever that this 'Edaljiite' would be another victim to taste penal servitude irrespective of the serious flaws in the case against him. The evidence could easily be challenged as several witnesses were on hand to rebut any connection between the cap, the pipe, the knife and Hollis Morgan. A butcher's assistant, employed in Bridgtown, had already informed the Cannock police that he threw a pipe bowl into a field near to the maiming and believed this was the one the police found; the cap was actually found several days before the Harrison maiming three quarters of a mile from the scene of the maimings; and the knife story was likely to fall to pieces as a carving knife, thought to be the weapon, found by the police on the railway line near Landywood belonged to a boy named Hughes, who lost it after having it sharpened. Testimony was also available to show Morgan had slept at the lodging house in Wolverhampton on the night of the maiming and not in Great Wyrley as he first thought; that he went to bed at 9.30 pm and got up at 6 am; and it was not possible for him to have left the house at any time during the night as the door

---

[575] Capt Anson to Blackwell, 20 Sept 1907, HO File 989 Pt 1; Gazette 31 Aug & 4/10/12/13/14/16/17 Sept 1907

[576] DM (Lon) 10 Sep 1907; Gazette 7 Sep 1907; Truth 19 Sep 1907

[577] Despatch 7 Sep 1907; DC 10 Sep 1907;

was locked and the key held in the pocket of one of the residents who slept in front of the locked door - no doubt a precaution to stop anyone doing a 'moonlit flit'.[578] Notwithstanding the utter fragility of the evidence against Morgan, the police were bent on continuing with the prosecution.

Morgan was arraigned at Penkridge police court on the 10th September in front of Lord Hatherton, dealing yet again with a local maiming case; H Staveley-Hill MP, who was acting on Captain Anson's behalf in Parliament; E A Foden, who was Lord Hatherton's estate manager; E V Vaughan and T Evans. Burke, the prosecutor, in offering up Morgan as the maimer, cited as evidence: the opportunity Morgan had for committing the crime, living as he did in the neighbourhood and having a bicycle to take him quickly to the scene of the slaughter; the cap and pipe bowl found at the scene of the crime belonged to Morgan; a knife allegedly sharpened by Morgan but not produced, which Burke claimed was like the implement used to commit the crime – an interesting claim since all the police had to do was conjure up an image of a knife and say Morgan had sharpened one similar to it; Morgan was a butcher and, as such, would have no feelings of revulsion for the destruction of life.[579] Previously, Captain Anson, Home Office officials, the Lord Chief Justice and Sir Charles W Matthews had rejected similar claims put forward by Conan Doyle against Sharp and/or Hart when they came under suspicion in 1903 since it brought every butcher into the frame.

Mr Wilcock, Morgan's defence counsel, was the legal agent for the Miner's Federation, taking on the brief as a result of the generosity of Mr Albert Stanley, the MP for North West Staffordshire, who knew the Morgan family and provided strong support for them – a pity that the other scapegoat, George Edalji, could not draw on equivalent support from someone like the influential Mr Stanley instead of attracting his antagonism. Wilcock had little difficulty in showing the evidence to be incredibly thin and attacked the prosecution of Morgan as maliciously inspired and he wanted the case dealt with at this hearing. Witnesses were available to testify that Morgan was at the lodging house on the night of the maiming. Evidence was also available, shades of Edalji, to show the "impossibility of him (Morgan) leaving the house at any time during the night." Rebuttal evidence for the cap and the alleged sharpened knife could also be presented. In a

---

[578] Gazette, 7 & 10 Sep 1907; DC 9 Sep 1907; Gazette 9 Sep 1907;

[579] DC 9 & 10 Sep 1907; Tribune, 16 Sep 1907; ES 9 Sep 1907; RN 15 Sep 1907

court room demonstration, Wilcock tried to fit the piece of pipe found at Morgan's lodgings into the pipe bowl found at the scene of the outrage but there was no match. Inspector Lewis admitted during his testimony that an expert had told the police the pipe bowl had never fitted Morgan's pipe.

The prosecution case was in tatters, the police had failed to provide a shred of evidence to build a case, yet the police refused to let the case lie down. Having made too many mistakes to back away now, the police tried to salvage from the ashes a vestige of justification for its actions and was backed by Lord Hatherton, who decided not to end the proceedings and allowed the charade to continue. To acknowledge another police debacle in the wake of the Wilson Committee's findings could only increase the criticism levelled at the Staffordshire police and this was something the bench had no intention of facilitating. Burke's demand for Morgan to be remanded in order for the police to acquire further evidence was allowed by the bench and Morgan, with cries of "Oh mother, mother" lasting several minutes, was duly remanded.[580]

Captain Anson, trying to distance himself from the impending disaster, informed the Home Office that within a couple of days of Morgan's arrest he had concluded the evidence was insufficient for a conviction. His remedy was to discard Morgan as soon as possible – interesting phraseology directed at a man thought to be wrongfully detained but, of course, Morgan did not qualify for the normal standards of decency as he was an 'Edaljiite'. The captain blamed the Wolverhampton police, but typically not to the faces of its officers, for acting unilaterally in arresting Morgan and, if a mistake was made, he (Anson) was completely blameless. He was trying to make sure that when the police case collapsed, he would be in the clear, despite encouraging Wolverhampton police officers in their actions by sending along extremely dubious 'evidence'. Captain Anson was covering his tracks while in full retreat and, with the possibility of a further blot on the Staffordshire police for participating in this farce, instructed his force not to arrest anyone without his permission unless it was 'a red hot cert'. A few days later, the erratic Captain Anson was not certain Morgan was the wrong man but irrespective of continuous vacillations, he expected Morgan to be released. In preparation for this prospect, he met with the prosecuting solicitor to determine the best way of discarding the prosecution with the least discredit to the Staffordshire

[580] DC 9 & 10 Sep 1907; ES 9 Sep 1907; RN 8 Sep 1907

police.[581]

The Scotland Yard detective, Collins, also recognised that Morgan was held on slender evidence and was likely to be discharged. He thought the remand was to give the police the opportunity to present evidence to justify charging Morgan and, if the evidence provided the means and opportunity, Morgan's pub talk might provide the motive[582] – a somewhat misguided declaration since the evidence submitted to the court was so easy to rebut and the 'pub talk' was nothing more than alcohol induced banter – a not unusual feature of the atmosphere of a public house bar. With this kind of perspective, Captain Anson might have been able to make an argument that Scotland Yard detectives were not that far removed from the 'elephant and tiger.'

With the case against Morgan dead and ready for internment, Collins came up with a new proposal for an undercover officer to watch any men discharged by Captain Harrison or any local lads convicted or suspected of cruelty to animals. He suggested placing an observation post in Great Wyrley railway station to watch visitors going to and coming from the vicarage.[583] But why did Collins want a surveillance of the vicarage? Did he think the vicarage was the centre of a cattle-maiming conspiracy with the Reverend Edalji acting as controller-in-chief of a gang of grudge-bearers and miscreants? Conan Doyle was not the only one writing detective fiction.

The Scotland Yard man's scheme for an undercover agent did not enthuse Captain Anson, who showed a marked reluctance for a Yard man to stay in Great Wyrley, perhaps worried that he might discover something untoward in the captain's relations with Sharp or Chris Hatton or possibly reporting back on the mess the Wolverhampton and Staffordshire police had made of the Harrison maimings. However, the Captain need have no worries on the latter possibility as the Home Office blamed the Wolverhampton police for messing up the case, overlooking the Staffordshire police's contribution to the 'mess'.[584]

When Morgan came up again before Lord Hatherton and the same bench on the 14th September, the prosecution had decided to drop the case but, in a fix and needing to extricate himself, the prosecutor played down the rashness of the Morgan prosecution and tried to justify the

[581] Capt Anson to Blackwell, 8 Sep 1907, HO File 989 Pt 1; Capt Anson to Simpson, 10 & 12 Sep 1907, HO File 989 Pt 2; Gazette 14 Sep 1907
[582] Collins to Drew, Metropolitan Police, 9 Sep 1907, HO No 294 File 987
[583] Collins to Drew, Metropolitan Police, 15 Sep 1907, HO No 294 File 987
[584] Captain Anson to MacNaughton, Scotland Yard, 10 Sep 1907, and HO Comment, HO No 294 File 987;

police's actions and his own demand for remanding Morgan at the first and second hearings by producing a crass and inane statement. Burke spoke of Morgan's box containing documents that could have compromised Morgan and others, and, if Morgan had been freed, he and his associates might have escaped. But it was known at the previous hearings that no such documents existed otherwise the police would have taken them when they searched Morgan's lodgings and Burke would have produced them to substantiate the case against Morgan. Not unexpectedly, when the case against the individual maimer collapsed the notion of other participants, a gang perhaps, rose to the surface albeit without a single shred of evidence. The conversation in the public house turned out to be a heated discussion about Edalji's guilt with Morgan saying that Edalji "was such a gentleman and such a nice young fellow that he could not possibly be guilty of the crimes and he hoped someone would commit more crimes while he was away." Also attributed to Morgan, during this alcohol induced touch of bravado, was an alleged admission of not being averse to doing one or two himself to get Edalji acquitted. This conversation occurred sometime between March and December 1906 but was only reported to the police in September 1907 following the Harrison maiming. This was naught but hearsay evidence as the informant was not called to substantiate the prosecution's claim to the court and, not unexpectedly, this hearsay was still allowed into the proceedings by Lord Hatherton. Despite the extensive verbiage produced by Burke, he was forced to admit, "We have no evidence" but still refused to offer Morgan an apology for the injustice of the prosecution. Wilcock attacked Burke's speech for being entirely devoted to excuse and he made short shrift of the prosecution's excuses.[585]

Morgan was discharged but, true to form, the police were again exonerated for their inadequacies. Just as the Wilson Committee chose an irrelevance to blame Edalji, Lord Hatherton did the same to Morgan by saying he was "responsible for what he had brought on himself by his own foolish statements."[586] This rebuke was administered without any evidence of the alleged conversation in the public house ever brought before the court; all that was offered was the hearsay evidence of a police officer in an alleged discussion with a public house licensee. Lord Hatherton had no right to assume Morgan used the words attributed to him and his insensitive and unjust criticism of Morgan was but an attempt to deflect attention from the extreme inefficiency of the

[585] Gazette 16 Sep 1907; WO 21 Sep 1907; DC 16 Sep 1907; ES 14 Sep 1907
[586] Truth, 18 Sep 1907; Gazette 16 Sep 1907

Staffordshire police for prosecuting a case with so many holes in it and his own inadequacy for allowing it to proceed.

Captain Anson was not in court to see yet another Staffordshire police fiasco come to an end but he made it clear later that Morgan, in making wild assertions, gave the Wolverhampton police good cause to believe him guilty – hardly sufficient grounds for the police to cause so much distress to the Morgan family and waste the ratepayers money, something that would have really peeved the South Staffordshire ratepayers a few years before.[587] Captain Anson's post-court comments give a good idea where the prosecutor's and the chair's condemnation of Morgan originated. The captain seemed to be running everything in South Staffordshire and none too well either.

(iii) The 'Yokelisation' of the Police

The press had little doubt that the outcome of the Morgan trial brought to an end the second attempt to find the author of all the outrages in Great Wyrley and, by bringing charges against an innocent man, the police had once again failed to apprehend the criminal. In displaying such contempt for Morgan, blackening his name with something alleged to have been said in a public house eighteen months before, Lord Hatherton and Burke came in for severe criticism. The Police Review saw both the Edalji and Morgan prosecutions as damaging the reputation of the police and held Captain Anson personally responsible for giving the impression that the conduct of the Staffordshire police was representative of the methods used by other forces throughout the country. 'Truth' was none too impressed either by the police in county districts, however, these deficiencies were attributed to the routine nature of their work, which provided little experience for unravelling obscure and abnormal crimes; and to the police's inadequate education and training. Those on whom the blame should rightly fall were the people of 'superior education' and 'station in life', that is, the magistrates and successive Home Secretaries, Gladstone and Akers-Douglas, who supervised the actions of the police and placed too much confidence in evidence raked together by the police in a partisan spirit. The London Evening News held a less than complimentary view of Staffordshire policemen, who with no great intelligence draw their weekly pay. While accusing them of a "healthy average of stupidity", the paper refrained from blaming them

---

[587] Capt Anson to ACD, 13 Sep 1907, HO File 989 Pt 2; Collins to Metropolitan Police, 9 Sep 1907, HO No 294 File 987

excessively, but raised the question of how "a yokel who is none the less a yokel for being a numbered and lettered official" was going to hunt down the criminal.[588]

The attacks stimulated an almost 'provinces versus capital' controversy with Wilcock, defence counsel, rising to defend the Staffordshire police, in an expression of local sub-patriotism. Wilcock, turning a blind eye to what had happened to his client, claimed the police had a difficult duty to perform and need not fear criticism even from London. Invoking the spectre of 'Jack the Ripper', Wilcock criticised the London police's failure to detect the murderer despite the victims being women and able to scream.[589] Captain Anson turned to the Staffordshire Joint Committee for assistance by asking it not to remain silent in face of these accusations, which was really a request for support for himself as he was the principal target in the firing line. He sought declarations of support not only for launching the Morgan prosecution, an absolute debacle, which he had already blamed on the Wolverhampton police, but also for the position he had taken regarding Sharp. In a report to the Staffordshire Joint Committee, he appealed for a public denunciation of Conan Doyle for interfering with justice and for accusing Sharp. Despite portraying Sharp as Doyle's scapegoat, when the hunt for the conspirators came too close for comfort, Captain Anson disclosed a complete lack of confidence in Sharp's innocence. Covering himself for any possibility of error or maybe it was an apprehension of being found out for not following through his suspicions about Sharp and Hart, the captain told the committee he could not guarantee that Sharp was absolutely guiltless of complicity in the maimings but Sharp was only one of many. An interesting comment considering the Staffordshire police claimed to have got their man – Edalji, and did not pursue a prosecution against anyone else for those crimes.[590]

The end of the Morgan affair was followed by a concerted effort on Captain Anson's part to retrieve a position he had been gradually losing since George Edalji's conviction. A truly vain hope from an equally vain man.

---

[588] Police Review 20 Sep & 4 Oct 1907; DE 16 Sep 1907; DM 16 Sep 1907; Truth 18 Sep 1907; EN 2 Sep 1907

[589] DN 16 Sep 1907

[590] Confidential document for members of the Joint Standing Committee from Capt Anson, 9 Oct 1907 in Capt Anson to Blackwell, 18 Oct 1907, HO File 989 Pt 1

Chapter XVII

The Last Hundred Days

(i)   The Captain's Friends and Foes

The shambles of the Harrison maiming, paraded under the title of *Rex v Morgan,* illustrated once more the sheer inefficiency of the higher echelons of the Staffordshire police force in submitting to the court the hotchpotch of items described by Mr Burke as the prosecution's evidence. Moreover, the continuation of the maimings and the timing of this one seemed to confirm that Edalji's guilt was naught but wishful thinking on the chief constable's part. Yet despite these new failings, Captain Anson was able to rely on support from a number of quarters: his aristocratic allies in the Staffordshire establishment always ready to carry out the captain's wishes; the 'ever-ready' Horace Edalji, who appeared to 'pop-up' at the most opportune moments for the captain; acquiescent Home Office officials who, however, were soon to embrace the distaste shown by certain legal officers of the State to Captain Anson's behaviour; and a surprising, indirect ally from the Edalji Support Committee, Yelverton, who did an unpublicised *volte face* on Edalji.

To distract attention from his and his men's shortcomings, Captain Anson drew on the main weapon in his arsenal – personal attacks on the integrity and sanity of his opponents. Sir Arthur Conan Doyle received the main thrust of his long harboured ill-feeling; members of the Edalji family were subject to the captain's usual off-handed disdain and unsubstantiated rumours against them; and Conan Doyle's two agents in South Staffordshire were accused of being liars and 'diagnosed' as lunatics.

Over the previous nine months since Conan Doyle's initial contact with him regarding the Edalji case, Captain Anson had shown some contempt for Doyle on several occasions. He now took the opportunity to spell out to the Home Office the source of his antagonism to Doyle, which he claimed was due to having been deliberately misled as to Doyle's real intentions,[591] although this appeared to be a cover for his deep resentment for not being placed in the public limelight, at least not in the way he expected. The captain had undoubtedly expected some

---

[591] Capt Anson to HO, 28 Aug 1907, HO No 278 File 987

favourable mention lionising his role in catching the South Staffordshire maimer upon completion of the famed Conan Doyle's article but had felt considerably let down by what he saw as a betrayal by the literary man in championing Edalji's cause. He illustrated his disparaging attitude to the Edaljis and to Sir Arthur in a spiteful way on the eve of Sir Arthur's marriage and the day after the ceremony. During the week following the collapse of the Morgan indictment two receptions were held. The first probably passed unnoticed by Captain Anson – a fête held on the 16th September in honour of Hollis Morgan's acquittal attended by fifty people, including the Reverend, Mrs and Maud Edalji.[592] The second, on the 19th September, was a reception held for Conan Doyle's marriage, attended by George Edalji. Prior to Doyle's wedding, Captain Anson unpleasantly remarked that if the Edalji family was to concoct any 'villainy', such as having a horse maimed, they would do it when Doyle was to be married; the most favourable time for them and the most awkward for him.[593] But how many of the Edalji family were involved in this imaginary plot and why they would wish to harm Doyle on the occasion of his marriage after his efforts in pursuing justice for George was left unstated by the captain. With George in Yarmouth and Horace thought to be "behav(ing) very nicely all through,"[594] this left only the Reverend, Mrs Edalji and/or Maud as the potential plotters – hardly a serious proposition but one tinged with the meanness of spirit so evident in the captain's attitude and behaviour towards the Edaljis. The chief constable attributed his own less than pleasant *Ansonian* personality to the Edaljis, an ill-used family as Conan Doyle once described them.[595] The day after Doyle's wedding, the captain's comments bore witness to his malice towards the bridegroom. Rather spitefully, Captain Anson wrote to Blackwell that had his (Anson's) criticisms of Doyle's 'theory' concerning Sharp's culpability[596] been added to the Attorney-General's opinion it would have made a really pleasant wedding gift for 'the man.'[597] He had obviously overlooked, or was unaware, that it was Sir Charles W

---

[592] WO 21 Sep 1907;

[593] Capt Anson to Blackwell, 26 Aug 1907, HO File 989 Pt 1

[594] Capt Anson to Blackwell, 17 Nov 1907, HO File 989 Pt 1

[595] ACD to Capt Anson, 5 Jan 1907, HO File 989 Pt 2

[596] Captain Anson had an inflated view of his own analytical skills because his appraisal of Doyle's hypothesis of Royden Sharp was as riddled with gossip and hearsay as was Doyle's case against Sharp. See Appendix I

[597] Capt Anson to Blackwell, 20 Sep 1907, HO File 989 Pt 1

Matthews who had loosened the mortar in the pillars of Doyle's case against Sharp.

With Captain Anson running true to form, one long-standing supporter of Edalji, none other than Yelverton, executed an unusual change of heart to embrace the Home Office's position. Yelverton was a surprising convert because for three years before Doyle came on the scene, he had laboured continuously and loyally on Edalji's behalf without a dissenting murmur. His baptismal epistle proclaiming his newly born faith was sent to de Rutzen, a member of the Wilson Committee and Captain Anson's relative. He attributed his conversion to information acquired during the campaign supplemented by more recent revelations, neither of which he chose to disclose. He voiced concern over the unfair criticism levelled at the Wilson Report and towards the Home Office, declaring his agreement with the main points in the report especially the assessment of the letters, "which played so important a part in the case before the jury." If Yelverton did have information casting doubt on Edalji's innocence before the free pardon was granted, why did he pursue the issues with the same crusading zeal displayed throughout? He was also a critic of the Wilson Committee and of the Home Office for its refusal to hold a Beck-style commission. Even the Home Office acknowledged "after the publication of the Wilson Report, Yelverton still believed Edalji to be innocent of writing the anonymous letters."[598] The Home Office thought that something had happened recently to cause him to change his mind or to express his true opinion and expected him at a later date to reveal his newly-referred-to information, which he never did. They thought it might have something to do with George Edalji dispensing with his services but that was in March 1907 and Yelverton was still campaigning for him well after that. Perhaps it took time for this personal snub to have an effect on Yelverton, causing him to turn tail and discard his previous conviction of the injustices perpetrated against George Edalji. Or, Yelverton may have originally entered the Edalji case with a pecuniary interest in mind and decided to call it a day when he realised compensation was not on the cards. Whatever the cause of his about-turn, it was Yelverton, who helped to keep the flag of the injustice done to Edalji flying from the mast until bigger guns came in. Yelverton's attitude throughout appeared typical of someone of whom it was once said, "what he saw as the truth (he) pursued to the bitter end, regardless of other people's interests or feelings and made him awkward for

---

[598] Yelverton to de Rutzen, 12 Sep 1907 and HO Comments, HO No 293 File 987

established conventionalities to assimilate."[599]

Yelverton might be an unforeseen, albeit indirect, ally for a cause less than honestly espoused by Captain Anson but it was no more than to be expected for the Staffordshire aristocracy to rally to the second son of the Earl of Lichfield in his hour of need. At the opening of the Staffordshire Quarter Sessions, the Lord Lieutenant, Lord Dartmouth, took the opportunity to defend the police from the verbal attacks and grave charges made against them in connection with a 'certain case' (George Edalji's). In a bogus even-handed approach but showing a partisan desire to carry out Captain Anson's wishes, the Lord Lieutenant heaped praise on the Staffordshire police for its justifiable action during these difficult and trying times. He also extended his favour to those people who gain respect for righting wrongs but this plaudit had narrow confines as it excluded Edalji's supporters who, in believing the police were acquainted with the identity of the real offender, adopted the mantle of judge and jury to implicate the whole of the county police force. Showing no qualms about misusing his office, the Lord Lieutenant remained absolutely silent on the difficult and trying times experienced by the victims of this miscarriage of justice, George Edalji and the Edalji family during the previous four years. This noble defence of the police might have garnered a little credit if His Lordship's address represented a principled stand on his part and was his own inspiration. However, Captain Anson was quick to tell the Home Office the speech was written mainly by Captain Anson for Lord Dartmouth to deliver, which he (Anson) thought was the best way of

---

[599] Yelverton Obituary, DT 6 July 1912 in HO No 293 File 987; Labouchere, owner of Truth magazine, called "Yelverton...a very bad lot...He lives by taking up small petty cases," and he provided some hearsay evidence to Gladstone concerning his predecessor, who apparently said that "when he (Akers-Douglas) was Unionist whip, Yelverton frequently asked to earn a £ or two for speaking at Unionist rallies. They (Unionists) would have nothing to do with him." Home Official officials passed comments, such as "It is very difficult to do justice in a cause championed by Yelverton" and "Yelverton is collecting money and sailing near the wind." The Lord Chief Justice warned the Home Office that "You must be very careful with Yelverton." This is conclusive of nothing of any real detriment to Yelverton but it gives an indication of his image amongst establishment figures. Labouchere to Gladstone, 25 Jan 1907, HO File 988; HO Comments, 5 Feb 1904 & June 1904, HO Nos 80 & 97 File 985; LCJ to HO, 11 Dec 1903, Ho No 26a File 984

dealing with the matter,[600] although it should not be overlooked that the Earl of Lichfield's second son might be inflating his own importance and influence.

Captain Anson's prejudice, so marked in his behaviour towards the Reverend, Mrs, Maud and George Edalji, bypassed the 'dutiful Oriental', Horace, 'punkawallahing' his way into the captain's favour by obligingly serving the captain's interests and, as a consequence, granted indemnity from his bigotry. As in 1905 when he was under fire from the 'Truth' articles, Captain Anson was again facing the firing squad and, *voila*, the 'nicely behaved' Horace's alleged correspondence of December 1903 was resurrected to throw light on the anonymous letters of the 1890s. Horace was the 'saviour of Great Wyrley' although the captain was relying on a supposition of Chris Hatton's that Horace had discovered George to be the letter writer and by threatening to expose him to their parents had halted the flow of letters in December 1892.[601] Horace had continued to be the bulwark against George while he remained at home but after Horace left the vicarage George picked up as before, although George showed remarkable patience by waiting for well over two years from his brother's departure before dipping his pen into the inkpot again. If Horace's claim were true, he performed an exceptional feat in 1892 in stopping George in his tracks and showing considerable discretion for a thirteen years old boy by keeping it to himself. Of course his claim had no substance, if he actually made it, because the letters carried on for a further three years after that as Captain Anson was only too well aware having written to the Edaljis about the letters in July 1895.[602] Such a claim also raises the question as to where Horace acquired the anonymous letter of 1895 allegedly shown to the defence team in 1903, if George's pen was at rest after 1892. If Horace was responsible for curbing George's pen who wrote the 1893-1895 letters, which the captain was well aware had continued to circulate during that time. When Captain Anson wrote to the Home Office relating how Horace stopped George "without saying anything to his parents and as long as Horace was at home no further trouble occurred,"[603] he was again demonstrating his disingenuity.

Chris Hatton was also said to have quoted from a letter of an

---

[600] Lord Dartmouth at Staffordshire Quarter Sessions, Police Chronicle 19 Oct 1907; Capt Anson to Blackwell, 18 Oct 1907, HO File 989 Pt 1

[601] Chris Hatton to Capt Anson, 30 Oct 1907, HO File 989 Pt 1

[602] Horace Edalji was one of four people claiming to have performed the feat of curbing George Edalji's letter writing in 1892!

[603] Capt Anson to Blackwell, 17 Nov 1907, HO File 989 Pt 1

undisclosed date sent to him by Horace, who apparently expressed surprise when Conan Doyle became involved in 1907. Horace wrote that, "He knew nothing of Doyle's interference until he saw it in the paper, otherwise he would have given him the 'tip'. If necessary I will let him (Doyle) know how matters stand. He has evidently been kept in the dark by Yelverton and my people."[604] The quote refers to Horace in both the first and third person, which may be an error in copying on Hatton's part or a careless fabrication by either Hatton or Captain Anson. But why did Hatton not send the original to Captain Anson?

Hatton apparently offered his services to coax Horace into contacting Conan Doyle but Horace never got in touch with Doyle,[605] which seemed rather strange on Horace's part because if he told the police, his parents, George's defence team and Chris Hatton, why not tell the person who became the leading light in the struggle to free his brother. Perhaps it was because he never told it to anyone. Horace's apparent surprise on hearing of Doyle's 'interference' and wanting to bring Doyle into the light, quickly went off the boil because it must have taken Horace anything up to nine months to register his surprise to Chris Hatton. Had Horace disclosed his surprise sooner than this, bearing in mind the Hatton-Anson pipeline, the information would surely have found its way into Captain Anson's hands much earlier than it did and he would most certainly have drawn it to the Home Office's attention.[606] Yet having made it clear that Conan Doyle was off track, Horace Edalji, not for the first time, let it be known he wanted nothing more to do with the affair.[607] How interesting to see that when Captain Anson was really in the firing line, information favourable to him suddenly came from Horace, who then made it clear he wanted absolutely nothing to do with the case. Horace appeared to be an extremely perceptive person – a touch of Oriental mysticism reaching out to Captain Anson in his hour of need!

Another significant tit-bit of information found its way to the Home Office via Captain Anson, drawing on the 1903 Horace Edalji-Chris Hatton one-way communication. Apparently when a post-trial

[604] Chris Hatton to Capt Anson, 30 Oct 1907, HO File 989 Pt 1

[605] Capt Anson to Blackwell, 26 Jan 1908, HO Files 989 Pt 1

[606] In fact, Hatton's alleged letter to Captain Anson was dated 30 Oct 1907 and was included in Captain Anson's letter to Blackwell, also dated 30 Oct 1907, which represented an exceptionally rapid onward relay to Blackwell, suggesting the alleged information was very recently 'acquired.'

[607] Chris Hatton to Capt Anson, 30 Oct 1907, HO File 989 Pt 1

defence, referred to as a *'post humous'* defence by Captain Anson, was advanced by Edalji's supporters claiming George could not have written the anonymous letters, Horace had allegedly said "no, that won't do, that line of defence will do more harm than good.   I don't think George killed the horses, but he did write the anonymous letters and it is no good basing a defence on unsound premises by maintaining that he did not write them. That would have been the soundest defence from the beginning."[608] This revelation allegedly made in the wake of the trial at the time of the Hatton-Cooper dialogue, surprisingly, was not disclosed either in 1903, 1905 or early 1907 until it was dug up by Captain Anson in November 1907 after a four year delay and fitting neatly into the hypothesis manufactured by Captain Anson – no killing of horses but writing anonymous letters. In fact, one of the letters attributed to Horace Edalji in December 1903 speculated that if George 'did the horses' it was for money, yet another pet 'money-inspired motive' from the Captain's stable, which he applied to George Edalji and to most people opposing his views.

Trying to defend Horace from a possible accusation of wanting to deliberately injure his brother, Captain Anson expressed the view that had Horace wanted to harm his brother's defence all he had to do was reveal the information before George's trial and a word from him would have made the conviction a certainty.[609] Despite Captain Anson believing his judicial assessment might have had every possibility of a favourable reception at the Staffordshire Quarter Sessions where he wielded considerable influence, the only information allegedly held by Horace Edalji dealt with inadmissible anonymous letters not from 1903 but from 1892 and not even Sir Reginald Hardy, under the tutelage of his 'aide', Brough, could have allowed those letters into evidence. Captain Anson was either unaware or being disingenuous because during the trial Horace had allegedly shown Vachell an anonymous letter conjured up out of nowhere, which was accompanied by the defence doing nothing to challenge the inadmissibility or the evidential worth of the 1903 letters. If Horace actually did show the letter to Vachell it was an obvious attempt to sabotage George's defence and not a fraternal act to protect his brother.

The isolation that Captain Anson attributed to George Edalji – a reason put forward for George committing the maimings, which in itself mocked the captain's attempt to place George in a gang of local 'roughs', was, according to Chris Hatton, an experience shared by all

[608] Capt Anson to Blackwell, 17 Nov 1907, HO File 989 Pt 1
[609] Ibid

the members of the Edalji family. Apparently, the only people whom the Edaljis could call friends were the Hattons, which, if true, was an indication of how barren was the soil of friendship available for the Edaljis to plough in the parish.[610] The captain's ready acceptance of this claim of friendship, if it was ever made, might be a manoeuvre to give credence to the alleged Chris Hatton-Horace Edalji communications by showing the Edalji family to be sufficiently close to one family in the area that confidences would be shared between members, including disclosing 'evidence' of a member's guilt capable of splitting the family. It enabled the captain to claim that Horace's 'evidence' was of the utmost importance, coming as it did from a source close to the family and something Doyle would not be able to explain away.[611] Even this claim of friendship between the Hattons and Edaljis was put to the sword by Captain Anson himself in correspondence to the 'lunatic', Beaumont, three months hence.

Hatton's compliance with the captain's requirements extended as far as agreeing to the latter's request to obtain a sample of Maud Edalji's handwriting in order to pin the anonymous letters on her but despite his enthusiasm to perform a further betrayal of another member of the Edalji family, Hatton failed to deliver the goods on this occasion.[612] Perhaps, his failure was due to having to come up with something concrete rather than merely being a purveyor of unsupported and uncorroborated 'opinion'. Following, so it seemed, in the path of his four year aristocratic confidante, Hatton believed that Royden Sharp "may have written one or two anonymous letters out of devilment."[613] This was an interesting comment since in fifteen years no one had been able to establish who was responsible; and coming as it did after Captain Anson's admission as to Sharp's 'innate mischief to imitate what others have done and are doing' and his susceptibility for anonymous letter writing that had led to Superintendent Barrett cautioning him as to his conduct.[614]

Why was Hatton so interested in assisting in George Edalji's downfall? Public spiritedness! Or was it really part of a long-standing grudge nurtured by the Hattons against the Edaljis with a convenient exception being made of Horace just as Captain Anson appeared to

---

[610] Chris Hatton to Capt Anson, 30 Oct 1907, HO File 989 Pt 1

[611] Capt Anson to Blackwell, 26 Jan 1908, HO File 989 Pt 1

[612] Chris Hatton to Capt Anson correspondence, 30 Oct 1907, HO File 989 Pt 1

[613] Ibid

[614] Capt Anson to Blackwell, 20 Sep 1907, HO file 989 Pt 1

have made. Were the Horace Edalji-Hatton letters an Anson conspiracy to prevent any consideration for releasing George in the same vein as the Anson-Loxton conspiracy was to arrest him? If Horace actually wrote the letters attributed to him, then that opens up the possibility of a Cain and Abel relationship between the brothers fuelling Horace's actions. One of J T Hatton's ten children being involved in a conspiracy against a member of a family, whose head caused difficulties towards Mr Hatton, cannot be discounted. A conspiracy can only be ruled out if everything reported by Horace Edalji, Chris Hatton and Captain Anson was true but too many question marks surround the 'evidence' provided by this 'public spirited' trio.

Captain Anson's plaudits for his 'nicely behaved' supporter can be contrasted with his tendency to express nothing but disdain for those who challenged his views, accusing them of being either maniacs or disreputable people and, in Doyle's case, suggesting that just as popes and emperors can be held in lunatic asylums why not Sherlock Holmes[615] and denouncing him as "an absolutely dishonest unscrupulous man."[616] A few months later, his spleen continued to be vented on Conan Doyle with references to him as an utter fool, a knave and insane.[617] These attacks were indicative of what Captain Anson was capable of doing. If he was prepared to attack and defame someone of Doyle's stature when communicating with Home Office officials, the chief constable's comments to his cohorts in Staffordshire County Council and the country set against a family with few friends or allies in Great Wyrley and who were the epitome of the captain's class and race bigotry were likely to know no bounds.

Even those in roles that could not reasonably be considered responsible for the state of affairs in South Staffordshire were not immune from Captain Anson's bile when he felt let down by them and he branded them as incompetent when failing to meet the 'high standards' he expected of them. Post office employees were dismissed as a wooden-headed lot who had no business delivering obnoxious postcards contrary to their rules and he proposed impounding the postcards. His solution imposed on postal workers the obligation, when clearing post boxes, to examine the contents to establish the presence of obnoxious postcards or letters and to find out where they were posted.[618] As a feasible means to detect the anonymous scribe, this

---

[615] Capt Anson to Simpson, 25 Jan 1907, HO File 989 Pt 2
[616] Capt Anson to Blackwell, 22 Dec 1907, HO File 989 Pt 2
[617] Capt Anson to Blackwell, 26 Jan 1908, HO File989 Pt 1
[618] Capt Anson to Blackwell, 18 Sep 1907 HO File 989 Pt 1

suggestion was on a par with the suggestion sent in anonymously some time before of postmen hiding in pillar-boxes to detect the anonymous scribe posting letters. Captain Anson's directive required every postman to open and examine every letter or become a handwriting expert to examine the writing on the envelope to link the letters to the scribe. The postal service would have come to a standstill in the chief constable's world.

(ii) Camouflage for the Captain

Faced with concerns in the real world and the growing disenchantment from more circumspect officers and officials in the corridors of Whitehall, the Home Office engineered majesterial recognition for the hard-pressed chief constable and the Staffordshire constabulary. On the 26th November, Captain Anson was appointed a member of the Royal Victorian Order, 4th Class, presented to him by the king, who only recently had granted Edalji a pardon. Upon receiving congratulations from Home Office officials, the captain conveyed his thanks for what he described as a problematic honour albeit receiving it with pride. Although acknowledging the award as trifling, it was obviously significant enough to the captain to interrupt his festive celebrations on Christmas Day to write the letter of thanks to the Home Office. The greatest benefit he thought the award offered was the rebuff it delivered to Doyle and his 'fellow conspirators,'[619] giving the impression that he thought the Edalji campaign was a mutiny amongst a group of rebellious subordinates. Captain Anson's own 'Indian Mutiny', which was incidentally celebrating the fiftieth anniversary of its outbreak.

Nor was George Edalji to be left out of the reward giving process albeit not from the generosity of the Home Office. The day after Captain Anson received his MRVO, George Edalji, on the 27th November, was reinstated to the rolls with leave to practice.[620] George's 'award' was equally significant for it was rare for a solicitor to be restored to the rolls and a convicted solicitor could not expect to be reinstated when an acquittal was based on a technicality, especially if the fact establishing his innocence disclosed collateral misconduct.[621] Consequently, a solicitor sending anonymous letters, including one threatening to kill an officer of the law, would find it extremely difficult, if not impossible, to gain readmission. This restoration was a

---

[619] Capt Anson to Blackwell, 25 Dec 1907, HO File 989 Pt 2

[620] Police Chronicle 6 Dec 1907

[621] Solicitor's Act 1888, quoted by Legal correspondent, DT 28 Nov 1907

clear demonstration of the legal fraternity, right up to its highest levels, rejecting the less favourable aspects of the Wilson Report – another rebuff for Captain Anson and Home Office officials.

Officers of the Law Society considered that Edalji's reinstatement would make it difficult for the Home Secretary not to reconsider compensation. However, the Home Secretary, like many since then, dug in his heels when having to admit that the police, local judiciary and Home Office officials had either fouled up or deliberately conspired to consign someone to the inside of one of His Majesty's prisons and to keep him there. Gladstone justified his decision not to grant compensation on the Wilson Committee's findings, which had in fact declared Edalji innocent and should not have been convicted while at the same time accusing him of bringing the trouble on himself.[622] So much for Reverend Edalji's faith in British justice and fair play!

The two events received very different assessments from the Police Review – showing an alignment quite at variance with what might be expected today. The award to Captain Anson, who was described as an honoured son of a noble family, the chief constable of Staffordshire and the prosecutor of George Edalji and Hollis Morgan, was thought ill-advised. If it had not been for the Edalji and Morgan cases, "the tribute would have been hailed by us with delight. But in view of the obvious facts, we regard the conferring of this distinction with regret. It appears as a 'solatium to a wounded friend'." Very philanthropically, the Police Review recorded that, "It is a sign of true greatness to discover one's mistake, to admit it, and rectify it. To such greatness we should never begrudge the membership of the Victorian Order." Conversely, George Edalji's reinstatement was seen as an act of justice, an acknowledgement that Edalji was wrongly convicted and had not been responsible for writing the anonymous letters; in essence, it was a condemnation of those responsible for his conviction.[623]

(iii) Lew Is and the Californian Sharp[624]

Attention had moved away from the Great Wyrley area after the publicity over the Morgan affair had died down and the battle of Great Wyrley, the 1892-1895 variety, was fought out at another transatlantic

[622] Gazette 28/29 Nov 1907

[623] Police Review 13 Dec 1907

[624] Lewis was Lewis Burgess Greenslade, born Witherbridge, North Devon, around 1851/2, who got himself into some kind of religious trouble in England.

venue, this time from the West Coast. The issue that arose to tantalise the two main belligerents and a number of onlookers illustrated that the tentacles of the case stretched several thousand miles from the meadows and coalfields of South Staffordshire to Long Beach, California. A newspaper cutting, an advertisement for Edalji's articles in Pearson's Weekly taken from a journal of the Scottish Churches and covered with religious and blasphemous comments scribbled in pencil around the margins, reminiscent of the God-Satan letters of fifteen years before, arrived on Conan Doyle's doorstep. The comments included, "George Edalji should leave it all to Lew Is"; "Day of judgement by the Lord God Lew Is"; "A hell of a bridegroom I'd be to tarry wouldn't I"; and containing many biblical references from Isaiah chapter 53, a chapter full of what might appear as a string of confessions, which were tailor-made for someone feeling guilt over Edalji's plight – "He had no beauty or majesty to attract us to him", "he was bruised for our iniquities," "he was led like a lamb to the slaughter", "By oppression and judgement he was taken away", "and the Lord has laid on him the inequity of us all." A card accompanying the cutting was also abounded with religious references to "Lew Is" and a logo in the corner featured "The Ark".

Acting on a hunch, Conan Doyle wrote off to the postmaster and to the police at Long Beach to find out if Frank Sharp, formerly of Cannock, England, was connected with 'the Ark' and if they knew anything about 'Lew Is'. The County Marshall at Long Beach, George Young, confirmed that Mr Lewis resided at 'The Ark', a cheap boarding house, and Frank Sharp had lived there but was now living in Santa Anna, Orange County, California, working for the Pacific Electric Rail Road as a track laying foreman.[625] Doyle had also reported the 'Lew Is' cutting to Home Office officials, who relayed the news to Captain Anson, who lost no time in sending a telegram to the county marshall at Long Beach. The captain later took the opportunity, as he did with everyone, to acquaint him with 'details' of the Edalji family including the 'history' of the waves of anonymous letters that had deluged South Staffordshire.[626] Captain Anson and Conan Doyle were both told that Lewis was a religious fanatic, often sending religious writings to people whose name he saw in newspapers and reading of Edalji's exploits must have prompted him to send the cutting. Both communicants were

---

[625] ACD to HO, 7 Oct 1907, HO No 297 File 987; George Young, Marshall to ACD, 2 Nov 1907, HO File 989 Pt 1

[626] HO Comment on Ibid; Capt Anson to G Young, 17 Oct 1907, HO No 297 File 987

informed that no connection could be established between Lewis and Frank Sharp other than that both had lived at 'The Ark.'[627]

The chief constable arranged for someone close to Frank Sharp to write to him. This was probably Miss B A Sharp, Frank Sharp's sister, who received a reply from Sharp saying he was a Welshman once resident in England but not her brother. In an extremely sensitive response, perhaps too sensitive for one stranger to write to another, Sharp expressed regret by saying he was "Sorry to crush your hopes in hearing from one who to judge by your letters you still love dear."[628] Captain Anson did not want the Home Office to disclose this letter to Doyle – a rather surprising desire for secrecy if it could clear up the issue unless the captain did not want Doyle to follow this up.[629] The Californian Sharp also sent a letter to Captain Anson denying being the man they were looking for and identifying himself as Fred Sharp. Reluctant to provide much detail about himself, he enclosed a photograph, which Captain Anson found unusual as he thought it would be easier for 'Fred Sharp' to have disclosed his birthplace rather than send a photograph. For some unexplained reason the captain accepted that 'Fred' Sharp might have difficulty in providing information on his background. Captain Anson sent the 'photo' to Mr Lloyd, in Welshpool, with whom 'Fred Sharp' had allegedly lodged in the past, and it was identified as Fred Sharp. The captain was convinced, or so he claimed, that the man was a stranger as the real Frank Sharp would not have answered. Hardly a convincing deduction since the real Frank Sharp might want them all off his back, to remain incognito, after all he had fled from South Staffordshire to avoid getting married and faced with a 'breach of promise' suit. [630] Nor did the captain provide any evidence of Sharp's letter or the police's so-called contact with S Lloyd of Welshpool. Not only that, when the county marshall wrote initially to Conan Doyle, he used the name Frank Sharp to identify the Sharp living at "The Ark'.

Captain Anson also received an undated letter from 'Lew Is the Light' claiming that Frank Sharp's presence at 'The Ark' was just a coincidence and he knew nothing about him. Nor did 'Lew Is' explain

---

[627] George Young, Marshall, to Captain Anson, 15 Oct 1907, HO No 297 File 987; George Young, Marshall to ACD, 2 Nov 1907, HO File 989 Pt 1
[628] F Sharp to Miss B A Sharp, Marle Hall in Llandudno, 11 Oct 1907, HO File 989 Pt 2; Capt Anson to Blackwell, 11 Oct 1907, HO File 989 Pt 1
[629] Capt Anson to Blackwell, 11 Nov 1987 HO File 989 Pt 2
[630] Capt Anson to Blackwell, 24 Jan, 9 & 13 Feb 1908 File 989 Pt 1; Greatorex , 1 Mar 1907, HO No 300 File 987

how the communication from 'The Ark' found its way to Conan Doyle but he might well have sent the cutting after being told the story by Frank Sharp without Sharp having any immediate hand in the matter.[631] Strange that this religious fanatic, always creating trouble, put himself out to give an explanation to Captain Anson but nonetheless it proved that Lewis or whoever wrote this letter knew someone at 'The Ark' called Frank Sharp. Doyle accepted that Lewis sent the cutting but thought Frank Sharp either wrote on the cutting himself or was the inspiration behind 'Lew Is' since it was too much of a coincidence for a letter on the Edalji case to come from a house where Frank Sharp was living without him having some part in it.[632] Captain Anson also thought it improbable that another Frank Sharp, by a mere coincidence, would be at the same address from where the newspaper cutting was sent with a reference to "A hell of a bridegroom I'd be to tarry wouldn't I", which the Captain thought might apply to Frank Sharp as did Home Office officials, who also believed it to be too much of a coincidence.[633]

Was it Fred or Frank Sharp? The man in California was 38 years of age, as was Frank Sharp of Cannock. Frank had left the UK for Mexico and was last heard of in California two years before.[634] Whoever it was in Long Beach, it provided nothing of relevance to the 1903 issues. What it did fuel was the debate surrounding the authorship of the 'God-Satan' letters of 1893-1895 and any connection those letters were thought to have on the events of 1903.

(iv) Vice Wrapped in Virtues Raimont

The 'Lew Is' issue was used as a magnet to draw Captain Anson into an imprudent bout of correspondence with Beaumont, one of Doyle's local informants of whom the captain held a most deprecatory view as he did of other minnows assisting his adversary. Beaumont managed to engage him in a discourse into which a person in the chief constable's position should not have entered. Hardly in keeping with his high office, the chief constable appeared irresistibly drawn towards this

---

[631] Lewis to Capt Anson, undated, in Capt Anson to Blackwell, 18 Nov 1907, HO File 989 Pt 1

[632] ACD to HO (undated) HO No 300 File 987: Capt Anson to Blackwell, 8 Dec 1907 HO File 989 Pt 2

[633] Capt Anson to Blackwell, 14 Oct 1907, HO File 989 Pt 1; Capt Anson to George Young, Marshall, 17 Oct 1907, HO No 297 File 987; HO Comment, HO No 297 File 987

[634] ACD to HO, 1 May 1907 & 18 Nov 1907, HO File 989 Pt 1 & 2

Anson-diagnosed 'lunatic' and was incautious enough to make a number of indiscreet admissions to Beaumont, whom he knew to be in the pay of Conan Doyle – a sign that the fall out from the Edalji case had really got to the chief constable.

Prior to this correspondence, Beaumont had spun the captain the line of a pact arranged between Royden Sharp and George Edalji in 1903 consisting of Sharp assisting Edalji to carry out the maimings and also supplying George with details of the people Edalji mentioned in the Greatorex letters. Missing from this disclosure were the terms of the pact and the reasons for the solicitor to align himself with the 'Third Mate'. Beaumont also disclosed that he mentioned this connection between Sharp and George to the Edaljis and, after they denied any such link, he had proven it to them, which put him in the family's bad books. Doyle, informed of Beaumont's claims, had given him the cold shoulder for the same reason.[635] Having told Captain Anson of his fall out with the Edalji's and Conan Doyle, Beaumont adopted what became a 'cat and mouse' game with Captain Anson but one unlikely to have been thought out for himself. He offered the captain some inside information on Doyle accepting that Lewis sent the cutting, not particularly significant information as Captain Anson was already aware of it, and he promised further information on what Doyle was likely to do in the future but this was an opening gambit for the real Beaumont-Doyle purpose. Taking on an obsequious demeanour by expressing his esteem for "your honour as chief constable," valued by Beaumont, so he claimed, as much as the reputation of Doyle, he went on to explain that his actions for giving information to both of them was for the "purest of motives." Beaumont disclosed receiving a letter from George Edalji informing him that unless the author of the 1903 anonymous letters was identified no compensation would be granted. Beaumont came to the punch line by asking the captain to honour a promise to show him the 'Greatorex' letter sent to the Isle of Man for comparison with a letter from George Edalji. An additional sop was waved in front of the captain by Beaumont by telling him of a new informant acquired by Doyle but for the present was unable to reveal any information. In conclusion, Beaumont advised him not "to relinquish vigilance for the present."[636]

Captain Anson made few references to Beaumont over the next six weeks but he did tell the Home Office that Beaumont was expressing

---

[635] Capt Anson to Blackwell, 18 and 20 Sep 1907, HO File 989 Part 1

[636] Beaumont to Capt Anson, 9 Dec 1907; Capt Anson to Blackwell, 8 Dec 1907; both in HO File 989 Pt 2

fear for what Sharp might do to him as George Edalji was now conspiring with Sharp, who had been told of the help Beaumont had provided to Edalji.[637] If the captain believed that such a conspiracy was possible then he had lost touch with reality. Beaumont was then reported as being "a dangerous man to have any conversation with simply because his brain is so overheated with Sharp." Captain Anson also wrote to Beaumont, "to rub well in the serious misunderstandings which he may cause by reporting things as facts which he is not clear about."[638] However, the captain seemed an easy target for Beaumont since he (Captain Anson) did not practice what he preached and was ambivalent over what Beaumont reported to him. He accepted that "old Edalji said Horace was a liar with the old old old story of the conspiracy against George Edalji" but rejected Beaumont's accusations against the Hattons of conspiring to injure George Edalji and that Mr J T Hatton exhibited unfair and prejudiced conduct in connection with Edalji's trial.[639] Captain Anson, in leaping recklessly to the defence of the Hatton's, indulged in a spot of character assassination concerning Mrs Edalji. The captain, his bile against the Edaljis overriding reason and good taste, mixing fact with fantasy, 'quoting' information allegedly brought to his attention by a man now beyond cross examination in any court of justice, having been dead for a month, wrote to Beaumont claiming that Mrs Edalji, in tears, had confessed to J T Hatton of having no doubt that George had written the anonymous letters.[640] As per usual the captain did not want the victim to be informed of the accusation and asked Beaumont to keep it confidential but he really did live in a fantasy world if he thought Beaumont would keep it to himself. Beaumont wasted no time in trotting off to bring Captain Anson's revelations to Mrs Edalji. In her usual genteel manner, Mrs Edalji dismissed the story as untrue. In a manner quite the opposite to the way the captain responded when his veracity or integrity was challenged, she wrote to the Home Office of the unfairness of such a statement being made so soon after Mr Hatton's death on the 5th January rather than in his lifetime and so preventing him from being confronted with the claim. Mrs Edalji, no stranger to Captain Anson's *modus operandi*, was aiming in the right direction when claiming this was "part of the secret

---

[637] Capt Anson to Blackwell/HO, 1 Jan 1908, HO File 989 Pt 1

[638] Capt Anson to Blackwell/HO, 26 Jan 1908, HO File 989 Pt 1

[639] Beaumont-Capt Anson Conversations, 2 Feb 1908, in Capt Anson to Blackwell 3 Feb 1908; Capt Anson to Blackwell, 16 Feb 1908, both in HO File 989 Pt 1

[640] Capt Anson to Beaumont, 4 Feb 1908, HO No 305 File 987

information" placed on the scales of justice that the Home Office had weighed against George Edalji.[641]

Home Office officials were less than pleased with the chief constable's indiscretions and sent Mrs Edalji's letter to him privately to see his reply. They were not particularly concerned with the injustice done to Mrs Edalji but thought that if he wrote any more letters to any of Doyle's other agents, like the one to Beaumont, he would soon succeed in reopening the whole question of his conduct of the case.[642] After reporting unsubstantiated hearsay conversations from a now dead witness and being brought to heel over it by Mrs Edalji, Captain Anson, showing no sign of contrition, wrote to tell her he was not prepared to discuss a letter concerning a dead man.[643] The captain gave the appearance of taking a chivalrous stand to the memory of a dead colleague as if it were one of his virtues but, having previously attributed unsubstantiated claims to this dead man, his cavalier dismissal of Mrs Edalji revealed nothing new – this was the approach he had adopted towards her twelve years earlier. Captain Anson's behaviour was hardly in keeping with the image of a gentleman and it contradicted the loftily held notion of aristocratic gentility displayed to members of the opposite sex. Of course, Mrs Edalji might not qualify for the finer points of social grace in the captain's eye, since she had gone off and married a 'Hindoo'. Captain Anson was truly a Victorian groomed gentleman and all that entailed when it involved those English ladies who married Indians. The chief constable's behaviour was the personification of the saying 'vice is often clothed in virtues raiment.'

Why was Captain Anson so keen to defend Hatton? Why not just ignore it since he thought Beaumont was mentally unbalanced and discreditable, and whom nine days previously he had called a dangerous man?[644] Was Captain Anson naive, arrogant or 'devil may care' in his attitude? Whatever it was, he had been rash enough to provide information, which he should have known would be sent post-haste to either the Edaljis or Doyle and who would not sit idly by and allow the captain's allegations to go unchallenged.

Captain Anson tried to bluff his way out of a situation that had raised concerns in the Home Office, by initially trying to divert attention away from it with the news that Beaumont wanted to tell Sharp of his part in the Doyle enquiries. With some relish, since he

[641] Mrs C Edalji to HO, 11 Feb 1908, in HO No 305 File 987

[642] HO Comment by Troup in HO No 305 File 987

[643] Capt Anson to HO, 16 Feb 1908, HO No 305 File 987

[644] Capt Anson to Blackwell/HO, 26 Jan 1908, HO File 989 Pt 1

thought Beaumont the inspiration behind many of Doyle's ideas, the captain encouraged him to do so and predicted that there would be some 'fat in the fire' if he did.[645] This was hardly consistent with keeping the peace but was par for the course for Captain Anson, who had previously expressed delight in knowing that Albert Stanley wanted to get his hands on George Edalji. When he did explain to the Home Office the indiscretions in his letters to Beaumont he defended the correspondence by claiming it had helped him to know what Doyle's agents were up to and, in true comic book style, appropriated a military phrase, namely, "you cannot carry war into the enemy's country without to some extent exposing your own flank and this conspiracy about Sharp could never be exposed by sitting still and passively resisting." He went on to inform Home Office officials of his decision to discontinue corresponding with Beaumont, adding, maybe a *mea culpe* to excuse his serious error of judgement, that when writing to Beaumont about Hatton's comment he did not expect Beaumont to keep it to himself. The captain tended towards a certain buffoonery exceeded only by his arrogance and lack of good taste.

Captain Anson was still unsure of what Doyle may have discovered, especially in the pursuit of Hart to turn King's evidence, and in the dying glow of the case was still poking among the embers for information from the Home Office. However, Doyle had arrived at the conclusion that nothing further could be done for Edalji - justice could not be served adequately without the help of the local police, or specifically Captain Anson, and neither the police nor the captain had any intention of helping. Nonetheless, Doyle felt some sense of achievement for clearing Edalji and getting him back on the rolls. Another benefit was the passing of the Court of Criminal Appeal Act, assisted by the miscarriages of justice in the Beck and Edalji cases.[646]

Conan Doyle's months of campaigning on Edalji's behalf, his revelations regarding Captain Anson's malice towards the Edaljis and the criticism heaped upon Captain Anson and the Staffordshire police in the press left its mark on the captain, a person who appeared almost obsessively to demand acceptance or acquiescence in his determination to damage the Edaljis. Following on from the vast array of negative publicity, Captain Anson decidedly lost his way and over the coming years showed a tendency towards increasingly erratic behaviour.

---

[645] Capt Anson to Blackwell/HO, 13 Feb 1908, HO File 989 Pt 1
[646] Capt Anson to Blackwell/HO, 13 Feb 1908, HO File 989 Pt 1; ACD to Blackwell, 29 Jan 1908, HO File 989 Pt 2; Gazette 23 Oct 1907; Truth 4 Dec 1907

Chapter XVIII

Laid to Rest

(i)   The Last Hurrah

With the issue 'settled', it might be expected that the secondary protagonists would exit the stage. However, the case was resurrected just over two years later and ran on and off for about a year, witnessing a more intense conflict between Conan Doyle and Captain Anson as they carried out their respective roles of Holmes and Moriarty.

In August 1910, Conan Doyle described Edalji's situation as a "national disgrace"[647] and a couple of months later approached his friend, Winston Churchill, the new Home Secretary, with a request to reopen Edalji's case but the Whitehall establishment in the form of Home Office officials advised Churchill against it.[648] Doyle's request found its way to Captain Anson, for whom any attempt to clear Edalji was taken as an attack on his own integrity and motives, which in effect it could reasonably be interpreted as such. Any action of this kind exposed the captain's Achilles heel – his inability to come to terms with anyone who had the temerity to 'cross him' and it seemed to be the spark that launched him into a tirade of abuse against Conan Doyle – an outlet for his brooding anger. The key to Captain Anson's brooding had the appearance of some kind of prep-school sense of hurt at being let down by Doyle, who, so the captain thought, had taken what he could from him when investigating the Edalji case and then did his best to turn it to his (Anson's) disadvantage.[649]

In November 1910, donning his official cap and using the stationery of the chief constable's office, he began to correspond with Conan Doyle and, when Doyle contested the captain's version of events, he responded with an extended letter raking up the Edalji sodomy issue by accusing Doyle of making a lying, offensive allegation of a peculiarly objectionable type to discredit him with Gladstone and then hiding behind "the poor miserable wretch Churton Collins," who was said to have originally put the allegation into Doyle's head. The captain again showed his penchant for quoting or attacking dead people,

---

[647] DT 6 Aug 1910

[648] ACD to Blackwell, 23 Oct 1910; ACD-Churchill Correspondence, 24 Oct 1910; in HO Nos 313/4 File 987

[649] Capt Anson to ACD, 14 Jan 1911, HO No 315 File 987

as Collins was tragically drowned in a bizarre way in 1908. Venturing into history, he complained of Doyle failing to inform him of his suspicions about Royden Sharp in 1907 and then went on to attack those suspicions as "a collection of arrant nonsense...never heard before a lawyer of repute as evidence in a criminal case."[650] This was one of the very few points that Captain Anson raised showing any sign of credibility because Doyle did present an insipid, unconvincing case against Sharp.

Captain Anson found it difficult to detach himself from Doyle's South Staffordshire 'agents', to whom the captain had been so indiscreet, and they also fell foul of the bile unleashed against them. Beaumont, apparently, now an incumbent of an asylum suffering from religious mania, was described as the lunatic reporting on Sharp's movements, a mental state also employed to describe Arrowsmith, who allegedly believed Sharp to be the Clapham murderer by interpreting an 'S' shaped scar on the face of the murdered man to stand for Sharp. Captain Anson also implied that Doyle was of the same mental state for accepting information from madmen. Doyle was also attacked for believing Frank Sharp's presence at the 'Ark' in California was more than a coincidence and the captain produced a rather limp debunking statement by claiming there might be as many as 150 Doyles and 550 Sharps living in Long Beach. Reaching even further back, the captain rejected as absolutely untrue Doyle's accusation of Royden Sharp having "a proved record of writing anonymous letters, of forgery, of diabolical mischief, and of bearing false witness", as there was no proven record of any of these things. Captain Anson had obviously not seen Sharp's school report where these particular faults were listed or even remembered the headmaster's comments to him.[651] The captain also appeared confused in suggesting Conan Doyle was indiscreet in allowing it to be known that he had altered his opinion of Edalji since it was Yelverton who had turned on Edalji in a letter to De Rutzen,

---

[650] Ibid

[651] In October 1910, Royden Sharp was convicted for stealing flowers from a garden. On another occasion, the judge, sentencing Sharp to 6 months imprisonment with hard labour, said "His character was extremely bad, he has been convicted of arson, of stealing on 3 occasions and of damage (and a)Cruel theft from (his) aged mother." CA 29 Oct 1910; ACD to Blackwell, 23 Oct 1910, HO No 314 File 987 Doyle, Sir Arthur Conan [1924] Memories and Adventures, Hodder & Stoughton, London, p221

Captain Anson's cousin.[652] When Doyle asked for an expression of regret from the Captain for accusing him of lying, Captain Anson rashly sent off a telegram to Doyle with the words, "Your statement to Home Secretary was a lie and I satisfied him it was," which was a rather churlish even childish response. Doyle drew the Home Secretary's attention to the "inexcusable language" used in an open telegram and he asked for action to prevent a recurrence otherwise he would go public.[653] When the captain's telegram and letter were passed on to Home Office officials, they thought his actions inexcusable and his comments on Churton Collins deplorable.[654] The behaviour was considered to be sufficiently serious by senior officials to warrant his removal from the post of chief constable. However, the Home Secretary was in no position to take this course of action since the only authority held by the Home Office was to withhold a certificate of efficiency from the Staffordshire police but it was difficult to do that merely on the grounds of Captain Anson's individual conduct. Problems might also arise if the captain refused to give an explanation and was backed by his Joint Standing Committee.[655] The Home Secretary, Churchill, thinking Captain Anson's communications discourteous and improper, could not ignore the matter since he had been drawn into it by being referred to in an open telegram. However, Home Office officials, despite admitting that Captain Anson was an impossible person and his actions characteristic of him, advised the Home Secretary that the only avenue open to him was to write a letter of censure if the captain's explanation turned out to be inadequate.[656]

Home Office officials, while curious as to why Captain Anson revived the sodomy issue after more than four years and still not really familiar with the nuances in the case or choosing not to be, thought the captain's letter was not a string of inaccuracies, as it was described by Doyle, but was offensive and in the worst possible taste. Captain Anson was acknowledged to be guilty of many indiscretions, particularly in the earlier stages of the case, but they defended him by digging up the indefensible claim of there being a number of 'errors' in the depositions. Nor did they believe that the chief constable or members of

---

[652] Capt Anson to ACD, 14 Jan 1911, HO No 315 File 987

[653] ACD to Churchill, 30 Jan 1911, HO No 314 File 987

[654] HO Comment 22 Feb 1911

[655] Blackwell to Troup, 3 Feb 1911, HO No 314 File 987

[656] HO to Capt Anson, 8 Feb 1911; HO Comment 8 & 9 Feb 1911; Blackwell to Capt Anson 16 Feb 1911; in HO Nos 314/314a File 987

his force deserved the obloquy heaped upon them.[657] Blackwell, holding the belief that Captain Anson had a grievance against Doyle for the accusations made against him and the Staffordshire police force in the press, was reluctant to recommend any drastic action or censure against the chief constable that did not take into account Doyle's malice or, at the least, blind stupidity in making the original accusation about sodomy.[658] Doyle's apology in 1907, given more in the interests of expediency while pursuing a pardon for Edalji rather than seeking to exonerate Captain Anson, who had shown himself capable of doing or saying anything against the Edalji family, provided Home Office officials with an excuse to back the captain despite the obvious disdain they felt towards him. Even when Captain Anson displayed the face that had confronted the Edaljis for many years, the Home Office still expressed some sympathy for him and could not, or would not detect the malice, or blind stupidity, dwelling behind his aristocratic face.

Oblivious to the disdain held by some Home Office officials towards him, Captain Anson retaliated by threatening to continue calling Doyle a liar as often as necessary until an apology was forthcoming and he refused to give an undertaking not to refer to the matter again. However, not being able to think clearly on the matter, he thought it unlikely it would be raised again and was willing to give a pledge not to do so but held back from giving an unconditional undertaking to hold his tongue.[659] Still in a real flap over the Edalji case, he gave the distinct impression of someone unable to cope with those who questioned his actions and motives and of allowing this to fester over a long time. The captain's reactions provided an insight into the kind of behaviour suffered by the defenceless Edaljis when facing the antagonism and intransigence of the chief constable.

Captain Anson was not the only one to replay the case. While the captain was releasing his fury at Conan Doyle for 'betraying a confidence' and for continuing to show support for George Edalji, Reverend Edalji latched on to press reports in an attempt to further his son's claim for compensation – the ultimate exoneration. In a letter to the Daily Telegraph, the reverend wrote of Archer-Lee, the 'Winslow Boy', receiving compensation for an unjust charge against him as was the charge against his son who received no compensation. In an editorial prompted by the reverend's correspondence, the editor

---

[657] HO comment, 9 & 22 Feb 1911, HO Nos 314a/ 315 File 987

[658] Home Office Comment, 14 Feb 1911, HO No 314a File 987

[659] Capt Anson to HO/Blackwell, 9 & 19 Feb 1911; in HO Nos 314a, 315, 316 File 987

informed his readers that any favourable decision for Edalji "would have involved the discrediting of a highly placed official with an aristocratic lineage", who lacked the vision to see, or at least to admit, the possibility of his making a mistake. Edalji's treatment was "a disgrace...and a blot upon our national escutcheon, the more so because of the racial origin of its victim"[660] – a sign that the editor was prepared to put the motive for the persecution of Edalji within the racial context of the period. When George Edalji himself pressed the Home Office for compensation, officials put it down to the influence of the Archer-Lee case, and Doyle's attempt to obtain compensation met with a refusal to re-open the case.[661]

The George Edalji case was dead and buried. Over the next forty five years, from time to time, attempts were made to breathe life into its comatose body but never again did it come fully to life. An occasional tremor could be felt but it was quickly anesthetised by officials, who probably had never heard the name Edalji.

(ii) Rattling a Few Skeletons

South Staffordshire made the news again in July 1912 when, after a break stretching from September 1907, cattle maiming once again returned to the area and was accompanied by a renewed spate of anonymous letters. Shortly before the outbreak flared up, Captain Anson was given early warning of the prospective outrages but doubted the authenticity of the information. The 'tip-off' was genuine enough and over a seven weeks period with numerous police keeping watch on the fields, six maimings occurred. Needless to say, with scapegoats thin on the ground, or if not in short supply relatively free from the fear of arrest following the Staffordshire police's previous bungling, the police failed to find the maimer or the scribe. A feature of this resumption of activity by person or persons unknown was the arrival of the usual bevy of eccentrics with bizarre schemes for identifying the perpetrator. A group of spiritualists and clairvoyants conjured up a description of a man sent from the watchers of the 'Great Beyond'; others thought the perpetrator was a bird of prey; or a malicious aviator; or a man disguised as a horse or cow.[662]

---

[660] Letter, Rev Edalji to DT and Editorial DT 11 Aug 1911

[661] G Edalji to HO, 15 Sep 1911, HO No 318 File 987; ACD to HO, 19 Oct 1911, HO No 320 File 987

[662] The Standard 6 - 11 Oct 1913; E & S 7 Sep 1912; DE 4 and 7 Sep 1912; Capt Anson to HO, 28 Aug 1913, HO File 45/24635, 227924/4

A year passed by without further incident until the Edalji case itself was resurrected in a book about Captain Darby by G A Atkinson, who presented the case as an issue revolving around two other protagonists, Conan Doyle and Captain Anson, which to all intents and purposes it had become since December 1906. The thrust of Atkinson's account was to claim that Edalji's side of the case was not fairly received and he thought it would be "a notable act of grace for the Government to review the case." Having promised Conan Doyle to approach the authorities but on a non-partisan basis, Atkinson, who claimed to like both Captain Anson and Conan Doyle, sought a meeting with Home Office officials. However, the Home Office turned its back on this invitation believing Atkinson's real object was to reopen the Edalji case in order to obtain compensation for him, especially as Edalji had written a couple of times in 1911 and 1912 on the issue of compensation.[663]

Within weeks of this correspondence, no government could have spent a moment of time on a miscarriage of justice and the injury inflicted on one man accused of butchering an animal, when across the channel the first steps were taking place to thrust millions of young men into a butcher's yard on the Western Front. During the Great War, the Wolverhampton Express and Star, no doubt seeking a diversion from the slaughter in Flanders fields, published the contents of the 1903 anonymous letters and expressed the view that the person responsible was a local man. The burghers of Great Wyrley demonstrated their parochialism via the Great Wyrley Parish Council, which, despite the wholesale bloodletting in France, including many local men, felt sufficiently aggrieved at this suggestion to petition the Home Secretary to restrain the editor of the Express and Star from "fanning the dying embers of fanaticism." The Home Office, having no authority for muzzling the press on such an issue, merely dismissed the petition.[664]

Shortly after the war was over, Captain Darby reappeared in 1919 after a five years absence,[665] he then retreated before going on the offensive again in 1923,[666] after which he disappeared for another eight years, re-emerging in 1931 with a new string of letters until he was finally caught in 1934. Enoch Knowles, who had no connection with the

[663] Correspondence between Atkinson and HO, 11 – 17 Jul 1914, HO File 45/24635, 227924/6 & 7

[664] E & S 13 Sep 1915; Correspondence between Sambrook and HO, 19 & 26 Oct 1915, HO File 45/24635, 227924/9

[665] Captain Darby (Enoch Knowles) had served in the trenches in France

[666] DE 5 Sep 1919; ES 14 Mar 1923

Great Wyrley area, admitted to being Captain Darby and was convicted in November 1934.

Following Knowles' conviction, an article by George Edalji appeared in the Daily Express under the title of the "Terror that Walks the Night", the local name given to the cattle maiming in 1903. Edalji disclosed a bizarre story told to him by a local man, who believed the maimings were committed by one or more boars released by their owners during the night, whom this informant claimed to have seen but apparently no one else did – a story thought by Edalji too fantastic to be true[667] but good material for detective fiction.

A few months later, prompted no doubt by the Knowles trial, Miss Young, a friend of George Edalji, now living in Welwyn Garden City, raised Edalji's case with her Member of Parliament, Sir Francis Fremantle. The MP, after looking through Edalji's papers on the case, contacted the Home Office asking for something to be done for Edalji, whom he thought had suffered wrongful imprisonment. The Home Office got in touch with the new chief constable of Staffordshire asking if Enoch Knowles could be responsible for the 1903 'Greatorex' letters. The chief constable contacted Captain Anson, who like an *eminence gris* or, more appropriately, a hibernating vulture, discussed the case with the new chief of Staffordshire police, who in turn swallowed his predecessor's well-rehearsed diet, cooked up and re-served on numerous occasions between 1892 and 1914. The passage of time allowed for new variations in the captain's account, bringing in the novel accusation that Reverend Edalji "bore very meekly the insinuations because he was aware of the letter writing activities of his son," overlooking the continual and strong protestations made by the reverend in defence of his son all those years before and contradicting Captain Anson's own admission in 1907 that he was not sure if George Edalji wrote all the God-Satan letters.[668] The ex-chief constable offered to discuss the case with Home Office officials, giving him the opportunity to rehash his arguments without any possibility of rebuttal – the kind of scenario suited to his talents and demonstrated so often before. Understandably, those looking at issues stretching back some forty years and relying on Captain Anson's distorted version took the bait willingly and the captain in his dotage with his bigotry intact gave a new lease of life to tired propositions. To accept that Captain Darby had written the 1903 anonymous letters would remove the grounds for the Home Office not granting compensation to Edalji. However, the Home

---

[667] DE 7 Nov 1934

[668] Capt Anson to Blackwell, 13 Oct 1907, HO File 989 Pt 1

Office saw no positive evidence to connect Knowles to these letters and relying on Captain Anson's contribution felt unable to reopen the case. Sir Francis accepted this and dissuaded his constituent from raising the issue through other channels. [669]

The issue was laid to rest and nothing more was heard from George Edalji, who came to his own personal end of the road in 1953, in the year following his brother's death. Edalji bequeathed his papers on the case to the Law Society but, surprisingly, an officer at the society had them destroyed. The writer, Compton Mackenzie, an old-time campaigner on behalf of Edalji, believed the papers were destroyed "to cover up those lawyers involved in a disgraceful miscarriage of justice."[670] Three years after Edalji's demise, three men, released from prison after being recognised as victims of a miscarriage of justice, were given, according to the Home Secretary, generous compensation.[671] This seemingly bland aside prompted Maud Edalji, now 74 years old, to emerge from the shadows of the garden city to raise the issue of the injustice meted out to her brother, given a pardon but no compensation. Time had obviously not mellowed the feeling of injustice that she harboured about her brother's treatment, although never before exposing this in the public arena. Maud went into the early details of the persecution of the Edaljis between 1892 and 1895, the

[669] Correspondence between HO and the Chief Constable for Staffordshire, Mar/Apr 1935; and Sir F Fremantle-HO Correspondence, 6 Mar to 22 Jun 1935, HO File 45/24635, 227924/15-17

[670] C Mackenzie to Stitt, 23 Feb 1970, Papers held at Wm Salt Library, Stafford

[671] The three men, Leonard Emery, Arthur Thompson and James Power, were convicted in January 1954 for grievous bodily harm to a police officer. One of three other men, who actually committed the crime, confessed to it in September 1955. An enquiry established that Emery, Thompson and Power were innocent. In granting a free pardon with compensation, Major Lloyd-George, Home Secretary, said "When a man has been imprisoned as a result of what turns out to be a mistake it is right that the State should make some payment as a symbol of its desire to acknowledge the error and to do what is possible to square the account between society and the individual." Interestingly, the fact that Emery, Thompson and Power had contributed to the miscarriage of justice by perjuring themselves at the trial did not count against them. Their perjury was in giving a fake alibi of their whereabouts at the time the offence was committed, which they did because one of the three men was on his way to commit other crimes of burglary and theft. Times 25 Jan 1956

1903 maiming, the arrest of George Edalji and the continuation of the maimings and anonymous letters after his incarceration. She pulled no punches when she described the Staffordshire police as "worse than useless, from Captain Anson downwards" for plotting George Edalji's downfall. Not confining herself to her brother's misfortune, Maud Edalji linked it to Adolf Beck, making the undeniable point that one benefit resulting from the sufferings of those two innocent men was the creation of the Court of Criminal Appeal.[672]

Maud stressed that her father, a Parsee, was dark not black and not a native of India but of Persia, exhibiting an approach to the race issue not unknown to people of Anglo and Indian origin of that era, who to some extent distanced themselves from other subject Black and Indian people of the British Empire. Yet, in what for her might be quite a startling accusation, Maud drew attention to the colour prejudice of Captain Anson, whom she accused of objecting to anyone who had a skin darker than most of the people. The significance of Maud's condemnation of Captain Anson's prejudice, now defined as racism, was that it was invoked by someone to whom this concept would only be used as a last resort, when all other reasons for the captain's behaviour had been scrutinised and rejected.

The Home Secretary's refusal to placate Maud Edalji by reopening the matter was not surprising bearing in mind a half-century had elapsed, and, as far as the Home Office was concerned, it was all ancient history. The Home Office recognised that Maud Edalji wanted nothing pecuniary; all she seemed to want was to draw attention to the injustice of her brother's experience – an extension of the attitude shown so determinedly by her parents in another era.

Maud wanted nothing more than for her brother's case to be fully investigated and, within the constraints imposed by the passing of a century; this account has been an attempt to do just that.

---

[672] Correspondence between M Edalji and the Home Secretary, Major Lloyd-George, 8 & 21 Feb and 29 Mar 1956, HO File 45/24635, 227924/18

Chapter XIX

Afterthought

Those responsible for the maimings and the anonymous letters will almost certainly never be discovered, unless papers secreted away revealing all somehow come to life – an unlikely prospect. George Edalji's personal papers may have provided more clues but were apparently destroyed by the Law Society as of little value![673]

Conan Doyle critically dismantled the case against George Edalji but offered little of substance to identify the real maimer. Although Royden Sharp, one-time apprentice butcher and mate on a cattle ship, and Jack Hart, a butcher who was also skilled in breaking-in horses, were more likely candidates, no substantive evidence was ever produced against them. Harry Green may have played a part, certainly in the killing of his father's horse, but was on his way to South Africa and living there when the other horses were maimed between November 1903 and August 1907. Another likely candidate was Thomas Farrington, seen in the vicinity of the crimes when the first two animals were maimed in 1903 and found guilty of killing two sheep in April 1904, after which there were no more maimings until August 1907 shortly after Farrington's release from gaol. However, this is naught but speculation and as in the George Edalji case there were no witnesses or constructive forensic evidence to tie in those suspects or anyone else for that matter to the series of maimings.

The anonymous letters produce a similar conundrum especially as they stretch for almost twenty years from their beginnings in 1888. The 1888/9 letters offered up two principal suspects, Elizabeth Foster and George Edalji, as the evidence inclined towards someone inside the vicarage as responsible. Foster, when found guilty of the offence, swore revenge on the Edaljis for her conviction and denied culpability up until her death in 1905. The letters between 1892 and 1895 may be unconnected with the previous letters and throw up a number of suspects, who may or may not be connected with each other. The first letters, crude in content and aimed principally at the Brookes' with the Edaljis thrown in due to the alleged friendship between Fred Brookes and George Edalji, looked to have been written by a schoolboy or

---

[673] C Mackenzie to Stitt, 23 Feb 1970, Papers held at Wm Salt Library, Stafford

schoolboys. The impression given by the contents of the letters pointed to Royden Sharp, who was in conflict with Fred Wynne and Fred Brookes, but this may have been a mask to hide the identity of the real scribe. Fred Wynne was suspected by both his headmaster and the police and suspended from school pending enquiries. Fred Brookes or George Edalji were two other suspects but why they would write crude letters about their own parents and sisters is difficult to understand and the pseudo-psychological explanations of George's alleged self-hate carry little weight. Surprisingly, Horace Edalji, who was never mentioned at all in any anonymous letters and thirteen years old at the time and close to Royden Sharp's age, was never considered a candidate despite being a member of an ethnic minority and living under the same regime as his brother. Perhaps, Elizabeth Foster, or kinfolk of hers, were serving up the vengeance promised to the Edaljis. Another batch of letters commencing about Christmas 1892, attacking numerous people in the parish and exuding a primitive Methodism was attributed by Conan Doyle to the Sharp brothers but nothing of substance was provided to support such a claim. A scholar with knowledge of Latin and French and a deep rooted religious paroxysm, pointing away from a member of the Anglican faith, must also be in the frame. One suspect was James Morgan, an educated man, part-time newspaper reporter, who seemed at odds with everyone in the parish, including Reverend Edalji and Mr W H Brookes, but who claimed to have no religious affinities. No explanation is available as to why the letters stopped in December 1895, but two people involved in one way or another left the area at that time – Royden Sharp went to sea and Sergeant Upton, whose behaviour in the enquiries in December 1892 left much to be desired, went to another police force. If George Edalji had been responsible for the considerable variety of letters flooding the area he would have to be extremely dexterous in handwriting, adopt or act out numerous personality traits, have an obsession with religion at variance with his Anglican background and be able to travel extensively around the Midlands.

In 1903, the first two anonymous letters and an insertion in the third letter were not attributed to George Edalji. The remainder were put at George Edalji's door but little reliance can be placed on this because the handwriting expert, Gurrin, was discredited for the principal part he played, by reason of a faulty analysis, in getting another innocent man convicted of deception. Several schoolboys, Greatorex, Stanley and Quibell, were all on the list of suspects. Royden Sharp, a recent returnee to the area, was due to be arrested on the 6th August 1903 for allegedly sending out crude anonymous postcards. Jack Hart, who had a deep-rooted antagonism to Edalji for his part in a libel suit brought against Hart, which cost Hart dearly, was also a candidate for some form of involvement. The authorship of several of the letters in 1903 may have been part of the conspiracy to entrap George Edalji conjured up between Captain Anson and Loxton, the solicitor, who sent out the 'Lover of Justice' letter. The Martin Molton letters in 1907 came at a less than fortuitous time for Edalji and it was unlikely for Edalji to be so reckless when campaigning for a pardon to have written them but the timing was advantageous to Captain Anson, with Royden Sharp on his payroll, who was trying extremely hard to discredit Edalji and block a pardon for him.

Trying to identify the maimer and the scribes was not a prime objective of this research, although to do so would have been a bonus. What evolved from curiosity led to some understanding of the particular experiences inflicted on the Edaljis during those turbulent years prior to George Edalji's conviction. George Edalji was not the first victim of a miscarriage of justice nor will he be the last but his experiences and those of his family have a particular bitter flavour.

Appendix I

Moriarty v Holmes ex-parte Sharp

Sir Arthur Conan Doyle and Captain Anson locked themselves into a bitter dispute over the Edalji issue related in part to their own concern in coming out on top – a dispute fought out on paper in a putative case against Royden Sharp, the mantle on which each sought to hang his prestige. In the saga, Doyle played the role of an ineffectual Sherlock Holmes while Captain Anson portrayed an equally ineffective Moriarty.

(i)   Sir Arthur Conan Doyle's Prosecution

Conan Doyle had played a significant part in securing a pardon for George Edalji by showing the implausibility of the myopic solicitor scouring the fields at night butchering cattle while successfully evading a posse of police standing guard in the area. Not only had Doyle exposed Captain Anson along with the Staffordshire police for the prejudice shown towards Edalji and the Edalji family but also highlighted the ease with which the police introduced, virtually unchallenged, evidence of the most dubious quality against George. However, Doyle failed to demonstrate a similar kind of rigour when examining the case against the Sharps and Jack Hart as he had done when exposing the deficiencies in the police evidence conjured up against Edalji.

Doyle's attention was drawn to the Sharps and Jack Hart by several local men and women: Fred Arrowsmith, whom Captain Anson in 1903 described as an honest man when supplying information to the police about Harry Green; Beaumont alleged by Captain Anson to have serious mental problems; Wynne, a recipient of anonymous letters in 1892 and an initial suspect for writing those letters as well as being a co-passenger with Royden Sharp when a railway carriage was vandalised; and Greatorex, Sharp's uncle and trustee of their father's estate, towards whom the Sharps held a certain animosity over the way he administered their finances. Information also came from a private detective agency, J Malcolm Fraser, whom Doyle commissioned to carry out enquiries independent of his local informants.

Doyle submitted details of his suspicions of Royden Sharp, the one-time apprentice butcher and third mate on a cattle ship; and Jack Hart, a butcher, who was skilled with horses; to the Home Office asking for the 'report' to be submitted to the Director of Public Prosecutions for consideration but for it to be withheld from Captain Anson. The points mustered to form his hypothesis on their guilt, forty-seven in all, were naught but a cocktail of local gossip, innuendo and supposition circulating in a locality rife with rumour, speculation and hearsay, and were little more than a collection of assumptions simply not hanging together. A sample of the 'evidence' brought to Doyle's attention by third parties consisted of: the existence of a route from the back of Sharp's house over open fields to Great Wyrley; a slaughterhouse frequented by Hart and believed to be a rendez-vous for a gang; a knife shown by Royden Sharp to Mrs Greatorex, which he claimed to be the type of weapon used for carrying out maimings; a claim made by Mr Mellor, a butcher to whom Sharp was once apprenticed in 1894, that Sharp maimed his (Mellor's) horse; a meeting up of the Sharp brothers in Cannock in the summer of 1906, which Doyle suspected was linked to George Edalji's prospective release from prison; a report from a Cannock tobacconist, Mrs Williams, about a warehouse boy, "Jimmy", one-time employee of Hart, who reported Hart as saying, "If we can't do any more horses we can fire ricks and get clean away" and, following the Green maiming, said, "I taught the chap how to do it, but a pretty mess he made;" a claim by Fred Wynne of hearing Harry Green often mention Hart's name as a member of the gang; links to Sharp in the anonymous letters and his record of writing such letters; and an assault on a young girl in 1903 alleged to have been carried out by Jack Hart and Royden Sharp, who were frequently seen together in 1903.

What real value could be placed on these reports? Mr Mellor, the butcher, failed to report the alleged injuries to his horse to the police at the time and his information on Sharp was relayed from Mellor to another butcher named Reynolds then to Arrowsmith and on to Doyle – a veritable chain of hearsay evidence collected by amateur sleuths. Mrs Sharp was said to have a tendency towards answering in accordance with the questioner's requirements, perhaps, attributable to her deafness. To Doyle's aide, she allegedly described her son, Royden, as a maniac but said the opposite to Captain Anson. Mrs Greatorex did not accept that the knife shown to her by Royden was the weapon used for the outrages. The Sharp brothers' meeting could only have consisted of Herbert, urgently recalled to Cannock; and Royden, since Frank was in the USA, and it may have had something to do with a family tragedy, Walter's recent death in South Africa, which Doyle seemed completely unaware of until well into 1907. The route over open fields to Great Wyrley was available to anyone and Hart's presence, as a butcher, at the slaughterhouse in the company of others was not out of the ordinary. As for the alleged assault in 1903, Doyle's proposal was for the 'attacked' child to be given a chance to identify Sharp – a none too sensible suggestion to think that identification by a child four years after a fleeting brush with an adult in a street had any legal or moral value. This was as unsound as some of Captain Anson's notions.[674] Other points in Doyle's portfolio were as unreliable as these and one member of the Edalji Support Committee, the renowned KC, Sir George Lewis, pointed out to Doyle the sheer inadequacy of this evidence before Doyle sent it off to the Home Office.

Extending his investigation to cover the anonymous letters, Doyle placed the blame on the four Sharp brothers for the whole series of letters flooding South Staffordshire from 1888 to 1903 and for the 1907 input from 'Martin Molton' and 'Lew Is' but his excursion into handwriting analysis was weak and vacillatory. Doyle studied the anonymous letters, noting they were written in a cramped and practically unpunctuated disguised style, the hand of an uneducated man, a foul mouthed boor, a blackguard with a smattering of education, irregular in his habits, having neither grammar nor decency, incompatible with George Edalji, living in a clerical atmosphere, of orderly habits and with no evidence of coarse speech, who was an educated man, writing with no errors in style or spelling, showing a set pattern of writing in an open and free style.[675] On the basis of this 'analysis', he believed Royden Sharp to be the coarse boy, who concocted the 1892 letters, with the other brothers either assisting or acquiescing. Herbert and Walter Sharp were said to possess the family gift of multi-style writing and Walter wrote verse, was blasphemous and boasted of his ability to imitate anyone's handwriting. Walter was protective of his younger brother and would more than likely come to his aid by threatening Fred Brookes, Fred Wynne or George Edalji or anyone else with whom Royden Sharp might come into conflict.[676]

[674] ACD case against R Sharp, HO File 988; Report to ACD from detective H Leatherdale, 4 Feb 1907, HO File 989 Pt 1; Correspondence between ACD and Capt Anson, in Capt Anson to Blackwell, Sept 1907, HO File 989 Pt 1; ACD to HO, 6 Feb, 23 Mar 1907 & 4 Apr 1907, HO File 989 Pt 1; Capt Anson to Blackwell, 8 Sep 1907 HO File 989 Pt 1; Capt Anson's notes on ACD letters, undated, HO File 989 Pt 2; Arrowsmith to ACD, 3 Sep 1907, HO No 300 File 987; ACD to Capt Anson, 5 Sep 1907, HO File 989 Pt 2; Sir G Lewis, in Green, R L [1983] 'The Uncollected Sherlock Holmes', Penguin, London, p119; Atkinson, G A [1914] G H Darby: Captain of the Wyrley Gang, T Kirby & Son, Walsall. p11; MM Letters, England: HO Case of G Edalji – memos and papers, B/p 2/4 (19)
[675] DT 11 June 1907
[676] ACD to HO, 7 Feb 1907, HO File 989 Pt 1

Doyle had brought together a number of incidents and a few coincidences to claim Royden Sharp was the source of the letters: in 1892, afflicted with the same malady attributed to George Edalji by Captain Anson, Royden Sharp had exhibited a 'propensity for anonymous letter writing' by sending scurrilous letters to the headmaster of Walsall Grammar School; also in 1892, Sharp set fire to Hatton's rick and several references to Hatton and rick burning were made in the 1893 letters; in 1893, Sharp attempted suicide and a suicide threat was referred to in an anonymous letter of 1903; several letters came from Rotherham, Sutton Coldfield and other places visited by Sharp in 1903; Sharp held a grudge against Greatorex senior, a reason put forward for getting Greatorex's son into trouble by sending out letters in his name; in 1895, Sharp left the South Staffordshire area to eventually serve on a cattle ship when Edalji's troubles ceased only to recommence after Sharp's return in late 1902; and several references were made to the sea in the anonymous letters in 1903.[677]

Great play was made of the connection to the sea and the abrupt ending of the previous letters in 1895 and their resumption in 1903 as coinciding with Royden Sharp's embarkation and disembarkation from a career at sea but Doyle was reading back from information already known about Sharp[678] – not fatal to an analysis but tending towards teleology. Speculating on Sharp's authorship of the 1903 letters, Doyle cited the references in the letters to Holton, Littleworth (doctor) Lyndop (colliery time keeper) Guy (local butcher) Harvey (colliery official) Phillips (shopkeeper) as proof of his guilt since they were all known to Sharp – an assumption that would indict most of the population of Hednesford.

Doyle was also convinced that Royden Sharp wrote the Captain Darby letters, which twenty seven years later were shown to be written by an outsider. The 'Aldis abuse letter', spelt 'Alldus,' of the 27th May 1907 was also thought as further evidence against Royden Sharp as the handwriting appeared to be identical to the writing of the 1892 coarse boy. However, to claim that the handwriting of the thirteen year old alleged co-writer of the 1892 anonymous letters was the same as the alleged twenty eight year old Martin Molton was stretching reality to breaking point but no more so than Home Office Officials, who linked the coarse boy's writing to George Edalji by the same criterion. The 'Aldis' letter brought crime detection to its 'apex' when tests were set

[677] 'Truth' 29 May 1907; ACD case against R Sharp, HO File 988; ACD to HO, 16 Jan 1907, HO File 989 Pt 1
[678] ACD to HO, 17/18 Nov 1907, HO No 300 File 987

for both George Edalji and Royden Sharp to spell out the name of the headmaster of Walsall Grammar School. Doyle administered Edalji's test, in which Edalji spelt the name as Allduss, Alduss or Aldreiss – rather curious for an educated man to give three variations. Captain Anson set the test for Sharp, whose spelling came out as Haldis. Doyle suspected Sharp by no means a scholar, of deliberately misspelling the name but inconsistently believed the scholarly Edalji's spelling was that of a man vaguely hearing the name – a very imbalanced interpretation. Captain Anson more reasonably thought that both Edalji and Sharp, believing the test to be a trap, deliberately misspelled the name.[679]

When it came to comparing the handwriting, Doyle identified the author of the 'Lover of Justice' letter, the 'Greatorex' letter of the 29th July 1903 and the Martin Molton letter as Walter Sharp but how Doyle came to rest on Walter was never adequately explained. A considerable difficulty arose for Doyle in identifying Walter as Martin Molton, whatever handwriting qualities he had or was assumed to have, because Walter died months before Martin Molton sent out any letters, which put Doyle over a barrel, as did the 'Lover of Justice' letter, a Loxton creation 'commissioned' by Captain Anson. However, it was on the analysis of the God-Satan letters that Doyle's inadequacy in the field of handwriting analysis was clearly shown but despite the holes in his hypothesis he retained an obsessive preoccupation with the Sharps. He was certain Martin Molton was God-Satan but this assessment like so many of Doyle's on the handwriting issue was far off the mark. At different times, he was convinced God-Satan was either Herbert or Frank, or Walter or Royden Sharp. At the beginning he thought God-Satan, Martin Molton and Herbert Sharp were one and the same. A week later, Doyle was convinced Royden Sharp was Martin Molton, then the deceased Walter Sharp became chief suspect, not arrived at by the type of handwriting but on the opinion of Greatorex, who could not imagine Frank or Herbert being the author but could believe it was Walter – a view 'confirmed' by Mrs Herbert Sharp, who claimed Walter was able to imitate anyone's handwriting and talked wildly about religion. Frank Sharp came into the frame when the 'Lew Is'

---

[679] Capt Anson to ACD, 11 Oct 1907, HO No 297 File 987; ACD to Capt Anson, 11 Sept 1907, HO File 989 Pt 2; ACD to HO, 7 Oct 1907, HO No 297, File 987, 15 Nov 1907, HO File 989 Pt 2 and 17 Nov 1907, HO No 300 File 987; ACD to HO, 29 Jan 1907, HO File 988; ACD to Blackwell, 18 Apr 1907, HO File 989 Pt 1; DT 24 May 1907; ACD to HO, Capt Anson to Blackwell, 18 Nov 1907, HO File 989 Pt 1; ACD to Blackwell/HO, 25 Nov 1907, HO No 300 File 987;

letter arrived. But then Doyle backtracked to light on Royden Sharp and in May 1907, Doyle was yet again convinced God-Satan had taken up residence on the Pacific Coast of the USA and was none other than Frank Sharp.[680]

Doyle's weakness revealed itself in a remark he made, after finding out that an uncle of the Sharp's had been accused of forgery by claiming that, "It is all in their blood."[681] Doyle's case was also constructed on the assumed defects in the family's characteristics than on any evidence deduced from the handwriting characteristics of which there was very little. Taking a leaf out of Captain Anson's encyclopaedia of 'denigratory terms for George Edalji and his supporters', Doyle described Royden Sharp as a dangerous intermittent maniac, feeble minded although rational in conversation, sometimes violent other times morose, with perfect ingenuity for intrigue and mystification.[682] The father, Peter Sharp, who died in 1893, was accused of being a drunkard; the mother was also a drunkard of dissolute habits; the uncle, Stanley Sharp, a porter at Hednesford station, was mentally deficient and physically peculiar, apparently having very large testicles!; Herbert Sharp was unemployed; Frank Sharp had absconded after failing to marry his betrothed and had a breach of promise suit outstanding against him; both Frank and Herbert Sharp were allegedly described as "immoral, drunken and reckless" by the Cardigan police; Walter had a weak physical constitution and was dead; and Jackie Sharp, the 6 years old son of Herbert Sharp, was not thought mentally bright. Doyle's conclusion after this biographical expedition was of the entire Sharp family being mentally and morally degenerate.[683] Interestingly, the father, Peter Sharp, was elected and re-elected as a member of the Cannock School Board on several occasions, therefore, the ratepayers of Cannock did not share this view of the Sharps, or at least one of them. The gem in Doyle's collection was the attribution to Herbert Sharp of religious mania, which he 'identified' as an index of family weakness that became 'murderous madness' in Royden Sharp.[684] Doyle's obsessive view of the Sharp family was as

[680] ACD to HO, 22 Jan 1907, HO File 989 Pt 1; 29 Jan 1907, HO File 988; and 17 Nov 1907, HO No 300 File 987; ACD to Blackwell, 18 Apr 1907, HO File 989 Pt 1; DT 24 May 1907

[681] ACD to HO, 24 Jan 1907, HO File 989 Pt 1

[682] ACD to HO, 17/18 Nov 1907, HO No 300 File 987

[683] Report to ACD from detective H Leatherdale, and ACD's Comments, 4 Feb 1907, HO File 989 Pt 1

[684] DT 27 May 1907

unsatisfactory as was Captain Anson's prejudiced obsession with the Edaljis.

Doyle's venture into the field of handwriting analysis was no more successful than any of the other contributions, lay or expert, produced in support of the Anson/Home Office line. This inadequate analysis compounded the errors in his other evidence against the Sharps, but he was not the odd one out in this field as no one seemed to have any expertise in analysing handwriting and all sides failed miserably in trying to establish a case against their favoured targets. It was like a detective story under construction where the author, having decided on the guilty party, made out a case against the wrongdoer. During the course of writing when the facts did not match the outcome of the plot, the author returned to the script to rework the evidence and rewrite the facts, as often as necessary, until they corresponded with the pre-determined end. This was a veritable world of fantasy masquerading as reality.

(ii) Captain Anson's Defence

While Doyle was putting together his case against the Sharps and informing the Home Office of his suspicions, Captain Anson claimed not to know whom Doyle had in his sights and he asked the Home Office to identity Doyle's suspect and provide him with the evidence upon which Doyle's theory was based. In fact, the captain had guessed it was Royden Sharp and without seeing Doyle's evidence had proclaimed Sharp to be absolutely innocent of the charges, referring to it as a 'monstrous allegation' and the sooner it "is disproved the better."[685] An interesting paradox of declaring Sharp innocent without examining the evidence unlike Edalji, whom the captain thought guilty first and the evidence then massaged to confirm this presumption of guilt.

The chief constable publicly admitted attaching no importance to Doyle's misleading 'weathercock theories' as the Staffordshire police acted only on facts upheld beyond a shadow of a doubt – a plus for the police if it were but true.[686] Captain Anson was demonstrating his limited perspective on policing practices by failing to understand that theories/hypotheses are tested by facts. His public declaration was merely chaff since if his requirement 'beyond a shadow of a doubt' was

[685] Capt Anson to HO, 23 Jul 1907, HO No 263, File 986; Capt Anson to Blackwell, 21 July 1907, HO File 989 Pt 1; Gazette, 30 Aug 1907;
[686] Gazette 30 Aug 1907; DE 30 Aug 1907

the criterion upon which the Staffordshire police based its work, or more specifically used by Captain Anson, then George Edalji would never have been arrested let alone finish up at the Stafford Quarter Sessions. Edalji was convicted on a 'weathercock theory' built on inadmissible evidence. Captain Anson's motive for not intending to investigate Doyle's prognostications had more to do with the possibility of unsavoury facts being discovered about the maimers, such as their identity, and to suppress the fact that Sharp was a police informant and probably a police 'postman.'

Captain Anson went on the attack against Doyle's three principal informants for leading him hopelessly astray, which was not without substance, but given the captain's track record towards any person favouring Edalji this criticism of Doyle's aides was hardly earth-shattering. The captain applied one of his ready-made categories to Beaumont and Arrowsmith - lunatics, and Greatorex was accused of harbouring bitter animosity towards Royden Sharp. However, this hostility was hardly surprising if Sharp created as many problems for Mr Greatorex as he did for his own father although it did cast shadows over the objectivity of Greatorex's information if not entirely precluding its validity. Captain Anson rejected any evidence provided by: the grudge-bearing Greatorex; the less than reliable Mrs Sharp and her character-deficient kin; Fred Arrowsmith, the 'lunatic' and not now the honest and reliable Arrowsmith whom the captain used to wheedle a confession out of Harry Green; and Beaumont, another lunatic, whom the captain took seriously enough to engage in a discourse on a number of issues.[687]

Captain Anson's rebuttal, like Doyle's 'prosecution' of the Sharps, was a *pot-pouri* of local gossip, innuendo, supposition and denials mashed together with a few matters of fact, and it characterised a similarly low evidential weight as did Doyle's contribution. However, the captain's response to Doyle's inconclusive checklist provided a lead as to who was in the police frame for the maimings and the anonymous letter writing. One or two points from Captain Anson's notes written in an exercise book sent on to the Home Office are illuminating. The captain admitted to believing that Hart assisted Harry Green in killing Green's horse and had been under suspicion for the other maimings. With Hart in the frame, there was no way in which Edalji should have been considered as a possible co-conspirator. Not only were their social backgrounds so different but Hart made it known he was a sworn

[687] Capt Anson-ACD Correspondence, Sep 1907, HO 989 File Pt 1; Capt Anson to ACD, 14 Jan 1911, HO File 987

enemy of Edalji for putting him to considerable expense over a libel case. The captain also dismissed the possibility of there being any evidence against Sharp for writing anonymous letters while attending Walsall Grammar School – a claim that he knew to be untrue since he was aware that Sharp was removed from the school for writing anonymous letters and for forgery, amongst Sharp's other serious shortcomings. The chief constable also acknowledged that Walter Sharp 'played pranks in the writing line' but, despite being aware of both Royden and Walter Sharp's involvement in writing anonymous letters and their possible responsibility for some of the 1892-1895 letters, he consistently blamed George Edalji.[688]

Doyle's identification of Royden Sharp as the scribe based on spelling mistakes in the letters was dismissed on the grounds that many people made similar mistakes – an interesting conclusion since one of the reasons the Captain put forward when arguing that Edalji was the author was spelling mistakes in the letters. He further sabotaged his own case against Edalji by making the point that the handwriting was so well advertised that anyone could copy it and his accusation of Edalji copying Sharp's 'r' fell down when he claimed thousands of people wrote like that and rhetorically asked if they were all guilty.[689] Captain Anson admitted that Sharp was mentioned as a possible suspect for sending out several obscene postcards in August 1903 when Inspector Campbell discussed with Greatorex, the banker, one of those postcards sent to the banker, but four years later the captain claimed the police never suspected Sharp. He made this claim to Conan Doyle while at the same time informing the Home Office of Sharp's susceptibility to writing anonymous letters such that Captain Anson had to despatch Superintendent Bishop to warn Sharp about it. With these 'dirty postcards', as he described them, still in his possession, Captain Anson, while identifying only one as 'unmistakably' in Edalji's writing, by using his handwriting analytical skills attributed them all to Edalji! He even acknowledged Royden Sharp's handwriting to have similarities with Martin Molton's and went as far as to say that if Royden Sharp was guilty of writing anonymous letters it was no proof of his committing the maimings – a view the captain also held of George

---

[688] Capt Anson to Blackwell, 2 Nov 1907 HO File 989 Pt 1; Capt Anson's notes of ACD Letters, undated, HO File 989 Pt 2; Mr Aldis to Capt Anson, 1 Jan 1893, in Capt Anson to Blackwell, 18 & 19 Nov 1907, HO File 989 Pt 1

[689] Capt Anson to Blackwell, 30 May, 22 Oct & 13 Nov 1907, HO File 989 Pt 1

Edalji but that did not stop him from prosecuting him. This also contrasted with his earlier claim to the Home Office that he was able to prove Sharp absolutely innocent, although no such proof was ever forthcoming from the chief constable.[690] The only reason for the captain refusing to accept any culpability on Sharp's part was a fervent and obsessive desire for the scribe to be George Edalji.

Captain Anson displayed an extraordinary protectiveness towards Sharp, a felon, and displayed an amazing degree of public spiritedness in his defence, in marked contrast to his attitude towards Edalji, a quiet, respectable professional man up until his arrest and, so it seems, all through his incarceration. Or was the captain's defence of Sharp an attempt to stifle Doyle who was opening up one can of worms too many. Of course, he may be acting on the principle that every one deserves the right to be thought innocent until proven guilty – a principle the captain failed to extend to George Edalji in 1892 or 1903.

Overall, Captain Anson portrayed Sharp, to the Home Office as a poor spirited, harmless individual preferring to live upon his mother's pension than working for a living. He dismissed any claim of Sharp and Hart being friends, relying, or so he said, on information supplied by Sharp, Mrs Sharp, Herbert Sharp and Hart, unless, added the chief constable, they were all wholesale liars – a caveat that should have carried some weight and seriously questioned the claims of the Sharps and Hart because the captain had already admitted that the Sharps and Hart were completely untrustworthy.[691]

Despite the lack of evidence and the chief constable's meanderings, he held Edalji responsible for the letters stretching from 1888 to 1903 because Edalji happened to be present in the area for the whole time, ignoring that many other people qualified on this criterion, including Walter Sharp, who was at home all the time. In fact, Captain Anson was of the opinion that several persons, at different times, were involved in writing forged anonymous letters in the Great Wyrley district – an interesting disclosure made by the captain, who had consistently paraded George Edalji as the sole writer throughout the whole period he was 'at large' in the Great Wyrley area. Digging

[690] Capt Anson to ACD, 2 Sep 1907, HO File 989 Pt 1 and 11 Oct 1907, HO No 297 File 987; Capt Anson to Blackwell, 28 May 1907, 21 July 1907 & 9 Jan 1908, HO File 989 Pt 1; Capt Anson's notes on ACD letters, undated, HO File 989 Pt 2

[691] Capt Anson to Blackwell, 26 Aug & 8 Sep 1907, HO File 989 Pt 1; HO Comment, 25 Nov 1907, HO No 300, HO File 987; Capt Anson to ACD, 5 Sep 1907, HO File 989 Pt 2

himself into a deeper hole, he declared it unsafe to attach too much importance to resemblances in handwriting, which may be intentional and the work of several hands, and he admitted that several persons in the area were sending self-accusative letters through the post, which was so easily done with little chance of detection.[692]

Captain Anson's own defence of Sharp was as inadequate as Doyle's case against Sharp but the onus was not on the captain to prove Sharp innocent but on Doyle's evidence to show guilt. The dispute between Doyle and Captain Anson over the Sharps proved nothing conclusive one way or another.

Captain Anson was not the one who sank Doyle's case against Royden Sharp as his criticism of Doyle's 'evidence' was equally weak and irrelevant and Doyle's case scuppered itself.[693] The captain acted 'like the cock that crows and thinks he has produced the dawn'.

(iii) Sir Charles W Matthews Contribution[694]

Doyle's rather insipid, insubstantive accusations against Sharp came under the careful scrutiny of an official in Whitehall, Sir Charles W Matthews, who pointed out the weaknesses, hardly an in-depth analysis but sufficient to refute Doyle's case. Matthews concluded: (a) for Sharp to confess to the deed and show the weapon to Mrs Greatorex in July 1903 giving her the opportunity to report him to the police was inconceivable and if Mrs Greatorex believed Sharp why did she remain silent before and after Edalji's conviction – a point drawing added strength from the fact there was no love lost between the Sharps and the Greatorexs; (b) Doyle's two different accounts of the words allegedly used by Sharp in this incident conveyed significantly different meanings, (i) "That's what the horses were done with" and (ii) "This is what they kill cattle with", the latter perfectly innocent considering Sharp was an apprenticed butcher and served on a cattle boat; (c) the anonymous letters contained no description of such a weapon; the

[692] Capt Anson to Blackwell, 21 Apr & 5 Nov 1907, HO File 989 Pt 1; Capt Anson to ACD, 11 Oct 1907, HO No 297 File 987 and 13 Sep 1907, HO File 989 Pt 2

[693] Harley, in 1985 claimed Captain Anson was responsible for debunking Doyle's case against Sharp, which was an overestimation of the merit of the Captain's capabilities. Harley, M, The Wyrley Maimings: Mr X Stands Accused, CA 18 Nov 1983

[694] Sir C W Matthews' notes on ACD's conclusion, 27 July 1907, HO No 266 File 986

reference to the sea and 'Tosh' Hatton, who was serving on a ship did not connect Sharp to the letters since he did not know 'Tosh' but George Edalji did; nor did Sharp's trip to Rotherham identify Sharp as the author of the Rotherham letters or any other anonymous letter; the phrases "I am as Sharp as Sharp can be," and "Ain't the gang as sharp, and a bloody sight sharper...." was met with the comment, "What of it?"; and references to committing suicide no more indicated Sharp than any one else in the neighbourhood; (d) Sharp's proven record of writing anonymous letters, of forgery, of mischief, of bearing false witness was no justification for accusing Sharp of a crime committed years later; (e) suggesting that Sharp, a butcher on a cattle ship, could commit 'blood-letting' crimes more easily than the ordinary man, meant that any butcher or anyone from a cattle ship could be justifiably arrested; (e) Sharp's living near to people named in the anonymous letter suggested only that Sharp was more likely to know their names than Edalji; (f) the girl's description of two men, allegedly Sharp and his dissolute butcher friend, Jack Hart, carrying out, or pretending to carry out the threats mentioned in the anonymous letter of September 1903 was not evidence for the crime committed on the 18th August; (g) Doyle could not make up his mind who wrote the 'God-Satan' letters, having accused then acquitted Royden, Herbert and later Frank Sharp.

While criticising Doyle personally for a certain impropriety towards Sharp, Sir Charles W Matthews thought Sharp had shown the behaviour of an innocent man after receiving the first anonymous letter of the 13th February 1907 urging him to confess. One of Doyle's aides in South Staffordshire was suspected of sending this letter, which was described as a discreditable act on Doyle's part but rebounding to Sharp's credit for handing the letter to the police. The overall conclusion drawn by Sir Charles W Matthews was that Doyle's charge sheet against Sharp contained insufficient evidence upon which to charge him – a view shared by the Attorney-General and by Sir George Lewis of the Edalji Support Committee, who had let this be known to Doyle earlier in 1907.[695]

Sir Charles W Matthews made a few errors: if the first anonymous letter – one not attributed to Edalji, had been taken into account there was a description of the weapon; 'Tosh' was known to Royden Sharp but even if he had not known him, 'Tosh' could still have been named by Sharp, because Edalji, not knowing the people mentioned in the letter who were living near to Sharp, was not excluded from writing the letters on that ground; and Sharp had tried to commit suicide in 1893,

---

[695] Attorney-General, 1 Aug 1907, HO No 269 File 986

which provided a link to the letters, but that in itself was nothing of substance. A couple of points made by Matthews, a plus for Edalji and a minus for Captain Anson were: (a) the 'discreditable act' on Doyle's part in conspiring to send an anonymous letter to Sharp and the praise given to Sharp for reporting the anonymous letter to the police, described as 'rebounding to his credit' equally applied to Captain Anson's actions against Edalji and Edalji's response. Sir Charles W Matthews was probably unaware of the Anson/Loxton 'Lover of Justice' letter to George Edalji – an equally discreditable act, which should have rebounded to Edalji's credit as he also passed it on to the police. Yet when George Edalji handed the anonymous letters to the police, this was construed by Scotland Yard as confirming his guilt when they measured his response to the motives of Dr Cream. Nor did Sir Charles W Matthews know that Sharp was working for Captain Anson in trying to track down George Edalji.

Sir Charles W Matthews was assessing the evidence with regard to the plausibility of bringing charges against Sharp based on Doyle's evidence and nothing else and the 'evidence' accumulated by Conan Doyle was insufficient for any judge not to have thrown it out without calling on the defence to rebut it.

Appendix II

George Edalji's Late-20th Century Critics.

In the hundred years that have elapsed since George Edalji's conviction, the case has received a brief mention in a number of biographies of Sir Arthur Conan Doyle's life and times and a few scattered contributions in crime anthologies. In the last twenty years, the case has been revisited[696] but no extensive work has reached publication, although a book on the case was promised for publication in the early 1990s. If such a work was published it is lost from view.[697] The late-twentieth century contributions have singularly failed to do justice to the material available on the case.[698] Instead they have concentrated on trying to exonerate Captain Anson and the Staffordshire police while condemning George Edalji as a miscreant and playing down Conan Doyle's significant role in exposing the deficiencies in the police and prosecution's case against Edalji. Little attention was given to the particular tribulations faced by the Edalji family that eventually led to the imprisonment of George Edalji for a crime committed by a person or persons unknown. When these works were published in the 1980s onwards, it was a difficult period for the police, facing considerable criticism from a variety of quarters for the type of policing used against members of ethnic minorities and, perhaps, these contributions should be viewed within the social milieu of the times.

---

[696] The most recent contribution was an article in three parts in the Cheslyn Hay Local History Journal, 2003/4. This contained some interesting points presented anecdotally, which have not been mentioned in any other source material to my knowledge, but without any detailed reference to the original sources. Cheslyn Hay Local History Journal, Winter 2003/Spring & Summer 2004

[697] M. Harley's promised book 'The Great Wyrley Mysteries: A Real Life Sherlock Holmes adventure,' Souvenir Press, was mentioned in a book about Sherlock Holmes by Dr P Lester. The case was also featured in a fringe play and on TV in the series "The Edwardians" in the 1970s. Lester, Dr P [1992] Sherlock Holmes in the Midlands, Brewin Books, Studley, p43-48

[698] A considerable amount of material is held at the Public Record Office at Kew.

Mike Harley,[699] who appears to have carried out the research upon which two other contributions were based, adopted an anecdotal approach in glorifying Captain Anson and disparaging Sir Arthur Conan Doyle, whom he criticised for helping to secure a pardon for a man guilty of criminal acts – the maimings and anonymous letter writing. In a more generous if patronising tone towards the famed literary artist, Harley wrote of a certain naïveté to be found in the writer of detective fiction, which enabled George Edalji to manipulate Doyle's generosity, trusting nature and propensity for being taken in. Harley was no doubt basing this claim on Doyle's later belief in fairies at the bottom of the garden. Such an assumption on Harley's part, while filling up space in an article, merely served to deflect attention from Doyle's critical and competent analysis of the crime for which Edalji was convicted and begs the question of how Edalji became aware of any deficiencies in Conan Doyle's psychological makeup and how he was able to manipulate those deficiencies. Harley would also have to explain how Edalji was able to 'con' the numerous solicitors and Kings Counsellors, lawyer MPs, university professors, lecturers, and many others from all walks of life, who, when confronted with the evidence, also came to the conclusion that a serious miscarriage of justice had occurred. If any influence was exerted between Doyle and Edalji it more likely came from Doyle, who talked Edalji into accepting the Home Office's watered down enquiry against the advice of the Edalji Support Committee, and if Doyle was 'conned' it was through trusting Home Office officials, who led him to believe that a public inquiry would take place while engineering a secret and limited committee hearing.

Doyle's highly detailed examination of the evidence made little impression on Harley, who considered the case against Edalji to have considerable merit but had been undermined by Inspector Campbell's sloppy procedures, which had diluted hard facts into circumstantial evidence. If only Captain Anson, using his clinical mind, had taken charge of the case himself, or swallowed his pride and called in Scotland Yard, a cast iron case could have been presented to the jury at Stafford. How the lack of evidence against Edalji, consisting mainly of uncorroborated statements from police officers, highly suspect forensic 'evidence' and a mass of inadmissible evidence, could have been so masterly converted into this iron cast by Captain Anson, to whom detective work was anathema, did not seem to warrant an explanation.

---

[699] Harley, M, Whodunnit & The Wyrley Maimings: Mr X Stands Accused, CA 18 Oct, 4, 11 & 18 Nov 1983; Harley, M, An Infamous Anson, Staffordshire History, Spring 1985

The reality was in fact quite different since Captain Anson, knowing of the grave discrepancies in the evidence, acquiesced in and was the driving force behind the prosecution of George Edalji in a 'Kangaroo-court style' hearing at the Quarter Sessions before a less than competent chair of the court – hardly an example of someone apparently viewed by Harley as something of a mastermind or super sleuth.

Harley tended to accept *prima facie* anything mustered against Edalji from any source – a few samples of his intake are as follows: having recognised that the evidence against Edalji was thin and circumstantial, Harley believed it to be sufficiently strong to convince the grand jury and trial jury of Edalji's guilt. He did not question the inclusion of a considerable quantity of inadmissible evidence nor the alteration of the time of the offence to the early hours of the morning of the 18th August in the prosecutor's final address to the jury for which no evidence was submitted to connect George Edalji. Up until then the prosecutor had argued throughout the whole of the trial that the crime had been carried out on the evening of the 17th August. Harley was silent about the evidence of the veterinary surgeon, which completely debunked the case against Edalji, who was sent to trial accused of committing the crime between 9 pm and 9.40 pm on the night of the 17th August but found guilty of carrying out the deed after 2.30 am on the following morning. The two minute spots of blood found on Edalji's coat, verified as mammalian of dubious age by Dr Butter, whom Harley referred to as "the well known eccentric GP", was, for Harley, conclusive proof of Edalji's guilt. At least in the dispute over the hair on the coat, Harley, in a backhanded fashion, gave Reverend Edalji the benefit of the doubt in not seeing them, not because the hairs were not there but because the Reverend's eyesight was so poor. Were Mrs Edalji's and Maud's eyesight equally defective? Generous enough to excuse Reverend Edalji's deficient eyesight, Harley did not show the same generosity to the reverend's son because he completely neglected George's myopia and astigmatism. Rejecting the argument that Edalji was too timid and nervous a person to carry out the maiming, Harley surpassed himself by attributing to Edalji the constitution of a horse as proven by his living to 77 years of age. Nor did Harley give any credence to the numerous lawyers, including senior law officers, who criticized (a) the evidence; (b) the prosecution's case; (c) the venue of the trial; and (d) the incompetence of the vice chair of the Quarter Sessions.

Harley also accepted without question the view that Edalji wrote the anonymous letters, basing his view on the trap set for Edalji by Captain Anson in sending out the 'Lover of Justice' letter, yet he failed to consider the possibility of other letters having their origins in the Anson/Loxton conspiracy nor did he mention the first two anonymous letters and the note on the enclosed envelope included in the third letter, none attributed to Edalji, which suggested at least three people were involved. Nor did he refer to the discrediting of the handwriting expert, Gurrin. However, he did give attention to the support for Gurrin's conclusions provided by the French and American 'experts' but made no mention of the serious faults, not too difficult to detect, in their contributions.

Referring to Doyle's contribution, Harley claimed that by putting his (Doyle's) views into concrete form, Doyle made it easy to show how lamentably defective were his methods of induction when applied to real life and he (Harley) firmly believed Captain Anson tore Doyle's theories of Royden Sharp's guilt to shreds. In fact, the chiding given to Doyle's hypothesis had little to do with Captain Anson's 'analytical' skills, its weakness was due to the inadequacy of the evidence mustered by Doyle that did not support the analysis, a mere set of disconnected points on a par with the captain's collection of equally unsupported, uncritical, statements against Edalji. The real debunker of Doyle's hypothesis was not the chief constable but Sir Charles W Matthews, who carried out a robust critical analysis.

Harley also denounced Doyle's belief in the so-called "unjust, racially inspired attacks on the shy reserved 'half-caste', (which) helped to obtain a pardon for a man certainly guilty of criminal acts and caused an innocent person to be unmercifully hounded by Cannock's version of the 'Baker St irregulars'" – an interpretation not agreed with by the Master of the Rolls, who restored George Edalji to the rank of a practicing solicitor. The race issue was an area where Harley showed considerable weakness. To Harley, the thought of persecuting Edalji because of the colour of his skin would never have occurred to Captain Anson nor would the police target Edalji because of colour prejudice. As happens too often, Harley inverted the racist dimension by placing the issue of racism within the mind of the victim, claiming that Edalji felt people looked down on him because of his Eastern origin – an attempt to identify racism within the psyche of the individual victim and not within the social and ideological structures of society. Harley's approach was a clear illustration of the limitations on his historical and sociological understanding of the late Victorian and Edwardian periods, noted for jingoism and racial prejudice towards the 'subject' races – phenomena that filtered down to all sections of the population. Add to that the increasing hostility shown towards the immigration mainly of Jews fleeing from persecution in Eastern Europe, which eventually led to the Aliens Act, and *voila* there is a seething witches brew of racial bigotry that needed little stirring.

Harley's assessment seems coloured by a deference to the memory of Captain Anson, whom he thought in possession of powers of decency, honesty and clinical deduction, not a view easily accommodated with the evidence of the captain's bigotry and malicious underhanded tactics, which his numerous letters to the Home Office were riddled with and were recognised as such by some Home Office officials.

Another writer, Lester,[700] leaning heavily on Harley, accused Doyle of allowing himself to be overly impressed by the professional status of George and Reverend Edalji, and once committed to the case could never admit to having been duped. Yet another interpretation playing on Doyle's alleged naiveté and vulnerability to professional people, overlooking that the Edaljis were hardly at the top end of the status hierarchy and Doyle consorted with people of considerably higher status – Winston Churchill was numbered among his friends.[701] If Lester's claim had any substance, why was Doyle not impressed by nor manipulated by other professional and high status people, such as the second son of the Earl of Lichfield, namely Captain Anson, with whom Doyle stayed in 1906, and who viewed Edalji as a thief, an embezzler, a fraud, a liar and, by implication as the alleged writer of anonymous letters, a crude, vulgar, immoral person verging on severe mental instability.

Lester accepted uncritically that George Edalji was the author of the 1892 anonymous letters and believed that when faced with the threat of exposure halted his 'mischief,' which considering four people claimed to have brought George Edalji's letter writing to a halt in December 1892, opens up the issue of who was responsible for the letters arriving at the vicarage and elsewhere over the next three years. Lester thought the letters suggested a neurotic disturbance associated with religion combined with a highly ambiguous attitude to his father. The religious rantings were indeed suggestive of some disturbance residing in the author but a more likely culprit was a person with an attachment to the tradition of primitive Methodism not someone with an Anglican background as was George Edalji's. As for any evidence showing ambiguity towards the scribe's father, Lester's methodology was based on the prior assumption that George Edalji was guilty of

---

[700] Lester, Dr P [1992] Sherlock Holmes in the Midlands, Brewin Books, Studley, p43-48

[701] ACD to Churchill, 24 Oct 1910, HO No 313 File 987

writing the letters. After reading that presumption of guilt back into the contents of the letters, assuming Lester read them, he came up with the proposition that George Edalji had an inner conflict over his father without presenting any credible evidence to support his hypothesis. Moreover, how does Edalji's alleged ambiguity to his father fit in with the attacks on Mrs Edalji and on numerous other people in the locality and other parts of the UK, including men, women, boys and girls.

Lester tried to make it seem plausible for Edalji to make the journey between the vicarage and the scene of the maiming by claiming that he would be crossing a field adjoining his home where he had lived all his life. He based his assessment of Edalji's alleged ability to negotiate the obstacle course, carefully described by Conan Doyle, by comparing the journey to the maimings with Edalji's daily return trips from the vicarage to New St Station, Birmingham and thence to his office in Newhall St, which though unstated was about 300 yards from the station, while not forgetting his occasional evening walks in the Great Wyrley area. If Edalji could perform this journey to work, which he was obviously able to do, Lester claimed he would have no problem in travelling along the route to the field, finding an animal, calming it down before disembowelling it – was Lester really being serious? A similar point upon a similarly dubious comparison was made by one ophthalmologist, a lone voice, in 1907. Perhaps Lester should have taken into account the other ten ophthalmologists in 1907, who arrived at different conclusions.

Lester also claimed that the thought of bringing disgrace on himself and his family over the debts he had incurred must have pushed George Edalji near to the brink of a mental breakdown and it was this state of mind that led him into making the wager and carrying out the deeds. This assessment, too, should be taken with a pinch of salt since it is a long jump from being in financial difficulties to being on the verge of a mental breakdown and wagering to kill eighteen animals in twelve months with all the attendant risks. Furthermore, if Edalji was about to suffer a nervous breakdown, how would Lester explain Edalji's conduct throughout the whole period of his incarceration before the trial and his calm and relaxed manner both during the hearings and his time in prison? Moreover, Lester unconditionally accepted that Edalji made that bet when no evidence was ever brought forward to substantiate an accusation that had no logic or credibility.

George Edalji's unsympathetic social environment and probable difficulties at school due to his colour were blamed for creating identity problems. George's life 'in a family of self elected celibacy, who had slept most of his life in the same room as his priestly father', led to the development of some unusual traits, such as the impulse to nocturnal expeditions to maim animals. Yet again, Lester has unequivocally accepted a claim made against Edalji, this time of nocturnal trips, without examining the motive behind those claims or the circumstances existing at the time they were made. Instead, Lester conjured up a simplistic pseudo-psychological solution paraded as an explanation for Edalji's guilt. If every person who was celibate or had 'unusual' sleeping arrangements or had types of behaviour not conforming to the 'norm' then went on to maim cattle, Britain would have resembled a vast abattoir working overtime. Another reason put forward to explain Edalji's venture into cattle maiming was racial prejudice experienced at school. At least Lester, unlike the others, acknowledged the existence of racism as part of Edalji's experience and although Edalji himself claimed that his father's origin did not "create any prejudice against us", it would have been difficult for him not to have had racist encounters in Victorian and Edwardian Britain. Even though Edalji played down this part of his life experience, it was another long jump between suffering this kind of victimisation and taking up marauding the countryside at night killing animals. Interestingly, while this author accepted that Edalji may have been the butt of racism from his peers he rejected any possibility of Captain Anson and the Staffordshire police having similar prejudices.

A fleeting contribution came from Dr Ward,[702] researching for a paper to be presented to the Police Federation in the 1990s. Dr Ward, intuitively since she provided no evidence, inclined to the view that the police fitted up Edalji for being a nuisance and winding the police up for years. She also claimed that Edalji wanted a reason external to himself to explain why his legal practice was going downhill and if he became the subject of notoriety and press speculation he did not have to look too closely into his own personal qualities for his failure. All he needed to do was to put it down to colour prejudice. This overlooked the fact that Edalji's practice was not the cause of his financial difficulties, those difficulties arose from his generosity and naiveté in financially aiding a fellow solicitor involved in a fraud. Edalji would need to be an extremely bizarre person to risk both imprisonment for a serious felony and being struck off from his profession in order to convince himself that any deficiencies he may have in conducting his business affairs were not his fault. Moreover, the suggestion that Edalji would blame any alleged failure on racism is an extremely dubious

---

702 Ward, Dr J [1993] The Story of George Edalji, paper to Police History Society Conference, at William Salt Library, Stafford

assumption and represents a late twentieth century tendency amongst apologists of racism, or those whose knowledge of racism is impressionistic, to deflect the issue of racism away from the actions of racists onto the supposed failings of the victim. As mentioned above, Edalji himself, though possibly minimising his own experiences in a society that was both deeply class and race conscious, never raised the issue of racism as creating a problem for him. It was his mother, Mrs Edalji, in 1904, and his sister, Maud Edalji, in 1956, who mentioned racism as an issue. To search for explanations in the individual pathology of the victim on whom to focus the blame rather than examining the wider social pathology operating against a victim such as Edalji distorts our understanding of what really happened to the Edalji family and to George in particular.

The only book to have devoted itself entirely to the Edalji case consisted of a collection of Doyle's articles published in the Daily Telegraph, in which the editors, R & M Whittington-Egan, took the opportunity in an introduction to comment on the case itself. [703] However, the editors' contribution offered little to our understanding, merely a 'fill-in' for the articles. Rather than making a suitably informed analysis as background material to the articles, the authors produced a piece noticeable for its verbosity and terminological weakness. Describing Edalji's origins in the words, "His Christian names and his patronymic reflect the two miscegenate halves of his birthright", they disregarded the fact that miscegenation is a concept describing breeding between two different species of animal life, hardly appropriate for the child of the Reverend and Mrs Edalji; "Reverend Edalji's marriage to an English woman had (not)...softened the resistance of his white flock to black sheep, neither had the multiplying of the union by three necessarily half-caste offspring" – apparently the authors, like Harley, were unaware that the term 'half-caste' is a hangover from the era of imperial rule during the Raj and denotes a lack of academic rigour since it has no sociological or anthropological significance.

The rumours circulated against the Reverend and George Edalji by, amongst others, Captain Anson were described as "the bizarre sleeping arrangements, redolent, indeed, of the custom of some far flung Samoan island - and (which) local gossip had its heyday in its enjoyable elaboration." They also make the point, of little relevance to the issues, that George Edalji was 27 years old and unmarried at the

---

[703] Whittington-Egan, R & M, (eds) [1985] The Story of George Edalji by Sir ACD, Grey House Books pp11 – 31

time of his "alleged martyrdom" and Reverend Edalji was "inordinately proud of his ewe-lamb." Why did they use the term 'ewe-lamb'?[704] If they found it necessary to make this kind of comparison, why not 'ram-lamb', unless they are implying some gender conflict in George Edalji's make-up. Typical of the whole tone of a weak and inadequate introduction, they refer to George Edalji, rather pettily and offensively, as being a "goggle-eyed adolescent of 17" when Captain Anson, described as a man of considerable distinction and certainly no fool, conceived an incredible animus against him. Edalji is also accused of bearing within himself the seeds of his own victimisation and they speculated that it would be no surprise "to learn that the Edalji family harboured a poltergeist infestation" – whatever that is supposed to mean.

The anonymous letters were depicted as a plague settling on the district "like a swarm of loathsome, stinging insects," at a time when a person or persons "set apart the humble beasts of the field...as if to bring to their knees the entire animal population of Great Wyrley." Although Captain Anson never produced any real evidence, the authors accepted that his claims against Edalji for the 1892-1895 anonymous letters had "some solid bedrock, something other than wildfire gossip and calumny." To bolster up the irrelevancies, inserted it seems to avoid the effort associated with scholarship, Edalji is reduced to an Agatha Christie character in 'Cretan Bull', saying "Even just lately things have been killed...Sheep, young lambs – a collie dog. Father locks me in at night but sometimes – sometimes – the door's open in the morning. I must have a hidden key somewhere but I don't know where I've hidden it."

Unable to find a real motive for the crimes, the Whittington-Egan's construct a pseudo-psychological motive in asking "What manner of freak is it that would come reeking out of the pages of Krafft-Ebing, shin over a padlocked gate on a dark night, lope across a field towards the shapes of warm, furry horses – grazing perhaps, or sleeping with folded legs and drooping muzzles, without a gruff word of reassurance and slit them quick along the soft, veined under-belly? Then satisfied, no doubt, and already savouring his next coup, slither away into the underbrush, just as his mentor, Jack the Ripper, had dislimned into the alleyways of the East End fifteen years before?" The clue for their motive lies with the name Krafft-Ebing, who wrote in the late 19th century on sexual psychopathy and aberrations in sexual life,

---

[704] Victor Hugo in 'Notre Dame de Paris' refers to young girls as 'ewe-lambs'

which might go some way to explain their use of the terms 'ewe-lamb' and 'poltergeist infestation'.

Conan Doyle's entrance in 1907 came as a result of a vacuum in his own life following the death of his wife in July 1906, reducing his intervention to nothing more than a 'therapeutic exercise' but described in terms combining Sir Walter Scott with Cervantes, thus, Doyle, "chivalric white plume tossing, and sporting the favour of Edalji, rides into the lists. Sometimes his lance rings true: sometimes it encounters windmills."

Doyle's trip to the scene of the maiming was described as "a circuitous ¾ mile route-march...experienced as an obstacle course worthy of Odysseus," and they criticised Doyle's analysis of Edalji's short sightedness for presenting Edalji as "a shuffling, mole-like creature in need of a knocking white stick," using this terminology to ridicule Doyle and minimise Edalji's short-sightedness. They went further by claiming that Edalji was hardly visually impaired since he attended school and law classes, served articles, researched and wrote a law book, and travelled routinely by train. However, this scenario was hardly comparable with maiming a horse during a rain-sodden night after following the 'Odysseus trail'. There was also the inevitable criticism of the lack of evidence to support Doyle's claim of colour prejudice as the motive for the harassment of the Edaljis, which was yet another example of contributors secreting themselves in an ahistorical vacuum by overlooking or ignoring the fact that the milieu of the late Victorian and Edwardian eras, the height of imperial splendour, was one of endemic jingoism and racism in Britain.

Two reasons for Doyle finding it inconceivable for a professional man to commit "such a beastly crime" were put forward by the Whittington-Egans. On the one hand, it was social and cultural, hidden deep in Doyle's upbringing where his "peculiar mother" reared him as a gentleman "upon the ideals of chivalry." On the other hand, it was psychological and due to Doyle's "weighty emotional investment...in the Edalji case (which) If by chance he had stumbled upon any evidence of Edalji's guilt, he might have extended into a further period of clinical depression." Doyle was also accused of displaying fervour and intensity, repetition, rhetoric and naiveté, in the wake of his wife's death, which caused him to overstate Edalji's case. It is true that Doyle may well have exhibited some of these qualities by overstating certain aspects of his investigation but this concerned his conclusions on the identity of those whom he thought responsible for the maimings and anonymous letters not in his destruction of the prosecution's case against Edalji.

The contribution from the joint authors drone on even to the point of bringing in Doyle's marriage, completely irrelevant to the Edalji case, but enabling them to make another literary insertion by describing Doyle's wedding reception as including "the rehabilitated George Edalji, a gargoyle figure against the silk and laces, like a phoenix emblem of the great man's renewed march through life." It is difficult to see how the author's references to Edalji's looks, 'goggle-eyed", "gargoyle figure," can make any contribution to understanding this case, unless, of course, like Captain Anson, they subscribe to the outdated Lombroso theory of physical attributes as an indicator of 'criminal traits'.

In the 21 pages of their introduction, the Whittington-Egans had taken the reader along a 'circuitous route march' with only three valid points surfacing, namely, that a strong defence counsel should have effectively challenged the prosecution for changing the time of the maiming; for raising the theory of a gang; and acknowledging it was wrong for a person to be incarcerated for three years on such unsafe evidence. Although serious question marks should be laid at the defence team over its failure to pursue the issue of Edalji's myopia and for not challenging the admission of the evidence concerning the anonymous letters, the Whittington-Egans overlooked the difficulty the defence had in countering the prosecution's changing of the time of the maiming and introducing the theory of a gang as these were made in the prosecution's final address to the jury, which followed on from defence counsel's address.

If the Whittington-Egan's introduction was not an 'account' of a serious miscarriage of justice, it might have some merit as a humorous caricature of an Edwardian melodrama laced with a *pot-pouri* from a number of literary sources. Perhaps that was its purpose!